**Information Engineering Systems Corporation**

pioneering solutions to your business and systems challenges

Corporate Capability Statement

Information Engineering Systems Corporation (IESC) is a consulting services and software products firm that specializes in Business and Information Engineering. For almost a decade IESC's experienced consultants have been delighting clients with their hard work, commitment, talent and attitude. Hundreds of commercial and government organizations have selected IESC to provide assistance in areas such as:

- business reengineering including business process reengineering
- data architecture and data management
- data reverse engineering
- data warehouse planning and implementation
- enterprise architecture planning
- enterprise client/server development
- quality rapid application development (Q-RAD)
- strategic information systems planning
- systems reverse and reengineering

Our products automate and accelerate many of the tasks and techniques associated with business-driven, model-based information systems and infrastructure development.

- *IE: Advantage™* supports the development of new information systems, the redevelopment of legacy systems, and the reengineering of business processes. Gartner Group stated "*IE: Advantage* is a Workgroup CASE tool with an Enterprise CASE mentality" because it automates business planning, data modeling (IE and IDEFIX), data access and business process modeling, object-oriented design, data reverse engineering, document and report generation, and more! Easy to learn and use *IE: Advantage* is the tool of choice for those who need an integrated, multi-user tool capable of handling your smallest or your largest project and everything in between.
- IESC's methodology product, *IE: Advisor™*, supports the improvement of your software development practices. By providing guidelines and examples of methodology techniques (data modeling, object-oriented design, etc.) this hypermedia reference product will help you increase the skill level of your systems development professionals while ensuring the timely delivery of quality software solutions. A missing ingredient in most CASE implementation, this powerful product will help ensure your success.
- The *IES: Universal Model™* product is used to accelerate the creation of a common, cohesive data architecture necessary to build a quality Data Warehouse and Executive Information/Decision Support Systems. The organization of the product into "Universal" business objects supports cross-functional, cross-organizational, object-oriented software development. Each business object can be quickly tailored to your specific requirement then implemented in a few weeks as a new information system.
- The *IES: Budget™* product is just such an implementation and illustrates the potential for the Universal Model in your organization in addition to being an exciting new product itself. *IES: Budget* supports the creation of multiple versions of budgets while linking business plans, budgets and work activities.

IESC can help you succeed with your most challenging business and information engineering projects. If you want to take a business-driven, model-based approach then IESC has the people and the products to help you produce results for maximum business benefit.

Information Engineering Systems Corporation, 201 North Union Street, 5th Floor, Alexandria, VA 22314
Telephone: 703/739-2242 FAX: 703/739-0074

Austin ◆ Dallas ◆ Pittsburgh ◆ San Francisco ◆ Seattle

Data Reverse Engineering

Other McGraw-Hill Books of Related Interest

AYER • *Object-Oriented Client / Server Application Development*

ANDRIOLE • *Requirements Management and Process Reengineering*

BAMBARA • *PowerBuilder: A Guide for Developing Client / Server Applications*

BERSON/ANDERSON • *SYBASE and Client / Server Computing*

DAVIS • *201 Principles of Software Development*

DOWN • *Risk Management for Software Projects*

JONES • *Applied Software Measurement*

LYON/GLUCKSON • *MIS Manager's Appraisal Guide*

MATTISON • *The Object-Oriented Enterprise: Making Corporate Information Systems Work*

MINOLI • *Analyzing Outsourcing*

SIGNORE/STEGMAN • *The ODBC Solution*

TILLMANN • *A Practical Guide to Logical Data Modeling*

TOPPER ET AL. • *Structured Methods*

Data Reverse Engineering

Slaying the Legacy Dragon

Peter Aiken, Ph.D.
Virginia Commonwealth University
and
Defense Information Systems Agency

How to harness organizational data
for reengineering and integration

McGraw-Hill
New York   San Francisco   Washington, D.C.   Auckland   Bogotá
Caracas   Lisbon   London   Madrid   Mexico City   Milan
Montreal   New Delhi   San Juan   Singapore
Sydney   Tokyo   Toronto

Library of Congress Cataloging-in-Publication Data

Aiken, Peter H.
    Data reverse engineering : Slaying the Legacy Dragon / Peter H.
Aiken.
          p.   cm.
    Includes bibliographical references and index.
    ISBN 0-07-000748-9
    1. Reverse engineering. I. Title.
TA168.5.A44   1996
    658.5—dc20   95-22598
                                                                              CIP

1 2 3 4 5 6 7 8 9   DOC/DOC   9 0 0 9 8 7 6 5

ISBN 0-07-000748-9

*The sponsoring editor for this book was Marjorie Spencer,
the editing supervisor was Jane Palmieri,
and the production supervisor was Pamela Pelton.
It was set in New Century Schoolbook by Peter Aiken.*

Printed and bound by R. R. Donnelley & Sons Company.

*This book is printed on recycled, acid-free paper containing a
minimum of 50% recycled, de-inked fiber.*

Contents

Detailed Contents

Part 2 Analysis   85

Chapter 6 Project Initiation Activities (Part 1)   87

Chapter 7 Project Team Initiation (Framework Activity 4)   101

Chapter 8 Project Initiation Activities (Part 2)   119

Chapter 9 Target System Analysis (Framework Activity 8)   143

Chapter 10 Project Wrapup Activities   161

Foreword

by Clive Finkelstein

I first met Peter Aiken two years ago at a joint seminar titled "Framework for Development" that John Zachman (the originator of the Zachman Framework) and I presented in Washington, DC for IT Managers and IT staff. He was concerned that many data modeling approaches focus mainly on the future needs of organizations using Forward Engineering, such as described in my books on business-driven Information Engineering (IE), and only limited coverage was given in the literature to the discipline of Reverse Engineering. We discussed many problems that organizations have in moving their existing systems (referred to as legacy systems) to client/server environments using object-oriented techniques and development tools. Such environments generally require redevelopment of those systems.

Therein lay a dilemma: for legacy systems invariably suffer from poor or incomplete documentation. While the business rules incorporated in those systems exist in program logic, they are generally not documented in business terms. But the business users who specified those rules many years ago have since moved on, been "downsized" or otherwise discarded. Furthermore, the systems design and program documentation may also be inadequate or incomplete—or worse ... may be out of date and therefore not reliable. The IS staff who developed those systems have also moved to greener pastures, or have otherwise been "outsourced."

In our discussion we both likened this situation to two disciplines: archaeology—the study of prehistoric remains—and anthropology—the study of primitive societies. The science of reconstructing long dead civilisations from bones and other debris they left behind is often the only way to learn how they lived. With no written history, there is often no alternative but to examine and analyse those bones and debris: to determine how they were used. We can then understand what was important to them. We can learn from the past, and where relevant we can utilise that knowledge for our future.

We then applied these analogies to the discipline of Reverse Engineering as it was used in the 1980s. The focus in that period was analysis of program code to determine program logic, and so business rules. Programs define HOW processing is carried out: they implement business processes. The data used by each program is apparent, but this is only a fragment of the entire data used in the business: analogous to bone fragments.

As bone fragments are difficult to comprehend until assembled into a skeleton, so also pieces of data are difficult to understand individually. But when assembled together in a data model we can see from those data fragments WHAT the business can achieve. We can then more readily determine HOW business processes work when we examine the program code. The result is clearer legacy understanding and documentation.

The analysis of legacy data bases and files, and of data structures in legacy programs, enables the development of legacy data models. These data models represent the business as it was, and allow the business processes as implemented to be understood more easily. As an up-to-date plan of a house makes it easier to extend or rebuild parts of that house, so also up-to-date legacy data models enable enhancements to existing systems, or new systems, to be developed and integrated with legacy systems that will not be changed.

Peter Aiken uses the term Data Reverse Engineering to emphasize the importance of data, and to differentiate his approach from other Reverse Engineering methods. As he described the technique, I saw its power. I encouraged him to share his insights with others. This book is the result.

When I first read the finished book, it was clear he had made an important contribution. Early on he establishes the case for a focus on data. He shows the application of Data Reverse Engineering in all stages as a series of Framework Steps, using three business scenarios introduced in Chapter 1 to illustrate. His approach is impressive. The legacy data models that result enable a good understanding of existing systems to be gained, as a firm foundation then for integration into data models that address the needs for the future using Forward Engineering.

Also as you read the book, the clarity that this data focus brings to the examination of program code and data structures becomes apparent. The result is better understanding of the business rules and the business processes reflected in the legacy systems, for migration to or redevelopment in other environments. These legacy systems thus can provide clear input to their successors: legacy systems to be redeployed in new environments are clearly documented for their redevelopment. And finally, those legacy systems that must continue in their current environment can be integrated with other newer systems so they can continue to provide value to the organization.

In the years following their initial introduction into organizations, legacy systems can become essential to their operation: they are mission-critical. Data Reverse Engineering ensures that the data, information, and business rules in those systems are all fully identified so they can be incorporated, as appropriate, into the systems that replace them.

Clive Finkelstein—Melbourne, Australia
Founder and Chief Scientist
Information Engineering Systems Corporation—Washington, DC

The Necessity of Data Reverse Engineering

by Elliot J. Chikofsky

The competitive international environment of the mid-1990s demands that an organization make the best use it can of its resources. Resources that can contribute directly to the organization's bottom line are of significant value. A resource that can be utilized for strategic and tactical advantage is invaluable. In the information-intensive age we have just entered, data is that invaluable resource.

Leveraging data

Some organizations have been very successful at leveraging the use of data. American Airlines, which introduced the first frequent-flyer program in 1981, proved the value of capitalizing on data about repeat customers. Besides rewarding key clients for brand loyalty, well-managed frequent-flyer programs provide a wealth of information about preferences, buying habits, and sales of companion products and services. This yields both current and historic information, on the individuals and on the group, from which patterns can be discerned and trends can be detected. When tied with program partners, such as hotels and car-rental companies, the frequent-flyer data opens important opportunities for marketing of packaged services and related products.

The same ability to leverage the use of data was demonstrated by the telephone company MCI when it introduced the first "Friends and Family" program in 1991. MCI capitalized on an understanding of its data and a computing situation that its principal competitor, AT&T, could not match at the time. MCI knew who its customers were because it handled the preparation of phone bills directly. MCI's customer records and telephone call logs were already being processed together. AT&T, on the other hand, billed its customers through the seven regional Bell operating companies and local phone companies. As a result of the Bell System divestiture, the local phone companies were intermediaries between AT&T and its customers. Unlike MCI, AT&T did not have the infrastructure in place to readily link customer identity with data on telephone calls.

With its existing billing operations and a firm knowledge of its available data, MCI had the mechanisms in place to detect and act on customer calling patterns. MCI turned this into a marketing coup by offering discounts when calls were made regularly between MCI customers. The result was a significant influx of new customers as existing customers became an adopted MCI sales force, encouraging their regular telephone partners to become MCI subscribers for the savings. This is a prime example of an organization capitalizing on an information technology–driven marketing opportunity.

These days, organizations adept at leveraging the use of data can be as near as the corner supermarket. In fact, they ARE the corner supermarket. With the introduction of bar codes and laser scanners, supermarkets sped up the grocery checkout process. In the same action, they revolutionized the grocery retail and wholesale business by providing a mother lode of data to be mined for tactical advantage. When your purchase is wrung up at the checkout stand, it is now recorded in the store's database. Besides allowing the store to monitor sales revenue and check inventories, the database itself is a product of the store. The data is of great value to the supermarket chain, wholesalers, distributors, and product manufacturers who readily purchase it.

The supermarket data tells much more than how many of each product were sold. Simple analysis reveals facts such as: how often sets of products were bought at the same time; how the quantity bought relates to the total size of the shopper's purchase; or, whether the store's customers were affected by local advertising and discounts. Leverage of this data leads to revised marketing campaigns and targeted sales promotions, including coupons printed right at the cash register.

A recent addition to the supermarket checkout as a tactical data source is the acceptance of credit cards, unheard-of for food purchases just a few years ago. Now, the customer identity is tied to the purchase. By combining data from appropriate sources, demographic information and purchasing profiles can become a potent source of information for direct target marketing. Already, it is not unheard-of for someone to purchase disposable diapers for a friend and then receive months of baby food offers and toy catalogs in the mail.

The ability to leverage data gives an organization advantages in many ways. Consider, for instance, customer service: having moved from Michigan to Massachusetts some years ago, my family missed a favorite Pillsbury product, orange danish rolls. We did not find them anywhere, though stores in the area carried other products of the same brand. Seeing a customer service address on one such package, I wrote to Pillsbury. Their response was a nice letter with a printout of every store within ten miles of my zip code that regularly received the item I was looking for. Here is an organization that knows its data and how to use it to make a customer very happy.

Recognizing the need

It is unfortunate that the success stories of leveraging data pale when compared to the untold failures and lack of effort across business and industry. Most organizations do not have a clue as to what their data is all about—never mind how to leverage it to best advantage. Without an understanding of the nature of their data, they have too much data and not enough information.

Data sources exist in an organization in many forms. Some are organized databases and files. Some kinds of data are locked in arcane structures in legacy systems whose designers are long retired. Other kinds of data are in quick little applications that someone threw together as a temporary fix five years ago and have been in use ever since. Then, there are the stealth data sources that the organization doesn't even know it has.

Today, organizations must change their information infrastructure quickly to satisfy rapidly changing needs. As the business climate changes, flexibility and response are key to taking advantage of new opportunities and meeting new goals. The rapid shift in hardware and software economics toward distributed, client/server, decentralized facilities has increased flexibility but also increased support challenges. It has also increased the need for a greater understanding of the data content and functional capability of the systems we are distributing access to. The data needs of the organization frequently require that information maintained in legacy systems be made available throughout the organization.

Yet, the data is only as good as the organization's knowledge of it. We have a vast store of potentially very useful information, already paid for by prior investment. If only we knew what was there and how to tap it. An organization needs to have the right data, know what it has, know where to find it, and know what it means. That is where Data Reverse Engineering comes it.

Reverse engineering is a process to achieve understanding of the structure and interrelationships of a subject system. It is a goal of reverse engineering to create representations that document the subject and facilitate our understanding it—what it is, how it works, and how it does not work. As a process, reverse engineering can be applied to each of the three principal aspects of a system: data, process, and control. Data Reverse Engineering concentrates on the data aspect of the system that is the organization. It is a collection of methods and tools to help an organization determine the structure, function, and meaning of its data. With that knowledge, the organization can develop meaningful plans to leverage its investment in data.

Not an option

Data reverse engineering is not an option. For many organizations, it is a necessity. Understanding the data that drives the business is, more and more, becoming critical to success. An organization needs to be competitive. It must get new products and services out ahead of, and better than, its competition. Many of those products and services are information products, and the rest are information-dependent products. The race to capitalize on the Internet and the World Wide Web by beating competitors to customer-generating services is an information-intensive contest. Organizations that understand their data, and through it their marketplace, are destined to fare best in both short-term responsiveness and long-term innovation.

There is another very pressing reason why organizations need to embrace data reverse engineering now. It's called the millennium date problem. As an industry, we know for certain that our computer information systems are fundamentally flawed. Hundreds of thousands of computer programs worldwide, billions of lines of code, and an unimaginable number of entries in databases and data files were written to store date values with a two-digit year format. When we enter the year 2000, comparisons involving two digit year values will invert their sign or change direction (greater/less-than result). This will crash many computing systems, produce devastating errors in calculations, and could create chaos in both business and safety-critical systems from banking and insurance to communications and air traffic control.

To avoid the millennium date problem, an organization needs to locate and correct hidden date problems throughout its information systems, computer programs, and data files. Finding all of the myriad ways in which dates are stored, encoded, and embedded throughout the business requires an understanding of the nature of the organization's data and a hard look at the systems which process it. In this regard, millennium solutions and data reverse engineering are complementary and codependent. The millennium problem provides the impetus for data reverse engineering, while reverse engineering provides the methods and techniques to discover the extent of hidden date problems needing action before the deadline.

The future belongs to organizations that understand their data and leverage its use to full potential. Data reverse engineering is key to that objective.

Elliot Chikofsky
Principal Consultant
DMR Consulting Group
Burlington, Massachusetts

Data Reverse Engineering in Information Technology

by Diann L. McCoy

Data reverse engineering (DRE) is a tool set of strategies and tactics for use in the fusion center of information technology (IT) operations. IT is itself a fusion of concepts and technology into one term. The book addresses current strategies of creating interfaces before the planned common operating environment evolves. The goals of standards, open systems, and common operating environment will always be evolving. DRE is the collection of strategies and tactics for the survivor's tool kit when operating in the "as is" world. In spite of the promises that the future will arrive tomorrow with standards that will obviate the drudgery of real work, the DRE tool kit is the one set of tools the IT data engineer can rely on during the long march of evolution.

Reengineering challenges are unique whether in small or large systems, or in small or large businesses and government agencies. DRE is the tool kit for any IT operative to make things work, when interoperability is required in the absence of a single standard system, or when multiple systems must be interfaced. While assessing the reality of the constancy of multiple data systems in an evolving and complex IT world, the Department of Defense (DOD) has endorsed DRE.

In October of 1994, then Deputy and now Secretary of Defense William Perry issued a direction indicating that organizations should include data reverse engineering as part of their overall approach to

1. Determining organizational information system requirements.

2. Evaluating their current inventory of systems.

3. Planning their migration paths to whatever future system they select.

In this book, Dr. Aiken has brought together the tool kit knowledge and tactics from the academic, business, and government data engineering operations to create an initial tool set for DRE. His activities working for the Defense Information Systems Agency (DISA) contributing to the development of a DOD Enterprise Model have qualified him to provide this type of guidance. In addition, I am pleased to have two other DISA, Center for Software staff members contribute to this book.

Diann L. McCoy
Deputy Commander
Center for Software
Joint Interoperability and Engineering Organization
Defense Information Systems Agency
Arlington, Virginia

Preface

From Sausage to Pig

One of todays most pressing information technology questions has been aptly asked by Christine Comaford: "How do you bring those creaky old applications into the modern world without spending an arm and a leg?" [Comaford, 1992]. I believe that for most organizations, data reverse engineering is a good answer. Data reverse engineering is an approach that can simultanously enable organizations to increase their:

- understanding and value received from organizational data assets

- ability to share data both within the organization and among strategic business partners

- organizational capablities to respond effectively to opportunities appearing in the environment

Perhaps the most memorable thing that's been said about reverse engineering is that it's about as easy as reconstructing a pig from a sausage [Eastwood 1992]. Why would anyone want to make a pig from sausage? Or for that matter, how does the study of existing systems contribute to the three goals listed above. That is the topic of this text. Studying existing systems can provide critical information and understanding that in turn can leverage and focus future systems development and/or enhancement. Buried within the system lie three types of organizational requirements: information, system, and data. Documentation isn't able to keep pace with the 5 to 7% functionality modification rate [Jones 1994] experienced annually by organizations. Often the systems are the most accurate source of this information, detailing the manner in which the systems support the achievement of organizational objectives. The leverage from reverse engineering can make the difference between project success and project failure. With a bit of experience, data reverse engineering projects can become a valuable means of beginning enterprise integration efforts.

Acknowledgments

> If you steal from one author, it's plagiarism; if you steal from many
> it's research.   *Wilson Mizner*

Writing a book is very much an opportunity. I have been fortunate to be able to take advantage of such an opportunity but I have also been privileged to work with two colleagues who collectively helped develop many of the ideas implemented on these projects. Russ Richards, the U.S. Department of Defense Information Architect, and Dr. Alice Muntz, Manager of Data Management Technology for Hughes Information Technology Company (HITC), got me focused on data reverse engineering as an important component of the Department's strategy for dealing with its legacy systems. They will continue to educate me once they write their respective books. Thanks, Russ! Thanks, Alice! Thanks also to a distinguished panel of foreword writers whose contributions I very much value.

- Thanks to Clive Finkelstein and to the folks at Information Engineering Systems Corporation, namely, Glen Hughlette, Dave Sturdivant, Dean Mohlstrom, Peter Ruiz, and Mason Washington, for their support over the years and for permission to use screen shots of their CASE product *IE:Advantage*. Clive's articulation of IE-related concepts help to push me to develop this material.

- Elliot Chikofsky's research and other activities have done much to motivate the relatively recent interest in reverse engineering. In his contribution, Elliot makes the case for data as an important strategy for managing systems evolution.

- Thanks to Ms. Diann McCoy, my boss's boss. Her leadership at the Center for Software is enabling and facilitating the implementation of these concepts throughout the Department of Defense.

Combined, I believe, these individuals have already made the case for data reverse engineering from industrial, academic, and governmental perspectives. My coauthors have contributed to and helped sort out my thoughts in many ways.

- Chapters 15 and 16 were coauthored with Pam Piper of DISA. Much of the basis for Chap. 16 was developed with Alice Muntz and Charlie Szymanski of the HITC Data Reverse Engineering Performance Team. I had subsequent discussions with Christian Ramiller, also from HITC. Finally, Pam Piper and I refined the discussion.

- Chapter 8 was coauthored by Major Michael Joseph III, as part of his master's program at Virginia Commonwealth University (sponsored by the Air Force Institute of Technology), and Dr. Amita Goyal also at Virginia Commonwealth University. The views expressed by Major Joseph are his own and do not represent Air Force or any other official positions.

- Chapter 13 was coauthored by Denise Heller from HITC. The example presented in that chapter is derived from her research into data integration.

- Chapter 19 was coauthored by Bill Girling (Manager of Systems, Dept. of Personnel and Training/Commonwealth of Virginia).

- Chapter 21 was coauthored by Scott Kozel (Systems Analyst, Virginia Department of Transportation) as part of his master's program at Virginia Commonwealth University.

- Chapters 12, 14, and 17 were coauthored by Richard Kirkbride (also from DISA). His views on value-added data administration helped me to focus on the management perception of data reverse engineering.

Thanks also to

- QED Publishing for permission to reprint the quotation on page 59 from S. Spewak *Enterprise Architecture Planning* © 1993 QED Publishing.

- *Data Management Review* for permission to reprint the quotation on page 60 from Connall and Burns "Reverse Engineering: Getting a Grip on Legacy Systems" © 1993 *Data Management Review*.

- *Database Programming & Design* for permission to reprint the quotations on pages 184 and 185 from Moriarty "Migrating the legacy: as the industry migrates to the PC, don't give up your mainframe products yet" © 1992 *Database Programming & Design*.

- *Harvard Business Review* for permission to reprint the quotation on page 189 from Haeckel and Nolan "Managing by wire" September/October © 1993 *Harvard Business Review*.

- *Datamation* for permission to reprint the quotation on page 205 from Appleton "Business Rules: The Missing Link" © 1984 *Datamation*.

- *Software Magazine* for permission to reprint the quotation on page 205 from Pfrenzinger "Reengineering goals shift toward analysis, transition; users adjust expectations as suppliers work on next-generation capture tools" © 1992 *Software Magazine*.

- *Software Engineering Strategies* for permission to reprint the quotation on page 350 from Ulrich "From Legacy Systems to Strategic Architectures" © 1994 *Software Engineering Strategies*.

During the manuscript review process, the Internal Revenue Service's reengineering gurus Julia McCreary and Sandra Yin both took time from their vacations to review drafts. The book has benefited enormously from their insights and helpful suggestions. Karen White of TASC and several anonymous reviewers also reviewed the text in various forms.

The HITC project team played a key role in developing and implementing the initial reverse engineering framework. I want to thank the dedication of C. Haley, D. Heller, D. Hobson, K. Kawakami, K. Janes, S. Lem, B. Nguyen, T. Pace, C. Ramiller, C. Szymanski, C. Tholen. I acknowledge their efforts contributing to the success of the data reverse engineering programs with which we have been associated.

Marjorie Spencer (editor of computing at McGraw-Hill) has been invaluable providing guidance to keep this project on and within budget. Ever consider taking a crack at software engineering, Marjorie? Thanks also to Jane Palmieri (our editing supervisor) for letting me play at the role of a novice composition editor.

I need and want to thank my many colleagues in the government, and in particular Tom Weber (also of DISA) for many stimulating discussions on these issues. In addition, Doug MacDonald, Marybeth Sission, Ann Polivka, Bruce Brown, Marco Johnson, Nancy Orvis, Linda Kjonnerod, Bunny Smith, Sandy Rogers, Robert Cooper, Carol Wilson, Ken Fagan, Jerry Cooper, Becky Harris, Bill Greyard, Lynn Henderson, all helped to provide other perspectives on the data reverse engineering process. Finally, thanks to my Department Chair at VCU, Dr. Richard Redmond, for creating such an excellent working environment. Thanks to my parents and especially my mother for the use of her dual-page Macintosh display. Also thanks to the Defense Information System Agency's Public Affairs Officer, Betsy MacDonald, for helping me to navigate through the proper channels. As a result of her efforts, I am able to attach the following message: "Cleared for open publication - subject to the following disclaimer: review of this material does not imply department of defense endorsement or factual accuracy or opinion (94-S-2334)." In order to acquire the clearance, I had to promise not use any DoD specific examples—consequently all have been made up and any resemblance to living, breathing systems is purely coincidental.

Finally, thanks to Jasmine for the subtitle, for showing me it is all possible, and for helping me to make it so!

Peter Aiken

Richmond, Virginia
August 1995
paiken@cabell.vcu.edu
http://128.172.188.1/isydept/faculty/paiken/paiken.htm

Context

context n.
1. The part of a text or statement that surrounds a particular word or passage and determines its meaning.
2. The circumstances in which an event occurs; a setting. (Middle English, composition, from Latin contextus, from past participle of contexere, to join together : com-, com- + texere, to weave; see teks-below.)

Synonym(s): No synonyms found for context.

Source: *American Heritage English Dictionary* © 1993 Houghton Mifflin Company

Part 1 describes data reverse engineering project contexts, terminology, typical motivations, and organizational steps that can be taken toward that goal. Accordingly:

Chapter	Summary
1	*Presents three data reverse engineering scenarios used repeatedly throughout the book, representing a range of project scopes and organizational approaches*
2	*Describes a number of data reverse engineering terms also used throughout the book and among practitioners*
3	*Shows how data and data-related issues can cause far-reaching organizational problems, motivating organizations to develop specific mature capabilities to address them*
4	*Defines a data architecture as a necessary strategy organizational asset and data reverse engineering's role in supporting its development*
5	*Answers the most frequently asked questions about data reverse engineering projects and presents a framework for project organization*

1

Three Data Reverse Engineering Strategies

The chapter presents examples of three basic data reverse engineering (DRE) strategies: *reactive* or *bottom-up* DRE, *proactive* or *top-down* DRE, and *middle-out* DRE—a hybrid strategy.

Reactive Data Reverse Engineering/World-Wide Airlines

For the third time this year, World-Wide Airlines monthly frequent-flyer statements are being mailed to 500,000 program participants without important information. Among other items, the statements (see Fig. 1.1) report the number of frequent-flyer miles accruing from the use of certain long-distance telephone company services. This feature alone attracts thousands of new inquiries about the program each month. The "mileage credit for long-distance usage" program feature and corresponding business partnership are considered by management to be part of World-Wide Airlines strategic advantage over the competition. Perhaps the only real drawback of the feature is that the program participants tend to be detail-oriented. With many participants soon to be inquiring about the missing information, additional customer service staff will be needed to handle the increased caller volume—this has happened before.

The statements should have been mailed 3 days ago. The alternatives were to either mail these statements out incomplete or wait another day with no guarantee that the information systems supposed to supply the information would actually produce it. Additional delay would impact preparation of the next month's statements. Because of previous experience, World-Wide management had enough recent historical data on the cost of customer service staff overtime required to respond to this type of incident to accurately forecast the costs. When no technical staff member was willing to predict when the

3

World-Wide Airlines Frequent Flyers Mileage Summary

Identification Number: 123 456 789
Additional miles to earn a free ticket: 4,099
Mileage Credited: 02SEP95 to 30SEP95: 7,471
1995 mileage accumulation: .... (*) 35,901
Mileage since enrollment: 215,901
                                 (*) Includes unredeemed mileage carried over from 1994

ACTIVITY SUMMARY:

Date	Flight	Description of Mileage	Credit	Miles	Bonus
13SEP95		Long-distance Mileage	60		
14SEP95		Bank-card Mileage	1393		
24SEP95	288	San Diego, CA-Detroit, MI		1956	
24SEP95		30% Exclusive, Bonus			587
24SEP95	474	Detroit MI-Richmond, VA		750	
24SEP95		30% Exclusive, Bonus			225
25SEP95		Rent A Car-San Diego	500		
26SEP95		San Diego Hotel	2000		

Figure 1.1   Information contained on a frequent-flyer mileage statement.

systems would be able to produce the information, management elected to mail the statements without the long-distance mileage, as a stopgap measure or as the lesser of two evils.

It was doubly frustrating that the customer service staff overtime would have to be added to the problem diagnosis cost. Besides, it was reasoned, the customers were probably getting used to this by now, and perhaps the caller volume would not be quite so high. Fortunately, this situation has a positive outcome. The chief information officer's (CIO's) long-term solution to the problem has been tentatively approved by World-Wide's executive management—pending an update of certain investment details. Management noted in the approval decision that if World-Wide's customers discovered that it spends between 60 and 80 percent of its information technology budget on system maintenance, the popularly held (and carefully cultivated) perception of the airline as a modern, technology based organization would be questioned. Thus, as soon as the executive management reviews an updated project investment proposal it will likely approve the airline's first data reverse engineering project.

World-Wide Airlines' first data reverse engineering project is designed to address the information exchange problems with its business partners. At the moment seven major interfaces are required to exchange information between World-Wide and its frequent-flyer partners. Interface 2 (bolded in Fig. 1.2) is the immediate problem area. Airline frequent-flyer program participants are rewarded each month with five times (5×) the number of dollars they spend each month with the long-distance phone company partner credited to their accounts as airline frequent-flyer mileage. Thus a participant spending $100 per month on long-distance phone calls expects to be rewarded with a credit of 500 additional miles on the monthly frequent-flyer program statement. Over the past few years however, the interfaces depicted in Fig. 1.2 have been somewhat problematic.

The current problem is associated with World-Wide's mileage accumulation and reporting system (MARS)—the system that accumulates the various types of mileage credits from the program partners and reports it to the program participants. Developed as one of the first of its kind, the system served its original purpose well, accumu-

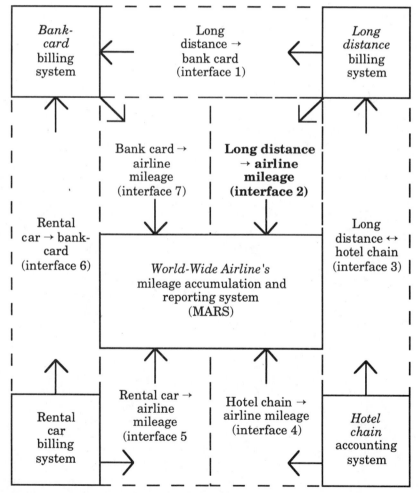

Figure 1.2   Interfaces required to support information exchange among five different organizations to produce frequent-flyer statements.

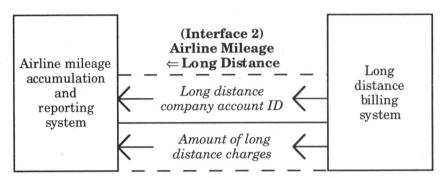

Figure 1.3   Close up of interface #2—long-distance billing system sends data to the airline mileage reporting system.

lating and reporting the monthly airline mileage for program participants. The system software was developed very rapidly to beat the competition. It consists of thousands of lines of unstructured, uncommented source code with almost no meaningful documentation.

As soon as frequent-flyer programs were introduced, it became clear that the participants demanded comprehensive partnerships with various rental car, hotel, bank-card, and other related organizations. Although the negotiations with the new partners were relatively easy to consummate, the technical process of exchanging information between the organizations proved more challenging. Integrating the additional information and functionality into the MARS was not an easy task in the first place and was made more difficult by the poor condition of the original programs. Again, the intense pressure to be first frequent-flyer program to offer these additional features caused the new functionality to be woven into existing tangled webs of code with substandard documentation, making a bad situation worse.

Problems initially occurred as unanticipated conditions caused the systems to fail. Patches, quick-fix solutions, or stopgap measures were applied to correct the problems but still worsening code conditions incurred sizable maintenance expenses as programmers and analysts struggled to keep MARS running. In addition, the partner organizations were making changes to their systems that interfaced with the MARS, and these changes often required corresponding changes in the MARS, which were implemented with great difficulty. A primary problem was defining the data items exchanged between the systems of the partnering organizations. Fig. 1.3 magnifies the interface between the long-distance company and the MARS. System value is added by successful information exchange. Automation was the key to MARS economic feasibility. Unfortunately the already brittle system interface has tended to fail if changes to (1) any piece of information exchanged, (2) the timing of the exchange, or (3) the information content are not coordinated with the cooperating partner. For example, if the long-distance company originally reported the "gross amount" of miles to be credited but now wants to report only the "dollars spent," it must secure agreement from World-Wide to coordinate the required MARS changes.

Both the long-distance company and World-Wide management recognize the value of the frequent-flyer program and support its existence. However, the long-distance company is in the midst of acquiring a number of its smaller competitors, bringing even more potential frequent-flyer participants to the partnership. Integration of the competitors' systems into existing systems requires almost monthly changes to the nature of the long-distance ④ airline interface. Lack of standardization creates expensively brittle operating conditions—regardless whether the amount of data exchanged is small or large. The result has been increasingly frequent disruptions in information exchange.

The airline CIO pushed for several months to obtain approval to reverse engineer the MARS (Fig. 1.4). Now it appears that approval

---

Proposal: Reverse engineer the mileage accumulation and reporting system (MARS) using data reverse engineering to obtain critical system information that will form the basis for the reengineering project

Project situation: Management has determined that the MARS has been unable to keep pace with the evolving requirements. Service demands will continue to grow as will the number of organizations with whom MARS exchanges information. A preliminary 30-day DRE system survey has been conducted. This project proposal is the result of the project scoping analysis.

Physical evidence assessment: Only two individuals with the organization today can understand the programs comprising the MARS. Fortunately they work for airline and are available to become project team members. Virtually all of the system documentation exists in their heads.

Project scope: In the initial phase, the project will require participation from the long-distance company. Eventually, all our business partners will be drawn into this effort to define common information exchange formats and technologies.

Anticipated results: Within 3 months, produce business rules and "to be" business and system requirements for a reengineered MARS. Also produce a list of potentially reusable software modules and other system assets so as to minimize the amount of MARS reengineer required. At that time, reexamine the project for continued feasibility. The goal is to migrate the MARS into a computer-aided software engineering tool environment so that future changes can be more effectively managed. In addition, this project will produce an evaluation of data reverse engineering as an analysis technique and indicate its potential value to the larger MARS reengineering project and to other airline information technology-based efforts.

Figure 1.4   Proposal for reverse engineering World-Wide's MARS.

will be granted. Other executives understand that requirements to rapidly produce MARS led to the present situation. They approve of the CIO's reengineering approach, which is to first examine the existing system to gain as much useful information from it as possible. The system information is captured and represented as models jointly developed with the long-distance company's system personnel. The models will enable the two organizations to precisely specify and communicate their information exchange requirements. Since the long-distance company is only partially through the process of integrating its former competitors, a number of other interface changes are planned. The models will help both business partners manage the changes everyone knows are coming. This is an example of reactive reverse engineering.

The project goals are modest. The CIO wants to explore the use of a new technology called *data reverse engineering* to see how it can help solve the problems associated with the MARS. Reverse engineering the MARS also represents an opportunity for the information systems (IS) group to gain experience with computer-aided software engineering (CASE) and reverse engineering technologies and methods. It is anticipated that using data reverse engineering to recover the existing business rules and system requirements and move them into a CASE-based repository will result in faster and more accurate access to information that could then be used to reengineer the MARS. The IS organization has already conducted a preliminary analysis to obtain the information used to determine the resources required to accomplish the project. It has secured the participation of individuals with information key to the project effectiveness as well as the participation of the long-distance business partner. If the project is successful, it will serve as a model for other reverse engineering efforts with the ultimate goal of reengineering the MARS and other troublesome systems.

Proactive Data Reverse Engineering/MiddleTown Health Care Facility Consolidation

As a result of attempted health care reform, a combined federal, state, and regional effort has resulted in the consolidation of several formerly competing health care facilities into a single operating unit. Clustered about the same geographic region (MiddleTown, USA), these health care facilities used to compete with each other for business in a market requiring technology-intensive equipment investment. For example, each health care facility had invested substantially in medical technologies such as magnetic resonance imaging (MRI) facilities. These facilities are now considered to be excess capacity. The MiddleTown health administration board now decides which health care facility will house a consolidated MRI facility, and the savings from not maintaining several separate facilities are used to increase services or reduce costs to the community.

In the same spirit of consolidation the MiddleTown board is looking to achieve similar savings by consolidating the functions of the individual health care facility IS organizations. Not having in-house expertise to conduct an evaluation, the board has hired a consultant on a 3-year contract (with options) to plan and manage the IS consolidation process. While receiving salary, the consultant's ultimate compensation would be based on a combination of the following:

- Net savings from retiring existing systems and introducing new, less costly technologies into the regional health care IS systems

- Satisfaction of all system users (information systems, management, end user, and health care facility customer) measured empirically at quarterly intervals

- Speed and smoothness of any resulting conversions

The board knew that this type of investment required both stable funding and a clear hand to direct the operation. It secured funding for a 3-year effort and was able to contract with the desired consultant. The stable funding source and the board's clear indication of a hands-off policy toward the project presented a perhaps once-in-a-lifetime opportunity for the consultant. By agreement with the board, the consultant will

- Supervise reverse engineering projects for selected hospital information components to obtain baseline information, including details of the current requirements being satisfied by the individual systems

- Develop a future or "to be" regional health care facility data architecture capable of meeting current and future needs

- Plan and implement the architecture by
  - Deciding which existing systems need to be upgraded, maintained, or terminated based on the basis of future needs
  - Accomplishing the transition from the present configuration to the future architecture while minimizing user community disruption.

Currently each of the formerly independent health care facilities has a separate IS group supporting multiple information systems. During project solicitation, the MiddleTown board decided that savings could be achieved by retiring duplicative or otherwise excessive systems services such as payroll, personnel, and administration. A preliminary investigation by the consultant agreed although it noted that two key findings—the (1) exact choice of which systems to retain and which to retire and (2) determination of the actual system requirements—could affect the net program savings quite dramatically.

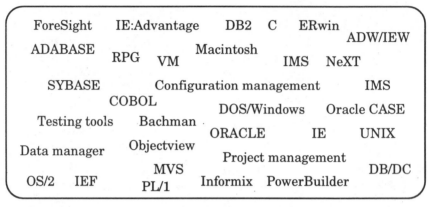

Figure 1.5   When facing enterprise integration challenges, data is often the most common element.

The consultant and the board agreed the consultant would submit recommendations and the board would retain an oversight role and stay out of decision making to mitigate the impact of political pressure on the board.

In a typical fashion, the individual facilities are composed of different and often incompatible operating systems, programming languages, and hardware from various vendors. Since most of the facilities never attempted to exchange information, there is little knowledge or historical basis for comparing the functionality of the various systems. The consultant is faced with the task of deciding whether to (1) retire the existing system now or in the future or (2) enhance the existing system so that it will meet future organizational needs. Such decisions require a master plan for guidance in individual projects. Figure 1.5 illustrates how, in certain situations, the data is the only common element in the complex legacy environment.

Figure 1.6 describes the proposed reverse engineering program as presented to the board. Figure 1.7 illustrates how the program will focus on assessing the condition of and extracting useful information from the existing systems. The program will be staffed largely by professionals recruited from the existing IS organizations. Project teams will be organized around functional areas by combining existing IS personnel with functional users and the consultant's data reverse engineering expertise. Plans call also call for a parallel organization-wide effort aimed at defining those information-based services that the new regional health care facility should provide.

A reconciliation operation will assess the differences between the "as is" and "to be" requirements. These differences will indicate those systems requiring full or partial reverse engineering efforts. The organizational data architecture will be developed using information obtained by reverse engineering selected systems and system components. Once the data architecture can be used as a plan to guide future reengineering efforts, selected systems will be reengineered to conform to the architecture. This scenario is a classic example of pro-active reverse engineering.

Hybrid Data Reverse Engineering/Governmental Pay and Personnel Project

This third data reverse engineering project is sized somewhere between the first two scenarios. The approach is neither top down or bottom up but instead a middle out approach to data reverse engineering.

Proposal: Establish a reverse engineering program (REP) as a limited duration, cross-functional, activity. The program activity will be staffed by members solicited from the existing IS staffs of the individual facilities. Reevaluate the charter and progress of this program quarterly.

Project situation: A regional alliance of health care organizations has been formed. Of particular interest, functionally duplicative systems exist. Part of the incentive behind the alliance was a reduction in the overall cost associated with supporting the combined organizations. This is the goal of the REP—established to help effect this transition as fast as possible! The entire organization is to be reengineered, and REP is to be prepared to begin operations supporting this effort within 2 weeks. Management is in agreement that the REP program goals should include (1) developing a data architecture suitable for use by the new regional facility, (2) evolving the current situation where each participating organization currently stores and use data differently to an enterprise-wide perspective using shared data to develop integrated information for the regional health care facility, (3) identifying the long-term needs including new technological infrastructure, and (4) evaluating and if appropriate moving to open systems and/or distributed systems.

Evidence assessment: Uncertain, but to date hardware and software from more than 20 different vendors have been identified—documentation is infrequent at best.

Project scope: Estimate multi-year effort required—3-year funding is authorized. This project could result in major changes in how technology is used in all levels of this organization.

Anticipated results: REP goals include (1) identifying candidate data reverse engineering systems within 2 months; (2) establishing a base set of organizational data reverse engineering metrics within 6 months; (3) within 24 months establishing and implementing an organizational data architecture based in part on data reverse engineering analysis; (4) producing accurate reverse engineering project costs within one year; and (5) delivering an accurate forecast for what can be accomplished during the remaining 2 years of the program and what will remain to be done. Eventually this unit must work itself out of a job.

Figure 1.6 Proposal establishing the MiddleTown health care facility reverse engineering program.

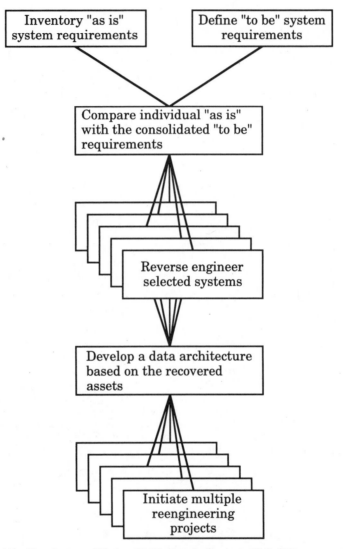

Figure 1.7   Plan for consolidating MiddleTown's disparate IS facilities.

The legacy environment consists of four systems: personnel and three legacy payroll systems resulting from a series of consolidations during the 1980s. In addition, focus the target the new system to be developed in a client/server environment. Personnel maintains the organization's personnel policies, standards, and guidelines; keeps personnel records for full-time and temporary employees and their corresponding positions; and administers group health plans for covered employees and their dependents. The system support is provided by the personnel management information system (PMIS).

First installed in 1978, PMIS contains all personnel records covering some 90,000 positions and 80,000 employees. Supplementing PMIS core functions are the following subsystems:

- The *recruit system*, which produces a biweekly-weekly report showing job openings

- The *personnel data analysis system*, providing selective extract information from PMIS files, which can then be used in conjunction with MAPPER to create customized reports

- The *benefits enrollment system*, used to maintain group health insurance information on 113,000 participants and 98,000 dependents

- The *wage employee system*, tracking the cost and utilization of temporary personnel

- Several smaller databases and their related applications, including
  - Minority and female talent bank
  - Employee suggestion program
  - Training records system.

Twice a month, the personnel system provides the various pay systems with tapes including salary rates, which are used to post salaries. After each payroll run, the pay systems provide PMIS with a copy of the expanded current earnings file, used to monitor wage employee activity.

PMIS runs on a large mainframe using commercial database management software. Including subsystems, it contains over 1000 programs, written primarily in COBOL.

Payroll systems cover the issuance of payroll checks. Organizational entities provide data for the three payroll systems both in print and via magnetic media. Some 130,000 paychecks, 70,000 of which are direct deposits, are processed by payroll on a semimonthly basis.

The pay systems are hosted on a different brand mainframe. Collectively the system contains some 750 programs for payroll only, 1000 programs for personnel only, and 135 programs with both payroll and personnel functions. COBOL and a vendor's proprietary procedural were used to write selected processes and screen edits.

A comprehensive system analysis cited a number of inadequacies in the current personnel and payroll systems. Examples include

- Redundant data entry into both pay and personnel systems, including the resulting reconciliation processes, are significant time and effort wasters. Many organizational components also maintain separate systems for specific human resource (HR) functions, requiring additional duplicative data entry.

■ Other shortcomings include lack of time-and-attendance functions, inadequate provisions for part-time or temporary workers, and limited support for recruitment and training activities.

■ All levels of users, from managers to clerks, require more comprehensive data in critical areas such as staff utilization, hiring trends, attendance monitoring, skills inventory, benefits utilization, and workers' compensation monitoring.

■ Future HR initiatives will be strongly benefits-driven. Current systems lack the flexibility to handle cafeteria plans, pay-for-performance, team incentives, and other modern personnel management practices.

The auditor has cited strong concerns regarding security structure and control problems inherent in the mainframe operating system hosting PMIS and has also repeatedly called for a single, integrated replacement for both the pay and personnel. Making extensive use of focus groups, the analysis identified over 300 required or essential HR business activities conducted by both pay and personnel, organized into the following functional areas:

■ Employment
  – Recruitment
  – Selection

■ Personnel administration
  – Employee relations
  – Salary planning
  – Classification and pay
  – Job evaluation
  – Benefits administration
  – Health insurance plans
  – Flexible spending accounts
  – Group life insurance
  – Retirement plans
  – Employee compensation
    changes

■ Payroll
  – Payroll administration
  – Payroll processing
  – Payroll interfaces

■ Organization and career
  development

■ Training administration
  – Career planning/skills
    inventory
  – Work group activities

■ Health and safety
  – Accidents and workers'
    compensation
  – Health and safety
    programs

Figure 1.8 contains the third data reverse engineering project proposal summary. This scenario illustrates a situation in which executive management and system personnel agree on the need for this reengineering project and on the reverse engineering approach.

A subsequent analysis of possible project risks yielded management's desire for a combined data- and process-oriented result capable of putting the organization in the best possible status for addressing the possibility of project complexities. Figure 1.9 illustrates three representative scenario complexities associated with the governmental pay and personnel scenario (#3).

Proposal: Integrate the three existing payroll systems as well as the pay and the personnel systems using information gained by data reverse engineering appropriate portions of the systems.

Project situation: As part of "downsizing," management has determined that the organization can no longer afford to support these organizational components in their current form—the pay and personnel functions will be combined. Neither information system meets current organizational needs—requiring disproportionate amounts of resources to maintain. A preliminary system survey has been conducted—this is the result.

Evidence assessment: Not adequate—already recognized as a factor contributing to the maintenance problems.

Project scope: Both information systems need to be replaced and both contain valuable organizational information. The three existing pay systems currently pay more than 50 different types of employees who are paid according to a schedule involving more than 15 different pay conditions.

Anticipated results: Within 15 months, produce business rules and "to be" business and system requirements for an integrated organizational pay and personnel system including the "to be" processes.

Figure 1.8 Governmental pay and personnel project: data reverse engineer and integrate the existing payroll and personnel systems.

	Identify critical success factors	Understand area(s) of greatest risk	Formulate risk alleviation strategies
Admin-istrative	Can an interorganizational data administration function be implemented?	Organizational inability (i.e., economic, technical, cultural) to master a demanding technical environment	Ensure that partners receive required training in relevant technologies in time to benefit
Techno-logical	Can the new partners implement the system in a cooperative distributed environment on-time and within budget?	Implementation of multi-platform system in a diverse technical and operational environment	Development of a flexible system architecture with both centralized and decentralized components
Oper-ational	Can the new system empower users to develop innovative solutions to meet their specific business needs?	Garbage in, garbage out (GIGO): automating existing processes and missing the benefits of advanced technology	Identify and prototype specific areas of risks associated with the transition from the "as is" to the future system

Figure 1.9 Governmental pay and personnel project complexity dimensions.

2

Definitions

Since definitions are particularly important to data engineers, this chapter presents and defines data reverse engineering, and a number of related terms in common use (and occasionally misuse).

Data Reverse Engineering Defined

A popular definition of *reverse engineering* provides some initial context. By calling it something like "the discovery of the obvious," some writers are attempting to convey the essence of a question that has often come from non-technical management:

> Why do you have to reverse engineer this system? Can't you just look at the documentation to get the information you need?

Too often the answer is "no!" Fortunate are organizations who have been able to keep their system documentation up to date. Most existing system documentation does not contain the information required to complete a DRE analysis because until recently, this type of information was not considered important to system development. Although reverse engineering is sometimes considered the discovery of the obvious, this isn't a useful definition.

When lecturing, I define the term *reverse engineering* thoroughly. I use charts pairing phrases from the Chikofsky and Cross [1990] reverse engineering definition with illustrations. Each pairing completely illustrates a part of the definition. The presentation of the lecture goes something like this:

Definition: *Reverse engineering* is the process	**Commentary**
Of analyzing a system	I ask the audience to notice the integral role tools play in some types of analysis. Some practices are difficult or even impossible without the use of certain tools. Successful projects depend on adequate computer aided software engineering (CASE) tool support.
Of identifying the system's components	Can you imagine what would be the state of modern medical practice if physicians had no concept of the body as a system composed of individual components? Patient treatment might be very different and perhaps not as effective.
Of identifying the system component's interrelationships	Understanding the interrelationships and interdependencies among system components leads to better understanding of the system behavior and performance.
Of creating representations of the system in another form	A key element of reverse engineering is the creation of a system model. Models are used to help understand complex system behavior. Computer-based models are also an excellent means for storing and formalizing organizational data. Finally, models permit evaluation of various scenarios or other outcomes produced by the model.
At a higher level of abstraction [Chikofsky & Cross 1990]	Modeling is also used to filter out extraneous detail. Model information can be considered basic or indispensable to understanding the system. Properly functioning models define an essential set of information. Models are used to monitor and then predict system responses to changing environmental conditions. Additional useful information is gained from the process of interacting with the model. The models developed during DRE analysis can and should be treated as organizational assets.

This definition has become standardized in the information technology community and usefully describes the general reverse engineering process. If the focus of a reverse engineering effort is on a system's data, the project should be labeled as *data reverse engineering* which can be formerly defined as: the use of structured techniques to reconstitute the data assets of an existing system. (The earliest reference I could find to the term *data reengineering* was [Ricketts et al. 1989] who defined it as standardizing data definitions and facilitating source code simplification.) In the next three subsections I'll clarify this definition by explaining the terms *structured techniques* and *data assets* and my use of the verb *reconstitute*.

Reverse engineering is predicated on the fact that requirements and designs are more easily understood than code; thus it is useful to obtain requirements or designs from code. In addition, it is more effective to transform old systems into a current CASE environment so all DRE projects have a CASE component. CASE allows for the management and reuse of existing process and data models which can then be used to facilitate changes in technology or vendor environments. Data reverse engineering has been successfully accomplished when the organization understands the current system sufficiently to facilitate subsequent redevelopment efforts at a suitable cost (adapted from Bush [1990]).

Structured techniques defined

Structured techniques are defined as model building techniques involving model construction and analysis of the existing situations and proposed solutions prior to actual system development [Pressman 1993]. Structured techniques provide analysts with tools enabling them to comprehend certain otherwise unfathomable situations. Structured techniques such as decomposition and abstraction permit the Federal Budget to be distilled to meaningful sound bites on the evening news. (It is also possible to decompose these things into meaningless bites.)

When I use the term *structured techniques*, the six specific characteristics permit analysts to understand the problem, guide them to a solution, and help them assess the results and payoffs in terms of organizational knowledge and investment. (These were passed along to me without attribution.) Thus, use of this term implies the following qualities. Structured techniques

1. *Allow the form of the problem to guide the form of the solution.* As opposed to those who have a tendency to view a problem from the perspective of a familiar tool. (Recall Maslow's observation: "If the only tool you know is a hammer you tend to see every problem as a nail.") Structured techniques are useful because they are adaptable to meet both changing understanding of requirements and increased understanding of the problem.

2. *Provide a means of decomposing the problem.* Problem decomposition has long been a part of structured techniques. To *decompose* something is to separate it into its components or basic elements. *Decomposition* is the process of dividing up large problems into smaller, more manageable problems. A solution to the large problem can be developed by solving the smaller problems.

3. *Feature a variety of tools simplifying system understanding.* Often these are graphics-based, permitting those who are not familiar

with DRE tools and terminology to quickly become engaged in the process. They quickly become contributing project team members.

4. *Offer a set of strategies for evolving a design solution.* Like management, data reverse engineering is an art as well as a science. This means to achieve the desired results it is necessary to understand the situation in the context of long range goals and draw on appropriate tools in response to evolving situations.

5. *Provide criteria for evaluating the quality of the various solutions.* There are two dimensions to the quality of DRE outputs: technical quality and validity. With a small amount of understanding, it becomes relatively easy to assess the technical project output quality. In addition, DRE outputs can be assessed for their correctness, and the end products can be—in essence—certified as accurate representations of the existing system by those working with the system.

6. *Facilitate development of a framework for developing organizational knowledge.* Data reverse engineering projects are capable of producing a lot of detailed information. It is a non-trivial task to organize and maintain these data assets to ensure their usefulness as inputs to other development efforts. Data reverse engineering depends on the availability of appropriate CASE-based technologies to function as repositories for the DRE project deliverables.

It is crucial to understand that the application of structured techniques is one of the key concepts that makes data reverse engineering economically viable. Data reverse engineering is also facilitated by near-standardized modeling languages and representations.

Data assets defined

It is always interesting to put down in print the meaning of a term you have used for many years. Such is the case with the term data assets. For starters, the term is not listed in most dictionaries.; nor does it appear in any of the five data administration glossaries that I have on-line [Martin 1989, Appleton 1985, Beese 1988, Inmon 1988, Narayan 1988]. The word *asset* didn't appear anywhere in the glossaries of the work just cited either. So I went to my on-line dictionary for a definition of this term (see Fig. 2.1). If assets are useful or valuable qualities, persons, or things, then *data assets* must be useful or valuable data. In the same manner as typical organizational assets, such as real estate, inventory, and financial and human resources, are useful and valuable, organizational data assets are useful or valuable organizational collections of fact and meanings [Appleton 1984]. The key point here is—all organizations have some data assets but not all organizations recognize data as an asset.

---

asset n.

1. A useful or valuable quality, person, or thing; an advantage or a resource: *An agreeable personality is a great asset; proved herself an asset to the company.*

2. A valuable item that is owned.

3. A spy working in his or her own country and controlled by the enemy: *"One of our assets working out of Leningrad managed to take a drive out of town"* (Frederick Forsyth).

4. assets. a. *Accounting.* The entries on a balance sheet showing all properties, tangible and intangible, and claims against others that may be applied, directly or indirectly, to cover the liabilities of a person or business, such as cash, stock, and goodwill. b. The entire property owned by a person, especially a bankrupt, that can be used to settle debts.

Synonym(s): No synonyms found for asset.

Figure 2.1 Definition of *assets* (Source: *American Heritage English Dictionary* © 1993 Houghton Mifflin Company).

Consider the following three examples of data items that might be considered valuable by an organization and thus organizational data assets.

■ The contact information and payment schedules of people who owe your organization money. (In a widely reported case, a major telephone company lost hundreds of millions of dollars when it lost track of customer calls for several months [Stapleton and Sarasin 1992].)

■ Certain information required by the Internal Revenue Service (IRS), Federal Trade Commission (FTC), Occupational Safety and Health Administration (OSHA) or other federal, state, and local governments. (How much would it cost to re-create all the information you regularly send to the IRS if this information disappeared one day?)

■ The phone numbers of customers who do business with your competition. (Specific means of obtaining this information as well as the associated ethical considerations are beyond the scope of this book.)

I use the verb *reconstitute* very deliberately (as, I assume, did Chikofsky and Cross [1990]), emphasizing the value-added nature of DRE projects (see Fig. 2.2). The next question might be: "Well, what kind of data assets might exist in an organization?" Some data asset examples might include the following items:

- Information that can expedite system maintenance efforts reducing the overall cost of system operation. Usually this is described as a form of enhanced system documentation capable of facilitating system maintenance efforts. Automated information systems are to a greater degree self documenting, if certain information (i.e., compilations) produced during development is still available.

- An organization-wide *data bank* cataloging the physical implementation and usage of data throughout the system. Data banks facilitate data sharing among organizational components. If the organization maintains a data bank, this information can also be valuable guidance to understanding the system before attempting to plan enhancements.

- Explicit and implicit prescripts used by the organization to achieve the mission. These include information ranging from pricing information to personnel references to strategic information monitoring techniques. These are the organizational *business rules* and they exist, whether explicitly defined or not. Business rules should be managed similarly to other data assets. Business rule development can be a primary data reverse engineering project focus.

The concept of data assets is broader than information produced merely as a byproduct of system development. Another key part of the definition of *asset* is the phrase "an advantage or a resource." Organizations are realizing that the value of data collected in information systems is such that both the data and the systems should be considered a valuable resource in the same manner as are organizational personnel. Properly developed, data assets can provide organizations with a competitive advantage [Haeckel and Nolan 1993, Berry 1994]. As such, organizational data assets deserve the same consideration as do other strategic assets such as manufacturing technologies, patents, and organizational skills.

Reconstitute defined

Organizational data assets exist in all organizations. Often they are embedded in the system; however, they must be analyzed (using structured techniques) and represented (in models) before they can be useful, let alone valuable to organizations. Unlike the terms *restore, recover, rebuild, reconstruct, reclaim, recondition*, the term *reconstitute* implies the addition of something valuable to the original assets to make them more useful.

Thus, data reverse engineering can be regarded as adding value to the existing data assets, making it easier for organizations to use and more effective as a tool. Data reverse engineering is and should be viewed as an empowering or enabling technology permitting, supporting, and facilitating the development of integrated systems. Integrated systems are a prerequisite to enterprise integration.

> **reconstitute** v.
>   To provide with a new structure: *The parks commission has been reconstituted.*
> Verb: To bring back to a previous normal condition. restore, recover, rebuild, reconstruct, reclaim, recondition, rehabilitate, rejuvenate

Figure 2.2 Definition of *reconstitute* (Source: *American Heritage English Dictionary* © 1993 Houghton Mifflin Company).

Data reverse engineering is the first step in enterprise integration. (For the present, consider the term *enterprise integration* synonymous with the terms *effective* and *efficient organizational functioning*.) Data reverse engineering is used to develop a data asset base of information that is then used as the basis for making decisions regarding the scope and timing of subsequent enterprise integration activities.

Understanding Related Terms

This section defines other terms commonly used in the context of reverse engineering projects including:

- Forward engineering
- Reengineering
- Business process reengineering
- Design recovery
- Restructuring
- Database reverse engineering

- Reverse engineering
- Legacy systems
- Software reverse engineering
- Redocumentation
- Software maintenance
- Product reverse engineering

Forward engineering, reverse engineering, and reengineering

Figure 2.3 is adapted from Chikofsky and Cross' presentation in their definitional article, "Reverse Engineering and Design Recovery: A Taxonomy" [1990]. Its compact presentation conveys a great deal of information. Many of the definitions cited in this section were presented in the same article. Consider first the distinctions between forward engineering, reverse engineering, and reengineering activities.

- *Forward engineering.* This is the process of using requirements assets to derive design assets and using design assets to derive physical code. Development flows from logical to physical.

- *Reverse engineering.* Reverse engineering activities are concerned with deriving their information from previously created assets (i.e., existing designs and code). It is the process of using physical evidence to derive design assets or using design assets to derive requirements assets. Development flows from physical to logical.

- *Reengineering.* Chikofsky and Cross' [1990, p. 14] definition of reengineering as "the examination and alteration of the target system to reconstitute it in a new form" has also become standardized in the information technology community. (The target system is the system to be reengineered.) Reengineering results from the coordination of forward and reverse engineering efforts. An important point to understand is that reengineering generally involves first some reverse and then some subsequent forward engineering activities. It might be useful to consider reengineering a type of information recycling aimed at that Chikofsky referred to in another article as "shortening the distance between actual and intended business operations" [Chikofsky 1990].

The gaps between the three categories of assets produced by data reverse engineering in Fig. 2.3: requirements assets, design assets, and code and documentation assets indicate that

- During reverse engineering, design assets are produced from code and documentation assets, and requirements assets are produced from design assets.

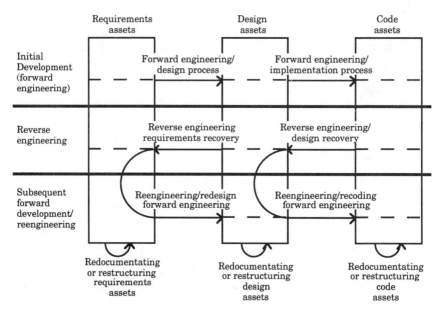

Figure 2.3 Definition of relevant terms (adapted from Chikofsky and Cross "Reverse Engineering and Design Recovery: A Taxonomy" © 1990 *IEEE Software*).

■ During forward engineering, the design is developed from the requirements (which are often not treated as assets) and the code and documentation assets are developed from the design (which are often similarly treated).

On the figure, gaps between the assets indicate the requirement for a certain amount of effort to be expended before a useful asset can be developed from its basis. This is due to the nature of the products produced. These products must exist in a relatively concrete state before they can be completely understood. For example, during reverse engineering a design—reverse engineered from the code/documentation—will not be useful until its development has attained a certain critical mass. Each data asset component needs to be defined as either related (or unrelated) to everything else in the model—the model needs to be complete before it is most useful. Developing and understanding common meanings for specific data assets will help, but not nearly as much as will understanding the defined data asset in the context of the remaining organizational data.

Legacy systems

A *legacy* is something handed down from an ancestor or a predecessor or from the past [AHED 1993]. Legacy information systems are the typical target of DRE projects. *Legacy systems* are defined as stand-alone applications built using a prior era's technology [Ulrich 1994]. They have been stereotypically and perhaps unfairly described as existing software systems whose plans and documentation are either poor or nonexistent [Connall and Burns 1993]. In 1983, Appleton sized the current investment in legacy systems at $400 billion resulting from 30 years' effort on the part of 500,000 IS professionals [Appleton 1983]. A more recent estimate indicates that organizations are spending $70 billion annually to maintain more than 10 billion lines of code [Lerner 1994]. In the 1993 annual Deloitte & Touche survey of more than 400 CIOs, respondents classified more than 70 percent of their applications as legacy systems [Deloitte & Touche 1994].

Legacy systems are often quite large and/or complex. Bucken describes a somewhat typical situation of an organization with 33,000 employees. The organization has an inventory of 1000 software programs containing 140 million lines of COBOL code. The average program was 17 years old in 1992 [Bucken 1992]. Another, more specific legacy system description was reported by Slonim [1994] and Tomic and Tilley [1995]. The IBM product called *Structured Query Language/Data System* (SQL/DS; also DB2/VM and DB2/VSE) was more than 10 years old in 1990, with some program modules more then 15 years old. It contains more than 3,000,000 lines of a proprietary IBM language called PL/AS organized into about 1300 compilation units [Buss 1994].

Many legacy systems evolved in response to user needs instead of being developed to support an organization-wide enterprise integration/strategic planning effort. Performance problems have arisen as user requirements have evolved, and the system developers have been unable to keep pace with the change requests [Software 1990]. One residual effect of the growth of end user computing activities [McLean et al. 1993] has been integration problems brought about by the localized process optimization. Few legacy systems have been properly integrated, resulting in high operational costs. Consequently, legacy systems have attracted attention because of poor performance characteristics or disproportionate resource consumption. In addition, increased corporate volatility resulting from mergers, takeovers, and other corporate restructuring has transformed a number of well-planned and well-implemented organizational systems into chaos [Ulrich 1994]. These factors have combined and as a result, many organizations are burdened with costly legacy systems .

A primary cause for concern is that (as Jones [1994] noted) software does not age gracefully; the rate of change of software is between 5 and 7 percent each year for as long as the software is operational and in use. Over time, the changes tend to degrade the program's original structure. Difficulty in understanding the system results in increased difficulty performing both maintenance and reengineering.

A common characteristic shared by legacy systems is that they are very difficult to replace. A recent GSA publication [GSA 1993, p. 6] reports two key factors:

- It is generally not cost effective to completely redesign the system from scratch. For example, suppose it would cost $1 million dollars to replace a legacy system with resulting savings of $75,000 a year. Many decisions makers would require a much higher payoff before approving the replacement of a system that may provide critical support for agency operations.

- To make matters more difficult, replacement of legacy systems causes disruption in the organizations. Replacement of a legacy system that integrates data/information will usually highlight the lack of integration of the program area's organization. Program area management will often resist reorganizing if the changes impact their organization. In addition, users accustomed to the existing will often resist moving to other systems.

Respondents to the annual Deloitte & Touche survey of CIOs [1994] indicated that nearly 70 percent of their applications were classified as legacy systems and 38 percent indicated dissatisfaction with these same systems, citing:

- Lack of access to management information (31 percent)

- Maintenance and enhancement difficulties (28 percent)

- Unresponsiveness to new business directions (24 percent)

- Systems excessively expensive to operate and maintain (13 percent)

- Inconsistency with technical direction (3 percent)

- Eighty-seven percent of the CIOs indicated they were taking "significant action" to improve or replace them.

Business process reengineering

A word of caution. The terms *forward*, *reverse*, and *reengineering* need to be reconciled with business process reengineering as described by Hammer and Champy [1993] and others. According to their business definition, *reengineering* is "the fundamental rethinking and radical redesign of business processes to achieve dramatic improvements in critical, contemporary measures of performance, such as cost, quality, service, and speed." A *business process* is defined as "the collection of activities that takes one or more kinds of input and creates an output that is of value to the customer" [Hammer and Champy 1993, p. 35.] It begins by "starting over"—envisioning the organization as if it could be created from scratch today. The focus is on identifying and supporting only value-added business processes. King epitomizes a popular conception of business process reengineering in Fig. 2.4.

Because of the popular use of the term *business process reengineering*, the following question often arises:

Why do you have to reengineer? Why can't you just start all over?

Often the data is protected by statute. This means that by law certain data items must be maintained for some period of time. In addition, as assets, the data often needs to be migrated from existing systems to those resulting from reengineering efforts. There is much value in the existing information assets that can be used as inputs to other development efforts — in effect, recycling the information.

A major focus during business process reengineering is definition, analysis, and refinement of organizational business rules. Selfridge et al. [1993] define *business rules* as requirements on the conditions or manipulation of data expressed in terms of the business enter-

---

Hold up a glass of water.
The optimist sees it half-full.
The pessimist sees it half-empty.
The reengineer sees twice as much glass as is needed.

Figure 2.4   Reengineering in a glass (adapted from King "How to Fail" *NAPM Insights* 1995).

prise or application domain. Business rules are a major source of bureaucratic inefficiencies because processes tend to be locally optimized instead of organizationally optimized. Sandifer and von Halle [1991] provide examples of the type of information maintained in business rule form:

■ The language used to describe and solicit information about business practices

■ Business practice metrics that provide a means of relating strategic organizational objectives to operational performance requirements

■ Links connecting business needs to data models

There are fundamental similarities between business reengineering and data reverse engineering. Data reverse engineering, grounded as it is in structured techniques, is designed to achieve the kinds of "fundamental," "radical," and "dramatically different" new systems needed to produce significant results. Using development processes free from preconceived notions inherited from the existing system is consistent with the "rethinking" and "redesigning" called for by business process reengineering advocates.

Software (or program) reverse engineering

How does software reverse engineering differ from data reverse engineering? Chikofsky and Cross' reverse engineering definition does not distinguish between the two. According to Biggerstaff et al. [1993, p. 27] software reverse engineering (a.k.a. *program code reverse engineering*) is achieved when

> A person understands a program when they are able to explain the program, its structure, its behavior, its effects on its operational context, and its relationships to its application domain in terms that are qualitatively different from the tokens used to construct the source code of the program.

The scope of software reverse engineering efforts is generally delineated by the software's application domain—its immediate environment. Local optimization is more likely to occur under these conditions. This application focus is illustrated with another passage from the same Biggerstaff et al. article, listing products extractable from COBOL programs.

> Reverse engineering is the process of decomposing an application into its components, primarily for documentation purposes. The objects that can be extracted from a COBOL application include program modules, paragraphs, links to called modules, and related data objects: data sets, logical files, records, data structures passed through the Linkage section, local data structures defined in Working-Storage, and the data elements that compose those data struc-

tures. Copybooks and common modules shared among programs can also be identified.   By analyzing database and on-line control statements, information about database structures, screens, and transactions can be extracted.

In Fig. 2.5, items 4 through 9 interact with each other, and so it is important to capture these relationships as well.   Figure 2.6 illustrates how project scope constitutes the primary difference between software and data reverse engineering.   For example, consider a system where the same data asset is implemented using different record definitions in dozens of different programs and is stored in multiple files.   Data cannot be completely understood by examining the application programs, program control language, and files separately.   Instead, the system as a whole must be analyzed.   Data reverse engineering is focused on enterprise-wide use of data, while software reverse engineering is concerned with understanding the processes implemented in a software program as they interact with an application domain [Hall 1992].

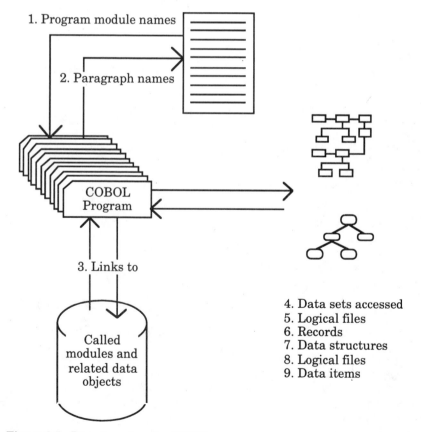

Figure 2.5   Reverse engineering COBOL programs.

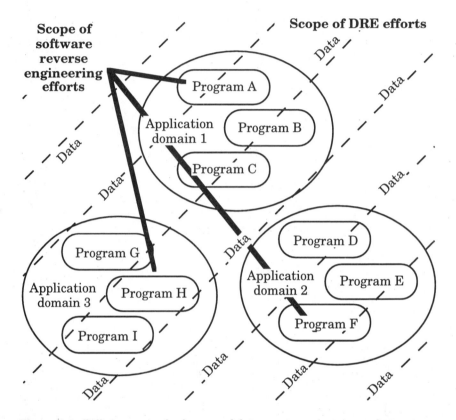

Figure 2.6   Differing scope of software and data reverse engineering projects.

Design recovery

Design recovery is "a subset of reverse engineering in which domain knowledge, external information, and deduction or fuzzy reasoning are added to the observations of a subject system to identify meaningful higher level abstractions beyond those obtained directly by examining the system itself" [Chikfosky and Cross 1990] (see also [Biggerstaff 1989]).

Redocumentation

Redocumentation is "the creation or revision of a semantically equivalent representation within the same relative level of abstraction—the resulting forms of representation are usually considered alternative views intended for a human audience" [Chikofsky 1990].   Redocumentation is the process of improving access to the information contained in organizational requirements, design, and code assets.

Restructuring

Restructuring is "transformation from one representation form to another at the same relative level of abstraction while preserving the
subject system's external behavior (functionality and semantics)"
[Chikofsky and Cross 1990]. Restructuring is the improvement in the
content of the information represented by data assets.   Chikofsky
and Cross [1990] also highlight the fact that data analysis is the importance of working with logical data models.   To draw a further distinction between restructuring and data reverse engineering, consider
how restructured code will not facilitate data migration, data sharing, or changing functional area business requirements.

Software maintenance

Software maintenance is defined as the "modification of a software
product after delivery to correct faults, to improve performance or
other attributes, or to adapt the product to a changed environment"
[ANSI/IEEE Standard 729-1983]. The focus of software maintenance
efforts is more generally associated with correcting aspects of the system that are causing it to malfunction.

Database reverse engineering

Database reverse engineering has been defined as "identifying the possible specification of a specific database implementation and possibly
also identifying how the implementation got to be what it is"
[Hainaut et al. 1993]. As many older systems do not use databases,
it is a subset of data reverse engineering and is applied in situations
where databases are used.

Product reverse engineering

Finally, consider the following—also correct—perspective of *reverse
engineering*:

> Reverse engineering is changing from a tedious manual dimension-
> ing or tracing process to a powerful engineering tool utilizing mod-
> ern digitizing equipment and CAD/CAM systems. Digitizing meth-
> ods, ranging from lasers, and video equipment, to coordinate meas-
> urement systems, measure the coordinates of points on a part con-
> tour.

Abella et al. [1991, p. 495] are describing an earlier but still widely
used meaning of the term reverse engineering.   Manufacturers have
become highly skilled at determining how the competition engineers
products.   In this context, reverse engineering is used to attempt to
expose innovative manufacturing or other techniques that the competition might be using to gain a competitive manufacturing advantage.

3

Organizational Data Issues

This chapter describes important organizational data issues. To varying degrees, organizational data issues adversely impact all organizations. They are seldom recognized as data issues, and organizations inefficiently spend resources attempting to solve the wrong problem. Whether fixing data problems or maintaining ineffective or inefficient systems, the net result is information systems that cost more than they should to operate. Extra costs are an inefficient use of organizational resources. Management is interested in maximizing the degree to which information systems support organizational missions. Addressing organizational data problems will lead to increased operational effectiveness because the flexibility of the information management permits its more effective utilization. Organizational data issues are often the result of complex technical and operational situations, perplexing decision makers and leaving them uncertain as to the best course of action.

Data and Information

Often the terms *data* and *information* are not well differentiated. Appleton [1984] presented a useful description of data as at least one fact paired with at least one meaning. Each unique combination of facts and meanings defines an individual piece of data. When data is supplied in response to a request, it becomes information. Different facts and meanings can be combined into data and supplied as information in response to different queries. Figure 3.1 illustrates this concept. An association created by a hospital sales representative links a fact—230 (units)—with a specific meaning—sales for a given time period—and is provided response to a standing request from the hospital sales manager. This information can be used by the sales manager to determine total commissions for the

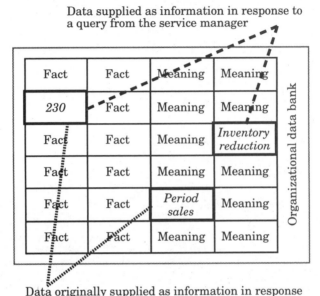

Data supplied as information in response to
a query from the service manager

Data originally supplied as information in response
to a query from the sales manager

Figure 3.1 Facts, meaning, data, and information.

period. The same fact—sales—can also be combined with a different meaning—a reduction in the inventory—by the hospital services manager to forecast inventory levels. (Other useful meanings for the same fact could include such measures such as advertising effectiveness, perceived product quality, or market penetration.)

In this manner, organizations are able to manage a relatively large amount of information by successfully managing a relatively small amount of data (for more on this see Moriarty [1992]). Organizations can afford to develop and maintain information systems in part because of the leverage achieved by this economy of scale. If technology didn't permit association of individual facts with multiple meanings, the cost of maintaining data comprising the required information would be much larger. In a similar fashion, resources invested in data quality can favorably pay off with relatively larger amounts of quality information. For example, facts and meanings can be combined into data items, data items can be combined into data models, and data models when related to other data models become data assets.

Data Quality Issues

Data quality concerns are driven by user requirements. In general, those requirements should be derived from the organizational mission and strategy, through tactical and operational levels, down to specific user requirements. Often this is the case, but sometimes user requirements are formulated outside the organizational strategy context. Thus, what are sometimes regarded as user requirements are often no longer relevant to the current mission and are thus not valid requirements.

There are two classes of data quality concerns. First is the quality of the facts. Is the number "230" the correct fact? Does it mean "somewhere between 220 and 240 units" or "exactly 230"? Does it mean that the sales representative hoped to sell 230 units by the end of the month but some orders are outstanding, or does it mean that the representative took orders for 230 units but this product averages a 10 percent product return rate?

Data definition quality is fundamental for subsequent analysis. The second concern is the quality of the associations implemented in the system and the manner in which the users implement their activities with the system. Consider how the situation would change if the system only permitted a three-digit number to be entered into the field corresponding to that fact and the sales representative wanted to associate the number 225,138 with it. While the "230" data might be precise enough to permit the services manager to forecast inventory levels, the data is probably no longer useful to the sales manager who is attempting to process data for the commission checks.

Organizational data requirements are often expressed in terms of various criteria including the following criteria: accuracy, completeness, consistency, extendibility, flexibility, modularity, reliability, relevancy, stability, timeliness, and validity. Figure 3.2 illustrates how these can be categorized according to content, form, and time dimensions. Data not meeting organizational requirements can suffer in a number of subtle ways. Consider an example—suppose that the sales reporting period is monthly. What should the sales representative report if only two weeks or so of data is available? If the representative waits to report the data until the entire month is available, the system might not meet organizational data timeliness requirements. If the representative reports the half month of data, the system might not meet data accuracy requirements.

Data Sharing as a Goal

Organizations experience data problems when data does not meet various organizational criteria. These problems are often brought to the awareness of organizational management when there are requirements for data to be shared among organizational components and it doesn't happen. Figure 3.1 also illustrates an example of data sharing as the fact "230" is successfully shared among the sales representative, the sales manager, and the service manager. The terms *shared data* and *data sharing* are frequently used to describe

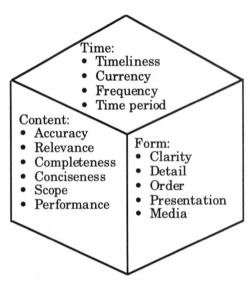

Time dimension

Timeliness	Provided when needed
Currency	Up-to-date when it is provided
Frequency	Provided as often as needed
Time period	Be provided about past, present, and future time periods

Form dimension

Clarity	Provided in a form that is easy to understand
Detail	Provided in detail or summary form
Order	Arranged in a predetermined sequence
Presentation	Presented in narrative, numeric, graphic, or other form
Media	Provided in the form of printed paper documents, video displays, or other media

Content dimension

Accuracy	Free from errors
Relevance	Related to the information needs of a specific recipient for a specific situation
Completeness	All the information that is needed should be provided
Conciseness	Only the information that is needed should be provided
Scope	A broad or narrow scope, or an internal or external focus
Performance	Information can reveal performance by measuring activities accomplished, progress made, or resources accumulated

Figure 3.2 Attributes of information quality (adapted from O'Brien *Management Information Systems: a managerial end user perspective* © 1993 Richard D. Irwin, Inc.).

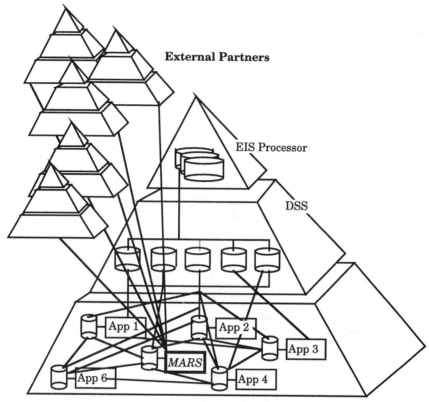

Figure 3.3   MARS legacy operational environment (App = application).

data meeting sufficient organizational requirements permitting it to be shared with other units. If "230" represents the amount of sales in thousands, the sales manager must identify an information source permitting commission checks to be processed. In order to be valuable enough to warrant the development of an exchange procedure, shareable data should meet organizational requirements for validity, accuracy, completeness, and consistency. Shareable data must also be relevant, reliable, and stable, or it will not be economically feasible to exchange the data. Simultaneously, shareable data must be maintained flexibly, modularly, and reliably in order to meet evolving requirements. Finally, it must be delivered in a timely fashion both within the organization and to its external business partners.

Since most legacy systems weren't developed to easily exchange data with other systems, they often don't! In the past, as information sharing requirements became known, systems were connected piecemeal. In the governmental pay and personnel scenario, three pay systems exchange data with a personnel system. Figure 3.3 shows the somewhat typical World-Wide MARS legacy operating environment resulting from several interconnected application programs

in different functional areas. More than a dozen program interconnections are shown at the lowest operational level. A decision support system (DSS) has been added at the tactical level permitting
some data to be extracted from files associated with the application
programs. DSS users can search some application data as they attempt to combine data among systems to address various unstructured problems (for more on DSS, see Sprague and Carlson [1982]).
As a further development, an executive information system (EIS) has
been added. The EIS is capable of facilitating access to data from
executive workstations. This pattern of information system evolution
results in separate classes of information systems and system users.
Separate data is developed and maintained to support decision making at operational, tactical, and strategic levels.

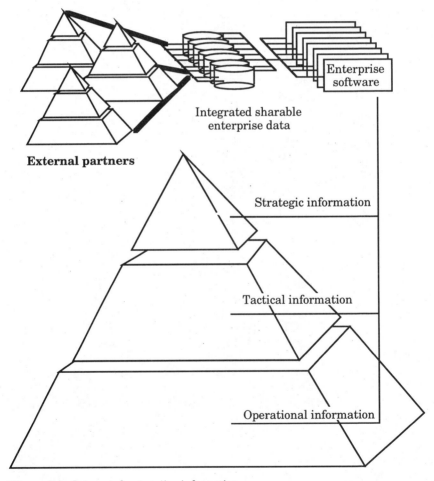

Figure 3.4   Integrated enterprise information.

Additional resources are required to maintain separate classes of information systems and used to support different classes of users. Achieving data sharing under these conditions has been difficult because of the tight coupling between organizational processes and information systems data encoded in the existing information systems as, for example, system data handling characteristics, program code, job control language, screen specifications, and edit checks. Changes to either processing or data require corresponding and often extensive modifications to the other. Perhaps more importantly, lack of standardized data and data structures across systems results in numerous brittle interfaces, resulting in situations where organizations are unable to make effective use of their own data [Pelton 1993, Aiken et al. 1994]. The inherent brittleness of this situation can be eliminated by separating process and data; the resulting situation is shown in Fig. 3.4. Instead of separate classes of software and of data, there is one class of access software and one set of organizational data capable of providing appropriate information in response to standardized queries from all levels.

Data and Models

Data is managed using models and is an important part of data reverse engineering. Data modeling is both a prerequisite and the means to achieving shareable data. An individual data reverse engineering project produces a number of model-based products. These are directly useful at solving system related problems. The model-based products become even more valuable as they are integrated with other organizational models. Figure 3.5 illustrates that data models must be integrated from the operational-level to the tactical-level models and further still to strategic-level models in order to ensure the model's correctness.

Recall from Chikofsky and Cross' [1990] definition of reverse engineering how models are used to help understand complex system behavior. Model information is basic or indispensable to understanding the system. Modeling is also used to

■ Filter out extraneous detail

■ Document requirements from existing evidence

■ Help discover business rules

■ Accelerate business process reengineering

■ Build and maintain institutional knowledge

■ Assist in organizational restructuring

■ Help estimate degree and scope of proposed system changes

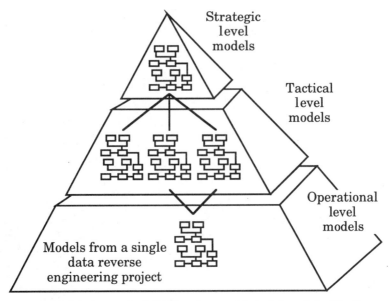

Figure 3.5 Models from a single DRE project need to be integrated with other organizational models.

- Increase the accuracy of design and implementation activities

- Store and formalize organizational information and

- Evaluate various scenarios or other outcomes produced by the models in the context of organizational strategy formulation.

Additional useful information is gained from the process of developing the model. Each model developed during DRE analysis can and should be treated as an organizational asset. Two classes of data are required to achieve shareable data. The first class has already been discussed—the specific combinations of facts and meanings combined as data. The second class is data about the data or what is referred to as *metadata* [Brackett 1994]. An example of metadata is the knowledge that the fact 230 is supposed to be associated with the meanings "period sales" and "inventory reduction." Both types of data are required to develop models. Modeling success is dependent on the quality of the data as well as the metadata.

Organizational Data Problems

The most important and prominent organization data problem category concerns data meanings. Before information can be exchanged among systems, all must be free of data meaning problems (see Fig. 3.6). For most systems these potential problem areas have been resolved within the scope of the system (local optimization). Problems occur as organizations attempt to exchange data between systems because the differing systems implement specific solutions to data problems that have not been integrated at the organization level. In the case of World-Wide Airlines' data problem, the names, field lengths, values, and so on are resolved within the boundaries of each of the long-distance company's various systems but the parent organization has not reconciled their implementation at the organization level. Thus, data and data exchanges can be a major source of problems.

Data synonym problems

Data synonym problems occur when facts and meanings have the same or similar names but different meanings. Consider two data items occurring often in legacy systems. The terms *person* and *individual* are both used in systems to represent a human about whom the organization desires to maintain information. Specific examples from the MiddleTown scenario include employees, customers, service providers, members, participants, individuals, patients, and so forth. If an organization wanted to know the number of individuals tracked by all systems, the individual formulating the query would have to understand the metadata in order to ask for the number of "persons" in one system and the number of "members" in another and so on. In addition, the query formulator would have to know which label to use with each system.

Data homonym problems

Data homonym problems occur when data items have the same name but different usage. An example of a data homonym would be what the long-distance company calls "charges." "Charges" to World-Wide

---

synonym n.

A word having the same or nearly the same meaning as another word or other words in a language.

Synonym(s): No synonyms found for Synonym.

-----

homonym n.

1. One of two or more words that have the same sound and often the same spelling but differ in meaning.

2. a. A word that is used to designate several different things. b. A namesake.

Synonym(s): No synonyms found for homonym.

Figure 3.6 Synonym and homonym definitions (Source: *American Heritage English Dictionary*, Deluxe Edition, Boston; Houghton Mifflin Company, © 1993).

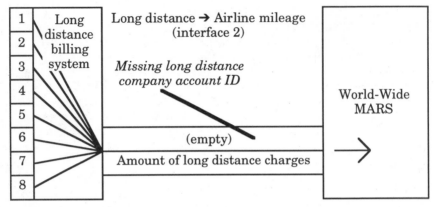

Figure 3.7 Close up view of the interface connecting World-Wide's MARS to the long-distance company systems. (This is a revised version of Fig. 1.3.)

Airlines are free trips that frequent-flyer club members make against their account balance. An inventory of the existing hospital information systems indicates "charges" also represents an accounting entry on the patient's record. A data homonym problem is currently the suspected cause of the MARS data problem. The current procedure is for each of the affiliated long-distance company subsidiaries to transfer information across the interface shown in Fig. 3.7.

Apparently, one of the long-distance company subsidiaries provided incorrect data to be accumulated by the long-distance billing system. The first system requires its data to be transferred manually, and the operator on duty was known to be sloppy about following established procedure and verifying the correct outputs of the standard queries. As a result of operator error, the system was asked to provide "account" instead of "ldaccount." The synonym "account" was the customer 's long-distance account—in this case—a number larger than the receiving interface field. The transfer utility substituted blanks for the actual data value. Other organization-wide problems resulting from legacy system evolution include the following (categories from Ricketts et al. [1989]).

Inconsistent field lengths

Inconsistent field lengths are used to maintain the same data. For example, does the system use a 5-digit zip code or a 9-digit zip code? Some systems use a 10-digit zip code, storing the hyphen between the 5-digit part and the 4-digit part. Transferring a 10-digit alpha-numeric zip code into a 9-digit numeric zip code can produce unexpected errors requiring manual intervention before attempting to re-load the data.

Inflexible field lengths

Inflexible field lengths are used to store expanding information. Consider the end-of-the-century dilemma for programs calculating something simple, like age, by subtracting the birth year (defined as a 2-digit number) "59" from the current year "95" (also defined as 2 digits). The program logic fails in the year 2000—as it does currently in isolated cases when users have tried to enter rather old birth dates such as June 18, 1899, because the programmers used a 2-year date field. Chikofsky (as quoted by Peterson [1993]) has provided another example. "Imagine making a phone call to another time zone at midnight and getting billed for 99 years of connect time."

Inadequate documentation

Nonexistent, missing, or dated documentation makes it difficult to determine the effects of modifying the data processed by a system. Suppose that you desire to expand the year field of all programs from 2 digits to 4 digits as your organization addresses the field-length problem described above. Determining how many programs will have to be modified and the effects of those changes is difficult when the documentation is poor.

Default data values

Inconsistent use of default data values also presents problems. Does a blank in the "married" field mean that the individual in question is single, or that the field never had any data entered into it (i.e., it is a missing value)?

Data Problems as "Hidden" Consumers of Resources

In all likelihood the major impact of organizational data problems is that they aren't recognized as such. When not recognized, data problems are not accounted for, tallied, analyzed, or treated as such. Data problems are often perceived as other types of problems and the data problem costs are intermingled with other costs. For example, the MARS-type problems are often described more generally as "computer problems" or perhaps as "system" problems. Those describing the situation as such do not correctly perceive the problem cause as an organizational inability to exchange data with a business partner: the long distance company. When data problems are not perceived correctly, are not addressed accordingly, and are not reported correctly there can be no organizational accountability and subsequent awareness of their true cost. Lack of organizational awareness of data as either an asset or as a potential problem often results in situations where resources are spent solving organizational data problems without either recognizing them as such or applying

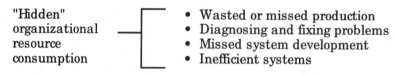

"Hidden" organizational resource consumption
- Wasted or missed production
- Diagnosing and fixing problems
- Missed system development
- Inefficient systems

Figure 3.8   Potential sources of hidden IS resource consumption.

the correct solution procedures to the problems. It's a little like attempting to diagnose an electrical problem inside a house with a hammer—an electrical diagnostic box would be a better tool choice.

All organizations spend some resources fixing problems in old systems. Some spend additional resources on systems that are no longer useful. The question is, how much? (When one considers that the financial services industry spends an average of $27,442 and the insurance industry spends $19,815 annually per worker on information technology—these number take on greater significance [WSJ 1995].) Figure 3.8 shows how data problems can contribute to "hidden" organizational resource consumption.

1. Users spend time running the system and producing incorrect outputs. In some cases the system will cease to function, providing a more visible problem indication. This would have been the case if the MARS data problem had been discovered as the monthly statements were being printed. Additional user time can be lost if production is reduced or idled during problem diagnosis and repair—for example, reducing or terminating production.

2. System maintainers must spend time diagnosing the problem. Generally, the amount of time spent diagnosing is influenced by the overall condition of the system documentation. Generally, the better the documentation, the more easily the content and applicability to the problem can be determined. Once diagnosed, the system maintainers spend additional time developing, implementing, and testing a solution.

3. Significant opportunity costs can be associated with problem solving activities as personnel are pulled off of whatever they were working on to assist. This generally impacts the project from which they were pulled. Figure 3.9 illustrates how the MARS project could impact another development project desired by World-Wide's information system organization.

4. A final class of resources are consumed by systems not optimized for organization-wide performance. In the past, many legacy systems were developed to support specific task-oriented perspectives. They were considered standalone systems supporting the (local) workgroup goals as opposed to the (global) organizational goals. One of the residual effects of the growth of end-user computing

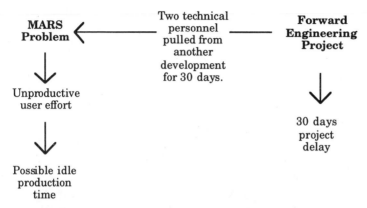

Figure 3.9 Effect of the MARS-type data problem on forward development (or other maintenance) efforts.

activities [McLeod 1993] has been increasing awareness of integration resulting from localized process optimization. Information systems have been developed to satisfy localized organizational needs is the absence of organization-wide technology-based information system planning. (For example, Hammer and Champy [1993] relate an example of local optimization where more than 50 manufacturing units supported individual purchasing functions. Providing a shared access corporate database produced savings of more than 150 percent improvement in on-time deliveries, 50 percent reduction in lead times, and 75 percent reduction in failure rates.) In some cases systems are kept operational by organizations no longer requiring their services but unaware of the changes in organizational requirements.

Although few organizations are able to account for the percentage of system maintenance costs attributable to data problems, system maintenance costs are forecast to rise to as much as 80 percent of organizational technology budgets during this decade (see Fig. 3.10).

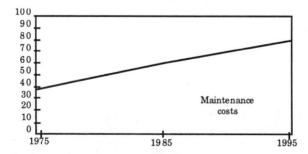

Figure 3.10 Rising cost of software maintenance (adapted from Pressman *Software Engineering: A Practitioner's Approach* 3rd edition, © 1993 The McGraw-Hill Companies, Inc.).

The cost of maintaining existing information systems consumes large portions of total information technology spending [Gibbs 1994]. Information systems operating in this context must be costing us more than they should to operate; in other words they could be run more efficiently. Some organizations may be able to achieve significant results by recognizing the extent of their data problems and addressing them programmatically as data problems.

Organizational Data Maturity

Organizational ability to achieve shared data generally increases in relation to information technology maturity (see Fig. 3.11). Like most industries, information technology has progressed through various growth periods that are used to assess organizational progress toward some ideal performance levels (see stages 1 through 6 in Fig. 3.12). The most frequently cited model of organizational information technology maturity is Nolan's "stages of data processing growth" [1979]. According to this model, each stage is characterized according to its

- Approach to its application program development and maintenance

- Organization of the information systems function

- System planning and control process

- User awareness levels

These stages provide a means of classifying organizational adeptness with the application of information technologies. Stage 5 is labeled "data administration." Organizations achieving stage 5 are characterized by their ability to share data internally and externally. Other stage 5 characteristics include appropriately low amounts of batch processing, emphasis of database applications, management awareness of data as a corporate asset, and joint key specialist-developer project management and accountability. Most organizations I've worked with have matured to stages 3 or 4 (this was also Nolan's assessment).

---

maturity n.
The state or quality of being fully grown or developed.
Synonym(s): No synonyms found for maturity.

Figure 3.11 The definition of *maturity* describes a state of development, free from positive or negative connotations (Source: *American Heritage English Dictionary* © 1993 Houghton Mifflin Company).

Growth processes	Application portfolio	Data processing organization	Data processing planning and control	User awareness
1 Initiation	Functional cost reduction applications	Specialization for technological learning	Lax	"Hands off"
2 Contagion	Proliferation	User-oriented programmers	More lax	Superficially enthusiastic
3 Control	Upgrade documentation and restructure existing applications	Middle management	Formalized planning and control	Arbitrarily held accountable
4 Integration	Retrofitting existing applications using database technology	Establish computer utility and user account teams	Tailored planning and control systems	Accountability learning
5 Data administration	Organization integration of applications	Data administration practices	Shared data and common systems	Effectively accountable
6 Maturity	Application integration "mirrors" information flows	Data resource management	Data resource strategic planning	Acceptance of joint user and data processing accountability

Figure 3.12 Nolan's six stages of data processing growth (adapted from Nolan "Managing the Crisis in Data Processing" © 1979 *Harvard Business Review*).

The basic requirements for being able to successfully invest in stage 5 technologies include

- Competitive environments requiring the strategic use of data
- Top management understanding of data as a corporate resource and corresponding investment commitments

- Significant progress toward the goals of standardized, shareable organizational data

- Information systems development characterized by and based on use of common data administration procedures and tools

The placement of stage 5 as the second most advanced technological maturity stage indicates that not all organizations have had the opportunity to evolve to the point where they can effectively implement organization-wide solutions to data problems; that is, there is a class of problems associated with information technology maturity that organizations have found difficult to properly address.

4

Data Architectures

A basic assumption among some new and potential dictionary users is that once a dictionary is installed, it somehow automatically provides instant control and benefits to the information management activities of an enterprise.

While a dictionary can allow users to effectively manage their data resource, it requires a significant amount of planning and preparation before it can be put into production. If an enterprise does not understand how or elects not to implement a dictionary system correctly, the results achieved will fall below expectations.

Figure 4.1 Automation alone is insufficient to ensure quality, shareable data. (Adapted from the *DB/DC Data Dictionary* G320-6017 © July 1978 by International Business Machines Corporation.)

Durell began his 1985 text [Durell 1985] on data administration with the material presented in Fig. 4.1. The description remains a key to obtaining support for an organizational function designed to perform the activities related to the data dictionary. In addition, the organizational data administration function has taken on a greater role: expanding beyond data dictionary maintenance into strategic planning. This chapter describes the role of DRE projects as most effectively performed as a coordinated component of an organization-wide data administration effort. An important data administration activity is the development of an organizational data architecture.

Organizational data administration functions are responsible for addressing organizational data issues. Data architectures support implementation of organizational strategy. Data reverse engineering projects typically play two types of roles in organizational data ad-

---

dexterity n.

1. Skill and grace in physical movement, especially in the use of the hands; adroitness.

2. Mental skill or adroitness; cleverness. [French dextérité, from Latin dexteritas, from dexter, skillful.]

Synonym(s): Noun: Skillfulness in the use of the hands or body. skill, readiness, prowess, adroitness, deftness, dexterousness, sleight.

Figure 4.2 Definition of *dexterity* (Source: *American Heritage English Dictionary* © 1993 Houghton Mifflin Company).

ministration efforts: a *reactive* (bottom-up) role correcting organizational data problems and a *proactive e*(top-down) role contributing to the organizational data architecture. Data reverse engineering projects are influenced in part by organizational data problems encountered and in part by data architectural development considerations.

Enterprise Integration Defined

In the *Proceedings of the First International Enterprise Integration Modeling Conference*, Petrie further defines *enterprise integration* in terms of improving the overall performance of large, complex systems. Improvements may be gained in areas such as processing efficiency, unit responsiveness, perceived quality, and product differentiation. Enterprise integration efforts seek to achieve improvements by facilitating the interaction among organizations, individuals, and systems Petrie [1992].

In today's turbulent competitive environments an organization's degree of enterprise integration can be defined as a state of organizational dexterity combined with organizational awareness of that dexterity (see Fig. 4.2). Dexterous organizations are more capable of responding effectively to opportunities appearing in the environment. Organizational dexterity can be measured by quantitatively evaluating the processes used to produce organizational outputs—for example, by assessing the time required to introduce a new product to the market or the resources required to process the accounts payable. The definition also indicates that accurate knowledge of an organization's capabilities can be as important as achieving the dexterity in the first place. Overestimating organizational ability to achieve desired objectives or performance can have disastrous results. Organizational dexterity is useless if not applied in appropriate contexts with reasonable expectations. The degree to which an organization can share its data—internally and externally—can be used to assess that organization's degree of dexterity. The amount of effort and resources required to achieve organization dexterity varies from situation to situation but is generally correlated with the use of structured methods and CASE technologies during system development.

Dexterity is typified by use of information technology to augment management's ability to assimilate and react in rapidly evolving situations [Haeckel and Nolan 1993]. Data sharing is both a key to achieving enterprise integration and the chief benefit. Perhaps the most intriguing role in enterprise integration is that of legacy systems. They both constitute the chief obstacle associated with achieving enterprise integration and simultaneously enable enterprise integration.

Consider the following assessment of the federal government's system development efforts from a 1992 General Accounting Office Report [1992]:

> In spite of more than $20 billion expenditures ... agency after agency still lacks critical information needed to analyze programs issued, manage agency resources, control expenditures, and demonstrate measurable results.

(See also Subcommittee [1989] and GAO [1979] for other related reports.)

While being blamed for disproportionate resource consumption, legacy systems can also be seen as valuable sources of information representing a promising means of leveraging the existing information system investment. Shared data is typified by organizational ability to use information as a strategic asset. However, assets are useless without knowledge of the asset characteristics in this case the metadata describing the data comprising the specific model in question. (Notice how the metadata becomes valuable as well.)

Enterprise integration is not possible without integrated enterprise information usually shortened to *shareable data*. Shareable data is a major enabler as well as an indicator of organizational dexterity. Organizations without shareable data spend greater amounts of resources producing the required information at the required time than do organizations with it. And they are unable to benefit from the shareable data. It is a prerequisite to effective use of enterprise information as a strategic asset and development of a data architecture as a major enabler of shareable data.

An *enterprise model* is a high-level map of a business that guides the development of computer systems and the executing of unautomated activities [Haeckel and Nolan 1993]. Organizational dexterity is measured, tracked, and assessed against objectives derived from enterprise modeling efforts. Enterprise models represent the means for managing the interaction between an organization and its environment. Models are used to establish distance periods of model performance (monthly, weekly, daily, etc.). Models are revised to reflect changes in the organization or the environment so that new behavior patterns can be understood. Once validated, in that they effectively predict aspects of future organization performance, the models can be used as a strategic weapon to evaluate alternate courses of action.

In addition, models can be used to identify opportunities to establish competitive advantage. Consider the following description of what Haeckel and Nolan call "managing by wire" [Haeckel and Nolan 1993].

> Models can be used to monitor and then predict system responses to changing environmental conditions. Just as heads up displays present selected abstractions of a few crucial environmental factors, like on coming aircraft, targets, instrumentation (and) communications technologies aid in evaluating and implementing alternatives, managers of organizations running by the wire respond to readouts appearing on the console, modifying the business plan based on changes in external conditions, monitoring the performance of delegated responsibilities, and sending directions to subsidiary units such as manufacturing and sales.

Figure 4.3 illustrates how data plays two roles during model development. Monitoring data provides a target characteristic to which the model is "tuned." When the model is operational, the data becomes the model inputs. Model development data is metadata needed to accomplish data engineering activities (such as name, definition, structure, encoding, source, steward requirements, business rules, models, designs, specifications, and repositories). Monitoring data is also used to report structural changes in real-world conditions such as the introduction of a new competitor into the market. Changes are applied to the model to maintain consistency between the model and its environment. Enterprise modeling can also be considered as the integration of numerous models existing at tactical and operational levels. Thus, models are the medium of communication for organizational data architectural development activities.

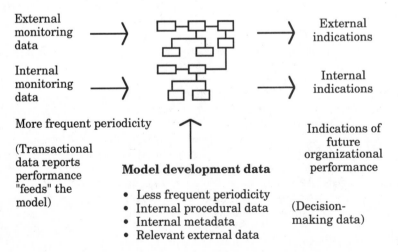

Environmental monitoring data

External monitoring data $\longrightarrow$ | External indications

Internal monitoring data $\longrightarrow$ | Internal indications

More frequent periodicity

(Transactional data reports performance "feeds" the model)

Model development data
- Less frequent periodicity
- Internal procedural data
- Internal metadata
- Relevant external data

Indications of future organizational performance

(Decision-making data)

Figure 4.3 The dual role of data in developing and utilizing models.

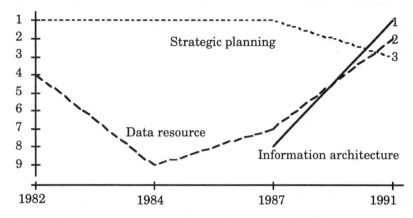

Figure 4.4 Relative importance of data, architecture, and planning issues identified by information systems professionals (adapted from Neiderman et al. "Information Systems Management Issues of the '90s" © 1991 *MIS Quarterly*).

Organizational Data Administration

The question becomes: How do organizations begin the process of evaluating and embracing appropriate technological components to facilitate enterprise integration components?   That is the job of the organizational data administration function.   When implemented as a coordinated component of an organization data architecture program, DRE projects enable data administration functions to contribute to increased system effectiveness and efficiency and achieve increased organizational dexterity.   This is accomplished with various types of DRE projects ranging from identifying and correcting operational data problems to larger-scale projects developed to contribute to organizational data architecture development efforts.   A data architecture is the tool used to accomplish the acquisition, structuring, and astute use of information, and a data administration program is the measure used by an organization to implement enterprise integration.

Data administration is the tool permitting organizations achieving stage 5 growth to address data issues with a structured, programmatic approach.   Guidance from data administration eliminates the need to deal with organizational data problems piecemeal.   A 1985 survey of *Fortune* 1000 companies indicated that more than 50 percent had formally instituted data administration functions and 40 percent of those were less than 4 years old [Appleton 1986].   Implementation of data administration functions continues to increase. Figure 4.4 shows four measurements of the relative importance of planning, data, and architecture issues between the years of 1982 and 1991 as perceived by organization technology management.   In 1991, information systems professionals Neiderman et al. [1991] rated the concepts of "data as an organizational resource" and the "development of a data architecture" as the top two key issues faced by the profession [Neiderman et al. 1991, Cooke and Parrish 1992]. The current strong interest in these three closely related issues indicates an attempt to address some of the organizational data problems that have been associated with traditional approaches to information systems development. Organizations are realizing that a lack of an effective data administration program can make information system modernization efforts prohibitively expensive. On the other hand, a strong data administration program can enable development of the systems required to support organizational strategy. A number of popular data administration works have been published (see for example Durell [1985], Finkelstein [1993], and Inmon [1992a]). For this book it will be useful to cite as a reference the normative data management model under development at the MITRE Corporation (see Parker et al. [1994]).

Part of the motivation behind the MITRE research is to produce a data management capabilities management model analogous to Nolan's stages of DP maturity and the Software Engineering Institute's (SEI) capabilities management model. In fact, if the MITRE research produces the anticipated results, organizations will have access to a map of how to get from stage 4 though stage 5 of the model. The normative data management model presents data administration as comprising four functions:

- *Data program management.* Establishing organizational data management goals on the basis of organizational information management program requirements and implementation-based feedback from the other three data administration functions. Figure 4.5 shows how data administration requirements are derived from enterprise-wide data requirements and functional user requirements. Some of these come from the legacy systems.

- *Enterprise data engineering.* Assists in the formulation of data management goals, develops enterprise data architecture, models organizational data sharing requirements, and integrates functional data assets at the enterprise level.

- *Business functional data engineering.* For each business function, identifies and organizes functional data needs, and ensures data sharing within a functional area.

- *Data operation.* Builds, operates, and maintains data assets developed to supply the needs of organizational information systems.

To illustrate the potential payoff of this work, consider the results achieved by 300 software professionals applying software process improvement over an 18-year period (as reported by Krasner [1994]):

- Ability to predict costs within 10 percent

- Only 1 missed deadline in 15 years

- Relative cost of fix defect is 1× during inspection, 13× during system testing, and 92× during operation

- Early error detection went from 45 percent to 95 percent during the period 1982–1993

- Product error rate (measured as defects per thousand lines of code) went from 2.0 to 0.01 during the period 1982–1993

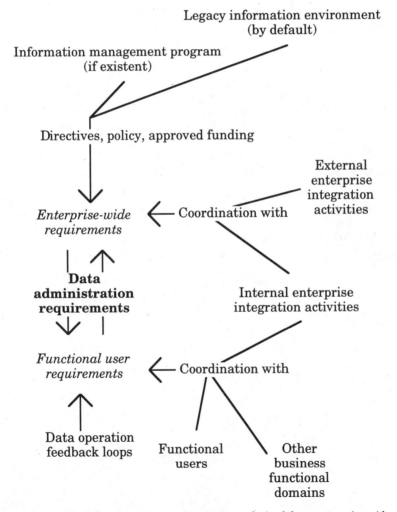

Figure 4.5 Data administration requirements are derived from enterprise-wide data requirements and functional user requirements.

Enterprise needs	DA function
Access to data in a useful format when and where needed	Provide timely access to needed data
Ability to adapt to changing business needs	Develop flexible, maintainable systems
Accurate and consistent data	Develop and facilitate use of integrated data and standards
Share data across the organization	Ensure data/systems integration
Contain costs	Cost effectiveness solutions
Information technology mission / Corollary	Provide quality data to those who need it / Productivity will result from focusing on quality but quality does not come about by pursuing productivity

Figure 4.6 Enterprise needs satisfied by the data administration (DA) function.

If similar results can be expected in the data area, great attention will be paid to the MITRE effort. Data administration is the organizational function ensuring information availability. Typical data administration functions include

- Developing and maintaining an organizational data bank for storing and integrating organizational data assets

- Developing and maintaining standard data products and models

- Encouraging the use of common procedures and tools

- Providing education, training, and consultation services to the organization

To put it another way, data administration is responsible for ensuring that the right combination of facts and meanings is maintained as models in a data bank to be able to respond to user queries made with common tools and procedures. Figure 4.6 illustrates how enterprise needs satisfied by the information systems function. The mission of the information system (IS) organization is to provide timely access to needed data with the understanding that productivity will result from focusing on quality, but quality does not come about by pursuing productivity.

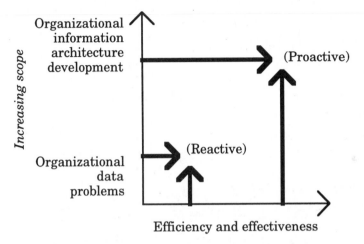

Efficiency and effectiveness

Increasing organizational information technology maturity

Figure 4.7   The range of data administration tasks.

Recall the previous chapter's definition that in order to be useful, data must meet various organizational criteria. The key to successful organizational data administration is identifying, understanding, and making successful tradeoffs among the competing organizational criteria. Thus, while data administration goals are reasonably consistent across organizations, each organization may require a different implementation plan to satisfy organizational objectives.

Organizational data administration activities can be classified as falling on a scale with dimensions ranging from primarily reactive to proactive. Reactive data administration activities are typically responses to recognized organizational data problems occurring as hidden data issues. World-Wide's problem with the MARS is one example. Proactive data administration activities typically occur in the context of the other data architecture activities such as enterprise data engineering, data program management, business functional data engineering, and data operation. Development of an organization data architecture would be considered a proactive data administration activity. It should go without saying that the more a data administration function can put efforts into proactive activities, the better prepared the organization will be to meet challenges of the competitive environment. Similarly, being forced to divert resources to handle reactive data problems will siphon resources away from proactive activities. More mature organizations will be able to devote more effort to proactive activities and less to reactive. Figure 4.7 illustrates this range of data administration tasks.

The same MITRE research has also provided a further definition of the term *data assets*. Parker et al. [1994] describe two types of data assets: (1) *data engineering assets*, labeled "metadata," which are

needed to accomplish data engineering activities (e.g., name, definition, structure, encoding, source, steward requirements, business
rules, models, designs, specifications, and repositories); and (2) *data
management assets*, which include data needed to establish and control enterprise data-oriented activities (e.g., policies, standards,
plans, budgets, metrics, and training feedback).

One last thought on data administration—it has tended to be the
location of the initial organizational investment in CASE technology
because of its heavy use of models and modeling techniques Tucker
[1993].

Data Architecture Defined

When fully utilized, organizational data architectuctures specifically
support not just organizational objectives but also the process of
supporting strategic decision making information systems. A more
important advantage occurs as organizations are able to use organizational information system assets to address specific questions.
Systems designed from a data perspective are better able to be rapidly reconfigured to respond to changing competitive conditions—more
rapidly becoming useful to unforeseen events. In addition, more in-
terapplication integration is possible because the data architecture
makes it simpler for these applications to communicate and exchange
data.

Spewak in his 1993 book, *Enterprise Architecture Planning*, compares the information systems portfolio of most organizations to a
southern California mansion called the Winchester House. The former home of Sarah Winchester, the mansion appears very much to be
what it is: a building where construction [Spewak 1993, p. xx of the
preface]

> continued 24 hours a day, seven days a week, month after month,
> year after year—for 38 years! ...highlights of the tour (now given)
> are such odd features as stairways that rise into ceilings, doors and
> windows blocked by walls, more passageways and halls than rooms, a
> four story chimney that falls short of the roof, and many rooms serv-
> ing the same purpose. ... Another comparison can be made of the
> Winchester House and the systems portfolio. There was no overall
> set of blueprints that showed what Mrs. Winchester wanted her
> house to be. Similarly, most systems organizations have no overall
> blueprints for the data, systems and technology needed to support
> the business.

With this type of development environment it is easy to see how
systems may no longer support organizational objectives. In many
cases the user requirements have changed since the systems were
first constructed (recall Jones' [1994] 5 to 7 percent annual system
requirements change rate). Organizations now compete in environments characterized by tight time constraints on the acquisition, interpretation, and response to and/or implementation of information

[Haeckel and Nolan 1993]. The traditional stovepipe method of systems development can no longer support organizations competing for scarce resources and customers.

Using another architectural analogy, Connall and Burns [1993] note how the modern day building of a large cathedral spanned 80 years and four generations of craftspeople asking the question: "Could it have been done without the blueprints?" Their description continues describing how, after the passage of time, information system [Connall and Burns 1993, p. 24]

> Plans and documentation ... are poor or non-existent, and the original designers and craftsmen are no longer available. The result is increasing maintenance costs and decreasing programmer productivity—a situation that is inefficient, wasteful and costly to our businesses. In other words, unacceptable.

The current state of legacy systems represents an impressive testimony to decades of creativity and engineering, especially when one considers we've had no blueprints guiding our evolution. Today, we understand more about system development activities then we did yesterday, and we have been studying these activities for only about 50 years. Productivity advances in CASE technology have transformed system documentation activity from a hated postimplementation chore to an essential component of system development. Systems are now so complex and tool-based technologies have advanced so far that the advantages of CASE-based system production of new systems are not in dispute. The focus has shifted to introducing the advantages of CASE technology to the systems constituting the legacy environment. The most productive function typically performed by data administration is the development and maintenance of an organization-wide data architecture supporting the development of information systems within the organization.

Data architectures are the blueprints or master plans used to guide the accomplishment of data administration goals and objectives. Information maintained by data administration in a data architecture includes the:

- Sources and uses of data

- Creation and use of data by specific processes

- Various organizational communication capabilities for delivering the information among data collections and uses

Figure 4.8 illustrates how data architectures are developed in response to organizational needs. Architectures are plans, guiding the transformation of strategic organizational information needs into specific information systems development projects. All organizations have data architectures, some are better understood and documented than others. The data architecture definitions referenced in the lit-

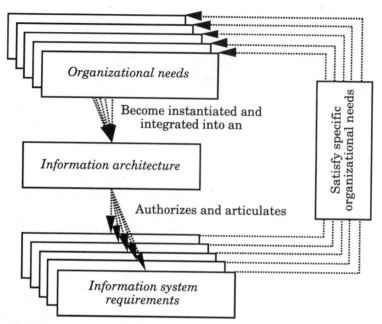

Figure 4.8 Organizational data architectures guide the transformation of organizational needs into information system requirements.

erature are derived predominantly from Zachman's work "A framework for information systems architecture" [Zachman 1987] (see Fig. 4.9) from Loosley [1992], Bruce [1992], Spewak [1993], von Halle and Kull [1993] and Whitten, Bentley, and Barlow [1994].

The Zachman framework describes data architectures as integrated collections of information pertaining to the complex process of developing information systems that are capable of effectively and efficiently meeting current and future organizational information requirements [Zachman 1987, Sowa and Zachman 1992]. Key also is the concept of organizing this information according to different perspectives or views from which different information-based products can be developed. As readers of the framework know, these views range from contextual to implementation detail specific perspectives of the data, functions, and communications specifications sufficient to accomplish the organizational mission. Figure 4.10 illustrates a data architecture with components developed as a set of guidelines supporting technological evolution of the enterprise answering the following questions:

■ How and why do the components interact?

■ Where do they go?

■ When are they needed?

- Why and how will the changes be implemented?

- What standards should be adopted?

- What vendors should be chosen?

- What rules should govern the decisions?

	Data (What?)	Function (How?)	Network (Where?)
Model components	Entities and relations	Processes, inputs, and outputs	Nodes and lines
The **ballpark** view is concerned with *organizational scope* and *objectives*	Lists of important business things where entities are classes of business things	List of processes the business performs where processes are classes of business functions	List of business locations where nodes are business locations
The **owner** view is concerned with modeling the *business units* in the organization	Entity-relationship diagram where entities are business entities and relationships are business rules	Functional flow diagram where processes are business processes and inputs and outputs are business resources	Logistics network where node are business units and links are business relationships
The **analyst** view is concerned with modeling the *information system specifications*	Data models where entities are data entities and relationships are data relationships	Data flow diagrams where process are application functions and inputs and outputs are user views	Distributed system architecture where nodes are IS functions and lines are line characteristics
The **builder** view is concerned with transforming the planner's *plan* into reality	Data designs where entities are segment and row combinations and relationships are pointer and key combinations	Structure charts where processes are computer functions and inputs and outputs are screen and device formats	System architectures where nodes are hardware and/or software and lines are line specifications
The **maintainer** view is concerned with understanding the *detailed representations of the system operation*	Database definitions where entities are fields and relationships are addresses	Programs where processes are embedded in language statements and inputs and outputs are control blocks	Network architecture where nodes are addresses and links are protocols
The actual system	Data	Function	Communications

Figure 4.9 The Zachman framework for information systems architectures (adapted from Zachman [1987] and Zachman and Sowa [1992] © 1987 International Business Machines Corp. Reprinted with permission from *IBM System Journal*).

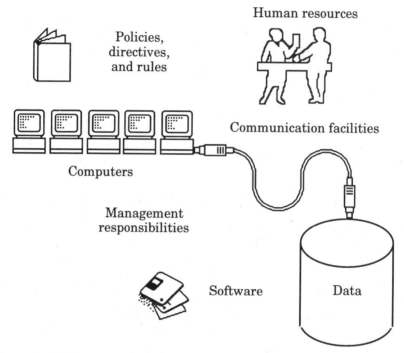

Figure 4.10 Data architecture components (adapted from Allen and Boynton [1991]).

- What policies should guide the process?
- What should be managed organization-wide?
- What should be managed locally?

Data architectures guide the implementation of data sharing and thus enable higher degrees of organizational dexterity. A *data architecture* is a framework permitting communication about thoughts and actions between IS and key specialists; it also facilitates communication with organizational management. Stored in this form, models are extensible, accessible, consistent, and traceable to physical structures in existing computer-based files and databases. A data architecture must also be transformable into an arbitrary number of user-oriented data structures to service end-user information requirements [Appleton 1983].

A *corporate data architecture* is an ordering or arrangement of an organization's data according to a master plan. A corporate data architecture permits management to respond to various corporate needs by facilitating access to data that is in a useful format and of known consistency and accuracy, when and where it is needed. In addition, a corporate data architecture gives organizations the ability to assess, adapt to, and share data across the organization in response to changing business needs.

The corporate data architecture is then a structure that models the data of the enterprise—it is an organization-wide architectural framework for developing information systems capable of supporting the achievement of organizational objectives. The most basic goal of such an architecture is to supply the information needs of the organization with systems developed using integrated information, systems capable of sharing data among themselves [Inmon 1988, Martin 1989].

Data architectures usually have two forms: the actual or "as is" architecture describing the current system state and a planning or "to be" architecture describing where the organization wants to be. The goal is to turn the as is architecture into the to be architecture. The problem is that many organizations don't have a formally defined as is architecture. That isn't to say that the architecture doesn't exist. It does. It just isn't documented, or better still, implemented as data assets in the enterprise data bank. (However, many data architectures result from evolution not planning.) And, yes, even if it isn't documented, a data architecture does exist, as does an organization's strategy. A corporate data architecture endows organizations with at least four types of capabilities:

- Identifying trends in performance by providing the capability for both periodic situation assessment and dynamic query formulation and environmental monitoring

- Correlating diverse data, in support of dynamic, strategic management

- Permitting management to evaluate the expected outcomes of various strategic scenarios using a corporate model with known strengths and limitations

- Defining and assessing progress toward corporate objectives

When sufficiently developed, the corporate data architecture becomes the language of strategic decision making. Dynamic information systems are required to support strategic-level organizational decision making.

Data Administration in Support of Organizational Strategy

In a 1989 article in the *Harvard Business Review* Henderson wrote, "Strategy is the management of natural competition ... it compresses time," equating, in this statement, the operation of business markets to organism-based competition for finite resources in the natural environment. Using the phrase "it compresses time," Henderson compares competition in the business world with the evolution of species

	Sun Tzu Wu [Wu 1944]	Liddell-Hart [1954]
Aim(s):	Frustrate the enemy's plans and prevent the joining of the enemy's forces.	The perfection of strategy would be to produce a decision without any serious fighting.
Elements and conditions:	Attack where the enemy is unprepared, appear where you are not expected.	Concentrate on movement and surprise, not on overcoming resistance.
Action:	If we wish to fight, the enemy can be forced to engagement ... all we need to do is attack some other place which the enemy will be obligated to relieve.	Take the line of least resistance and expectation while depriving the enemy of freedom of action.
Basis:	You can be sure of succeeding in your attacks if you attack places which are not defended and you can be sure of the safety of your defense if you hold only positions that cannot be attacked.	While hitting, one must guard and the enemy must be off guard; also one must possess alternative objectives.

Figure 4.11 The essence of strategy as applied in business contexts.

in the natural (biological) world. Strategy is a defense against the biological process of "natural selection" [Henderson 1989, pp. 142–143]. It is the means used by organizations to anticipate and preposition themselves in anticipation of possible future events and outcomes instead of reacting to them as they occur. Wayne Gretzky, the ice hockey great, has been often quoted with an eloquent definition of strategy—something like "he skates to where he thinks the puck will be."

The evolution of the study of strategy in organizational contexts can be traced back to a study of war, the competition between humans [Evered 1983]. Combined in Fig. 4.11, two descriptions of war-based strategy provide the essence of strategy as it has been sometimes successfully applied in business contexts. The essence of successful strategy indicates two components:

1. Conservation and judicious but decisive use of resources

2. A rapid cycle situation assessment-response formulation capability

The same as every organization has an "as is" data architecture, so too [Porter 1980, p. xiii], every firm competing in an industry has a competitive strategy, whether explicit or implicit. This strategy may have been developed explicitly through a planning process or it may have evolved implicitly through the activities of the various functional departments of the firm. Left to its own devices, each functional department will inevitably pursue approaches dictated by its professional orientation and the incentives of those in charge. However, the sum of these departmental approaches rarely equals the best strategy.

This is the same concept as localized workgroup optimization at the expense of organization-wide optimization. Organizations coordinating efficiently, conserving resources, and simultaneously monitoring the environment for events to occur or opportunities to present themselves will more likely succeed in competitive environments. The winners in strategic competitions are those positioned to take advantage of opportunities and well prepared to rapidly implement the necessary steps. The losers are well aware of what happened but lack the understanding of why it was able to happen.

A more blunt assessment than the IBM disclaimer that began this chapter is one by Ackoff [1981] describing most corporate planning efforts as being "like a ritual rain dance: it has no effect on the weather that follows, but it makes those who engage in it feel that they are in control. ... Most discussions of the role of models in planning are directed at improving the dancing, not the weather." As shown by its stage 5 status, the implementation of organizational data architecture as a major element of organizational strategy is a nontrivial proposition. The successful development of an organizational data architecture requires a degree of information system development:

■ More often spoken about than sought after

■ More often sought after than achieved

Strategic planning without the benefit of a data architecture is just a ritual rain dance. To illustrate this point about the degree of integration required among organizational components, consider the following proposition:

> Everything the organization does should be done to achieve specific objectives in support of the organizational mission.

This is strategic management distilled to its most basic principle. Next, consider a logical extension of the proposition:

> Every information system asset in the organization should be focused on supporting the attainment of specific objectives designed to achieve the organizational mission.

Information systems are expensive investments. If they aren't supporting organizational objectives, then how is consumption of those resources justified? IS management is becoming increasingly conscious about demonstration systems support of both primary and subsidiary organizational objectives. Consider the following two assumptions: (1) data problems reduce overall information system effectiveness; and (2) largely because of assumption 1, IS resources are not being used to directly support attainment of objectives designed to achieve the organizational mission.

If either of these two assumptions is true, then IS professionals have a reason to be concerned. In this age of "sizing" and outsourcing, IS professionals need to be concerned with both the perception and the actual progress toward the degree to which the resources under their operation support organizational mission achievement. Measures other than size of the data processing organization need to be developed and monitored to enable more effective IS operations (see Brynjolfsson [1993], Clark [1992], and Moad [1993a, 1993b]).

Data Reverse Engineering in Support of Data Administration

Consider the current situation. Organizational information system needs are changing rapidly to cope with rapidly evolving environments. Thus even if we could define current requests by the time the systems were delivered, they wouldn't meet the current needs because the needs the system was developed to meet had evolved at the standard 5 to 7 percent. Increased amounts of data and multimedia-based data types, program data independent development, and immature data management techniques combine to complicate this problem for the organizational data administration function.

The only solution is to adapt to flexible organizational information technology (IT) infrastructure structure capable of rapid responses in changing conditions. Data reverse engineering is a system-level technique that can be applied successfully in many data problems. Because data reverse engineering is based on structured analysis techniques, it produces products that are fundamentally model-based. This means that data reverse engineering products can be applied directly to the problems at hand but the products can be stored in the organizational data bank and used again on future projects.

The most immediately useful output from DRE projects is new and improved system documentation for existing systems. Transforming the current documentation from paper to a CASE environment results in the maintenance of requirements, design, and implementation in an integrated environment that surpasses existing system documentation in terms of accuracy and usefulness.

Figure 4.12 illustrates two classes of DRE projects. Data reverse engineering projects can be characterized by a range—from projects with a narrowly defined, problem-solving focus to those more broadly focused on architectural development. Figure 4.12 illustrates this range, showing how these two classes of projects play roles supporting organizational data administration activities. Narrowly focused projects can be used to solve specific organizational data problems,

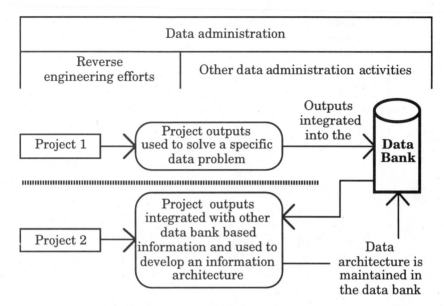

Figure 4.12   Two classes of DRE projects

while more broadly focused projects can be designed to contribute to
the development of an organizational data architecture.   Project 1
can be considered representative of the MARS project proposed in
Chap. 1.   The focus of this project is to develop a long-term solution
to the data problems associated with the accumulation and reporting
of the long distance company mileage credits.   The MARS project is
proposed as a way to develop a solution to the current problems.
The results are integrated into the organizational data bank in anticipation of future use.

Figure 4.13 illustrates this point using the MARS project.   Data
and other types of models will be the primary outputs.   These will be
used to solve the problem prompting the reverse engineering analysis.   Both the models produced and the solution development history
are stored in the data bank.   In a separate step, the models are integrated into the organizational data architecture.   Once properly
integrated, these models can be accessed for use in appropriate future architectural development projects.   The results are integrated
into the organizational data bank in anticipation of future use.

Data reverse engineering is the technology used to effectively extract information from legacy systems and structure it in a more manipulable form as a data architecture component.   The shift will continue away from task oriented views of software applications and
toward integrated shareable data.   Data reverse engineering projects
enable organizations to accumulate vital knowledge about the enter-

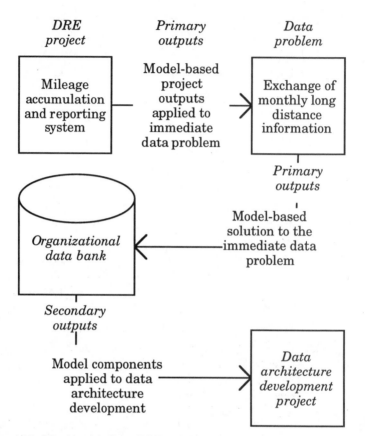

DRE project | Primary outputs | Data problem

Mileage accumulation and reporting system

Model-based project outputs applied to immediate data problem

Exchange of monthly long distance information

Primary outputs

Model-based solution to the immediate data problem

Organizational data bank

Secondary outputs

Model components applied to data architecture development

Data architecture development project

Figure 4.13   Direct and indirect DRE project outputs.

prise. Data reverse engineering can be a cost effective component of existing data architecture planning, because outputs often can be used in multiple enterprise integration processes.

In addition to providing information used to construct the data architecture, DRE projects also provide an information base used for making specific technology-based investment decisions. Data reverse engineering represents a practical approach to implementing information engineering concepts in organizations with a portfolio of legacy systems. Figure 4.14 illustrates the symbiotic relationship between DRE projects and data architecture development activities.

Data reverse engineering projects can be used to provide information-based "fuel" for architectural efforts. As the primary type of information fuel, models are computer manipulable representations of information used to represent complex system behavior. They exist in both the physical context of a CASE tool environment and the virtual context of the organizational data architecture. Models represent potentially powerful information management tools. Models are the primary means used by the data administration to ensure that it is able to develop and deliver systems.

Data reverse engineering projects support the efforts of the data administration function to develop an organizational data architecture. A data architecture is required in order for data administration to provide effective support for organizational strategy. Figure 4.15 illustrates the DRE role in the development of an organizational data architecture.

Use of the models in subsequent architecture development activities is an example of the class of secondary DRE project outputs. Other secondary outputs include the following:

- *Data sharing*. Reverse engineering plays a key role controlling redundancy, fostering reuse and dependability, improving operational performance, and reducing costs, and also promotes data shareability and maintainability.

- *Modeling*. Modeling is prerequisite to data standardization, documenting existing data resources and providing a baseline used to estimate degree and scope of proposed changes. Once developed, models can be used to quickly solve data problems.

- *Reengineering*. Reverse engineering provides the basis for improving the "solution set" (forward engineering) for current or changing business requirements. It facilitates reengineering and creation of new applications.

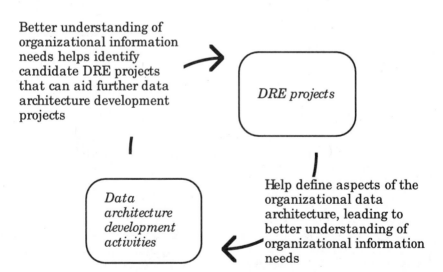

Better understanding of organizational information needs helps identify candidate DRE projects that can aid further data architecture development projects

DRE projects

Data architecture development activities

Help define aspects of the organizational data architecture, leading to better understanding of organizational information needs

Figure 4.14 Symbiotic relationship between DRE projects and data architecture development activities.

Legacy systems

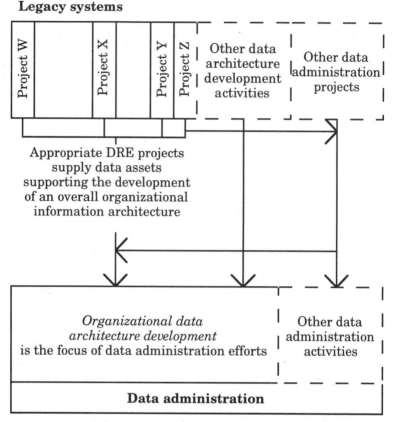

Figure 4.15 The role of data reverse engineering as a component of data administration activities and data architecture development. (The dashed boxes indicate other aspects of both organizational data architecture and strategy development not addressed here; see Durell [1985], Finkelstein [1993], von Halle and Kull [1993], Sowa [1992], and Zachman [1987] for more information on these activities.)

■ *Organizational integration.* Data reverse engineering is often a good first step towards the broader objective: increased organizational integration. It can also be used to salvage and prepare "straw" requirements (i.e., initial-version, candidate) in preparation for subsequent enhancement.

Similarly, reverse engineering project outputs provide excellent "reality checks" for validating portions of the corporate data model. Consider an organization needing to validate requirements in the pay and personnel area. If two systems are considered for data reverse engineering, it becomes an easy choice to schedule the system in the personnel area to complement the requirements validation effort. Outputs from this project can be used as inputs to "feed" the development of a portion of the corporate data model and other data administration efforts.

Thus, data reverse engineering plays a key role controlling redundancy; fostering data reuse and dependability, shareability, and maintainability; improving operational performance; and reducing costs by

- Cutting down on the cost of data inventories by improving data quality

- Enhancing the shareability and maintainability of data particularly in cases where data is shared across functional areas

- Promoting integration of data models as a prerequisite to achieving large economies of scale associated with shared data

- Accomplishing structuring and mapping of data facilitating migration to other languages or platforms

- Improving data quality and accuracy by permitting data sharing across areas or applications using a single point of entry

- Enhancing data shareability and maintainability across functional areas by reducing the "islands of automation" syndrome

Data Reverse Engineering in Support of System Maintenance

Sooner or later every IS organization is faced with major decisions concerning required system maintenance. Typically they must choose from the following five alternatives:

1. (Continue to) do nothing.

2. Perform maintenance to the system.

3. Reverse engineer the existing system to develop improved data assets and associated documentation.

4. Reengineer the system.

5. Replace the system.

Since system failure is often a characteristic of system maintenance problems, ignoring the problem (choice 1) is seldom an option, as is the other end of the spectrum—replacing the system (choice 5). If resources were available to replace the system, why would a maintenance problem exist? Organizations are thus faced with continuing choices of whether to invest their dollars in system maintenance (choice 2), enhancing their systems through reverse engineering analysis (choices 3 and 4), or completing the reengineering cycle by first reverse engineering and then forward engineering the system. Reconsider the projected $75,000 annual savings projected by the General Services Administration illustration [GSA 1993] in Chap. 2, and it is easier to see the value of data reverse engineering if it takes an investment of only $250,000 to create the savings. Data reverse engineering can play two possible roles when choosing between the five options.

- Portions of the system can be reverse engineered to improve the system data assets and associated documentation.

- The potential contribution that DRE outputs can make to a system reengineering effort should be examined.

5

Frequently Asked Questions

Frequently asked questions (or FAQs, in Internet terms) have become regular parts of on-line discussion groups. New participants joining a network discussion group are generally expected to locate and read the answers to the FAQs. The answers to FAQs are generally in a text file containing information that puts the discussion topic into perspective. By obtaining and reviewing the FAQs, both the new participant and the discussion group can avoid wasting bandwidth discussing standard terminology, definitions, context, acronyms, and so on. Reading the answers to the FAQs saves everyone in the discussion group time and effort. Similar to the information contained in the answers to the FAQs, DRE project team members will eventually encounter someone who wants the 5-minute version of the what and why of specific DRE projects (e.g., why a team member needs access to certain information). Team members are charged with communicating accurate and useful information. It is in the team leader's and the team's interests to ensure that all project team members know the answers to FAQs about DRE projects. In order to function most effectively as a team, all members must share the same understanding of the project purpose or goals and the means of achieving them. Perhaps more importantly, the project information will be explained in a consistent manner to those external to the project team. The project team cannot be overinformed. Every team member needs to be able to give a coherent version of the following claim:

> If we invest \$W into data reverse engineering system x, it will save us \$y within z months (or it will result in the following benefits such as increased system functionality or lower system maintenance costs) because ...

The most typical forms of DRE FAQs and answers are presented in the following sections.

What is data reverse engineering going to do to the system?

Since it is the process of analyzing an existing system, DRE will do nothing to the target system. It typically is used to produce improved system documentation, enhancing system understanding. The outputs from these projects can be used to develop organizational data architectural components.

Can you give a 2-minute explanation of how it is accomplished?

We need to develop validated models of aspects of the target system. Candidate models will be developed representing things such as system data items, the relationships between those items, and organizational business rules. These models will be analyzed, reviewed, and improved by selected key specialists in their roles as project team members. Revisions and refinements will be made to the models as new or clarified information comes to light as a result of these sessions. Systems benefit from better quality systems documentation and from increased understanding, and we gain the ability to formally apply this knowledge in overall enterprise integration efforts. The analysis will permit us to develop valuable organization data assets from target system information. (Recall that data assets are specific combinations of facts and meanings of value to the organization in the same fashion as are human or financial assets.) These data assets will be stored as models in the organizational data bank along with other relevant project information. The models are integrated with other models as required. When a sufficient quantity of models have been integrated, the information in the data bank is capable of providing useful, consistent, and coherent information to all levels of organizational decision making, thus making us a better-functioning organization.

What do you mean by *validated models*?

It is appropriate to explain the term *validated* here. *Validation* is the end process of joint key specialist–data engineer model development. After the data assets have been developed, they are carefully certified and ascertained to be a correct representation of what they were asked to produce by the project team and other specialists. Validated data assets enable the development of shareable data because the term validated indicates the project team has verified the correctness of the data assets.

How can these data assets be used?

Shared data assets contribute toward the development of metadata and shared data, contributing towards a higher degree of organizational dexterity. Increased organizational dexterity can be used to alter the basis of competition in our environment [Cash et al. 1992]. What organization wouldn't

- Benefit from better organized, more accurate, and more useful system design, and requirements documentation?

- Like to reduce system maintenance costs?

- Want to gain more service from existing information systems?

Are you going to be in the way?

When posed by someone affiliated with the target system, this question translates into "What role do you want me and my organization to play in this project?" The answer depends on who is doing the asking and the type of role that person will likely play in the project. A database analyst for a popular product might be needed only occasionally to answer specific technical questions. On the other hand, in cases of unfamiliar application environments, greater technical participation is often required to achieve economic feasibility. This may mean as much as half-time participation for some system technical and functional personnel for much of the project duration. Specific levels should be determined after completing the preliminary system survey as part of the project planning activities.

Why do you need to talk with my people?

System management needs to understand; their functional and technical personnel are in possession of valuable information about the system. Participation by these individuals can reduce the amount of time and resources required to accomplish the project by a factor of 10! The DRE project team acknowledges that their time is also at a premium and that the proposed project must be worked into their existing schedules. Data reverse engineering has tended to be labor intensive. Participation by individuals representing functional, technical, and systems functions is often required to achieve economic feasibility. At times these specialists possess better quality information than does the system documentation.

How is data reverse engineering related to other system development activities?

The first activity of data reengineering is often also an economically feasible prelude to enterprise integration activities, because the outputs produced are useful in other data architecture component development activities. This topic is covered in detail in Chap. 15, "Enterprise Integration Information."

When will the data reverse engineering products be ready?

Before performing a preliminary system survey, the answer is "We don't have enough information to make that precise determination, but once we have completed the preliminary system survey, we'll be able to develop useful project estimates." After the preliminary system survey, it is possible to develop a useful estimate of the number of weeks the project will last.

Are you better at this than software engineers are at delivering software on time and within budget?

Skeptical because of poor track records at delivering useful systems on time and within budget, managers are often seeking assurance that projects will not turn into nightmares because of poor planning or execution and that the required outputs will be produced. Project team members need to demonstrate to users that the products developed will be immediately useful and can be produced within the specified time frame. Good track records can be very reassuring in these situations. Unfortunately, the first time you do one of these projects you won't have access to the type of information required to develop useful estimates. For the first project, it is possible to begin, acquire data, and then develop the desired estimates before reaching the halfway point.

Why do we need you to help us—can't we do this ourselves?

We need to establish a partnership for two reasons: (1) unaided, the work can be technical and detailed; and (2) data reverse engineers are also specialists and can keep our interactions with your people (the functional, technical, and system specialists) to a minimum by forming a project team partnership. We have formed the team such that each team member contributes toward the project goals in the most effective combination—for this set of circumstances.

What is the nature of this partnership?

We ask your people where to look for information. We analyze the information and develop data assets for your people to examine, refine, and eventually validate. This is done by asking specific questions, through structured interviews, or using formal model refinement and validation (MR/V) sessions. We also need their knowledge of the system for selected activities during project initiation and project wrapup activities.

Why are you looking at the old systems?

We are doing this for any combination of the following reasons:

- Often the existing system will be the only reliable source for the business rules that a planned system must support.

- The information gained can be applied to economic build, rebuild, or buy decisions.

- We wish to examine some of the existing software components for possible reuse.

- A new or proposed data asset requires validation.

- We need to obtain information that will reduce system maintenance costs by adding functionality, correcting errors, and enhancing documentation.

Why do you need a CASE tool?

With the industry "rule of thumb" being one success story for every 10 CASE tool implementations, it is no wonder some organizations are shy of the CASE implementation [Eliot 1994]. CASE tools provide a feasible means to capture, organize, structure, and present the system information that is the focus of the DRE activities [Aiken 1989]. In general, DRE projects also require CASE tool support in order to be economically feasible. Organizations may still be faced with the technical and cultural hurdles associated with organizational CASE tool implementation, but DRE projects provide a means of evaluating CASE tool implementation in organizational contexts.

What do I get out of it?

The most immediately useful products produced by DRE analysis have been described by some system managers as "a superior set of system documentation delivered in a format where we can more easily keep it up to date." This is often an easier project selling point than attempting to make the longer term argument of the associated data architecture–enterprise integration goals covered in the previous chapters.

amorphous adj.
1. Lacking definite form; shapeless
2. Of no particular type; anomalous
3. Lacking organization; formless
4. Lacking distinct crystalline structure
Synonym(s): adjective—having no distinct shape. shapeless,
            unformed, formless, inchoate, unshaped.

Figure 5.1 Definition of *amorphous* (Source: *American Heritage English Dictionary* © 1993 Houghton Mifflin Company).

What are the data reverse engineering project challenges?

Data reverse engineering projects typically do not exist below certain thresholds of project characteristics. These projects generally address situations that are

- Complex in nature—manipulating large amounts of information

- Large in scope—involving the relationships between literally thousands of objects

- Information-intensive—maintaining detailed collections of information about things of concern to the organization

Data reverse engineering project challenges have occurred because of the amorphous characteristics of software and data (see Fig. 5.1). Software and data aren't tangible, and consequently it has been difficult to value them as assets. Rugaber [1992] described reverse engineering as—in part—addressing gaps between the concrete world of physical and computer implementation and the abstract world of high-level descriptions. These gaps form the basis for the DRE project challenges:

- Determining the quality of the evidence required to successfully achieve the project goals

- Acquiring the minimum key specialist participation levels to ensure project economic feasibility

- Identifying and addressing stakeholder priorities

- Educating participants to the cumulative value of data assets

What do you mean by "the cumulative value of data assets"?

The last item is particularly important. Since we are developing a knowledge structure with these data assets, the relative value of the first data assets produced (or any single group of data assets) is less that the value resulting from the combination of two or more groups of data assets. The data assets produced are worth much more to an organization after they have been integrated with other data assets than as isolated groups. The goal is to understand how everything relates to everything else. Fig. 5.2 illustrates the cumulative nature of the of data assets. A DRE project produces data assets consisting of data items combined into models. Once validated and integrated with other organizational modeling efforts, the models become the basis for data architecture development. Data architecture is a required component for achieving enterprise integration.

What are the data reverse engineering project critical success factors?

Knowing and understanding the nature of DRE critical success factors permits management to assess the gross feasibility of candidate reverse engineering projects and to accurately understand the nature of progress and problems associated with ongoing projects.

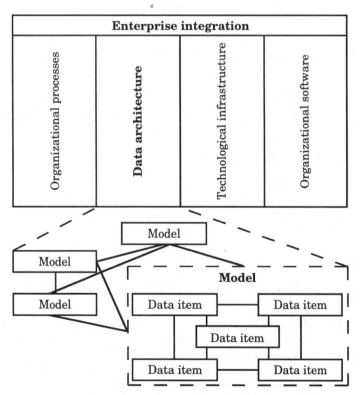

Figure 5.2   The cumulative nature of data assets.

As applied to DRE projects, use of success factors:

- Permits project managers to determine those factors on which attention must be focused

- Provides a means of accurately measuring those factors

- Defines the amount and type of information required to accurately track each factor

Since DRE is often part of a broader system reengineering effort and is dependent on the availability of appropriate CASE technologies, and since other researchers and practitioners have already developed critical success factors for both systems reengineering and CASE tool implementation, it seems appropriate to build on these existing efforts. Seymour's "critical success factors in reengineering legacy systems" [Seymour 1994] concentrate on overcoming certain recurring problems, while Ulrich's "software reengineering critical success factors" [Ulrich 1992] define necessary conditions for project success. A good recent accounting of CASE tool implementation critical success factors has been provided by Eliot [1994]. Finally, Chikofsky [1990] has supplied a list of reverse engineering project criteria indicating reverse engineering as a candidate when you

- Get more out of a project than the effort you put into it

- Can or must retrieve information that has become lost

- Will actually use the data assets developed

- Will develop data assets that are useful to other enterprise integration efforts

- Can benefit from new, useful perspectives on the system

- Can discover hidden system defects or impacts

- Can enable reuse of system components

- Will take some action because of it

Practitioners have focused largely on technology-driven aspects of data reverse engineering. These, while important, are not sufficient to produce the desired data assets. It is important to avoid, what Seymour [1994] calls the "silver bullet" syndrome: misunderstanding on the part of organizational resource management as to DRE project goals and strategies leading to differing and confused expectations. Like CASE and many other popular concepts, DRE cannot be accomplished with a single project. Management must be aware of degree of commitment required. Securing organizational commitment, key specialist project buyin and commitment, and system development capabilities are required. This is most easily accomplished when

■ Management recognizes needs for drastically different information, the value the current information, or improvement in organizational dexterity.

■ A strategic plan is in place for reengineering, system consolidation, and enterprise information, resulting in integration with other enterprise integration processes.

■ Reverse engineering is accepted and incorporated into system development, maintenance, or operational plans.

■ A blueprint framework linking the reverse engineering project to organizational strategic planning is in place.

Project management success factors key to successfully implementing DRE projects include

■ Project team factors
  — Formation of a capable project team
  — Acquiring minimum key specialist participation levels
  — Ensuring proper levels of infrastructure support for performance teams ·
  — Team has appropriate infrastructure support
  — Successful, clean, and concise communication with other performance team members and those external to the project

■ Methodology factors
  — Developing organizational DRE expertise
  — Unambiguous analysis targets
  — Reusable and/or customizable implementation model
  — Clear delineation of activities within overall process
  — Identifiable objectives, dependencies, and deliverables

■ Organizational factors
  — Avoiding the analysis paralysis that has sometimes accompanied large projects and risk averse project management
  — Understanding and managing within the complexity of the legacy environment
  — Overcoming organizational resistance to change
  — Measures of impact—must be clearly understood by management; these are required to demonstrate that continually useful outputs are generated by the project

■ CASE tool factors
  — Intelligent investment in appropriate tools
  — Project team training and education
  — Integration vehicle for tools, techniques, and methods

---

framework n.

1. A structure for supporting or enclosing something else, especially a skeletal support used as the basis for something being constructed.
2. An external work platform; a scaffold.
3. A fundamental structure, as for a written work or a system of ideas.

Synonym(s):   No synonyms found for framework.

Figure 5.3 Definition of *framework* (Source: *American Heritage English Dictionary* © 1993 Houghton Mifflin Company).

— Sophistication with automated support permits project teams to devote less time to the mechanics of analysis and more time to the actual analysis
— Successful application of CASE technologies

How would you explain the data reverse engineering project framework?

As you can see from the definition (Fig. 5.3), *frameworks* provide guides for assembling physical structures and conceptual idea organization. Project frameworks help define the boundaries and other characteristics of complex or information-intensive projects. Frameworks permit project teams to associate facts and to facilitate project knowledge development. Creating a project-specific DRE framework similarly helps others place project activities conceptually in context. The framework concepts presented here evolved from an earlier version developed for use on a series of related DRE projects (see Aiken et al. [1994]).

Figure 5.4 presents DRE projects as composed of 13 activities, making up three project phases: initiation, implementation, and wrapup. Each activity produces a specific output. Acceptance of the output delivery signals completion of the activity. For example, the fourth activity, "initiate project team," results in the output labeled *published team directory*. Each output is designed to ensure that each activity accomplishes specific outputs. While the framework phases and activities are usually implemented sequentially, the actually ordering is project-specific and thus somewhat flexible. Readers can use this material as a starting point and develop their own organization and project specific DRE frameworks. Once developed, other parties involved in the DRE projects can use the frameworks to evaluate their own roles and responsibilities as well as evaluate the feasibility of specific reverse engineering projects. Since there are a wide range of DRE outputs associated with various levels of effort, it is important to define project specific objectives capable of complementing other development-improvement-reengineering efforts.

Chaps. 6 to 11 (in Part 2 of this book) describe the framework activities.

#	Name	Output
	Initiation phase	
1	Target system identification	Candidate target systems
2	Preliminary coordination	Target system points of contact
3	Evidence identification and access	Target system evidence catalogs
4	Project team initiation	Project team directory
5	Preliminary system survey	Project estimate data
6	Project planning	Project planning data
7	Project kickoff	Project charter
	Implementation phase	
8	Target system analysis (repeated until completed)	Characterized by MR/V cycles
8.1	— Cycle planning	Focused plan for next cycle
8.2	— Evidence acquisition	Structured evidence
8.3	— Evidence analysis	Candidate data items
8.4	— Straw model development	Data items organized into models
8.5	— Model refinement and validation	Clearer, more accurate with validated models
8.6	— Model storage and organization	Accessible models and associated information
	Wrapup phase	
9	Data asset packaging	CASE tool-based data assets
10	Data asset integration	Integrated data assets
11	Data asset transfer	Shared and shareable data assets
12	Project metrics collection	Additions to the project metrics database
13	Framework/methodology refinement	Continually improving framework/methodology

Figure 5.4 Overview of a three-phase, 13- activity DRE framework.

Analysis

> **analysis** n.
>
> 1. The separation of an intellectual or substantial whole into its constituent parts for individual study.
> 6. Systems analysis. [Medieval Latin, from Greek *analusis*, a dissolving, from *analuein*, to undo: *ana-*, throughout; see ANA- + *luein*, to loosen.]
>
> A close or systematic study.
>
> Synonym(s): Noun—the separation of a whole into its parts for study; resolution, breakdown, dissection.

Source: *American Heritage English Dictionary* © 1993 Houghton Mifflin Company.

The chapters in this part describe the process of DRE-specific systems. This process consists of the three-phase, 13-step approach described in Chap. 5. Outputs from the project initiation phase are described in this part because they are used as inputs to the other two project phases. All other project outputs are discussed in Part 3. Accordingly:

Chapter	Summary
6	*Describes the first part of project initiation activities (1 to 3) as identifying a candidate target system, coordinating the project with other organizational activities, and identifying and gaining access to the required evidence*
7	*Is devoted entirely to DRE activity 4—constituting a project team*
8	*Describes the second set of the project initiation activities (5 to 7): performing the preliminary system survey (PSS) to understand more about the target system while obtaining information required to develop the project estimate, planning the DRE project using the information acquired from the PSS, and kicking off the project*

(continued)

Chapter	Summary
9	Describes the process of analyzing the target system as a series of modeling cycles
10	Describes a number of project wrapup and evaluation considerations
11	Examines available tool support for DRE projects

6

Project Initiation Activities (Part 1)

Successfully implementing DRE projects depends first on identifying, understanding, and addressing any administrative, technical, and operational complexities. This is the focus of project initiation activities: a series of activities developed to ensure only feasible projects are proposed. While project initiation activities do not consume significant organizational resources, this step is crucial to ensuring that the analysis is correctly focused. Fig. 6.1 illustrates the DRE framework activities constituting the project initiation phase (activities 1 to 7). Dotted lines illustrate potentially useful feedback loops among activities. Project initiation can last as long as 30 days depending on the complexity of the legacy environment and the size and scope of the proposed project. This chapter discusses framework activities 1 to 3, Chap. 7 focuses on framework activity 4—project team initiation, and Chap. 8 covers framework activities 5 to 7.

Target System Identification - Framework Activity 1

The first issue is which (if any) systems should be considered for reverse engineering at this point in time. While functional communities can and have initiated DRE projects, responsibility for identifying candidate legacy systems for reverse engineering typically rests with the organizational data administration function (often working in concert with the information system development and maintenance organizations). Candidate legacy systems are primarily identified as a result of two ongoing data administration activities:

- *Information system portfolio monitoring.* This activity assesses the strengths and weaknesses of the organization's information technology investment in an attempt to identify major project areas.

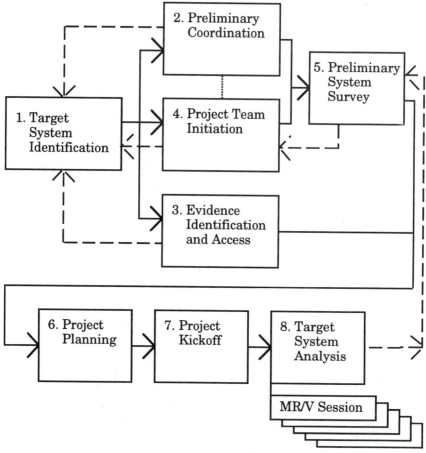

Figure 6.1 Project initiation phase activities (dotted lines illustrate potential feedback loops).

- *Organizational data architecture development.* The process of developing an organizational data architecture requires contributions in the form of strategic, tactical, and operational system models; DRE projects can provide much of the model content.

Figure 6.2 illustrates one approach to target system identification applied in the health care facility consolidation scenario. The left column is a list of "problem" systems maintained by the information system (IS) maintenance group. Continuous monitoring of the portfolio's effectiveness and efficiency results in individual system or system component performance assessments. When asked to rank according to specific criteria, system management can produce a list of the worst-performing systems. The systems are labeled "problem systems" because either they do not provide sufficient information quality or their operation consumes disproportionate organizational resources. Figure 6.2 indicates that the office automation, the pay, and the patient administration systems are the three biggest maintenance problems. Systems that might also be included on this problem list include systems

- With large maintenance problems

- Facing data migration challenges

- Valued in strategic data exchange with organizational partners via interorganizational information systems or electronic data interchange

- Specifically identified as critical to achieving integrated enterprise information via shareable data

- To be eliminated as part of a merger with another organization possessing systems with apparent duplicative functionality

Since these categories are neither comprehensive nor mutually exclusive, systems can belong to multiple categories and should be evaluated according to their respective attributes. Just because a system is a poor performer doesn't mean it is a candidate for data reverse engineering. For example, DRE is less likely to be useful in a situation in which the data is maintained as a flat file and is processed using batch file transactions. And DRE will not correct performance problems unless it is part of a larger organizational reengineering effort.

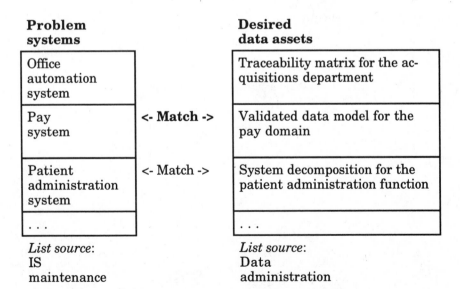

Problem systems		**Desired data assets**
Office automation system		Traceability matrix for the acquisitions department
Pay system	<- **Match** ->	Validated data model for the pay domain
Patient administration system	<- Match ->	System decomposition for the patient administration function
. . .		. . .

List source:
IS
maintenance

List source:
Data
administration

Figure 6.2 Desired data assets matched against a list of "problem" systems.

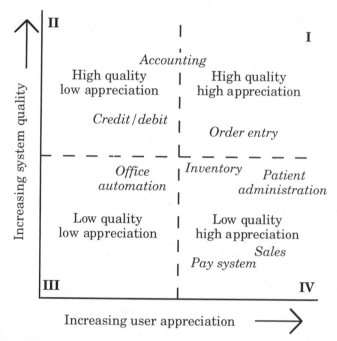

Figure 6.3 Identifying systems for reengineering (adapted from Sneed "Planning the Reengineering of Legacy Systems" © 1995 *IEEE Computer*).

Verdugo [1988] presents another means of rating *programs* for reengineering suitability. Adapted for *system* use (from Sneed [1991b and 1995]), it is presented as Fig. 6.3.

- In quadrant I, systems rating high in quality and appreciation should be maintained.

- In quadrant II, systems high in quality but low in appreciation should be left alone.

- In quadrant III, the systems low in quality and appreciation should be combined.

- In the remaining quadrant IV, systems should be evaluated for reengineering.

These guidelines can be used as a reality check, providing an additional assessment of the proposed project suitability.

Usually "problem" systems are associated with reaction-type data administration problems. Data administration involvement in data architecture development and enterprise integration provides insight into organizational information needs. The data administration function can monitor for opportunities to develop or enhance certain portions of the data architecture or contribute other information to enterprise integration efforts. The column on the right side of Fig. 6.2 shows the data administration's assessment of the three most immediately useful desired data assets which include:

- *Traceability matrices.* These are electronic indices enabling users to trace data items from the logical system model to the physically implemented system components developed during system design or design recovery activities by linking logical data items and file elements—in this case for the acquisitions functional area.

- *Pay system model.* This system model is required by the business process reengineering effort scheduled to begin shortly. When complete, this data asset will provide precise data item definitions for organization-wide reference in systems development contributing to shared organizational data.

- *System decomposition.* This is a type of system model produced as part of the DRE project planning. System decomposition models show the system as the sum of individual components. System decompositions are often represented as model views.

The list produced by the system maintenance group could be evaluated against a set of specific data assets required for enterprise integration activities. Obvious matches indicate good starting points for more detailed study. For example, Fig. 6.2 indicates a need for patient administration system decomposition and that the system may require large proportional amounts of resources to keep it running. It is certainly a good candidate for data reverse engineering.

Coordination with other data architectural development activities can also influence the order in which system components are analyzed. Consider the task of planning a project designed to obtain data assets from a health care management system. If the data architecture group was planning to develop the portion of the model dealing with HEALTH CARE WORKER CREDENTIALING, it might make sense to analyze the PROVIDE CREDENTIALING component of the FACILITY QUALITY ASSURANCE subsystem ahead of other components to extract the business rules embedded in the PROVIDE CREDEN-TIALING system component. Once recovered, the business rules could be used to validate and extend portions of the enterprise model dealing with rank and promotion.

For this example, a higher priority project is indicated by bolding the word "match" in Fig. 6.2. The pay system is also ranked second on the list of problem systems. Recall the governmental pay and personnel systems scenario from Chap. 1. Suppose the pay related component of the enterprise model was initially developed at a high level of abstraction—the definitions seem correct but are not detailed enough for use at the operational level. More information is required to establish linkages between the high level architectural components and the "to be" system. The missing detail will be gained by DRE portions of the existing pay system. Because of the timeliness and the dual functionality, this is a higher priority DRE candidate. In an interesting result, 41 percent of the organizations responding to the widely reported CSC/Index survey indicated that the reengineering choice was "obvious" [CSC 1994]. So at least for some organizations, identifying the focus of reengineering is easy.

The output of activity 1 is the identification of one or more candidate systems targeted for possible data reverse engineering. In the "matching" example used in this chapter, there are two good potential candidate DRE projects. Once the candidate systems have been identified, they can be further screened for project suitability as described in Chap. 17, "Evaluating DRE Investment Opportunities."

Careful selection of the first project (see Fig. 6.4) can set a good tone for future DRE efforts. Organizations might be unwilling to attempt another project if the first one fails to produce the desired results. When attempting to select the first DRE project, it is important to keep the following considerations in mind:

- *Be visible.* Everyone will be watching the progress of the first project; publicize the project progress, outputs, and lessons learned.

- *Be clear.* Some may be skeptical about the organization's ability to achieve the desired enterprise integration goals since they are often one step removed from DRE project objectives.

- *Be sponsored.* Be certain to design a project with a clear mandate.

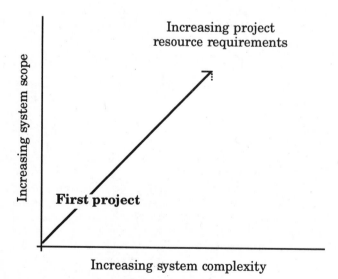

Figure 6.4 Keep the first project simple.

■ *Be relevant.* Design a project that the entire organization can relate to and benefit from; everyone will understand the improvements to the benefit, payroll, personnel, etc. systems.

■ *Be obvious.* It helps to demonstrate a payback within a relatively short period of time (I like 24 months) when persuading management to invest in the resources.

■ *Be team-oriented.* Carefully select a winning team. Some will be anxious to participate; evaluate their qualifications, and, if they match your needs, get these people on the team.

■ *Be conservative.* Design a project where you feel the payoff is quite evident. Pick a project where you will be able to produce multiple data assets for multiple other enterprise integration activities.

The last item represents a potential opportunity to demonstrate multiple uses of project payoffs. The best possible project outcome is to promise to positively affect multiple other development efforts and then deliver on the promise. Scenario 3 in Chap. 1 (government pay and personnel) is an example of a DRE project producing three payoffs:

■ Better understanding resulting from the CASE tool-based system documentation.

■ A data model now resident in the organizational data bank.

■ A system decomposition for use in the "to be" process reengineering.

Figure 6.5 shows how a single DRE project can produce multiple outputs useful for other enterprise integration activities. (This process is detailed in Chap. 15.)

In order to develop useful (realistic) project estimates, managers must first have data on how long it takes their organization to perform DRE analyses. This is similar to the problem of obtaining a bank loan or credit card for the first time. Few organizations are willing to lend to someone with no credit history. Unless some organization takes a chance and provides the beginning borrower with an opportunity to prove creditworthiness by extending a small loan, no one would ever get credit. Similarly, with the first DRE project someone will have to convince management to make that first, tentative investment in data reverse engineering. This means that management must possess sufficient understanding of enterprise integration goals, or at least of data reverse engineering. Additional issues include:

■ *Developing a means of accurately estimating DRE projects.* The model is useful after the first project is completed and becomes more useful with the addition of data from subsequent projects (for more on this subject, see Chap. 16).

■ *Project team member reuse.* Organizations can build on experiences by establishing a group within the organization dedicated specifically to reverse engineering and using it as a core team (especially the data engineers) that goes from project to project.

■ *Use of consultants.* If consultants are employed, the general plan should be to transfer the DRE knowledge and practices to your organization as, over time, the contractor role switches to oversight and then to occasional consultation.

When presenting a candidate project for consideration by system management it is important to highlight the technology transfer that occurs as a result of participation in a DRE project. This includes

■ An introduction to and understanding of the role of CASE tool development

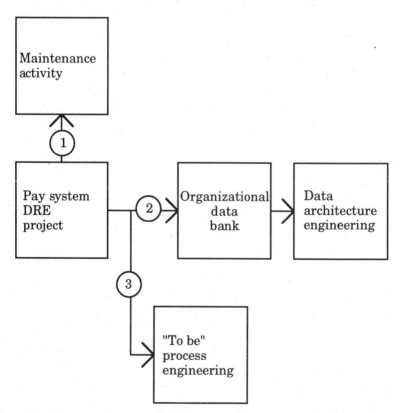

Figure 6.5 Outputs of a single DRE project can positively impact other enterprise integration activities.

■ Benefits of CASE-based system implementation

■ Experience with structured modeling techniques

■ Better understanding of data administration concepts

■ Increased awareness of target system capabilities

There is one final consideration factor, this one concerning approval thresholds. Design a project that won't require high levels of organizational resource management approval. Consider performing the DRE projects as a series of "byte-sized chunks." Structure the initial projects so they stay below a significant approval level to build up some results before making a significant investment. For example, suppose that your organization has to get all projects over $50,000 approved by the vice president for finance (or the CIO, or administrative vice president, or whoever ...). Implement a few DRE projects under the threshold. Let them successfully complete, and then go to the organizational decision maker in question, present the project outputs, illustrate the benefits, and then ask permission to continue. You probably have a better chance of gaining approval than if you went to that same individual with a request for several hundred thousand dollars worth of DRE projects and were unable to articulate the benefits as easily and well as the hospital data administration function did in the scenario 2 proposal justifying the establishment of the DRE program for the regional health care facility.

Preliminary Coordination - Framework Activity 2

While private sector DRE projects can have less complicated approval processes, a significant number of government systems need to be reverse engineered. Consequently, I'll spend just a few paragraphs describing some coordination considerations because I expect some public sector readers will be interested. If you can, imagine the following situation, occurring as a possible worst version of scenario 2:

> The organizational resource manager in charge of selecting the DRE project didn't consult the target system's project management office before hiring a contractor to data reverse engineer the target system. The contractor hired to data reverse engineer the target system discovered that another contractor—a competitor—had a development contract for the system. As a result, the development contractor was reluctant to share information with the reverse engineering contractor.

When you consider that some systems are shared among dozens of agencies, the possibility for coordination difficulties is apparent. Under these circumstances it is important to become politically savvy or at least ensure that someone on your project team has sufficient background to keep project team members away from political issues. I was once reverse engineering a system when we received a stop development order from a powerful Congressperson! (The project team debated for only 15 minutes or so about whether the order applied to us because it specifically called for all "development efforts" to cease. We decided it would be a lot of fun explaining DRE to a Senate Subcommittee and therefore the order didn't apply to the DRE project.) Data reverse engineering projects and organizational data and IS-related issues tend to cross functional area boundaries. Consider, for example, the governmental pay and personnel scenario where the organization has defined "pay" as a functional area separate from the personnel functional area—a common practice. Does this mean that the payroll system belongs to the pay functional area? If so, then what is the formal role of the personnel functional area who "loads" the payroll data? The point is to walk carefully.

The cross-functional nature of DRE makes it crucial to secure management approval to access the skills and knowledge of the key specialists prior to forming the reverse engineering project team. This leads to three "rules of thumb" for project team formation:

- Each system stakeholder's objectives must be identified and prioritized. The reverse engineering objectives and priorities must be synchronized (in synch) with and agreed to, by the stakeholders.

- Without coordinated buyin, a reverse engineering project cannot be successful. High-level management approval is necessary but not sufficient. Middle-level management and systems personnel must also understand and support the reverse engineering project objectives, or else organizational "rice-bowl" politics may jeopardize project success.

- The negotiation, planning, and buyin processes must be done *before* the project starts.

As the scope and size of the project grow, so does the amount of resources required to fund the effort. Proportionately larger project investment requires higher level authorization and increasing amounts of project coordination. *Coordination* is generally defined as a state of harmonious interaction. Data reverse engineering projects depend on this coordination to ensure that planned project goals can be met in a timely fashion.

Preliminary coordination begins well before the project team is formed or any target system analysis occurs. This activity involves identifying and contacting all parties who might have an interest in the proposed DRE project—at the very least, appropriate representatives of the system trinity. The initial contact involves describing to the system users and system stakeholders, DRE concepts in general, and the proposed project in particular.

During any preliminary discussions, the data engineers are constantly on the lookout for specific "show stoppers" or project specific considerations indicating project unfeasibility. For example, a system engineer who is the "only person who really understands the system" and who is unavailable could present information access difficulties and prevent project success. This is an example of a project specific characteristic that

■ Could likely be encountered in the regional health care facility consolidation scenario (Scenario 2, Chap. 1)

■ Could be (but isn't) part of the governmental pay and personnel scenario (Scenario 3, Chap. 1)

■ Is a part of the MARS scenario (Scenario 1, Chap. 1)

It doesn't do much good to secure organizational resource management approval if you don't have functional system management approval. In general, it is best to verify that key specialists have the motivation to take on a project and then go to seek management approval. Barring discovery of any specific "stopper" items, it is appropriate to draw up a list of contacts for the various functional areas of those personnel who should be involved in the proposed project. Identification and selection of a candidate project influences the composition of the project team. For example, in the MARS scenario, use of an obscure operating-system environment requires an expert to facilitate system understanding.

For a variety of reasons, it is possible to eliminate many infeasible projects during activity 2. The output of activity 2 is a proposed DRE project that has passed both organizational needs and preliminary coordination screening. As a consequence of passing this preliminary screening, the project organizers will have developed one or more points of contact for the candidate target system. These are the individuals with whom the proposed project must be coordinated.

Evidence Identification and Access - Framework Activity 3

The next step is to identify, catalog, and establish access to the required project evidence. The phrase "establish access to evidence" has a broad definition, including explicitly obtaining access to specific individuals participating as key specialists. At times they possess better quality information their heads than the system documentation. Ideally, obtaining access to evidence can range from accessing the proper individuals, to getting the right file format of the outputs from the system data dictionary, to getting access to the proper versions of the printed systems documentation. To demonstrate the range of evidence categories, seven are illustrated in Fig. 6.6.

Understanding the state of the evidence permits data engineers to determine the amount of effort that should be spent studying it (no point in studying with wrong information). One final point, on the state of the evidence. Many organization have legacy systems that are decades old, using older technology hardware or obscure programming languages or environments. The most difficult challenge is the case of the "home grown" environment. Thus, the relative value of good-quality evidence increases as the technical environment becomes less common.

The first concern is the shape of the evidence. Part of Rugaber's [1992] reverse engineering description addressed the gap between the desired coherent and highly structured system description and the actual system whose structure may have deteriorated over time or not even been captured in the first place. (Recall Jones' [1993] assertion that software changes at a 5 to 7 percent annual rate.) So the first question becomes "What is the shape of the evidence?" Individual pieces of evidence can be classified as being in one of three possible states:

- *Synchronized.* Synchronized evidence is documentation that accurately represents the current state of the system. Synchronized is the most desirable evidence classification state. System documentation that is produced using a CASE tool is most likely to be synchronized. It is also, unfortunately, the rarest.

- *Dated or otherwise of imperfect quality.* If documentation exists, it is often outdated or of poor quality. Dated system documentation was created to reflect the system as it existed at a point in time, but changes have been made to the system since the documentation was created. Dated system documentation might have been

Evidence category	Examples
Domain specialists	Domain knowledge from the specialists, business rules
Processes	Functional descriptions, process models, code, user manuals
External data	Screen, report, interface specifications, interfaces to other systems
Conceptual data	Logical data models
Internal data	Program variables, data element lists, tables, file layout structures
Policies	Directives, guidelines, planning statements
System	Program source, object code, job procedures, libraries, directories, test cases, schemas, copylibs, make files, link maps, I/Os and other documentation, data

Figure 6.6 Project evidence categories.

created with a CASE tool but could also be paper-based. Locating
the evidence can also be quite a task. Systems with dated documentation are likely to have maintenance problems. Most evidence used in DRE projects falls in this category.

■ *Not useful or not available.* Of course, the worst possible case occurs when documentation was never created in the first place or
was subsequently lost.

These states are useful for describing evidence—whether it exists on
paper, in a CASE tool environment, or in someone's head. It is critical to understand the role of physical evidence in reverse engineering.
One of the data engineer's goals is to minimize the time spent intrud-
ing into the key specialist's regular work schedule. This is accomplished largely by "doing homework" studying the evidence. The
closer the system documentation is to being synchronized and accurate, the easier and more economical will be the DRE project.
      A common misperception is that DRE projects can be accomplished
by examining the existing system documentation. System documentation is often out of date and therefore of limited or no use. For
some projects, documentation is often a necessary but not sufficient
requisite to feasible reverse engineering. The characteristics of many
projects do not permit DRE to occur is on the sole basis of system
documentation.
      Data reverse engineering is dependent on appropriate key special-
ist participation and is most effectively accomplished somewhere between two extremes—having the key specialists provide all information via modeling cycles and reviewing the system documentation.
For example, because key specialists know the value of the existing
documentation, they can save data engineers hours of futile analysis
by just indicating what information is documented in specific volumes
or what written documentation is accurate.   Key is to identify,
achieve, and maintain appropriate balance between relying on key
specialists and written documentation.
      Further, *validated* system models cannot be produced without key
specialist participation. Data engineers cannot effectively produce
validated system models without key specialist assistance. The role
of data engineers is to derive candidate system models for subsequent refinement and validation by system users. There are two dimensions of evidence collection: duplication difficulties and competition for access (see Fig. 6.7).
      The activity goal is to identify and obtain access to adequate rep-
resentation of the evidence for subsequent analysis. The output of
activity 3 should be the initial set of evidence specifications required
to achieve the proposed project goals and plans for acquiring them.
Consider these evidence catalogs as pointers to evidence that should
eventually exist in the project data bank. In addition, they can be
used to track the status of individual pieces of evidence as synchronized, dated, or not useful, and assess the overall state of the sys-

tem's evidence. The evidence specifications should consist of a list of the primary resources to be used on the project. The evidence access plan should indicate precisely what information is required to complete the project and how the project team will obtain access to the information. All project information is stored in the project CASE-based and physical project data bank for subsequent reference.

	Not difficult to duplicate	Documentation is not useful and therefore not in demand (copy anyway)	CASE-based documentation is duplicated by copying files (obtain copy of CASE tool and duplicate required files)
	Difficult to duplicate	Documentation does not exist on paper (extract from key users)	Documentation is useful but difficult to duplicate and therefore in demand (photocopy at night when evidence is not in use)

(left axis, vertical label: Effort required to duplicate)

Competition for access

Figure 6.7 Dimensions of evidence collection.

7

Project Team Initiation (Framework Activity 4)

Assuming that you manage to identify a candidate target system, pass any preliminary coordination hurdles, and favorably assess the evidence quality, you next put together a project team capable of accomplishing the tasks required to achieve the project objectives. Activity 4 involves forming the project team, defining participation levels, and scheduling modeling cycles. Once constituted as a project team, these individuals must collectively perform the preliminary system survey (as well as the remainder of the project), and they need to understand the overall project goals and enterprise integration strategy. Project team initiation includes training and otherwise educating the project team members with any required background information, methodology requirements, as well as acquisition of and training on CASE tools, etc. Understanding the roles and responsibilities of the various team members will help readers identify candidate administrative, technical, and management team members for specific reverse engineering projects. This chapter describes the types of investment various DRE project stakeholders are making, the composition of the project team, and the functions of the project team, and suggests some default matching between project team members and project team roles and responsibilities.

Project Stakeholder Concerns

My earliest encounter with a depiction of the system trinity concept came from a systems analysis class that I taught in 1989. The text [Eliason 1987] illustrated how standard roles in system analysis did not follow a typical "service provider–client" role as do many other formal service arrangements such as that of defendant and lawyer. Instead, organizational infrastructure–related projects are characterized by a three-part interaction consisting of

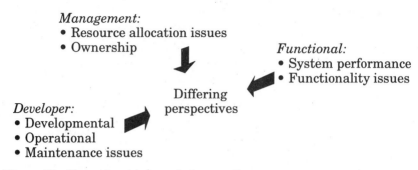

Figure 7.1   The system trinity project perspectives.

■ Developer perspectives

■ Key functional area perspectives

■ Organizational resource management perspectives

Figure 7.1 illustrates this three-part interaction resulting in differing perspectives that characterize DRE projects.

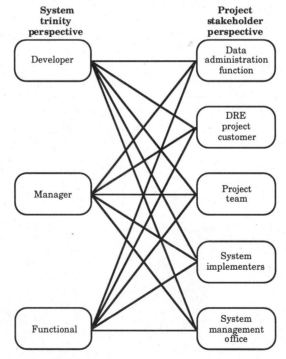

Figure 7.2   Data reverse engineering project stakeholder groups represent multiple and potentially complex interests.

Stakeholder	Concern(s)
Data administration function	■ What will help us invest in projects wisely? ■ How can we demonstrate our contributions?
DRE project customers	■ How can we invest operational resources wisely? ■ How can we improve system effectiveness? ■ How can we assist functional system use?
Project team	■ Why am I needed for this project? ■ How can I do a good job if I don't understand? ■ Can I represent my workgroup?
System implementers	■ How will we learn more about system operation? ■ When will we improve system documentation? ■ How do we minimize system maintenance?
System functional management office	■ How can we avoid appearing to have been deficient? ■ Why should we allocate resources to these projects?

Figure 7.3   Project stakeholder group investment concerns.

It is important to understand the project perspectives held by various types of stakeholders. These concerns are addressed through participation on DRE project teams. Explicit representation of various perspectives facilitates formulation of clearer project goals and smoother planning and operation. As shown in Fig. 7.2, five types of DRE project stakeholders each represent some aspect of the system trinity perspective. Primary stakeholder concerns are summarized in Fig. 7.3 and addressed in more detail in the following paragraphs.

Data administration function

In the ideal case, organizational resource management feels strongly enough about the value of organizational data assets to support a chief information systems officer (CIO). Where the organizational information system function has matured to stage 3 or 4, the data administration will be represented on the project team. A CIO isn't required to initiate DRE projects because not all such projects will initiate with the organizational data administration group. A sizable number have been initiated at the insistence of users. In these cases, the key specialists convinced organizational management of the viability of this approach.

Generally, however, organizational data administration is faced with the task of evaluating candidate projects in which to invest.

The data administration function suggests the projects that will yield the most in terms of investments. Although it cannot have future knowledge of the exact payoff, it is possible to assess likely scenarios. In addition, the data administration function is responsible for creating and maintaining the appearance of success. Since data administration programs have proved difficult to "sell," is it important that data administration programs—particularly newly formed or rejuvenated ones—demonstrate timely cost effectiveness. Data administration program management faced with these conditions often feel pressed to produce results early to quiet any critics and secure program stability.

Data reverse engineering project customers

In DRE projects it is crucial to identify and address all customer-related concerns. All participants are customers and must understand both the nature of their respective investments in DRE and the value of the results. Project team members in particular and management in general need to understand that DRE projects benefit many customer types including

- *Management,* by providing reduced system operation costs and progress toward enterprise integration goals

- *Key specialists,* by providing benefits related to improved system knowledge because the information created is easily accessible with the enterprise data bank

- *Developers,* by receiving data administration development and experience in DRE projects

Project team

Project team members develop a vested involvement in the project's success as they become aware of their own key role in developing the project models. This is especially true for non-data-administration project team members.

System implementers

System implementers are those individuals responsible for operation, maintenance, and enhancement of the target system. There are systems with little or no key specialist involvement in system operation and maintenance, leaving the development group as the primary representative of the system implementer perspective. Heavy key specialist involvement in system activities indicates a key specialist participation equal to that of the development group. By investing in DRE projects, system implementers hope to be reimbursed in the form of opportunities to

- Learn more about the system operation

- Increase the quality and quantity of CASE-based, verified system documentation

- Reduce maintenance costs

- Increase the effectiveness and efficiency of system operation

Functional system management

In some instances, systems have oversight boards (with names such as "Consolidated Pay and Personnel System Program Management Office") managing the organizational investments in the system. Functional area management are the customers of the services provided by the system—they serve as the system management—determining how the system resources are applied in response to the service requests. System management will be asked not only for the services of technical, functional, and system specialists) but also possibly to postpone development projects required by users to permit the DRE project. These groups can range from informal user groups to formal, contract-driven bureaucracies charged with contract management. The purpose of these oversight groups is to ensure wise application of scarce system resources to meet user needs while retaining the organizational perspective in decision making. They balance organizational needs against system user needs and coordinate system activities to maximize organizational objectives. System functional management team member concerns with investments in DRE projects can include the following:

- *Their own credibility and professionalism.* Some in program management offices have seen the attempt to data reverse engineer their system as a sign of failure on the part of their office. It isn't. It illustrates how far we have come as an industry and what we now know about system development.

- *Reallocation of personnel.* Often program management is requested to reallocate personnel from forward development activities—which has then often created confusion as indicated by statements such as:

    You mean I have to take an analyst off of the interface development project because you need their assistance tearing the system apart? I don't get it. You are impacting my development schedule!

Regardless of the availability of personnel, the program management office (or the equivalent) generally requires coordination and approval prior to explicitly investing resources in the project. System management must be certain that it can justify the investment to the community of system users it serves.

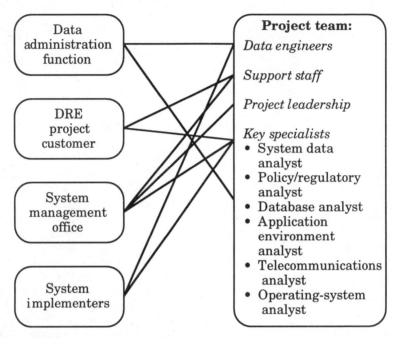

Figure 7.4 Project team composition.

Project Team Composition

There are four types of DRE project team members, as shown in Fig. 7.4:

■ Key specialists

■ Technical specialists/data engineers

■ Leadership

■ Support staff

From an organizational investment perspective, project team members have been asked to participate on what could develop into a significant undertaking. The project goals and objectives may or may not conflict with the individual project team member goals or the goals shared by their functional area perspectives. To do a good job, they need to understand their respective project roles. Figure 7.4 also shows how each of the four project team roles (described in the following subsections) represents the other four stakeholder groups. Project team members are the interface with various parts of the system's operational environment. They communicate directly with the target system user community as well as with management.

Key specialists

Every system has key specialists. For DRE projects you want what Nardi [1993] calls "gardeners." They are also known as "superusers" and "power users." Regardless of the label, these are users who have developed a better-than-average understanding of the target system. Their expertise surpasses that of the rest of the user community. They are the ones to whom everyone else turns when they encounter system problems.

Key to project success is identifying and obtaining at least available minimal key specialist participation. Because the most effective individuals needed to perform reverse engineering analysis are often the key specialists, DRE projects are potential competitors with other system related projects.

Their principal role is to facilitate the transformation of facts known about the system into knowledge stored as models. For example, the system may have an individual who functions as the primary technical expert, a person who understands the intricacies of the physical implementation of the system, the one to whom everyone turns to answer complex questions. It is just as logical for that person to be a part of the team developing system enhancements as it is for the same individual to be a part of the reverse engineering analysis team. Because of the cross-functional domain of some DRE projects, project team members can be working on DRE projects in functional areas other than their own. The pressure on organizations to trim their staffing levels puts even greater demands on the services of these individuals. It is often critical to identify individual(s) possessing the following technical understanding:

- *System data specialists.* These individuals understand how to get the system to produce the required results. They are the ones other users seek to answer questions such as "what types of transactions do I enter to back out 13 weeks of pay for an employee who has already resigned?"

- *Policy or regulatory specialists.* These include individuals versed in the terminology or lingo of specialized domain areas such as the Federal Acquisition Regulations or the Americans with Disabilities Act, as well as various federal, state, and regional regulations. They are needed to trace and document the relationships between relevant law, policies, regulations, procedures, and practices, and specific system components implementing the "guidance."

- *Database specialists.* These individuals possess analyst knowledge of the implementation of physical data management for the system. Their knowledge extends to physical representation issues such as whether the data is actually deleted or just marked as deleted.

■ *Application environment specialists.* These individuals are cognizant of the program-language (PL) capabilities. Some projects will benefit from the participation of individuals knowledgeable in PL and other systems programming environment characteristics.

■ *Telecommunications specialists.* In systems such as the MARS where the distributed nature of the desired system architecture ensures that telecommunications will play an important role, the participation of a telecommunications analyst can facilitate team understanding of relevant telecommunications related aspects of the system operation. This is required if there are telecommunication aspects such as electronic data transfer involved in the system operation.

■ *Operating system specialists.* Sometimes systems are implemented in familiar programming languages but on unfamiliar hosts. Operating system specialists can quickly address any specific problem areas or questions. This is required if operating system specific characteristics impact the project. For example, granting access to models in digital form on an unfamiliar operating system often also requires an operating system analyst to help with the extraction.

Figure 7.5 illustrates the primary role of the various specialists in reverse engineering activities. The more technical team members, data, programmer, and operating system specialists, play key roles facilitating the transformation from the target system to design and the functional team members translating from design to requirements. Key specialist availability levels are assigned according to the level of participation available, as shown in Fig. 7.6.

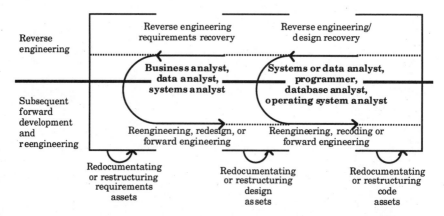

Figure 7.5 The primary roles of key specialists (adapted from Chikofsky and Cross "Reverse Engineering and Design Recovery: A Taxonomy" © 1990 *IEEE Software*).

Availability level	Participation
Full time	Key specialists are actively participating as a full-time member of the project team. Full-time participation usually requires under 20 hours per week.
Part time	Key specialists are designated as available to answer questions during certain times of the project but are not expected or perhaps needed at all project meetings.
Limited	Key specialists are designated as being able to participate in a limited number of (usually 5) days of attendance at modeling cycles. Usually these individuals are in high demand, but their presence at the sessions will greatly contribute to the project team productivity.
Very limited	Key specialists are in such demand that they are available for only abbreviated or partial model refinement or validation session attendance.
Not available	Project feasibility must be reconsidered if key specialists are unavailable.

Figure 7.6   Key specialist availability levels.

Figure 7.7 illustrates some suggested ranges of key specialist participation in DRE projects. Project team members will probably devote about one-third to one-half of their weekly schedule on average to the DRE projects. This actual use of time will vary from just a few hours per week to three-quarters of a week during the model validation-refinement sessions. Figure 7.8 shows typical key specialists' involvement over the course of 16 one-week-long modeling cycles.

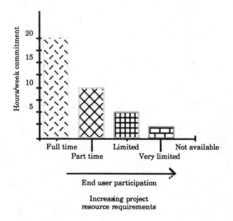

Figure 7.7   Ranges of key specialist participation in DRE projects.

	Full time		Part time		
Cycles per week	Hours per week	Days per week	Hours per week	Days per week	Event
1	10	2	10	2	Project kickoff session
2	5	3	2	2	Occasional consultation
3	5	3	2	2	Occasional consultation
4	20	3.5	10	2	MR/V session 1
5	5	3	2	2	Occasional consultation
6	5	3	2	2	Occasional consultation
7	5	3	2	2	Occasional consultation
8	20	3.5	10	2	MR/V session 2
9	5	3	2	2	Occasional consultation
10	5	3	2	2	Occasional consultation
11	5	3	2	2	Occasional consultation
12	20	3.5	10	2	MR/V session 3
13	5	3	2	2	Occasional consultation
14	5	3	2	2	Occasional consultation
15	5	3	2	2	Occasional consultation
16	20	3.5	10	2	MR/V session 4
Total	145	49	72	32	

Figure 7.8   Typical key specialist involvement.

As mentioned previously, a major DRE project challenge area is concerned with ensuring that certain system experts are able and motivated to participate on the DRE project team at sufficient levels to ensure project feasibility. If certain pieces of evidence are physically missing, the only alternative might be to gain access to someone familiar with the system and its development history. Lack of adequate documentation can lead to larger required minimum participation levels. This can be partially offset by having knowledgeable key specialists available to compensate for the lack of documentation.

In situations with low-quality evidence, participation of these key players can also make the difference between project success and project failure. Occasionally, personnel with the required knowledge have not been immediately available and have been coaxed back from retirement. Data reverse engineering projects can depend on the availability of key specialists.

Data engineers

Data engineers are supplied by the data administration organization. They are the technical personnel most familiar with both data administration functions and DRE techniques. As such, they provide guidance to the remainder of the project team. Required areas of analyst and/or project experience include:

■ *Data reverse engineering experience.* Given the nature of DRE projects, organizations will probably benefit from concentrating—that is, developing staff DRE analysis among a few individuals—rather than attempting to educate everyone a little bit.

■ *Data modeling experience.* In general, one to three experienced data modelers are required depending on the size of the projects. These individuals should probably have computer science credentials or demonstrated information engineering project experience. Data engineers are the type of computer engineers you want working on your projects.

■ *People interaction and leadership abilities.* Data reverse engineering is a people-oriented business requiring enough face-to-face information exchanges as to require data engineers to have good people skills.

A guiding principle in all system analysis work is to be as unobtrusive as possible to the key specialist community. Although, key specialists are project team members, they deserve to have planned, predictable, and pleasant interactions with other project team members. Data engineers begin projects by gathering, reading, and indexing copies of existing system documentation. These are examined in detail with the goal of establishing "straw" or initial versions of the data products. These are presented to the user in refinement and/or validation sessions.

Support staff

Because of the information intensive nature of DRE projects, adequate support staff is absolutely required. Proper levels of clerical support can also increase the effectiveness of the DRE efforts by a factor of 10. Duties of support staff include the following:

■ *Performing librarian functions.* Cataloging and maintaining all collections of physical evidence and adding the information to the project CASE data bank.

■ *Coordinating or facilitation functions.* Facilitating meetings, taking minutes, arranging logistics, transcribing session minutes, entering relevant information in the project data bank, and operating a CASE tool during modeling cycles. Quite often professional facilitation skill can be employed to keep the various modeling cycles progressing effectively.

■ *Duplicating, cataloging, and data translation functions.* Often system documentation is in short supply. In situations where manuals can be obtained only overnight, it is often more effective to duplicate copies.

Consider, for example, the amount of resources wasted by having data engineers copy manuals. These services should be provided along with "professional-strength" hardware and software facilities. While I don't advocate wasting trees, there will be situations in which certain documentation is so valuable that it is available only overnight. It should be nothing to hand this document to a project team staff member with the instructions, "Please copy this, enter it into the library, and return the package to me by tomorrow morning." Other additional infrastructure-related tasks might include translating a mainframe produced data tape of system information into a format suitable for import to a workstation.

Qualified support staff is often provided by the data administration function while the information system organization provides the hardware and software. There have been cases of system management supplying support staff in an effort to get the project started.

Leadership and key management representatives

Ultimate responsibilities for project success must rest with an empowered project manager. As appropriate, the manager may come from the data administration group or, with a bit of experience, from the functional community. The project manager is largely responsible for strategic-level project leadership, including resource allocation decisions, project scoping, and model analysis issues. In most cases the project manager has a dual reporting line: to both the data administration functional management and the functional system management.

Project Team Functions

Figure 7.9 shows general involvement for project initiation activities, indicating limited key specialist and decision maker involvement before project kickoff; larger checkmarks indicate heavier involvement. Collectively, the project team is responsible for producing project estimates and outputs, scheduling, and otherwise ensuring project success. Specific functions and outputs are covered below.

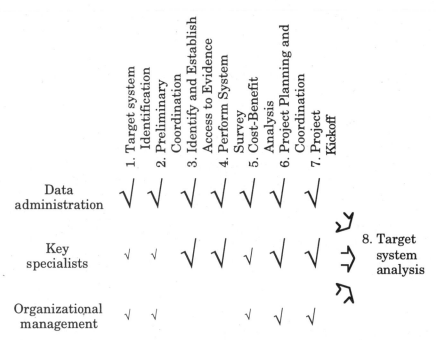

Figure 7.9   Relative project team member involvement during project initiation activities.

Modeling

Modeling in the DRE context is defined as a representation of data items and their relationships and attributes in a general sense, independent of software, hardware, or other implementation considerations [Martin 1990 and Narayan 1988].   Modeling is accomplished using appropriate combinations of documentation analysis, question/answer, questionnaire or oral interview sessions, and more formal model validation and/or refinement sessions. Models are used to represent information extracted from the key specialist or technical representative project team members during the sessions.

Data analysis

Also accomplished during the modeling cycles, *data analysis* is described by Martin [1990] as refining complex data structures into simpler, more stable structures. Data analysis is based on rules designed to ensure flexible and anomaly-free data designs. This is key to the process of ensuring that designs are free from preconceived notions inherited from the existing system.

Reporting

As indicated previously, team members are the project's interface with the rest of the organization. The better informed the project team members are about project progress as well as the goals, the better informed will be the organization. In the same manner, the project team is responsible for timely and accurate reporting of progress and resource utilization.

Information gathering

Project team members are key to effectively and efficiently locating and delivering project information, largely in the form of physical evidence consisting of bits of evidence representing the physical implementation of the system. Much of the evidence exists in the knowledge of certain individuals associated with the system and must be extracted during phone or other brief consultations, structured interviews, or formal modeling cycles.

Coordination

As illustrated previously, project teams must carefully coordinate with other parts of the organization. Key specialists can be particularly valuable, with their knowledge of the functional user community helping avoid missteps.

Project management

While the internal organization can vary, collectively the project team is responsible for all aspects of project management. This includes monitoring for cost, monitoring for schedule, and for technical quality.

Quality assurance

Finally, collectively, the project team is responsible for and empowered to perform appropriate project quality assurance functions. Quality assurance activities occur continuously throughout DRE projects. In addition, activity 13 includes a project self-analysis to facilitate and encourage organizational learning from project experiences. Figure 7.10 illustrates how one CASE tool vendor has implemented methodology specific quality assurance functions as part of the tool. Figure 7.11 shows a sample of one of the report outputs indicating a specific modeling error and recommending a solution.

Suggested Project Team Member Roles and Responsibilities

This section is intended to assist in the process of developing DRE team member roles and responsibilities. Key is to retain the idea that DRE project teams strive to use symbiotic knowledge with

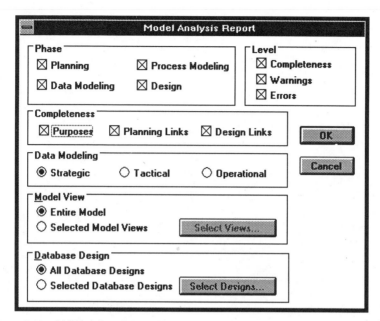

Figure 7.10 CASE tool model quality assurance support. (Source: Dialog box from IE: Advantage Universal CASE tool © 1991-95 Information Engineering Systems Coporation, Alexandria: VA.)

- Data engineers understanding the modeling techniques

- Key specialists understanding the content of the information that needs to be modeled

Suggested project team member roles and responsibilities are illustrated in Fig. 7.12. Regardless of the final division of duties and responsibilities, it is critically important that all parties reach an understanding of the definition of the roles and responsibilities. Key specialists share responsibility with data engineers for information and data acquisition.

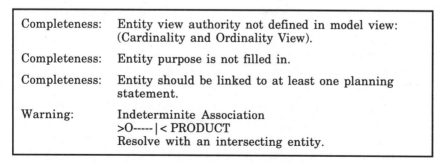

Figure 7.11 Sample model quality analysis output.

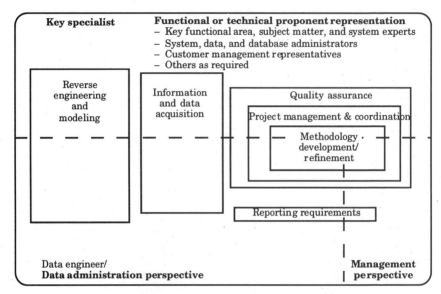

Figure 7.12   Project team member roles and responsibilities.

They support the DRE, data modeling, and data analysis portions of the project. The quality assurance, project management and/or coordination, and methodology refinement are typically shared among all three types of project team members. The reporting requirements belong to those from data administration but are coordinated with those representing organizational management.

A DRE project team constituted to address a system in the health care facility consolidation scenario is illustrated in Fig. 7.13 (see also Fig. 7.14). The sample team was developed for a situation where a contractor is to be employed to perform some of the DRE activities—desirable in situations where organizations would like more guidance developing their first project(s).

This activity will be completed when each team member has verified the correctness of the information contained in the project team directory. A published team directory consists of contact information, telephone, fax, e-mail address of committed team members, and authorized points of contacts. It also describes roles, participation levels, and communication protocols—all these within the context of the DRE project framework. The output of activity 4 is a proposed DRE project team with a specific charge, usually something like

> Perform a preliminary system survey designed to derive information required to develop useful data reverse engineering project estimates.

The project team formation indicates that organizational resource management has been convinced of the project's worthiness and desires to perform the initial analysis required to develop useful project estimates.

Project team member	Quantity	Hours/Week
Key specialist participation	3	60
Data administration analyst	1	40
Data engineer	2	80
Clerk or scribe	1	40
Project manager	1	40
Program management officer	1	10
Total	9	270

Figure 7.13   An example six-person DRE project team.

Name	Organization	Role	Participation level	Phone	Fax	e-mail	Address
Karen L.	Hospital administration	Key functional area specialist	Full-time	. . .	.	. .	. .
Diane C.	Hospital systems	Key system language specialist	Full-time	. . .	.	. .	. .
Ray B.	Development contractor	System data handling specialist	Full-time	. . .	.	. .	. .
Bill D.	Hospital administration	Program office management	Half-time	. . .	.	. .	. .
Peter H.	Project manager	Data adminis- tration	Full-time	. . .	.	. .	. .
Sheri L.	Reverse engineering contractor	Data engineer	Full-time	. . .	.	. .	. .
Kathy J.	Reverse engineering contractor	Data engineer	Full-time	. . .	.	. .	. .

Figure 7.14   Data reverse engineering project team directory.

8

Project Initiation Activities (Part 2)

This chapter describes the last of the DRE project initiation activities as performing the preliminary system survey, planning the project, and project initiation.

Preliminary System Survey - Framework Activity 5

Imagine being told you are to head up a DRE project for an unfamiliar system and then asked to produce a plan showing schedules and milestones. How fast could you produce the required information? In order to realistically plan for a given DRE project, it is advisable to invest first in a preliminary system survey (PSS). The PSS is a project scoping exercise designed to help assess the magnitude of the proposed project. It is used by the project team to develop useful project estimates. Since this activity generally requires key specialist participation, authorization to involve them is often required. The survey is developed to provide enough information about the system to develop a cost-benefit analysis and detailed project plan—the outputs of activity 5. To do a good job, that is, to learn enough about the system on which to base future plans, regardless of the project size, allow an upper limit of between 2 to 4 weeks of dedicated preliminary work. It is more appropriate to answer the question:

How much will it cost me to data reverse engineer system X?

with the response:

It will cost you at least the cost of a preliminary system survey to find out.

than it is to make uninformed judgments that might return to haunt the project sometime in the future.

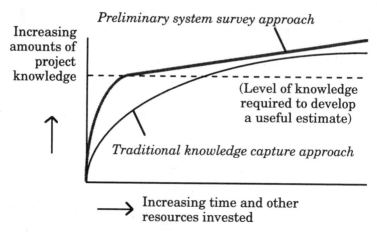

Figure 8.1   The PSS attempts to acquire project information more rapidly than the traditional approaches allow.

By definition, DRE projects are explorations; Chikofsky [1990] has described them as archaeological in nature. This analogy extends to the PSS—an initial inquiry as to the nature of the system to be examined by the reverse engineering analysis.

The dashed line in Fig. 8.1 indicates some level of knowledge required to develop a useful project estimate about a proposed project. The thin black line illustrates increasing amounts of knowledge obtained via a traditional approach to estimating DRE projects—first "guestimating" the project, obtaining management approval, and then beginning work on it. As soon as work begins, the project team begins to amass considerable project knowledge. Unfortunately, this increased knowledge often uncovers additional complications, invalidating the original estimate and creating potentially difficult situations for the project management. The solution is to perform a PSS of the target system, more rapidly gathering information about four key project variables characterizing individual DRE projects. Figure 8.2 illustrates how PSS based data is used to develop project estimates.

The PSS approach is shown as the wider gray line on top in Fig. 8.1 indicating requisite information is obtained more rapidly, and that better project estimates can be developed. (See also Fig. 8.3 for a list of typical PSS objectives.) The cost-benefit approach to evaluating potential investments in DRE projects is also developed by the project team. After ensuring that the project team understands the basis of cost benefit analysis, the team determines the various decision criteria and populates the decision structure with data. A set of assumptions are developed and evaluated with current knowledge. The area of the largest uncertainty is identified as the area of greatest project risk; the focus of the next phase is on reducing the project

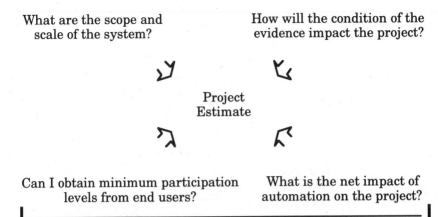

Figure 8.2   Four characteristics of DRE project cost.

risk. As the project proceeds, the assumptions and therefore the cost-benefit analysis are periodically reviewed and updated. Assuming that the cost-benefit analysis is favorable, project planning begins.

The PSS information is combined with organizational reverse engineering productivity data and other situation-specific considerations to develop project estimates and determine project estimates (see Fig. 8.4). The system survey is an attempt to develop an accurate baseline assessment of the project characteristics:

- What are the scope and scale of the system?

- How will the condition of the evidence impact the project?

- Can I obtain minimum participation levels from key specialists?

- Determine and catalog specific information required to accurately estimate the time, personnel and other resource requirements for the project.
- Assess and catalog the quality and availability of the existing evidence.
- Synthesize the available information into meaningful project size, evidence, participation, and automation characteristics.
- Where possible, interpolate, derive, infer, or otherwise obtain and/or correct missing or substandard information.
- Document the process—especially actions taken in activity 4.

Figure 8.3   Sequential preliminary system survey objectives.

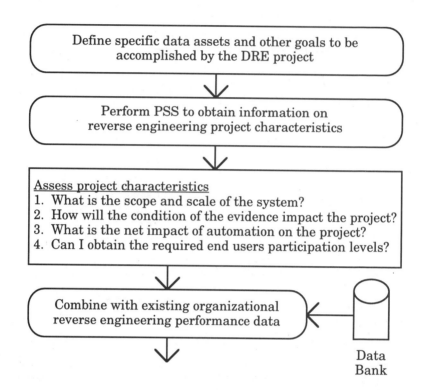

Figure 8.4 The process of obtaining useful reverse engineering project estimates is based on information obtained from the PSS.

■ What is the net impact of automation on the project?

Useful DRE project estimates can be developed if adequate PSS information (listed in Fig. 8.3) is obtained about the project: participation, size, evidence, and automation characteristics. As shown in Fig. 8.4 the project characteristics developed during the PSS are applied to organizational performance characteristics to determine the project estimate. Note how two project characteristics present opportunities for cost reduction.

An overview of the process of accomplishing a medium-sized PSS is shown in Figs. 8.5 and 8.6. The survey begins by identifying and securing the participation of key specialists. Having secured key specialist participation, the project team focuses on developing and validating a system context model and functional decomposition. This can be accomplished through a series of workgroup sessions. The sessions refine and validate models produced by the project data engineers. The four project characteristics become the first organizational models created from the candidate DRE project and should be stored in the project data bank for anticipated future use. Descriptions of the project characteristics to be determined are shown in Fig. 8.6. An overview of the system survey process is shown in Fig. 8.7.

Development and validation of a system model view decomposition hierarchy

The key is to decompose the target system, permitting development of a phased approach to uncovering required information in an orderly fashion. This is accomplished by using the system decomposition (SD) as a map to the system, providing both a common description of the system and progress indication. The most tangible of the PSS is a validated "as is" or existing SD. The SD is derived by the project team using structured decomposition techniques. It is subsequently used as a guide to indicating likely data modeling views that will be created as part of the DRE analysis.

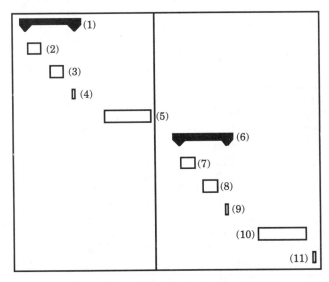

ID	Name
1	PSS Phase 1
2	Gather and study evidence
3	Perform selected interviews
4	Prepare for next week's session
5	Model refinement-validation session 1
6	PSS Phase 2
7	Gather and study evidence
8	Perform selected interviews
9	Prepare for next week's session
10	Model refinement-validation session 2
11	Presentation of results

Figure 8.5 Typical DRE project scoping schedule.

Description	Question(s) to be answered by the PSS
System characteristics are gross measures of system size and complexity	To determine the relevant dimensions of the system to be data reverse engineered: ■ Is it a small compact system used by a small group of users (such as a group decision support system)? ■ Is it a small compact system used by thousands of users [such as an automatic teller machine (ATM) control program]? ■ Is it a large distributed interorganizational information system such as an airline reservation system?
Evidence characteristics are measures of the expected contribution of the evidence to the overall project information	How will the condition of the evidence impact the project? System documentation will range from not useful to useful. Additional factors such as the state of organizational knowledge, version control, and configuration management must also be factored in. Some evidence exists as knowledge in the heads of key specialists.
Participation characteristics are assessments of how much key specialist participation will help the project	■ What is the expected contribution of the key specialists to the project? ■ One key form of participation is executive sponsorship—do we have it? ■ Have we identified and secured at least minimal participation of key specialists? Participation by these individuals can make the difference between feasible and infeasible projects. ■ In some circumstances it will be desirable to transport (virtually or physically) key specialists who work in different parts of the world—are they available? ■ Multiple stakeholders make it important to consider all participants' perspectives—have we?
Automation characteristics are computer-aided impacts applicable to the DRE project goals	To what degree will automation in the form of CASE technology or other reverse engineering tools contribute to the effectiveness and efficiency of the analyses? ■ No support: No automated tools support the platform/language combination. ■ Fully supported: The popularity of the system created a market for the automated tool support.

Figure 8.6 Project characteristics addressed by the preliminary system survey.

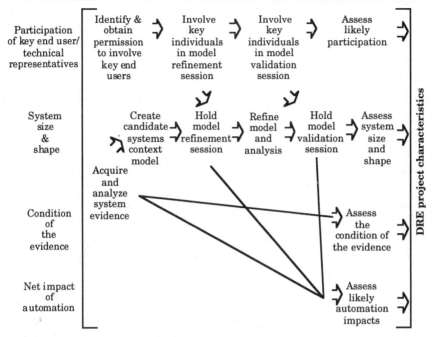

Figure 8.7   Preliminary system survey overview.

Models can contain information about literally hundreds of data items. System decompositions are used to focus analysis on some smaller number of entities, sparing data engineers and other project team members the enormous task of considering all data items in the model simultaneously. *Model views* are defined as inverted-tree structures indicating how system components decompose into processing primitives. A model view may be used as a filtering device to permit analysis of complex material in groups of related items. The entire data model can be described as the sum of the system decomposition components.

Once complete, a SD also functions as a map of the processes currently supported by the system. As the system is reengineered, the SD will be transformed into a representation of the desired or "to be" system. The steps creating a SD include

1. Acquiring and analyzing relevant system documentation. Since one of the reverse engineering specialist goals is to be as unobtrusive as possible outside regular meetings, the proper place to begin is with system documentation. It is acquired and analyzed with assistance from the key specialists as appropriate (i.e., meaning whether they are available and useful).

2. Careful examination of the system documentation usually permits the data engineers to develop a straw or candidate version of a

system decomposition hierarchy. System documentation is analyzed to determine the basic business processes supported by the system. The SD should contain one view for each basic process supported by the system. The initial version of the SD is developed by the data engineers with assistance from the key specialists as appropriate. As shown in Fig. 8.8, each process is broken down into subprocesses.

3. The candidate SD is presented to the rest of the project team at a model refinement session. The session goals are to refine the candidate model into an accurate representation of the system. The focus of the session is on increasing model completeness with a secondary emphasis on model accuracy.

4. On the basis of the critique from the model refinement session, the SD is revised by the data engineers.

5. Once the model has been revised to conform with the results of the refinement session, it is presented again to the project team. When validating the SD, the participants carefully examine the initial SD with the goal of refining it to be as accurate as possible. At this second session the emphasis is on validation of the system representation. *Validation* means a consensus has been reached by the project teams that the SD is complete and accurate.

The resulting model decomposition becomes a framework for developing the models. It becomes the basis for further analysis. The system complexity can be assessed by examining the framework. Once validated, the dimensions, quantity, and capacity of the system can be gauged from the completed model. The system scope is measured according to the number of processes supported by the

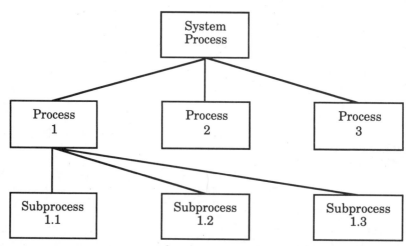

Figure 8.8 The top three levels of a generic model view decomposition hierarchy.

Level 1	Level 2	Level 3
Pay and personnel	Employment	Recruitment
		Selection
	Personnel administration	Employee relations
		Employee compensation changes
		Salary planning
		Classification and pay
		Job evaluation
		Benefits administration
		Health insurance plans
		Flexible spending accounts
		Group life insurance
		Retirement plans
	Payroll	Payroll administration
		Payroll processing
		Payroll interfaces
	Development	N/A
	Training administration	Career planning and skills inventory
		Work group activities
	Health and safety	Accidents and workers compensation
		Health and safety programs

Figure 8.9   A three-level decomposition of the model views from the governmental pay and personnel scenario.

system. These can be determined by the levels of decomposition and the number of views created to support the bottom level of the hierarchy. Examples from two of the scenarios are illustrated in Figs. 8.9 and 8.10, showing examples of a relatively simple and a relatively complex SD. Space considerations forced the second figure into a two column layout. This SD from the health care scenario is also incomplete, illustrating 54 out of a total 72 views. The validated SD is used to define and illustrate the total number of essential business functions supported by the system. For the health care scenario the business functions include: patient administration, patient appointments and scheduling, nursing, laboratory, pharmacy, radiology. The SD serves as an organizing framework as the system components views are separated. The data contained in the SD is used to size the system, scope the project, and define candidate logical data model views. The SD is a relatively inexpensive yet useful data asset to produce. It is important to track and store this type of information, making it available to appropriate subsequent activities especially material evaluations and other project feasibility analysis.

Health care system

1	Patient administration		
1.1	Registration	6	Radiology
1.2	Admission	6.1	Scheduling
1.3	Disposition	6.2	Exam processing
1.4	Transfer	6.3	Exam reporting
1.5	Medical record	6.4	Special interest and teaching
1.6	Administration		
1.7	Patient billing	6.5	Radiology workload reporting
1.8	Patient affairs		
1.9	Patient management		
		7	Clinical dietetics
2	Patient appointments and scheduling	7.1	Establish parameters
		7.2	Receive diet orders
2.1	Create or maintain schedules	8	Order entry and results
2.2	Appoint patients	8.1	Reporting
2.3	Record patient encounter	8.2	Enter and maintain orders
2.4	Identify patient		
2.5	Identify health care provider	8.3	Obtain results
		8.4	Review patient information
3	Nursing	8.5	Clinical desktop
3.1	Patient care		
3.2	Unit management	9	System management
		9.1	Logon and security management
4	Laboratory		
4.1	Results reporting	9.2	Archive run Management
4.2	Specimen processing		
4.3	Result entry processing	9.3	Communication software
4.4	Laboratory management	9.4	Management
4.5	Workload support	9.5	Site management
5	Pharmacy	10	Facility quality assurance
5.1	Unit dose dispensing	10.1	Provider credentialing
5.2	Controlled Drug Inventory	10.2	Monitor and evaluation
5.3	Outpatient		

Figure 8.10 A relatively complex model view decomposition hierarchy of a health care management system from Chap. 1, scenario #2.

A preliminary inventory and assessment of the condition of system evidence

Where in between the two extremes does this system lie? Are the system changes completely undocumented? Or has the organization been able to apply the resources required to keep the documentation synchronized with the system changes? The second system survey output is an assessment of the availability, accessibility, and condition of the system evidence. This output is usually developed as a by-product of the SD development. The assessment is best accomplished by examining the documentation first hand, performing a series of comparisons with the existing system to verify correctness, and following the change history with the documentation changes to get a feel for the system volatility.

This task is a good place to practice some sensitivity because it involves, in part, assessing and reporting on the state of the system documentation. System documentation usefulness assessments have sometimes been uncomfortable to systems management who might wish for the resources required to keep their system documentation up-to-date. Concentrate on the facts without judging. Future enthusiastic participation of systems management on the project team is likely to be a key determinant of project success.

Assessment of key specialist participation levels

The third goal of the system survey is to, as much as possible, verify the anticipated participation level of the key specialists. The importance of obtaining executive sponsorship becomes evident when requesting significant amounts of key specialist time. The process of holding the two model refinement-validation sessions will provide evidence as to any possible discrepancies between proposed and actual availability. Strong attendance and participation at the sessions are more likely indicators of future project success.

Key specialists have been quickly educated to perform some data engineering functions (i.e., entering project information directly into the project data bank). This form of support can be used to leverage the project team efforts. It represents an opportunity to save considerable project time and presents a nice opportunity to perform some technology transfer as the key specialists discover how much easier it is to maintain CASE-based system documentation.

The net effect of automation on the project

A consulting organization I know tells customers that reverse engineering will cost them *about one dollar for each line of code.* I always wanted to introduce them to the folks I know who program in MUMPS (Massachusetts General Hospital Utility Multi-Programming System), a programming language whose programmers take pride in their ability to write entire programs as single lines of program code. This consulting organization was charging to run code through a DRE tool designed to programmatically extract certain types of information. For certain projects this application of automation will provide rapid access to the required information. If the environment is somewhat standardized (COBOL), there is more likelihood of automated products supporting the analysis. There are fewer automated tools supporting MUMPS and other less popular system environments. For other DRE projects, this type of analysis will be infeasible or not useful. Thus automation has the potential to hurt as well as help in DRE projects. Similar to available key specialist participation levels, automation should also positively affect DRE project estimates. The goal is to determine the potential technological leverage in light of likely project goals.

The *automation impact* can be defined as the degree to which automated support affects the productivity of either the model validation-refinement sessions or the effectiveness of the model development activities. However, since automation can have a positive effect only on those occasions where project benefits outweigh project costs, it is more useful to speak in terms of a net automation impact. *Net automation impact* is the amount remaining after the costs of automation are subtracted from the benefits.

Automation characteristic	Example
Weeks of project-specific analytic tool learning curve	Having to learn a different CASE tool because original system models were developed using something other than the current tool
Weeks of project-specific CASE or reverse engineering tool development	Deciding that it will be effective to develop a tool specific to a project (e.g., to read and/or analyze nonstandard data structures)
Programming language effect on productivity	Systems were developed using obscure programming language or otherwise experiencing a nonavailability of language expertise benefit from increased participation from programming-language specialists
Platform or operating system effect on productivity	Projects where systems were developed in obscure platform or operating system environments experience similar relationships between participation and productivity
Data management system effect on productivity	Projects where systems were developed using popular data management systems can require less expertise than situation where nonstandard data management systems were employed

Figure 8.11 Automation characteristic components.

Component/ subcomponent	Description	Range
Evidence/ Categorize specific pieces of evidence as existent or nonexistent	These relate to the volume of evidence requiring analysis—typically includes such items as pages of code, file-based data items, reports, screens, fields, data structures, schemas, business rules.	The detailed examination of the physical evidence required to produce a validated SD also provides enough knowledge of the evidence to assess its impact on the project.
Evidence/ Categorize specific pieces of evidence as in documentation in synchronization with the system state or documentation	Existence of evidence is good news to the data engineers. Evidence that is synchronized with the current system state is better.	System documentation is ■ In synch with the current state of the system ■ Not in synch with the system state.
Amount of evidence (relates to system complexity)/ These variables describe the scope of the system	Does the system produce paychecks from a transaction type input or does the program handle all of the accounting functions related to the production of payroll, IRS reporting.	N/A
Confounding factors/ Language	COBOL is easier; MUMPS is more difficult	N/A
Confounding factors/ Data handling system	VSAM, DB/2 easy; Samuel not so easy·	≥ 1 indicates this increases the overall resources required to do the project.
Beneficial impacts/ Adequate participation by key specialists	Adequate participation by key specialists can be the project specific variable with the biggest single impact—having all of the above can be useless without this.	Availability and coverage are the two dimensions.
Automation	Amount of automated assistance available, both from the host environment and from any CASE or other reverse engineering tools employed.	Should reduce the overall project dimensions through automation of key analysis aspects.

Figure 8.12 Project characteristic components.

	Typically available statistic	Desired statistic
Files	■ Number of files ■ Number of data items for each file	Number of hours required to analyze files
Reports	■ Number of reports ■ Number of data items on each report	Number of hours required to analyze reports
Screens	■ Number of screens ■ Number of fields on each screen	Number of hours required to analyze screens
Data structures	■ Number of data structures ■ Number of data items on each data structure	Number of hours required to analyze data structures
Business rules	Organizational procedures manuals	Number of hours required to analyze business rules
System documentation	Number of pages of documentation	Number of hours required to analyze system documentation
Code	Number of pages of code	Number of hours required to analyze code
Total	Total number of data items	Number of hours required to analyze all data items
Overall	Effective data item analysis rate per hour	How long it will take to complete the project

Figure 8.13   Desirable physical evidence statistics.

Working in an unfamiliar operating system environment can adversely affect the productivity. So can working on an antiquated CASE tool or manually. Specific components of the automation characteristic are presented in Fig. 8.11. (The last three items can be offset by the participation of a corresponding key specialist in the programming language, platform, and data management areas.) Figure 8.12 shows information that should be included in the PSS decomposed into components.

Base line - relative condition and amount of evidence

Analysis of the relative condition and amount of evidence consists of inventorying the number of system data items. Figure 8.13 shows some of the possible forms of the physical evidence. It also presents the typically available statistics and the desired project planning information. For example, when assessing the task of analyzing the code, the typically available statistic is the number of pages of system documentation. The more desirable information for this metric is the number of hours required to analyze code. But over a series of projects organization will develop algorithms and expertise to make these and other metrics more useful. The data that results from this action is one or more evidence categories with some measure(s) of the condition and amount. The data can also evidence synchronization and evidence existence measures.

System programming language as a confounding factor

If the DRE project characteristics require an analysis of the source code, the specific programming language requiring analysis can adversely impact the project. A language factor can be assigned according to the class of programming language (see Fig. 8.14). Again, the more popular the programming language, the more automated tools supporting DRE are available. Negative impacts associated with programming languages can stem from the difficulties acquiring the key specialist participation for less popular system or operating environments. The degree of platform-specific support for the DRE project can also confound the analysis. Throwing an MVS operating system specialist at a Unix workstation can be confronting, to say the least. Working with an unfamiliar operating system environment can adversely affect productivity.

Language category	Example
Structured high-order language	COBOL
Unstructured high-order language	FORTRAN
Commercial off-the-shelf assembly language	Burroughs Assembly
Unstructured commercial language	MUMPS
Commercially unsupported language	GWAR

Figure 8.14   Categories of system languages.

Data handling system as a confounding factor

A data handling system factor can be assigned according to the category of data handling system. Similar to the programming language classification, the more obscure, obsolete, or otherwise nonstandard the data handling system, the more difficult it can be to access information (see Fig. 8.15).

Data handling system category	Example
Relational DBMS	DB2
Hierarchical DBMS	IMS
Network	IDMS
Cots file management system	VSAM
Non-commercially supported file management system	NIH

Figure 8.15   Categories of data handling systems.

Impacts due to key specialist participation

Participation requirements for each of the following categories must be defined and the participation of individuals possessing the required knowledge secured:

- Effect on productivity due to database expert participation.

- Effect on productivity due to functional participation.

- Effect on productivity due to application program expert participation.

- Net effect on productivity due to domain expert participation.

The outputs of the PSS—the project estimate data—should include the following:

- Project goals

- Personnel commitment

- Return on investment

- CASE tool requirements

This data is accumulated and provided for analysis during project planning activities to determine feasibility and project schedules. In addition, a master list of questions, issues, assumptions, and so on, should be established at this point and maintained throughout the project to ensure that all considerations are addressed and all issues or conflicts are documented and eventually resolved.

Project Planning - Framework Activity 6

I found the following two statements on the Internet one day:

1. Carelessly planned projects take three times longer to complete than expected.

2. Carefully planned projects take four times longer to complete than expected, mostly because the planners expect their planning to reduce the time it takes.

Aside from the writer's obvious cynicism, the statements still acknowledge the importance of formal project planning, regardless of the project context. Two measures are appropriate for measuring DRE projects:

■ Number of weeks of project team effort

■ Number of project team members and participation requirements

The system decomposition and key experts are queried to determine the total number of core business functions supported by the system. These are evaluated for overall complexity and are then combined with a functional analysis rate per hour. The result is an estimate of the number of weeks required to accomplish business function decomposition.

The system survey provides a baseline estimate of the number of total data items to be analyzed in order to be produce the desired project outputs. If the system survey provided indications that the target system maintained information about 200 entities, and if your previous DRE experience indicated the project teams could define 30 entities during a standard week-long modeling cycle, then the total estimated schedule would be a total of seven modeling cycles or around 28 weeks of total project time. The selection of targets and time frame for measurement will be specific to each organization.

Project specific reverse engineering objectives can be developed for the proposed project. Specific project objectives will determine the desired nature of the reverse engineering project team identifying candidate administrative, technical, and management team members for specific reverse engineering projects. Using information gained from the preliminary system survey, a finalized project scope will be developed such as

This data reverse engineering project will produce validated logical data models of the data assets contained in the subsystems A, D, and E of the system—the data models will be used in the forward engineering parts of the system.

The project team needs to standardize on and understand a DRE project methodology, develop a concept of operations, and adopt operational conventions and protocols. In addition, the team may need to acquire the hardware and software required to support the project. Access to additional infrastructure support items such as intelligent copy support should also be secured at this point. (I know of instances where this activity has taken many more months than it should have.) Outputs from this activity include operationally validated DRE procedures, means of assimilating the tool and model usage data, and an operational concept of operations.

Project planning involves reevaluating initial project assumptions with the PSS data. Again, key specialist and decision maker involvement is required. First they need to be updated on the relative value of the project on the basis of information from the PSS and cost-benefit analysis. In addition, they must be given the chance to reevaluate the anticipated resource commitment. Management and key specialists alike will feel better about their respective participation if they understand the nature of the commitment during the planning stages.

Since DRE projects are information-intensive, it is a good idea to establish preliminary coordination rules and conventions up front. The project team is interested in spending as little time as possible writing reports and briefings. There are many ways of accomplishing this reporting. A technique I have used in the past has been to have the first portion of any modeling cycle devoted to briefly recapping the project goals, assessing progress toward the goals, and outlining the specific goals of this modeling cycle. Interested management should attend these sessions regularly to track project progress. Regardless of the specific details, the project team and respective management must come to agreement as to the specifics of reporting with the goals of minimizing its impact on the project.

Productivity measurement

A quick word about productivity measurement. The last thing in the world I would suggest is development of quotas with regard to productivity variables and additional reporting mechanisms. Data engineers must collect and report their own data via standard work breakdown structure reporting codes and other existing time management and reporting vehicles. (Throw a redundant data collection device at these individuals, and it will definitely get thrown back!) Collect the evidence at postproject review sessions (framework activity 13) by counting the number of model components created and dividing by the hours allocated for analysis. Over time these numbers can be used as accurate predictors.

Management perception

The costs to properly reverse engineer systems and the value of the reverse engineering products are consistently underestimated by management. A common misperception is that we just "run the code through a CASE tool and the tool will produce new systems." It has been challenging to convince management that reverse engineering is a broader and more complex task than just "restructuring the code."

Price, quality, and speed considerations

My friend Michael Adams prints the back of his business cards with the following three words:

Price   **Quality**   **Speed**

When asked, he tells clients to choose two of the three. You can have a great price and quality at the expense of speed. If you desire greater speed, you must reduce your price or quality expectations. If you desire greater quality, you must trade some price and/or speed.

DRE projects are subject to these same tradeoffs. The important thing to keep in mind about DRE projects is that they have this incremental nature about them. Figure 8.16 shows how price, speed, and quality tradeoffs involve stepped functions. For example, since DRE projects are performed by project teams, the addition of a second project team will require at least the cost of the project in savings due in increased project throughput. It costs one specific amount to produce unvalidated models and another to produce validated models. Spending an amount sufficient to fund one-half of the amount required for asset validation will not produce a half-validated asset. It produces unvalidated models, so save the money.

The primary cost for DRE projects turns out to be time. DRE project costs are composed largely of the cost of the project teams plus a few one-time costs. One-time costs can include items such as CASE tool support and workstation purchases. Finally, project overhead costs may need to reflect any associated travel, lodging, clerical support, copying, cataloging, etc. Of course, the key is to remember that these projects are performed by teams and that any one team member's nonparticipation can reduce the overall effectiveness of the proj-

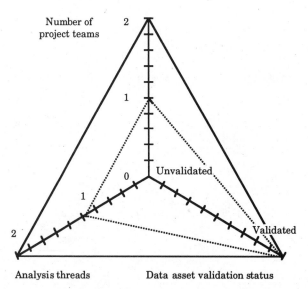

Figure 8.16 DRE price, speed, quality tradeoffs—this project is characterized by a single analysis thread and performance team with validated data assets being the desired result.

ect team. The stability of the project team provides management a solid basis for planing project expenses. Consider the hypothetical example in Fig. 8.17 illustrating the cost of a medium-sized project team. The personnel resource cost is $3500 per week; multiplying the $3500 total times 14 four-week-long modeling cycles provides a project team expense of at least $49,000.

The technical quality of the models produced by DRE is relatively easy to sense but perhaps a bit more difficult for an outsider to judge. There are two aspects of DRE project technical quality:

■ Project team ownership

■ The correctness and completeness of the models produced

At a point about a quarter to a third of the way through the project, a key specialist jumps up during a modeling cycle to grab the pointer or chalk or some other symbolic element of control and begins to make corrections to the model being refined or validated. Watch for it. This is the point at which this key specialist demonstrates ownership of the project outputs by making changes to them using the modeling technology itself. If this activity hasn't happened by the halfway point in the project schedule, this might be a good time to reassess the process to see if the desired results are being produced. If the key specialists have demonstrated ownership during the modeling cycles, there is an increased likelihood that the project outputs will be of usable technical quality. Consider the symbiotic nature of the project team partnership. The data engineers facilitate the development of the requisite models, but the model content is controlled largely by the key specialists. If they are confused as to their role or are unable or unwilling to participate, it is unlikely that they will be able to adequately support the project team activities.

Cost factor	Quantity	Hourly cost, $	Hours per week	Total $
Key functional specialist	2	30.00	20	600.00
Key technical specialist	1	30.00	20	600.00
Data engineer	1	30.00	40	1,200.00
Scribe	1	10.00	20	200.00
Facilitator	1	15.00	20	300.00
Clerical	1	15.00	40	600.00
Total	6		200	3,500.00

Figure 8.17 Model refinement-validation session cost factors.

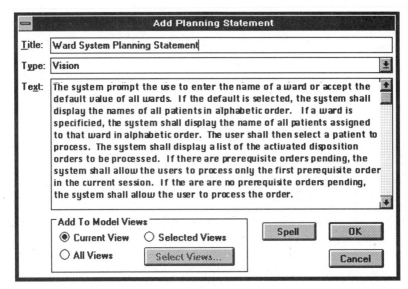

Figure 8.18 Good-quality purpose statements indicate good data asset quality. (Source: Dialog box from IE: Advantage Universal CASE tool © 1991-95 Information Engineering Systems Coporation, Alexandria: VA.)

Beyond judging the quality of the interaction and productivity of the modeling cycle, the soundness of the models produced can be assessed reasonably rapidly. Simple checks such as the completeness of the associated purpose statements, the degree of data analysis (or attempted data analysis) performed, and the visual appearance of the graphical models can flag a poor quality data asset. Figure 8.18 shows a good quality purpose statement displayed by the project data bank from the health care facility consolidation (Chap. 2, scenario 2). Note how the planning statement also embodies a business rule directing the sequence in which the orders are processed. Each modeling technique used during the modeling cycle has associated quality and completeness factors that can be used to assess model technical quality.

The next planning step is to develop a task completion schedule indicating task details, completion dates, and descriptions of the required activities. The DRE project planning outputs include a task schedule, organizational resource commitments, a project-specific DRE framework, and DRE procedure.

■ *Project activity schedule.* The project activity schedule specifies project activities, completion dates, and descriptions of the required outputs.

■ *Organizational resource commitments.* These specify identified organizational resource commitments, ensuring that the project has viability and proper organizational resource management endorsement. Resources include both personnel and other organizational investments such as CASE technology.

■ *Project specific DRE framework.* When planning a DRE project, it is useful to examine the proposal in the broader contexts of enterprise integration and data architecture development. The key to effective use of DRE projects is to obtain as much leverage as possible with them by providing data assets simultaneously useful to both data architecture development and enterprise integration processes. This means making certain that project outputs are delivered in time to be useful to other enterprise integration process requirements as well as available to assist data architecture development processes. The framework provides a means of developing project plans for the project specified in terms of variations from the framework. The project framework defines what specific needs a particular DRE project will address, particularly in light of the data administration and enterprise integration efforts.

■ *Project specific DRE procedure.* The procedures used in past projects have been analyzed for effectiveness and efficiency. Changes to any communication protocols, reporting and operating procedures, project methods, and conventions are incorporated in light of the project framework so that the individual project can be as productive as possible.

Developing data reverse engineering project objectives

Three different types of destinations for the data assets developed from data reverse engineering projects include those shown in Fig. 8.19.

Project Kickoff - Framework Activity 7

Planning, coordinating, and executing the project kickoff meeting is an important phase for any reverse engineering project. The project kickoff meeting marks the transition from project initiation to project implementation and the start of target system analysis. Project kickoff provides a good opportunity to demonstrate organizational resource management's understanding and commitment to the project. The checklist below contains four items to be addressed prior to the kickoff meeting. Each item can be used to define a project kickoff critical success factor.

1. Have I identified and conferred with authorized representatives of the key specialists and of organization resource management?

2. Do I have confidence that the representatives understand and are, in turn, able to articulate project objectives in the context of enterprise integration goals?

Destination	Scope	Example
Project related objectives	These deliverables are used immediately by subsequent project phases.	Better information about the target system resulting in more useful project estimates.
System performance related objectives	The destination of this class of outputs is restricted to the target system.	Improved system documentation.
Data architecture related objectives	Scope of use is confined to the data administration function and affiliated database operations.	Consider a project enhancing the enterprise model to permit real-time evaluation and response to competitor pricing structures. The marketing department may be attempting to expand the customer base making use of improved data on customer trends.
Enterprise integration related objectives	The most effective use of project outputs is in other enterprise integration projects.	Entries describing the entities to be used to develop an information system designed to give the organization a competitive edge in its strategic environment.

Figure 8.19 Classifications of DRE project deliverables.

3. Do the members of the project team understand project context commitment (in terms of participation time)?

4. Does organizational resource management understand the nature of the investment they are making in this enterprise integration activity?

The output from the project kickoff activity is the project charter. This is typically formal authorization from management charging the project team with performing the DRE project and indicating a willingness to fund the project at sufficient levels to ensure its success. Typically included are the outputs produced by the project initiation phase as well as the project goals and anticipated return on investment.

9

Target System Analysis (Framework Activity 8)

"A journey of a thousand miles must begin with a single step."
— CHINESE PROVERB

This chapter describes target system analysis—DRE framework activity 8. Target system analysis is cyclical in nature; modeling cycles are repeated until the project has achieved the desired results or the project has become infeasible. Modeling cycles are used to derive the models from the evidence analyzed. This is the activity most people associate with DRE projects. Modeling cycles can occur in various formats involving contemplative solitude, to phone consultation, to structured interviews, to formal model validation-refinement (MR/V) sessions. Figure 9.1 details the modeling cycle in the context of the DRE framework.

Modeling Cycles

The process of analyzing the target system begins before the PSS is initiated. The PSS information is used to develop a project estimate indicating in part the number of modeling cycles required to produce validated models. "Getting to know more about the people, situations, and clarifying all that you already know about it" [Koberg and Bagnall 1972, p. 32] are the two basic themes for each modeling cycle. Key is to determine what model component will reduce uncertainty by the greatest amount and make it the focus of the next modeling cycle.

Once the PSS is completed, project approval is gained, and the project kickoff has occurred, it is time to get down to the business of data reverse engineering the target system. Figure 9.2 indicates the activities and participants during modeling cycles. With a few exceptions, management's role is confined to cycle planning activities. Key specialist participation is required during cycle planning, evidence analysis, and MR/V activities. Data engineers largely take the lead, planning modeling cycles, and guiding and facilitating the project. Experienced modelers and data engineers will prove their value as team members as they facilitate the application of DRE technologies.

Initiation Phase (detail omitted)			
Implementation phase			
#	Name	Process	Output
8	Target system analysis (repeated until completed)		
8.1	Cycle planning	■ Evaluating and incorporating previous cycle results ■ Identifying area of highest risk of lack of knowledge ■ Specifying analysis targets and a plan for the current modeling cycle	Focused plan for obtaining desired results from the next cycle
8.2	Evidence acquisition	■ Collecting evidence ■ Cataloging evidence ■ Structuring evidence ■ Looking for missing evidence	Organized evidence
8.3	Evidence analysis	Analyzing the evidence for appropriateness and model development potential	Candidate data items
8.4	Straw model development	Creating candidate models	Data items organized into models
8.5	Model refinement/ validation	■ Identifying changes in the model as a result of errors, new knowledge, and normalization ■ Documenting changes and further refining models ■ Validating models using appropriate techniques	Clearer, more comprehensive, more accurate, validated models
8.6	Model storage and organization	Collecting, cataloging, and structuring models for archival and configuration management purposes	Accessible models
Wrapup phase (detail omitted)			

Figure 9.1 The modeling cycle.

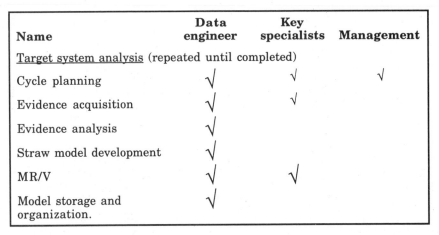

Name	Data engineer	Key specialists	Management
Target system analysis (repeated until completed)			
Cycle planning	√	√	√
Evidence acquisition	√	√	
Evidence analysis	√		
Straw model development	√		
MR/V	√	√	
Model storage and organization.	√		

Figure 9.2 Modeling cycle roles–activities matrix.

Figure 9.3 shows a modeling cycle format. From a project team perspective, there are two key activities associated with DRE projects: extracting information and organizing and structuring the information into models. Extraction and structuring are performed in a sequential, iterative manner, with successive phases influenced by the results of previous phases. During each modeling cycle:

■ A specific subset of evidence to be obtained is identified.

■ One or more techniques are used to obtain the requisite information.

■ The information is then structured into a format designed to achieve the goals of the specific reverse engineering project.

■ These results are evaluated and the next iteration is planned based on the results of the previous iteration(s).

This sequence of obtaining and structuring the reverse engineered information is repeated, with successive iterations influenced largely by the results from previous iterations, until the reverse engineering project goals are met.

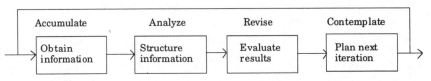

Figure 9.3 Conceptual modeling cycle overview.

#	Name	Output
Initiation phase (detail omitted)		
Implementation phase		
8	Target system analysis (repeated until completed)	
8.1	Cycle planning	MR/V cycle plan
8.2	Evidence acquisition	Structured evidence
8.3	Evidence analysis	Candidate data items
8.4 8.5 8.6	Straw model development Model refinement-validation Model storage and organization	Models and associated information
Wrapup phase (detail omitted)		

Figure 9.4   Target system analysis outputs.

Data reverse engineering analysis is a structured technique, performed using a systematic approach and to some degree supported by automation. For each cycle, specific information is obtained using one or more reverse engineering analysis techniques. Information is then structured into a format developed to meet the goals of the modeling cycle. Planning for the next phase is based on the results and level of effort required to obtain models from the previous phase(s). This sequence of obtaining and structuring the reverse engineered information is repeated until project goals are met.

These activities transform information into models. A class of automated tools is associated with each type of activity; extraction tools can be used to obtain information from existing systems, and information structuring tools typically are data banks falling into the dictionary-encyclopedia-repository class of CASE tools and are used to maintain and facilitate access to enterprise integration information. Extraction and data bank tools are described in Chap. 11. Figure 9.4 summarizes the target system analysis outputs by activity. Each specific output is described in Part 3 (Chaps. 12 to 15).

Cycle planning - activity 8.1

The modeling cycle begins by planning for the upcoming analysis activity. Most find it convenient to use week-long modeling cycles. The previous cycle's results, lessons learned, new information sources, and new data are evaluated. The results to date are compared to the results desired by the project plan. Normally the focus of the next modeling cycle addresses the area of greatest risk and/or uncertainty, identifying and understanding the information that has the potential to most influence the remaining analysis. The focus of the modeling cycle is usually expressed in terms of target system model components defined during the PSS. The project team selects some subset of the evidence as the focus of an upcoming modeling cycle. A subset is required because, like building construction, it is more practical to attempt to develop models by assembling data items into models and then combining the model into an architecture than it is to attempt to put all of the pieces together simultaneously. The project team develops a plan to model this subset during the next cycle. The cycle plan can also be influenced by key specialist availability or other considerations.

Naturally, the first question is where to begin. Use the SD to define a good starting place. Selecting a SD component that is relatively self contained can keep the initial analysis relatively uncomplicated. This permits the project team to achieve a rapid success in the same manner that assembling the edges of a puzzle makes it easier to complete the remainder. Another consideration in selecting a starting place is the quality of the documentation. For example, if the documentation for the system component "Personnel Administration" from the governmental pay and personnel scenario (Chap. 1) was superior to other parts of the system—it makes sense to begin the analysis by examining the best information sources. The special case of interface analysis offers additional information opportunities discussed in Chap. 13 in Part 3.

Figure 9.5 illustrates the application of this process. The SD for a portion of the Patient Administration system (first shown as Fig. 8.10) has been used to plan the project modeling cycles. Please note that it isn't likely to take a week to complete each component. Instead, previous experience indicates these modeling components can be developed at a rate of one per week on average. Actual results, while varying, averaged out to the number of cycles used on the original estimate as shown in Fig. 9.6.

System	Model component	Modeling cycle
Personnel	Employee relations	Week 11
administration	Employee compensation	Week 12
	Salary planning	Week 13
	Classification and pay	Week 14
	Job evaluation	Week 15
	Benefits administration	Week 16
	Health insurance plans	Week 17
	Flexible spending accounts	Week 18
	Group life insurance	Week 19
	Retirement plans	Week 20

Figure 9.5 Schedule showing the modeling cycle for which each model view is scheduled.

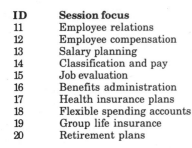

ID	Session focus
11	Employee relations
12	Employee compensation
13	Salary planning
14	Classification and pay
15	Job evaluation
16	Benefits administration
17	Health insurance plans
18	Flexible spending accounts
19	Group life insurance
20	Retirement plans

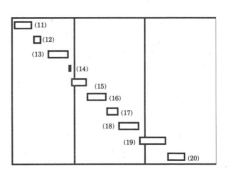

Figure 9.6 Actual progress reported for the same project, although varying considerably from the original plan, averages out to the project estimate.

Since project costs are composed largely of project team costs, monitoring for project schedule largely also accomplishes monitoring for cost. The PSS provides a base for estimating the resources required to obtain the desired project output(s). Project management has a relatively simple task to consider when monitoring for cost.

■ First, was the amount budgeted for the one time costs sufficient? By the time the modeling cycles had begun, the startup costs should have been spent and the products acquired. This can be determined by assessing the productivity of the modeling cycles. If the one time cost items have been acquired and are in use and the project team is, for example, demanding more access to the CASE technology, corrective action is called for.

■ Assuming the startup costs were sufficient, the other type of cost monitoring involves comparing the planned against the actual progress. If the project has completed the 7th of 14 one-week modeling cycles and the project team has modeled more than the planned number of data items, the project would seem to be ahead of schedule. On the other hand, if the project team has discovered numerous data items that must be developed in addition to the planned work load, it is unlikely that the project could be considered ahead of schedule or under budget.

Finally, it is important to define some tangible interim deliverables that can be shown to management throughout the project so that they can be convinced you're getting somewhere. Interim deliverables are essential to keeping management convinced and interested in sponsoring the projects. These interim deliverables need to be included on the initial milestone charts.

Evidence acquisition - activity 8.2

The next activity is to collect and analyze the evidence relevant to the focus of the upcoming modeling cycle. After all, you don't want to study irrelevant documentation. The goal of evidence acquisition is to obtain information about the target system. The evidence can occur in many forms, including business rules, domain information, system specifications, and data structures, as well as other forms of systems specifications. Evidence can also come in the form of technical as well as functional specialist participation, paper-based and electronic versions of system documentation, and any other sources capable of providing the required information. Included in this information to be analyzed could be such items as existing system documentation, database schemas, and notes from interviews with key specialists.

The existing evidence is surveyed for applicability. Anything possibly containing information required for the upcoming modeling cycle is surveyed for appropriateness. The portion of the evidence corresponding to the target component must be separated from everything else. This subset is then "marked" for analysis and acquired if it hasn't been so already. Digital evidence is stored in the project data bank. All other evidence is stored in the project library.

Evidence analysis and straw model development - activities 8.3 and 8.4

Evidence analysis and straw model development are difficult to separate in practice. Although they are two distinct activities, most analysts switch back and forth between them in a seamless, integrated fashion.

The data engineering policy of introducing as little disruption as possible into the daily activities of the key specialist community and system management indicates that it is beneficial to create the models prior to meeting with users. Model preparation is done in advance to leverage the use of the key specialist participation on the project. This is in keeping with the concept of a data engineer's symbiotic relationship with the key specialists as shown in Figure 9.7.

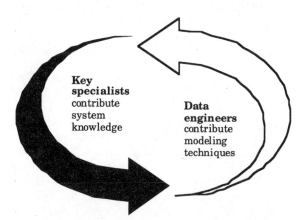

Figure 9.7   Symbiotic relationship between data engineers and key specialists.

Initial preparation of the models consumes more time than does the validation process. By having the data engineers prepare the models ahead of time, key specialists do not have to sit through the model creation process. Instead, the key specialists review the candidate models, consider the appropriateness of the representation on the basis of their own understanding of the target system, and make suggestions for improving the model quality and/or accuracy.

When analyzing evidence data engineers often have two choices:

■ *Examining it on the spot.* The data engineer can examine the evidence where it is normally kept, such as visiting a well maintained system library and easily accessing the required piece of documentation. In cases where standards don't exist, the engineer can bring a CASE tool to other locations and create system model components on the spot. This process could involve entering or copying certain information into the CASE tool. Each piece of evidence is linked to internal model components to ensure traceability.

■ *Making a copy.* In some situations it is best to copy the documentation and bring it to a project library for subsequent analysis. If the documentation is poor, it may make more sense to copy and perhaps enhance the quality of the existing evidence. One example of quality enhancement is to create an index for a stack of diagrams that were copied and returned to the users with the new index integrated into the documentation.

Evidence analysis can occur synchronously or asynchronously and face-to-face or via telecommunication utilizing technologies such as videoconferencing, and electronic mail (e-mail). Selection of a specific technology is up to the project team, who will also keep track of the technique's effectiveness as part of the project records. An interesting example was a situation where the key specialists had to leave a planned interview to respond to an urgent call; instead of walking through each model component, under these circumstances the individuals briefly discussed the changes, and the discussion was tape-recorded and entered into the project laboratory for subsequent analysis. The technique's success initiated use of taping for portions of the remainder of the projects.

Candidate versions of the models are developed as a result of extensive study of relevant documentation. Today's CASE technology enables data engineers to create and modify the various models in real time. The addition of notebook computing technology permits data engineers to bring the models with them as they visit the key specialists. As much as possible, the project CASE tool-based data bank should be updated in real time during those activities. Updating the model information in real time offers close feedback benefits similar to those offered using rapid storyboarding technology for systems development activities [Andriole 1989, Madsen and Aiken 1993].

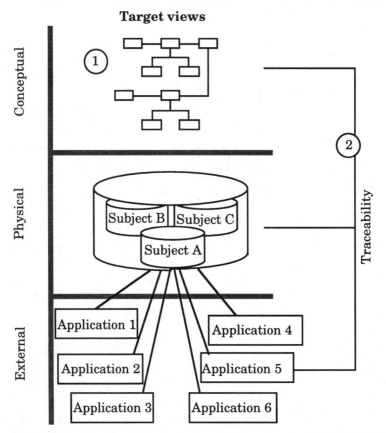

Figure 9.8 Linked (or related) three-schema views based on the ANSI/X3/SPARC three-schema architecture.

Analysis of evidence permits the data engineers to develop straw or proposed or candidate versions of modeling cycle target system components. Figure 9.8 illustrates the results of evidence analysis and model development activities.

1. The model of the system or systems components are derived using a combination of evidence describing the system data as it is stored on disk and utilized by application programs.

2. The links are developed, associating model components with application programs and with use of the physical data stored on the disk.

Data reverse engineering project goals motivate the development of models of specific data. These data assets most often take the form of logical data models but can also include the previously mentioned system decompositions and other model types.

#	Name	Model status
Initiation phase (detail omitted)		
Implementation phase		
8	Target system analysis (repeated until completed)	
8.1	Cycle planning	Assessed
8.2	Evidence acquisition	Created
8.3	Evidence analysis	Analyzed
8.4	Straw model development	Modeled
8.5	Model refinement/ validation	Refined
8.6	Model storage and organization	Accessible
Wrapup phase (detail omitted)		

Figure 9.9 It takes a data asset at least two modeling cycles to be validated.

Data models indicate the interrelationship between data items. Data modeling and associated traceability formats are covered in Chap. 12. Data modeling is a subject covered in depth by a number of other authors. For information on the specifics of data modeling, see Finkelstein [1993], Martin [1989], or Ross [1987].

The output of these combined activities is a candidate set of models and associated components describing a modeling cycle target system component. It contains draft information that data engineers have modeled and want key specialist support for in refinement and validation activities.

Model refinement and validation - activities 8.5 and 8.6

MR/V activities use constructive criticism to improve data item and model content and accuracy. The goal of model refinement is to transform candidate models proposed by the data engineers into more comprehensive and accurate models. MR/V activities occur with a different format. During model validation, the focus is on validating the accuracy of the model component; during validation, the models are again presented to the requisite key specialists in the appropriate format. This time the purpose is to validate the model's accuracy. Validation is a statement by the project team that the models produced accurately depict the current state of the system. Figure 9.9 shows how data items require at least two cycles to be validated. The first cycle refines, while the second validates the components.

Model refinement and validation sessions can be accomplished using a variety of formats:

- *Question / answer sessions.* Typically these occur as data engineers encounter issues requiring clarification or other analysis problems. They are scheduled with the key specialists, and, if possible, the questions are provided in advance. They typically last just a few minutes either face to face or via e-mail or phone conversation.

■ *Structured interviews.* Similarly scheduled ahead of time with the topics provided to the interviewees in advance, these are more prolonged versions of question/answer sessions aimed at focused, efficient information transfer. Interviewing and other brief forms of focused interaction are especially useful formats for model refinement sessions as key specialists clarify specific points not completely understood by the data engineers. One example I observed had to do with the data item "length of service." Different divisions of the organization defined this data item in different ways. The difference turned out to be an important issue when considering issues such as retirement.

■ *Model refinement and validation sessions.* Modeling sessions are variations of joint-application development efforts with key specialists developing the models in conjunction with experienced data engineers [Carmel et al. 1993]. The candidate models are presented to the project team in a formal modeling session. The session is designed specifically to get the right people together to consider the accuracy and completeness of the candidate models. Users are then asked to attempt to make the documentation wrong. (Once they understand that this shortens the overall process, they readily adapt to this alternative perspective.) The models are refined based on information from the interaction of data engineers and key specialists during the modeling cycle.

Data engineers consider the various improvements suggested during the cycle, incorporating changes, refinements, and new information into models. Particular attention is paid to structural changes of models indicating fundamental types of knowledge have been captured and were missing from previous cycles. Each is carefully documented. The overall considerations and implication of the changes are considered for accurately and completeness. The models are modified and prepared for the next cycle.

Data model normalization should be a part of the model refinement-validation process. Normalization is the process of taking validated user-data engineered models and creating a representation in the most flexible possible design. The goal of normalization is to represent the logical data in the most flexible state and reduce the possibility of modification anomalies. The normalization procedure can be used to develop additional information (such as system requirements and business rules) from the evidence.

The goal of both the constructive criticism and the normalization related model improvement are to develop models accurately representing the system. These are validated models—*validating* implying a confirmation that the models are accurate and complete. The outputs of the two activities are refined and validated models of the target system.

Model storage and organization - activity 8.7

Once validated, the models are stored in the project data bank for use in subsequent modeling cycles. (*Remember:* We are attempting to learn how everything relates to everything else and can use the validated data assets to define other currently undefined data assets.) In addition, as appropriate, the data bank contents can be made accessible to other enterprise integration activities as validated references, examples, and organizational business rules. The outputs from activity 7 are the validated models accessible in the project data bank and any links associating specifications with evidence stored in the project library.

Modeling Cycle Example Using a Validation Cycle

Figure 9.10 illustrates typical stakeholder perspective involvement in a week-long modeling cycle with a single formal day-long MR/V session, shown in Fig. 9.11. This cycle is occurring toward the end of the project, and its purpose is to validate a relatively large portion of the model. There are a number of different possible ways to accomplish the modeling cycle objectives, such as, for example, splitting the day-long session into two half-day sessions and performing a total of two cycles during the same week. Planning details should be left to the project teams.

Activity	Data engineer	Key specialists	Mgt.
Target system analysis (repeated until completed)			
Monday (morning) Review of (1) project goals, (2) progress to date, (3) plan for the week	√	√	√
Monday–Tuesday Review and refine candidate models, and document changes	√	√	
Wednesday Day-long model refinement session	√	√	
Thursday–Friday (morning) Further refine models	√	√	
Friday (afternoon) Project team huddle to plan for next week	√		

Figure 9.10 Modeling cycle example roles and activities.

Monday–Tuesday	Wednesday	Thursday & Friday
Planning and preparation for model validation session	Model validation session	Incorporating and evaluating MR/V session results — Cataloging — Analyzing
	Validate data assets using MR/V session	— Structuring
Collect and analyze evidence		Documenting changes and further refining data assets
Create candidate models		Identifying changes in the model as a result of new knowledge
		Identifying area of highest risk of lack of knowledge

Figure 9.11 An example week-long modeling cycle containing a modeling session.

There is considerable preparatory work required to manage an effective modeling cycle. In this example, I have allowed one-and-one-half days' preparation for a day-long modeling session on Wednesday. The models are presented to the remainder of the project team at the model validation session. Since the models are prepared by the data engineers, they typically present the models to the key specialists. Collectively the project team then examines each data item individually as well as the model as a whole with a critical eye. Links associating the logical model components to the physical system and to policy guidance and so on are examined for correctness and completeness. The session goal is to use constructive criticism to improve the data asset information content and accuracy.

Applicability of Mythical "Man-Month" Considerations

The nature of DRE projects, and specifically the availability of key personnel, often narrows the options facing DRE project managers. This chapter closes with a discussion of modeling cycle planning and coordination considerations. In addition, I'll be using the more correct term, *person month*, from here on.

In 1975, Brooks published *The Mythical Man-Month! Essays on Software Engineering*—probably the most quoted information systems project management book. (This followed a journal article on the same topic [Brooks 1974].) Brooks described five primary causes for delay in large systems development as:

- Project estimation technology and unrealistic optimism

- The mythical "man month" (person month)

- Lack of courteous stubbornness

- Poor progress monitoring

- Dealing with schedule slippage by adding person (human) resources

Collectively, these five factors are also responsible for much of the delay associated with DRE projects and knowing how they actually cause project delay helps managers avoid similar situations.

Project estimation technology and unrealistic optimism

Apparently, things have not changed much in the two decades since *The Mythical Man-Month* was published. Heemstra [1992] recently conducted an analysis of software development practices. Results indicated that the 14 percent of organizations who used software estimation models produced no better project estimates than did those who didn't use models or other formal methods. Jones, in a more recent article [1995, p. 73], states that "at least 85% of the world's software managers jump into projects with hardly a clue as to how long they will take." When you couple inexact estimating techniques with the assumption that the project will proceed in an orderly fashion, according to the latest schedule, and that the project activities will take only as long as they are expected to take, it is not difficult to see why perhaps developing useful estimates and schedules have been problem areas for many types of large-scale projects. Useful DRE project estimations can be produced once an organization has completed its first project; see Chap. 16 for details.

The mythical man-month:
parallelism in data reverse engineering projects

Person-month considerations are important to DRE projects as well. Because of its correspondence with modeling cycles, it is more useful to use *weeks* as the base unit of measure—so Brooks' term "month" becomes "week." Team weeks can be calculated by the sum of the participation of the various project team members. Brooks' truism has been often repeated.

> While cost remains the product of persons working on projects—progress toward project objectives is not.

Adding more people to a project doesn't necessarily produce the desired results; in fact, often the result is more delay. Typically, DRE projects require a high degree of coordination between the project team members as well as a high communication volume. Increasing or significantly altering the mix of project team members requires increased communication in order to compensate for any reduction in coordination. Parallelism is achievable, but the addition of a second project team is determined by

■ *The size and type of project startup and PSS costs*. These include balancing between having both teams participate on the system planning and survey activities versus the cost of bringing them up to speed. Bringing project team members up to speed can include training on the technology, learning about the project domain, understanding project goals, and the development approach to the solution.

■ *The integration requirements*. How difficult is the task of integrating the work of the multiple project teams? Integration difficulties can manifest themselves in a number of ways, including

— *The costs of purchasing CASE tools*. These can cost potentially thousands of dollars per copy regardless of whether the CASE tools are purchased at the rate of one per team or one copy for each team member.

— *Data bank support for project coordination*. Coordinated access to the project data is required to support parallel project teams. This is because the likelihood of a data item occurring in multiple models is high. Coordination mechanisms allow project teams to access a common data bank containing integrated project information.

In addition, availability of key specialists to multiple project teams can be a consideration. The key specialists have felt overwhelmed by participation on two coordinated project teams. Figure 9.12 shows how a schedule can become overloaded. In addition, this assumes that the key specialists are able to participate full-time.

Decisions on project team size are typically concerned with the number of project teams. The obvious place to begin DRE projects is with a single team. A reverse engineering project estimate might indicate a total of 26 weeks to perform DRE for a system. However, the relative progress of other enterprise integration projects will be delayed unless the results can be achieved in half that time or 13 weeks.

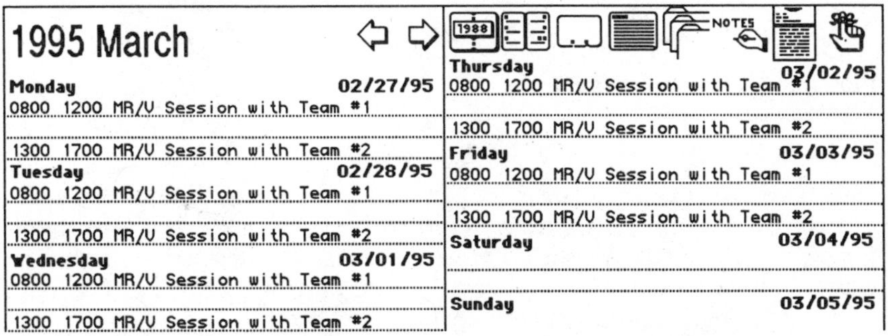

Figure 9.12 The planning calendar of an overextended key specialist attempting to participate on parallel project teams.

High overhead associated with project startup and survey or integration activities indicates a greater need for the parallelism to pay off. Although work progress can be altered, having to vary the project resources in team sized increments instead of individual increments. This forces a step function. There is one exception—the addition of some forms of clerical staff can speed progress by increasing the amount of time team members are able to concentrate on analysis activities and decreasing the amount of time they must perform tasks such as copying, searching, and using tools.

Lack of courteous stubbornness

In spite of our apparent inability to produce useful estimates for large-scale development projects, we nevertheless have not exhibited enough of what Brooks so correctly termed "the courteous stubbornness." Courteous stubbornness is required to provide management with enough knowledge to enable them to make intelligent resource allocation decisions required to produce quality products. At the time, Brooks acknowledged that to allow one-eighth of total project time was more than usual and still barely enough to produce useful project planning information. Data reverse engineering project initiators must convince management of the following items:

■ The DRE process will prove a useful investment.

■ Until we have completed at least one project, we cannot begin to provide useful project estimates.

■ The work cannot be hurried.

In addition, management must understand the cumulative nature of analysis product development. Spending of half of the resources required for a specific product does not produce half of the final product. Instead, as Brooks again pointed out you are more likely to end up with an undercooked egg than an omelet. The DRE project team must ensure that management is aware of this and must politely insist on being allowed the time and resources required to successfully complete the project or avoid starting it altogether.

Poor progress monitoring

If you don't know where you are going—any road will do.

This is another Chinese proverb. If you don't have a plan, it is very difficult to determine whether you are on or off track. Progress monitoring not only tells you about your progress but also provides indications as to the accuracy of your planning efforts. Data reverse engineering projects are estimated in terms of project team weeks and modeling cycles. These two measures can be used to monitor progress. If the project estimate called for the development of 100 data items and at 13 weeks into a 24-week project the project teams have developed 25 data items, we can surmise that, regardless of whatever else is going on, this project is behind schedule.

Dealing with schedule slippage by adding project teams

This might be the best learned lesson resulting from Brooks' work. Project management does seem to have learned the lesson of Brooks' Law—which he admittedly oversimplified as

Adding manpower to a late software project makes it later.

Projects now have a tendency to be late because we do an awful job of estimating, when we bother to estimate at all. But we, as an industry, have at least learned that there is nothing to gain and much to lose by throwing additional persons into the projects. We tend to say "Oh well, it's late." The darkened block labeled "Back Briefing" on Fig. 9.13 illustrates that late addition of another project team more often than not results in more delay than would have been encountered had the additional team been included from the start. While suggestive, this example illustrates that additional time required to bring the second team up to speed and further additional time required to integrate the separately developed model components into a single set of project outputs exacerbate the slippage.

Single-Team Plan

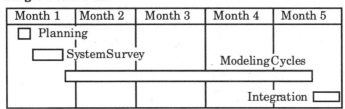

Effect of adding a team in mid-project

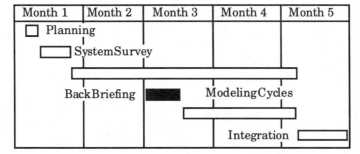

Figure 9.13 Effect of a mid-project project team addition.

Chapter

10

Project Wrapup Activities

Once the modeling cycles are complete, there are a few additional activities to be completed before the project can be considered complete. Additional activities that must be completed after the modeling cycles are finished include packaging, integrating, and transferring the data assets; collecting project metrics; and evaluating and refining the framework and methodology on the basis of the project metrics. The first four activities address the issue of making the data assets created by the DRE project more useful to other enterprise integration activities. For example, if the data for the MARS (Chap. 1, scenario 1) is cleaned up, it still must be made useful to the enterprise as a whole. Without that activity, major data administration and enterprise integration benefits will be lost. In order to complete asset packaging and bring closure to projects, several additional tasks are required. These include creation of indices to the material stored in the data bank, printing associated graphical representations of the data assets developed, and attaching a list of unresolved issues and other unfinished business. The chapter closes with a look at the information that might be evaluated at the end of a DRE project with the idea of improving the existing processes.

Data Asset Packaging - Framework Activity 9

Data asset packaging ensures that data assets are correctly packaged for delivery to other enterprise integration activities. Two formats are particularly useful:

1. A format that everyone on the project can point to and say something like "The data assets created on this project are documented on this binder, and the data administration group can help you obtain electronic access to them."

2. An electronic, CASE tool-based format stewarded by the functional community and maintained by the data administration group. In

organizations that have implemented CASE on an organization-wide basis, this information is readily accessible to other uses.

Because DRE projects are dependent heavily on CASE tool support, much of the data asset packaging activities occur continuously as the validated data assets are added to the project data bank. These activities are generally completed by the data engineers. The outputs of activity 9 are the validated data assets documented and packaged in usable and accessible format. From these the organization is able to develop term usage standards. When models are "published" in the organizational data bank, these models will be considered as organizational data assets.

Data Asset Integration - Framework Activity 10

Because of the cumulative nature of DRE project outputs, the data assets developed during DRE projects can be made more valuable by integrating them with other data assets developed during the course of enterprise integration activities. Data asset integration involves, for example, explicitly addressing identical data items, data synonyms (where different terms have similar meanings), and data homonyms (same pronunciation but different meanings). This activity's goal is to resolve instances of data confusion and place the target system models in perspective relative to other data assets. Outputs from activity 11 are integrated data assets made more useful to the remainder of the organization through the data administration program. (Data asset integration is described in more detail in Chap. 15.)

Data Asset Transfer - Framework Activity 11

Framework activity 11 is formal recognition and enforcement of the fact that most DRE projects produce outputs that are required by other enterprise integration activities. Figure 10.1 illustrates how a single DRE project can produce 5 different assets useful to other enterprise integration activities. Potential data asset transfers include the following:

1. There should be regular exchanges of information with any concurrent infrastructure evaluation activities.

2. Data assets may be exchanged with "as is" process reverse engineering efforts.

3. System-related technology constraints and opportunities captured during DRE activities often provide a wealth of requirements information to subsequent infrastructure customization activities.

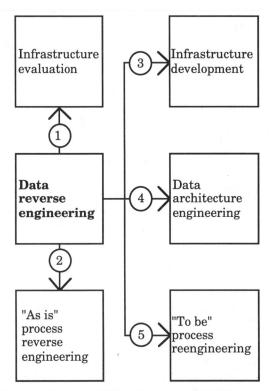

Figure 10.1 Outputs of a single DRE project can positively impact multiple enterprise integration activities.

4. Validated data assets are developed with the presumption that they will be integrated with the corporate data architecture.

5. An inventory of existing data assets, containing the type and form of data currently maintained about specific people, places, things, concepts, events, and so on.   This is useful in business process reengineering activities.

Making data assets available to other enterprise integration activities may well be the most important aspect of DRE projects.   Making data assets available can involve changing the media, location, and format of data assets to match requirements of other enterprise integration activities.   For example, while it isn't a desirable situation, certain situations may arise where organizations are using different CASE tools and the data assets can be translated from one tool format to another via various import/export utilities.

Other assets transfer situations may occur when the enterprise-level models may need to be extended for linkage to operational concepts or additional data assets may need to be developed to resolve cross functional integration issues. The outputs of activity 11 are data assets delivered on time, within budget, and meeting their intended purpose of proving useful as inputs to other enterprise integration activities.

Project Metric Collection - Framework Activity 12

After the project is complete, it is time to collect metrics to assess the overall project productivity. This information is used to establish and refine organizational DRE productivity information used in both planning individual reverse engineering projects and strategically assessing enterprise integration efforts. Data to be collected concerns:

- Information describing the overall analysis throughput

- Assessment of the key specialist participation

- Reactions of systems management to the project

Framework-Methodology Refinement - Framework Activity 13

One of the most important project closure items is collecting and recording the project metrics, any refined procedures, tool and model usage data, and operational concepts. The outputs from framework activity 13 are focused on assessing and improving both the framework and the methodology. These are stored for subsequent analysis. Each DRE project should be reviewed in full hindsight with the idea of learning from the successes as well as the unexpected occurrences.

The results are improved procedures, data on tool and model usage, and the framework-methodology assessment. The nature of DRE projects and all enterprise integration activities is such that the benefits increase in value as they grow toward a sufficient critical mass—recall the cumulative nature of data assets. In other words, the net worth of the project outputs cannot be evaluated immediately after the project is completed because the overall contribution of these outputs towards data administration goals and enterprise integration activities can become apparent only in the context of longer term reengineering activities. Thus the outputs of activity 12 become another set of measurements in the overall enterprise integration project metrics data collection. Specific framework-methodology refinements are considered in the following subsections.

Changes in cycle nature

Four specific changes in the modeling cycle activities should be considered. Figure 10.2 shows how the relative amounts of time allocated to each task during the modeling cycle change over time. (The figure illustrates how the preliminary activities occur prior to the start of the first modeling cycle in order to obtain the PSS information.)

■ *Documentation collection and analysis.* Over time the focus shifts from evidence collection to evidence analysis.

■ *Preliminary coordination requirements..* Coordination requirements can be particularly high in situations where managers are unaware of the project context or the target system's role in enterprise integration activities. Once target system analysis commences, coordination requirements can diminish significantly.

■ *Target system analysis.* Just as the documentation and collection and preliminary coordination activities decrease, the amount of effort that can be devoted to target system analysis should increase steadily; shifting away from collection activities and toward analysis activities.

■ *Modeling cycle focus.* By performing a little validation and more refinement each session, the focus of modeling cycles shifts correspondingly away from refinement and toward validation activities.

Data asset traceability completeness

Developing and maintaining the completeness of the traceability matrices is an important and challenging accomplishment. Since few CASE tools capable of maintaining the required associations exist, it is likely the organization will have to develop their own version using, for example, spreadsheet, word processing, and database technologies. As the organization becomes more proficient at DRE, the utility and ease of developing the traceability matrices will increase.

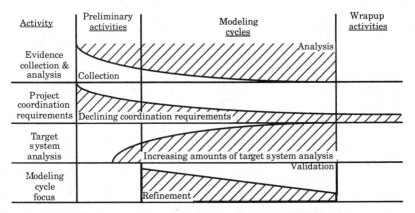

Figure 10.2 Relative use of time allocated to tasks during DRE projects.

Version control and data asset management

Version control has traditionally been associated with maintaining backup copies of systems. If changes to a system didn't work, the pervious version could quickly replace the one containing the modifications. Generational versions were also kept in case the current system became unusable. In addition to the two uses mentioned above, DRE projects encourage data engineers to exercise a different type of version control—this one concerned with the evolution of the components that make up the models. Using data bank organizing and structuring facilities, individual components of the data assets can be tracked as they evolve. For example, the original definition of a data entity might have changed over time. Versioning mechanisms permit developers to understand the *evolution* of these assets as they *evolve* over time—an important aspect of business rule analysis. One other key point concerns the relative value of data assets. Data assets management becomes increasingly important as the value of the data assets belonging to the organization increases.

Evolution of structured techniques

Figure 10.3 indicates that structured techniques have evolved steadily of the years. (The evolution of structured techniques is well presented in a 1991 article by Keuffel in *Unix Review*.) The one thing you can count on is more evolutionary change. Attempts to minimize changes to application programs is what motivates us to attempt to manage data separately from processes in the first place. Consequently, you should anticipate changes in both your structured methodology and your CASE tool. Key is to learn a certain group of techniques and know when to apply each one. Remember: It's not so much how to apply a methodology that counts; it's knowing when it is most useful to apply a specific methodology, so look for strengths in all methodologies and determine how they can be applied to each individual project at the most appropriate time.

1965	"Programming considered as a human activity" by Dijkstra [1965], ■ Identified self-modifying code as a source of lack of clarity ■ Introduced GOTO problems and functional decomposition.
1966	"Flow diagrams, turning machines and languages with only two formation rules" [Boehm and Jacopini 1966] proved that any flowchart can be constructed out of the standard three, one entry/one exit constructs iteration, selection, and sequence.
1968	NATO introduced the term "software engineering."
1972	"A technique for software module specification with examples" by Parnas [1972] introduced pseudocode and described a major problem as lack of techniques for precisely specifying without revealing internal information. This indicated it was desirable to model a program prior to programming.
1974	"Structure design" by Stevens, Myers, and Constantine [Stevens et al. 1974] presented a graphical notation describing behavior of modules and a taxonomy of module types.
1978	"Structured analysis and system specification" by DeMarco [1978] introduced data dictionary, minispecs, and pseudocode.
1986	"A rational design process and how to fake it" by Parnas and Clements [1986] asserts that big systems cannot be designed in a top–down fashion but that documentation must be produced as if it had been done top–down.
1988	"Understanding and controlling software costs" by Boehm [1988] introduced an system development life cycle advocating iteration between analysis and design with concentration of efforts in area(s) of greatest risk.
1988	"Modern structured analysis" by Yourdan [1988] introduced object orientation to structured analysis.
1989	Coad introduces object-oriented analysis [Coad and Yourdon 1989].
1989	"Information engineering" co-authored by Finkelstein [1989] and Martin [1989] defined crucial linkages between organizational strategic planning and information systems development.

Figure 10.3 A very brief history of structured techniques (adapted from Keuffel "House of Structure" © 1991 *Unix Review*).

Chapter

11

Tool Support

Computer aided software engineering (CASE) is defined as "tools and methods to support an engineering approach to software development at all stages of the process. By '"engineering approach' we mean a well-defined, well-coordinated, and repeatable activity with widely accepted representations, design rules, and standards of quality." [Forte and Norman 1992, p. 28]. Sneed [1991b] has documented a number of examples of how the cost of reengineering can be reduced by the proper application of automation, citing such success stories as investing $1,200 to reengineer a 25,000 statement

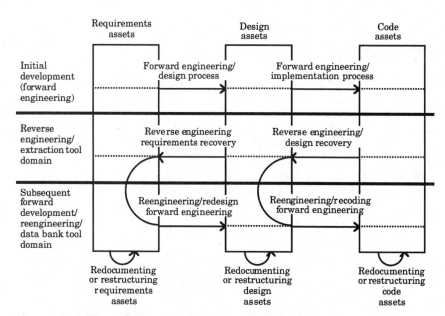

Figure 11.1 Uses of DRE tools (adapted from Chikofsky and Cross "Reverse Engineering and Design Recovery: A Taxonomy" © 1990 *IEEE Software*).

COBOL program [Sneed 1991b]. (See also Sneed [1984], Sneed and Kaposi [1990], Sneed [1991a], and Sneed [1995].) Similar positive results are to be expected by the application of automation to DRE projects. Figure 11.1 shows two classes of automated CASE tools useful for DRE projects:

- *Extraction tools.* These are used to obtain requirements information from existing systems.

- *Information structuring tools.* These are typically part of the data bank class of CASE tools.

Each is described in this chapter, which concludes with an assessment of CASE tool support for DRE projects.

Data Reverse Engineering Tools

The software engineering tools market continues to grow. Sharon [1993b] reports more than 300 vendors offering more than 1000 software engineering tools and the U.S. Department of Defense's Software Technology Initiative recently released a report surveying more than 200 reverse engineering tools [Sittenauer et al. 1994]. Jones [1993] notes that a measure of the power available to software engineers has increased by two orders of magnitude during the last 30 years; combined, these account in part for robust industry growth. Another factor has been the increased amount of support for what information systems (IS) organizations are doing a lot of: combined maintenance and reengineering. This reflects industry trends away from new systems development and toward reengineering. Many "new" development projects are replacements or enhancements of existing systems, anyway.

Jones [1994] notes how the current situation with respect to software engineering is a response to "the highest skilled manual content of any engineered product since skilled manual labor is expensive, in short supply, and not altogether predictable in terms of results." Figure 11.2 presents a basic CASE tool schema indicating both horizontal and vertical relationships (adapted from Jones [1992], who noted inadequate or deficient CASE tool support in the areas of project sizing, planning, and estimating; milestone tracking and project measurement; maintenance planning and estimating; prerelease defect tracking; and defect analysis). These features are similarly unsupported in the DRE tool world as well.

Figure 11.3 presents another view of the modeling cycle originally presented as in Fig. 9.3, showing the respective tool domains for extraction and data bank tools discussed in the following section. Figure 11.3 shows these two activities distributed across a week long modeling cycle.

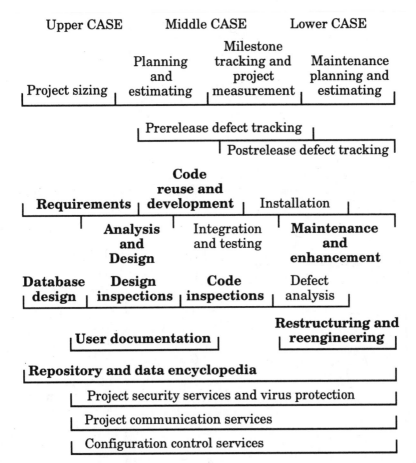

Figure 11.2 CASE technology schema (adapted from Jones [1992]).

Extraction Tools

Extraction in the DRE context is the process of deriving or obtaining specific evidence from the target system. The first place to look for the evidence is the system documentation. Sometimes, however, the requisite data doesn't exist in the system or the associated documentation. It may have been lost or become obsolete, or it may never have been created in the first place. In these instances, information must come from key specialists and often from the system itself.

Extraction tool motivation

Extraction tools are used to obtain information from target systems. Information useful to DRE projects comes from many sources, including: system documentation, system programming language code, key specialists, policies, and rules and regulations. Automation should be applied to the extraction process anywhere it is economically viable. Figure 11.4 shows how extraction tools can be used to support certain information extraction activities. In many circumstances, information can be extracted using commercial off-the-shelf software packages specifically designed to read through, for example, file access formats. These packages can read popular formats, for instance, and create such data assets as entity relationship diagrams, decomposition hierarchies, and structure charts [Sharon 1993].

Extraction tool users

Extraction tool users are likely to be data engineers and associated support staff. In certain situations a key specialist may have gained

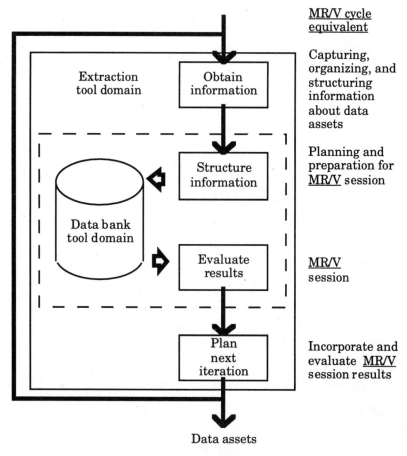

Figure 11.3 Data reverse engineering tool domain.

or wants to gain experience with a particular tool; for the most part, however, data engineers will be using the tools to fill a precise need.

Extraction tool uses

The primary goal of extraction tools is to develop models from the extracted information. Current tools are limited to producing specific outputs from specific inputs. Figure 11.5 shows a classification of extraction tools. Extraction tools are typically designed to document structure embedded in system codes.

Running system components through these tools will typically give you the documentation you might have had in the first place if it had been created. The tools listed are generally implementation-specific, delivering useful outputs when running on the correct software version of the correct operating-system platform. Correctly applied, they can provide some level of automated support to analysis and modeling activities.

Extraction tools can also be used to help develop DRE project estimates. Especially in the well developed environments such as COBOL and C, a number of commercial extraction tools are currently used to assess the complexity and structure of application programs. These measures permit data engineers to determine the relative degree of difficulty involved in attempting to extract the desired data assets. Numerous industry-standard metrics can be used to determine complexity, structure, maintainability, and testability of current systems. Metrics can be used to calculate the deterioration of a system [Jones 1994]. This information provides insight into the system's status and can be used to identify reengineering candidates.

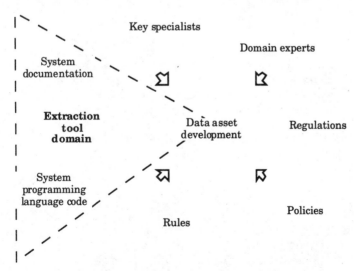

Figure 11.4 Extraction tools support focuses primarily on systems documentation and system source code as sources of information for extracting data in DRE projects.

Category/Tool purpose	Tool output
Restructurers / Detect poorly structured code fragments, replacing them with structured code	New code that is more understandable and therefore more maintainable than the original
Cross-referencers / List variable references	Lists of variable references—it is often useful to have these available on disk so they can be searched electronically
Static analyzers / Detect anomalous constructs such as unused variables and dead code	Draws attention to unused or unusable sections of program code
Text editors and other reformatting tools / Support system browsing and readability through use of indentation, bold facing, capitalization, etc.	Permits more rapid understanding of system code through use of editors, etc.
Redocumenters / Create documentation better representing the structure of the program	New program documentation providing more information than existed in the original source code listing
Transformation tools / Transform system code from one implementation or one version to another	A version of the system code in the new language or new version

Figure 11.5 Categories of extraction tools (adapted from Rugaber [1992] and Sittenauer et al. [1994]).

Extraction tools can be quite effective and the models produced, quite valuable. The products produced are too often printouts; that is, there are no machine readable model components produced. Full benefits from automation are derived from use of CASE tools where models produced can be directly entered into the project data bank. The interfaces between extraction tools and the organizing and structuring tools are typically brittle because current tools are limited to producing specific outputs from specific inputs.

Extraction tool use situations

Extraction tools can provide some of the information required to create candidate data assets for a particular modeling cycle. Extraction tools are used in situations where they are available for use and provide at least part of the required information. Tool availability is a key concern. Often a tool will exist, but the organization won't have acquired a copy in time. For example, the PSS will have indicated the usefulness of this tool but it wasn't ordered in time.   Careful planning will ensure that needed tools will be available.

Extraction tool requirement considerations

Because of the nature of each specific tool, it is impossible to specify requirements for each of the hundreds of extraction tools.   Instead, each specific tool must be evaluated according to situational cost-effectiveness.   For example, a specific extraction tool may be able to read the required source code, producing unnormalized entity relationship diagrams and program structure charts.   However, the tool doesn't interface with the project data bank.   In addition, a $5000 price tag may discourage its use on the project.

Data Banks

All project information including data entity, data attribute, and data relationship definitions is managed and stored using the project data bank.   An immediate benefit of this integration is enhanced communication among performance team members.   The structure of the data bank facilitates information sharing among the selected performance team.   This includes "library checkout" support for work combining and work partitioning.

Motivation for a data bank

Data banks are facilities providing both a place for storing data and for structuring the data into information when requested.   As soon as developers realized that computers could be used to produce graphical representations of development products that were easier to produce than hand drawn products, they began to develop computer-based tools supporting system development activities.   The motivations were pretty straightforward and the same as for systems development tools:

- Using the computer to produce diagrams, reports, and other development products made sense because the products could be generated repeatedly without the overhead associated with unautomated production means.

- The original products could be changed, modified, or enhanced by modifying the representations stored in the computer and, again, produced at a fraction of the effort required to completely reproduce the initial version.

- Change histories could be maintained by the computer, providing a means of tracking product evolution.

- Computer-based analysis could be performed on the stored representations, permitting more comprehensive analysis to be performed on the computer-based representations than was possible on the unautomated products.

During systems analysis, the analyst is learning about the system. The volume of detail and terminology can easily overwhelm the analyst. The project *data bank* is a means of collecting, organizing, and controlling the details. The organizational data bank serves as the central library for integrating individual project data bank metadata.

The original name of these facilities was a *dictionary*. Dictionaries were developed as a place to maintain consistent definitions. The concept was then widened to include more than just definitional material, and the label was changed to *encyclopedia*. The current term seems to be *repository* but *warehouse* is also becoming popular. Is it any wonder there is confusion? The latter two labels seem particularly inappropriate considering the passive connotations of the definitions. I prefer the term *data bank*. The name reinforces what I have been saying all along—the value of the assets compounds in relation to the addition of assets to the data bank. You decide for yourself what to call them. The definitions follow:

■ *Dictionary* (computer science). (1) A list of words stored in machine-readable form for reference as by spelling-checking software; (2) An electronic spelling checker.

■ *Encyclopedia*. A comprehensive reference work containing articles on a wide range of subjects or numerous aspects of a particular field, usually arranged alphabetically.

■ *Library* (computer science). A collection of standard programs, routines, or subroutines, often related to a specific application, that are available for general use.

■ *Repository*. (1) A place where things may be put for safekeeping; (2) a warehouse; (3) a museum; (4) a burial vault; a tomb; (5) one that contains or is a store of something specified: "Bone marrow is also the repository for some leukemias and lymphomas" (Seth Rolbein); (6) one who is entrusted with secrets or confidential information.

■ *Warehouse*. (1) A place in which goods or merchandise are stored, a storehouse; (2) to place or store in a warehouse, especially in a bonded or government warehouse.

Data bank uses

Data banks have two primary uses:

■ Organizing the information about the development project so that it can be easily located by those wishing to reference or modify it.

■ Providing facilities for structuring the data items into the models for refinement, validation, and use in other development activities.

Initially the uses of this facility were limited to specific development projects. However, as concepts such as data architectures matured, it became obvious that these facilities could and should be used to support data architecture development activities. That is, to facilitate coordinated development of integrated activities, the information should be accessible on an enterprise-wide basis. To illustrate one aspect of this type of organized and structured information, recall the subject of version control discussed previously. Versioning capabilities are required to permit changes to the model reflecting changes in organizational policy as well as model evolution.

As awareness of the capabilities of computer-based tool support increased, the uses of these computer-aided system development tools expanded. Software developers are now accustomed to having access to a centralized, automated facility where they can store information about a development project. For more than a decade, CASE tools have included the following uses of these facilities.

■ *Facilitating coordination among project team members.* Project team members can divide up the work and use the facility to store information they have created during development activities. Other project team members can access this information to determine how other project team members have performed their analysis.

■ *Serving as a single point of reference for information about the development project.* Project team members performing development activities can access terms and information produced during previous development phases.

■ *Serving as the project documentation facility.* The facility has the ability to maintain project information so that anytime, anyone, during system development or maintenance, can easily produce the required information.

A description of the information storable in a data bank comes from Martin [1989], who includes

■ Organizational goals and strategies

■ Data and process models

■ Business rules

■ Report and screen designs

■ Program and data structures

■ System specifications

Facilities supporting this sort of integrated system information could be used to answer questions such as

■ What systems access employee information?

■ How many systems will require modification if we replace all uses of the term *vendor part number* with an internally generated *part identification*?

■ Who is responsible for assigning product identification numbers to new products?

■ Where are the locations of all copies of the new reporting systems located?

Organizational management uses these facilities to retain their competitiveness in the marketplace. The integrated information maintained in these data banks permits systems to be developed more rapidly and at lower cost. Lower cost permits resources to be shifted from system development activities to other activities such as product enhancement and/or differentiation. Systems can be developed to more closely support organizational goals.

Key specialists will appreciate systems developed for them that more closely meet their needs. Perhaps more importantly, key specialists will appreciate systems delivered to them that are more easily modified, permitting them to more rapidly meet the changing needs of their application domain.

Because of the existence of enhanced system documentation, and traceability features, system developers are able to concentrate more on developing new systems supporting the organizational goals, and less on correcting problems associated with existing systems. The model-based nature of the information stored permits them to develop models useful beyond the immediate scope of development activities and demonstrate the advantages of model-based development techniques.

There is an additional motivation for data bank use. Most current CASE tool development activities are confined to development groups. Data bank technology will help encourage others to investigate the feasibility of this technology.

Data bank users

Data bank tools are used by a wide variety of technical specialists, administrators, etc., depending primarily on the level of maturity the organization has achieved and on the specific capabilities of the tool. These users are broadly listed in Fig. 11.6. Key to data bank tools is the concept that all users are working from the same information base. Using the traceability features, users can see not only how

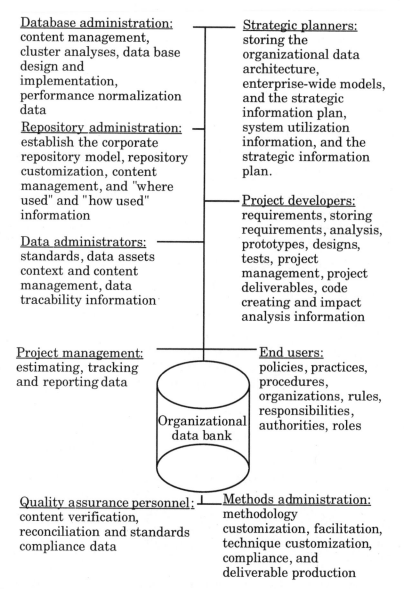

Figure 11.6 Data bank users (adapted from Selkow [1990]).

their information is represented but also how others make use of the data in differing contexts.

Data bank requirements

Unlike the situation with extraction tools, it is possible to specify some generic requirements for data bank tools. These include:

- *Model traceability.* The first requirement is traceability as described in Chap. 9.

- *Access and security requirements.* These include organization-wide on-line, real time access to the information via a suitable computing platform. As the place where corporate assets are maintained, the data bank tool becomes a meta-asset, or an asset containing information about organizational assets. Appropriate security facilities both permit access to those who require it and prohibit it to those who shouldn't have it. Multiple user and multiple platform access are typically important requirements.

- *Change management* and version control. Changes in both the definition of data asset components and the structure of the organizational models contained in the facility must be traceable, reversible, and implementable at the smallest level of component.

- *Customizability and applicability.* Since no single tool can provide all features to all users, it is more likely that users will have success with tools permitting modification of their characteristics so that a single tool can handle diverse organizational use requirements.

- *Open architecture.* Interfaces to other tools including extraction tools, forward development tools, and external report generation or query tools permit organizations to develop their own specific reengineering environments.

Secondary data bank goal is to provide a basis for subsequent decision support or executive support systems development.

Data Reverse Engineering Tool Considerations

There are a number of additional considerations that should accompany any substantial investment in CASE technology.

- The manner in which CASE technology has been used previously in the organization.

- Understanding that CASE technology and DRE projects are inextricably linked.

- The type of CASE tool architecture best supporting the DRE projects.

- Understanding the nature of the link between the number of copies of CASE tools purchased and the productivity of the DRE projects.

■ The degree to which the technology supports or enforces methodology issues.

■ When using multiple tools, ensuring that the data exchange mechanism is sufficient to transfer all information between tools in the required direction.

CASE tool usage

CASE-based development has typically been restricted to new development projects. This is because new projects are typically the only ones that can generate the critical mass required to support the investment in CASE technologies. Maintenance situations haven't permitted the development of the information base required to migrate into the CASE environment because most maintenance efforts are considered too short to justify the long-term investment required to learn and adopt CASE. Models don't tend to exist for systems you want to purchase or for older systems. This situation requires reversal of this mind set. Since DRE projects are typically infeasible outside a CASE environment, an organization's first encounter with DRE can also be considered a good opportunity to investigate the role of CASE technologies within the organization. If it hasn't already adopted CASE, then this makes an intelligent first step toward migrating to a CASE-based development environment.

Count on a payback period for CASE of 3 to 5 years for a CASE investment. Once a CASE-based development environment has been configured, an organization must determine how much of its application portfolio will be managed through the data bank. Any application developed outside the CASE tool environment is part of the legacy. As well put by Moriarty [1992],

> If your slick, new relational database application was developed without the benefit of the environment, then it's as much a part of the legacy application as the batch system you've been patching together for the last 10 years.

CASE tool architecture considerations

Many CASE tools are migrating toward a workstation environment because of the increased number of features available. This doesn't mean there aren't quality mainframe-based CASE technologies available. The decision of which CASE technologies to invest in should include consideration of access, ease of use, and functionality considerations as well as price. For example, a mainframe-based tool costing $100,000 per copy might compare favorably against having to purchase 12 copies of an $8000 per copy workstation-based tool.

In addition, you must be careful when determining where reverse engineering tools should reside. While LAN (local area network)-

based CASE tools make complete sense for forward engineering, I don't believe the same economies currently exist for the reverse engineering software. Consider the following decision situation (adapted also from Moriarty [1992]:

$75,000 can purchase an IBM mainframe reverse engineering tool with extensive impact analysis capabilities for COBOL applications. Once installed, any person with access to the mainframe can use this tool—no additional hardware is necessary. For the same amount, a LAN-based reverse engineering tool can be licensed for approximately 10 workstations. While the PC product's graphical environment is definitely more user-friendly than the text-oriented mainframe tool, the PC version can be used by only 10 people at a time, requires an investment in a server hard drive of probably at least one gigabyte to contain your COBOL program source code, and program source must be downloaded from the mainframe, which can be a time-consuming process. If you're interested in understanding the paragraph structure of a COBOL program, the mainframe product's analysis is often completed before the program's source code has finished being downloaded to the LAN. Furthermore, many organizations have yet to invest in LANs and workstations for their programmers. In this case, what's the advantage of downsizing?

CASE tool access management

CASE technology isn't cheap. Investing in it can be a major cost factor, particularly for the first DRE project. How many copies of a CASE tool should be purchased? Obviously, at least one for each project team operating. Some circumstances might dictate that a project team have access to multiple copies of a CASE tool because of the need to run parallel teams. Purchasing additional copies of the tool can reduce contention and permit faster modeling. For an overview of the costs involved in CASE implementation see Huff [1992]. These costs may make the first DRE projects more difficult to justify.

Methodology considerations

Some CASE tools have control over which features of a methodology or programming language are supported, and some constructs found in programming languages such as COBOL have been deemed as unacceptable for structured development and are often not supported. However, reverse engineering tools must be able to parse and analyze any construct available in the source language, and the data bank must be able to maintain the results of the analysis. Key specialists who know the programming language's capabilities to be reverse engineered must be actively involved in evaluating reverse engineering products. In addition, CASE tools have tended to be either overly methodology driven or not at all supportive of methodologies. Finding the correct balance between the two extremes is important.

Lack of integration between extraction and data banks

Extraction tools are not always integrated with the available data banks. This means that while the extraction tools can produce data assets, often these assets are paper based, existing on printouts, and must be reentered into the data bank manually. This clear need for integration is evidenced by recent moves by major vendors to acquire popular extraction tools [Pfrenzinger 1992].

Some Conclusions about Tool Support for Data Reverse Engineering Projects

The current crop of tools touted as reverse engineering solutions focus on associated physical data structure and variables of code segments. This is useful in identifying how physical schema are created, updated, read, and deleted, but it is not sufficient to construct the logical and conceptual external views of data requirements. Even if the functional and technical specialists help the reverse engineers clean up the analysis products, the products do not include, for instance, the links to physical evidence provided in the traceability matrices and model management support described previously. More importantly, using such tools in isolation may be as damaging as performing inadequate, inaccurate, or incomplete systems or software requirements engineering. Recovering a normalized logical data model together with the associated business rules, policies, and physical data structures still requires human-performed analysis. CASE tools may augment the analysis to provide initial understanding of physical implementation of the system, but CASE tools do not currently provide "the" solution for recovering the data items. In addition,

- C, COBOL, FORTRAN, ADA, are the most popular languages supported by DRE tools.

- CASE technology does not provide visibility into the design of large, multitasking multithread systems.

- CASE technology does not automatically identify architectural components or interconnections.

- Better tool support is needed for assessing software portability considerations.

- Emphasis on automated documentation generation could result in better system understanding.

- Lack of integration with other tools presents significant data integration problems.

Figure 11.7 presents an adaptation of Sharon's [1993] tool classification scheme showing how each tool category can be used in DRE projects.

- Current tools provide necessary but not sufficient support functions for reverse engineering.

- Key is to first develop an organization-specific methodology for data reverse engineering to define the project requirements and then examine available tools. Let tool selection be influenced by your needs, and not the other way around.

Finally, few organizations look to their information system organizations as sources of revenue or to start new business ventures. However, Francis [1990] describes how one organization (Kimberly-Clark) has recently commercialized a product developed by its internal information systems department. The product (K-C Enable/DB2) converts programs developed to support Datacom/DB to IBM's DB2 database. One-time solutions can be packaged and sold on the market, creating an ongoing revenue stream from the reverse engineering activity.

(*Note*: There are several excellent collections of information on the hundreds of reengineering tools available. Interested readers can follow up using information provided in Chap. 20.)

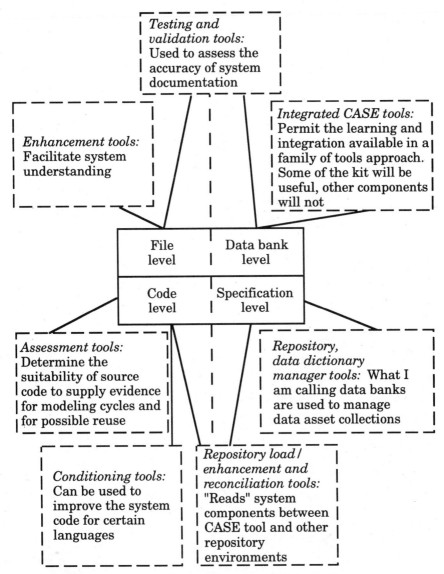

Figure 11.7 Categories of software engineering tools contributing to data reverse engineering projects (adapted from Sharon"Software-Engineering Tool Classification" © 1993 *IEEE Software*).

Outputs

output n.
1. The act or process of producing; production.
2. (a) An amount produced or manufactured during a certain time; (b) intellectual or creative production: literary output; artistic output.
3. (a) The energy, power, or work produced by a system; (b) *computer science*—The information produced by a computer from a specific input.
To produce or manufacture (something) during a certain time.
Synonym(s): Noun—the amount or quantity produced. product, production, yield.

Source: *American Heritage English Dictionary* © 1993 Houghton Mifflin Company.

This part of the book describes data reverse engineering (DRE) project outputs. There are two classes of outputs: outputs directly affecting the target systems and outputs useful in data architecture development and enterprise integration activities. Accordingly:

Chapter	*Summary*
12	*Describes the direct outputs of DRE projects including data items and models, term usage, traceability matrices, data asset inventories, and business rules.*
13	*Describes indirect outputs including data integration, data exchange projects, and data evolution.*
14	*Describes DRE project outputs contributing toward organizational data architecture development.*
15	*Describes DRE's role in enterprise integration activities.*

Chapter

12

Direct Outputs

A wide range of DRE project outputs are possible. For some projects, it will be cost effective to produce subsets of the possible outputs. In other cases, a complete set of outputs will be required to meet project-specific data administration and/or enterprise integration objectives. This chapter provides information describing available DRE project outputs. This enables readers to evaluate possibilities and make each DRE project as effective as possible. Accordingly, this chapter describes

- The general destination of outputs from DRE projects as a combination of the target system, data administration, or enterprise integration activities and how their respective needs influence the types of project outputs to be produced

- Project outputs for framework phases II and III of DRE projects (phase I activity outputs were covered in Part 2)

- Management of the DRE project outputs

Output Uses

Two types of knowledge result from reverse engineering projects. The first is reference material such as enhanced systems documentation. The promise of obtaining better system documentation can be sufficient to justify an investment in data reverse engineering. The second type of information results in a better understanding of the system on the part of the key specialists. Both types are capable of facilitating increased effectiveness of organizational information system resource investments.

The successful organization, the dexterous organization will have what Haeckel and Nolan [1993, p. 126] describe as a high corporate

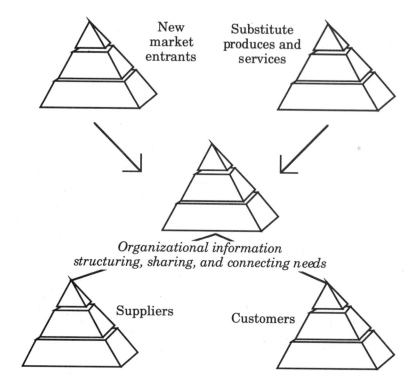

Figure 12.1 Required corporate IQ is driven by an organization's environmental complexity (adapted from Porter [1980]).

IQ, or abilities to deal with complexity by capturing, sharing, and extracting meaning from marketplace signals:

> In most large companies, a low IQ results from change occurring so rapidly that keeping computer applications up to date is neither feasible nor affordable. Low IQs are particularly prevalent when processes have been automated over decades without any framework to integrate disparate applications and databases.

Figure 12.1 illustrates how the relationship between an organization's competitive environment and the corresponding organizational IQ results in three specific sets of operational requirements.

1. *Information connecting requirements.* These are driven by the number of information sources; *connecting* in this context is defined as the ability to access knowledge and information.

2. *Information sharing requirements.* Driven by the volume and complexity of the organizational information sharing and integration requirements, *sharing* is defined as the ability to integrate and share information.

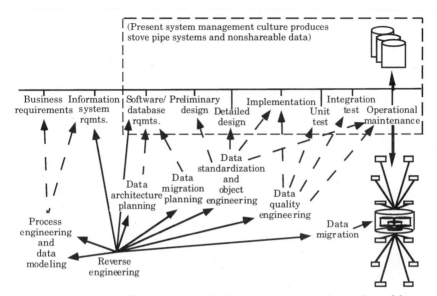

(System reengineering incorporates enterprise integration and data administration strategies, producing integrated, shareable data assets)

Figure 12.2 Reverse engineering information has uses throughout the life cycle (adapted from Aiken et al. [1994]).

3. *Information structuring requirements.* Driven by the number and types of relationships between elements to be coordinated, *structuring* is defined as the ability to extract meaning from data.

Organizational models are the currency of organizational IQ. Figure 12.2 presents another perspective on DRE project output uses. It illustrates the relationship between reverse engineering products and other system development activities and shows the outputs exchanged among DRE projects and other activities. Dark lines are direct effects, and dashed lines are indirect influences (see the next chapter, Chap. 13), presenting an overview of DRE project outputs and subsequent usage. The arrow contents are described in the matrix in Fig. 12.3.

Figure 12.4 shows the outputs passing from DRE projects to the target system, as well as data administration and enterprise integration activities. In addition to the benefits to the target system, DRE outputs accrue to data administration activities that, in turn, feed enterprise integration activities. This is an example of process quality depending largely on the quality of the inputs. Poor-quality inputs will limit the data administration and enterprise integration activity quality because all of these outputs build on each other. Data administration, in turn, obtains its inputs largely from DRE efforts and other development activities—acknowledged with the dash-lined "other activities" box. Data reverse engineering project outputs are used primarily to develop reference material provided to data administration function, which, in turn makes it available for other forward engineering project efforts.

Enterprise integration activities are built on data administration outputs and other enterprise integration activities—shown on the figure as the other dash-lined box. (Box size is not indicative of contribution.) Thus DRE plays a key role in data architecture development activities, which, in turn play a key role in enterprise integra-

Enterprise Integration Activity	Project output								
	Model view decomposition hierarchies	Logical data models	System and organization term usage	Traceability matrix	Data inventories	Process effectiveness reports	Methodology effectiveness reports	Technology insertion opportunities	Tool usage reports
Project feasibility analysis	↵	↵	↵	↵	↵	↵	↵	↵	↵
Data integration activities	↵	↵	↵	↵	↵	↵	↵		↵
Infrastructure evaluation	↵				↵			↵	
"To be" process engineering	↵	↵	↵		↵			↵	
System requirements engineering	↵	↵	↵	↵	↵	↵		↵	
Data evolution planning	↵	↵	↵	↵	↵	↵		↵	
Data architecture development	↵	↵	↵	↵	↵			↵	
Data quality assurance	↵	↵	↵	↵	↵	↵	↵		↵
Object engineering	↵	↵	↵	↵	↵	↵	↵		
Data security architecture	↵	↵	↵		↵				

Figure 12.3 Relationship between reverse engineering products and other system development activities.

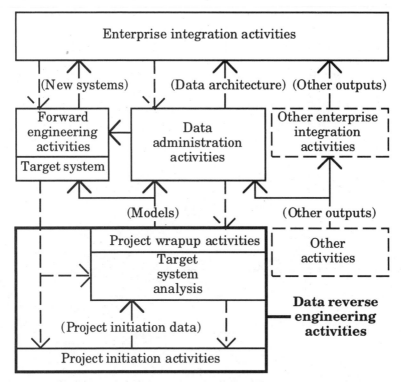

Figure 12.4 Multiple destinations of DRE project outputs.

tion activities. Various data assets have multiple uses for these two activities. Figure 12.5 builds on concepts presented in Fig. 12.2. The matrix is read as follows: the information derived from DRE outputs (e.g., data inventories column 5 is used by all enterprise integration processes). Notice how all DRE outputs are included in the project data bank. Figure 12.5 also indicates whether each specific DRE output is mandatory or optional. Mandatory items are required to produce technically sound models.

Often optional outputs can be omitted to achieve greater project throughput. Producing fewer outputs can permit DRE projects to be planned more rapidly in order to meet other data administration and enterprise integration goals. In many cases the information required to produce these optional deliverables is captured, anyway. Postponing portions of the analysis to a later time is another form of leverage and can be effective as long as not too much time passes between capture and analysis. If maintenance or other changes are applied to the system, the documentation will be out of sync with the physical evidence until it is updated.

Mandatory	Data bank	Enterprise integration process	Data architecture process	Data reverse engineering project	Project planning	Project feasibility analysis	Inputs to: / Outputs from step:
							Survey:
Y	L				L	L	Project estimate data
Y	L				L	L	Performance team directory
Y	L				L	L	Organizational requirements
Y	L				L	L	Master list of considerations
	L				L	L	Catalog of information resources
Y	L	L	L		L	L	Model view decomposition hierarchies
							Planning:
	L		L				Task schedule
Y	L		L				Organizational resource commitments
	L		L	L	L		Project specific framework
Y	L		L	L	L		Project specific procedure
							Project:
	L	L	L	L			Data models
	L	L	L	L	L	L	System and organization term usage
	L	L	L	L			Traceability matrix
	L	L	L				Data inventories
	L				L	L	Process effectiveness reports
	L				L	L	Methodology effectiveness reports

Figure 12.5   Data reverse engineering project outputs and usage (adapted from Aiken et al. [1994]).

Initiation Phase Outputs

Figure 12.6 illustrates the cumulative nature of phase I activity outputs. Each activity produces outputs (shown in italics) used as inputs by the next activity. The system decomposition is the primary exception; it is used continuously during target system analysis as a project roadmap. Feedback and refinement information flows permitting overall phase I improvement possibilities are shown using dotted lines. It makes sense to use the same data engineers on both the reverse and forward activities as they'll produce the documentation they know they will need and will be more familiar with the project. Project team outputs are often specifically developed for immediate reuse by the same individuals who created them. Knowing that they will be using the outputs to plan and guide the project forward engineering activities, the preparers are typically careful. They

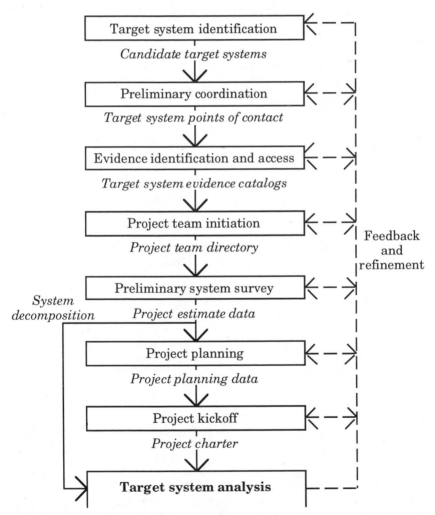

Figure 12.6 Project initiation outputs are used as inputs by target system analysis activities.

Activity 1: target system identification	One or more candidate systems targeted for possible DRE—selected on the basis of overall contribution to enterprise integration or in response to reactive organizational data problems
Activity 2: preliminary coordination	■ Elimination of infeasible candidate projects ■ Candidate target system ■ Points of contact
Activity 3: evidence identification and access	Target system evidence catalogs—lists of ■ Domain specialists ■ Processes ■ External data ■ Conceptual data ■ Internal data ■ Policies Required to reverse engineer the system
Activity 4: project team initiation	Project team directory containing ■ Contact information ■ Project team roles ■ Participation levels ■ Communication protocols
Activity 5: preliminary system survey	Project estimate data containing enough information about the system to develop a useful project estimate
Activity 6: project planning	Project planning data ■ Project activity schedule ■ Organizational resource commitments ■ Project-specific DRE framework ■ Project-specific DRE procedure
Activity 7: project kickoff	Project charter ■ Formal project authorization ■ Project goals ■ DRE outputs to be produced ■ Anticipated return on investment

Figure 12.7   Phase I project initiation activity outputs.

will rely on their own shorthand notations, and their familiarity with the system characteristics will permit them a small amount of leeway with respect to preparation of initiation phase outputs. It would be redundant to repeat the information describing Phase I activity outputs—instead I'll summarize it in Fig. 12.7.

While the accuracy of these outputs is probably high because the preparers are also the most direct users, the quality must be sufficient to satisfy data administration reference material requirements,

```
Entity:              BED

Data Asset Type: Principal Data Entity

Purpose:             This is a substructure within the Room
                     substructure of the Facility Location.   It
                     contains information about beds within rooms.

Source:              Maintenance Manual for File and Table Data
                     (Software Version 3.0, Release 3.1)

Attributes:          Bed.Description
                     Bed.Status
                     Bed.Sex.To.Be.Assigned
                     Bed.Reserve.Reason

Associations:        >0-+ Room

Status:              Validated
```

Figure 12.8   Validated data entity.

which are generally more stringent than those imposed by forward
engineering requirements.   Any sort of testing or other quality assessment measures can then be performed by the data administration group. This occurs prior to making them available to organizational data bank users.   Control and maintenance of the organizational data bank also facilitates the process of identifying customer
usage of data administration products.   Project material required by
forward engineering activities can be checked out from the data administration function.

Implementation Phase Outputs

Implementation phase outputs include: data items, models, system
and organization term usage, traceability matrices, data asset   inventories.

Data items and models

Data items are facts about persons, places, or things about whom or
which the organization collects information. Facts collected are called
attributes.   Attributes are grouped into units known as *entities*.
Facts must be combined with meaning to represent data.   Attributes
associated with entities become data.   Additional data is obtained
from the way entities are "related" to each other. Figure 12.8 shows
an example of a single validated data asset, in this case from a
health care management system scenario describing the organizational concept of BED. Notice that the entity metadata is composed of

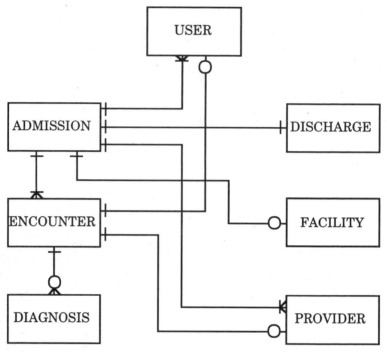

Figure 12.9   Data map of the DISPOSITION view.

- A purpose statement describing why the organization is maintaining information about these "business things" [Ross 1992].

- Sources of information about it.

- (A partial list of the) attributes or characteristics of the entity.

- Associations with other data items; this is read as ROOM contains zero or more BEDS.

In order to fully integrate the information required by this it is also important to understand the concept of ROOM. In systems development, data item meanings have been implied by the use of data items, rather than being represented explicitly. While some data item meanings seem obvious (such as bed), much data has no obvious meaning.

As described in Chap. 3, data architectures provide a set of blueprints describing the organization in terms of its data. Data architectures consist of models consisting of data maps and supporting reference material. Data models are the output most commonly associated with DRE projects. The motivation for their widespread use is that data modeling is a prerequisite to achieving shareable data—a major data administration goal. Portions of all data models deal with reference material. When it reaches the enterprise data bank this reference material must be in a suitable form for other projects to access it; that is, it must be integrated with the rest of the material. Data models have two primary components: the data map(s) and the reference materials consisting of entity lists and definitions. The data maps are typically entity relationship diagrams (ERDs). Data maps model the structure of data as a network of interconnected entities and are used as structured shorthand to represent and communicate patterns simplifying the modeling subjects.

Figure 12.9 is a data map of a single view of the disposition function (system decomposition component 1.3) from the patient administration component (1.0) of the health care management system scenario originally presented in Fig. 8.10. It shows the relationships existing between the seven entities constituting this particular view. The required definitions supporting the data map are shown in Fig. 12.10. Combined, the two figures convey the following information:

- At least one but possibly more system USERS enter the DISPOSITION facts into the system.

- An ADMISSION is associated with one and only one DISCHARGE.

- An ADMISSION is associated with zero or more FACILITIES.

- An ADMISSION is associated with zero or more PROVIDERS.

- An ADMISSION is associated with one or more ENCOUNTERS.

- An ENCOUNTER may be recorded by a system USER.

- An ENCOUNTER may be associated with a PROVIDER.

- An ENCOUNTER may be associated with one or more DIAGNOSES.

Entities and attributes represent the basic structure of the data. The lines connecting the entities together denote *relationships* between the entities. Rather than being structural in nature, relationships represent restrictions to the order in which the data can be added to the structure. The resulting structure is organizational knowledge.

As part of the physical implementation, data structures have multiple roles. Data structures extracted directly from the system are typically transient data variables used to store processing results from stored data elements. Processing associated with these structures is typically an implementation of business rules or low-level mathematical algorithms (e.g., sort). Data structures are also used to hold data presented as on-line screens or reports. The logical models should contain links that can be used to map to data elements stored in databases or files. Hence, data structures defined in existing software and data dictionaries, if they exist, may represent only some of the required conceptual, external, or physical data element views.

Attributes can also be shown on data maps, but more detailed maps require different information content considerations because fewer entities and relationships can be displayed on a single page or computer screen. Understanding the definition of the entities and attributes and the interrelationships is prerequisite knowledge to achieving shareable data. In today's environment, lack of shared data can make it impossibly expensive to maintain, let alone expand, existing organizational IQ levels, and much less to develop new functionality.

Data modeling notations used can differ but not to the extent of preventing data model information exchanges. Modeling techniques differ chiefly according to how entity relationship lines are drawn. Some notations use single- and double-arrow terminators, some use single lines and crow's feet (an inverted arrowhead), and some simply use single lines with numeric labels. Some notations allow multiple relationship lines to be joined, while others require an intermediate entity to be defined. Some have a notation for mutually exclusive relationships; others do not. Depending on these subtleties, translation between model types can be nontrivial and valuable information can be difficult to translate.

ADMISSION	Contains information about patient admission history related to one or more inpatient episodes.
DIAGNOSIS	Contains the International Disease Classification (IDC) of code representation and/or description of a patient's health related to an inpatient code.
DISCHARGE	A table of codes describing disposition types available for an inpatient at a FACILITY.
ENCOUNTER	Tracking information related to inpatient episodes.
FACILITY	File containing a list of all facilities in regional health care system.
PROVIDER	Full name of a member of the FACILITY team providing services to the patient.
USER	Any user with access to create, read, update, and delete DISPOSITION data.

Figure 12.10 Data map definitions for the DISPOSITION view.

System and organization term usage

One use for data models is facilitating system and organizational term usage understanding. This understanding is key to sharing data. If I use the term "runway length" and define it internally as the measurement in *feet*, a pilot who thinks in *meters* would be very interested to know its unit of measure as well as the source of the data. One function of the organizational data bank is to maintain the organizational and system usage standards—in this case so that everyone uses the same units of measurement and avoids potentially fatal accidents.

Traceability matrices

One of the most valuable outcomes of data reverse engineering, traceability information, is maintained using traceability matrices. The matrices are used to identify and document the correlation of items contained in the various models. Model traceability is crucial to model validation. Part of the model validation process involves establishing and maintaining traceability. Traceability is a key concept in DRE because it provides a means of validating the models. There are two aspects of traceability:

■ Links between evidence source and model components.

■ Links between model components and the physical components implemented in the system.

In the data bank the models need to be developed in three distinct but integrated views:

1. *Physical or application program view.* This is the "computer view" of the data as it is implemented and has to be accessed from application programs. Unless data redundancy has been eliminated, there may be multiple versions and instances of data items in the system.

2. *External or key specialist view.* This is how the data manifests itself to the key specialist community (i.e., portions of screen displays). Users have many external views of data.

3. *Conceptual or data administrator view.* This is how the data appears to the data engineers and how the data engineers present it to the external community as an enterprise data architecture component.

Figure 12.11 illustrates how the external view, the conceptual view, and the physical view are linked. Unlike the simplistic linkages portrayed between the three different views shown in the figure, the actual process of mapping data items to corresponding data items in other views is much more detailed—literally linking hundreds of data items to hundreds of other data items.

Using these capabilities, links can be developed associating and integrating project information. Consider the large amounts of information maintained in links between logical model components, physical system components, and various other sources. They include

- System functional requirements, policy, and guidance that exists in the application code

- Functional dependencies, associated operational, tactical, and/or strategic requirements

- Business-domain information

- Organizational data distribution

- Data architecture components

- External model views, physical model views, conceptual model views, and business rules

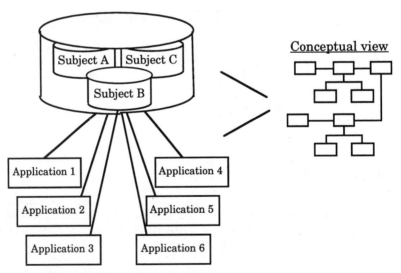

Figure 12.11 Linked (or related) three-schema views of target environment are just one type of useful linkage capable of being a project output (adapted from Aiken et al. [1994]).

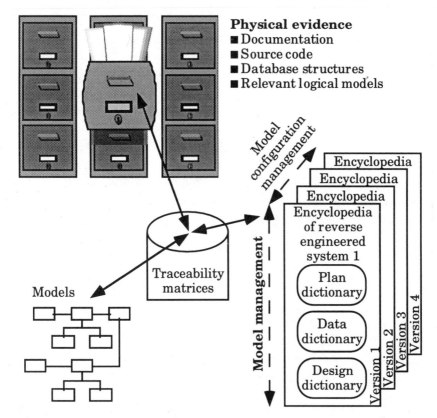

Figure 12.12   Data reverse engineering approach to model traceability (adapted from Aiken et al. [1994]).

To enhance traceability, model components are linked to the evidence revealing their existence (system manuals, source code, directives, interview results, etc.). Electronic indices are developed to link evidence stored in the data bank with evidence stored in the project library. Finally, each version of the data items stored is kept so the project team and subsequent readers can examine the various refinements that occurred during model development.   Figure 12.12 illustrates just part of this traceability, showing linkages between models, physical evidence, and model components.

Figure 12.13 shows another aspect of traceability, in this case showing

■ The sources of information about the organizational entity PATIENT

■ The model views it appears in

■ The source of information used to defined the entity

■ Links to system design components

```
Entity:          PATIENT

Category:        Principal

Model Views:     PATIENT ADMINISTRATION not defined
                 DISPOSITION Shared Read, Update
                 ADMISSION Shared Read, Update

Purpose:         Contains the demographics information for an
                 individual requesting care at a FACILITY

Source:          MR/V session of 3/15/95 and the Health Care
                 Management System Data Dictionary

Attributes:      ssn #
                 name
                 sex

Design Links:    PATIENT.ROOM

Associations:    >|----•< ADMISSION
                 >|---|< MARITAL STATUS
                 >|---•< PROVIDER
```

Figure 12.13   Traceability information.

■ Associations to other entities

The recorded linkages make the traceability matrices critical for
validating the correctness of data models derived from physical evidence. When traceability matrices reach a critical mass of knowledge, they can be used to assess the impacts of organizational and
environmental changes. The traceability matrices can also be used
to plan data evolution from legacy to future reengineered systems.
Using advanced CASE tools, the logical data models can be used to
automatically create table structures for the selected database, while
the traceability matrices are used to develop the mapping required to
migrate data from the legacy systems to the appropriate tables in
the new system.

The matrices are also maintained to substantiate requirements
for specific data model components by linking them to specific author-
izing statutes, regulations, policy guidance, and so on. Matrices are
used to perform impact analysis when subsequent requirements
changes occur. The matrices identify how specific data items relate
back to specific legacy system components. A data item appearing on
a screen can be traced to the data model components and to specific
information system components where it appears. In addition, the
requirement specifying the creation of the data item and other key
information such as which enterprise goals the data item supports
are also available.

CASE-based representation of this information can facilitate system understanding and lead to immediate payback in terms of system maintenance reduction. Traceability matrices are useless without models. Thus they are typically considered as part of the model. Models, however, are useful without the traceability matrices. Thus the traceability matrices are an optional DRE output and can be eliminated from the project goals. However, marginal costs are associated with their development, and the information developed is valuable. The project sponsor usually attempts to have projects funded at sufficient levels to permit development of traceability matrices.

Data asset inventories

This type of output is really another model component; however, this information is in much demand from other enterprise integration activities. Data inventories consist of accurate catalogs of organizational metadata such as an inventory of existing data items containing the type and form of data currently maintained about people, places, things, concepts, events, etc. of interest to the organization. The inventory can help "to be" process reengineering activities to evaluate alternative organizational process architecture configurations. For example, an existing database of competitor responses to organizational competitive moves might support a more aggressive pricing strategy of an organization. Data asset inventories passed to "to be" process reengineering efforts can guide the selection of or confirm the feasibility of newly defined processes. The catalogs are typically maintained as CASE-based data models with associated flexibility in permitting users to design their own output types.

Business rules

Appleton [1984, p. 145] has stated:

> The problem is that most businesses assume that the rules controlling their data are consistent, when in fact they aren't. This is why management gets inconsistent, unreliable, conflicting, and contradictory information.

Pfrenzinger [1992] elaborated on this definition, stating:

> Much discussion has been given to efforts to salvage code from an existing system, but the focus has recently shifted to recovering a system's business intent. This information can be used to create an entire "as-built" requirements document or to selectively recover individual business rules to assist in system redevelopment.

Business rules are a relatively new but powerful type of data asset capable of linking data items to processing requirements. Ross [1994] notes how it is possible to view an organization as a collection of rules, each organization possessing thousands that govern its behavior and distinguish it from other organizations. *Business rules* are defined by Sandifer and von Halle [1991, p. 453] as a "statement written in natural language describing terminology, definitions, rules or policies about information that is used in conducting the enterprise's business." They also present four primary classes of business rules (several extensions are possible for each category):

1. Those pertaining to entities include entity definition, identification, and cardinality.

2. Business rules concerning the interrelationships between entities include relationship identification rules, relationship cardinality rules, relationship justification rules, relationship optionality rules, and relationship referential integrity rules.

3. Attribute business rules include attribute definitions and attribute domain rules.

4. The fourth class of business rules don't relate directly to entities, attributes, or relationships but nevertheless promote increased comprehension of the organizational functioning.

Because business rules often provide guidance for organizational managers when conducting daily business, they are a major source of bureaucratic inefficiencies because processes tend to be optimized locally rather than on an organization-wide basis. Business rules embody organizational knowledge about "business things" that people need to know information about: entities. The relationships between these entities are also represented as business rules in the organization. In reengineering contexts, business rule management serves as an opportunity to uncover suboptimal business practices by providing starting points for the development of system models that can be used to optimize business practices.

Approaches to business rule development are similar to the approach to target system analysis described previously (e.g., see Sandifer and von Halle [1991])—in fact, so similar that the two activities, DRE and business rule development, are most effectively combined into target system analysis.

Figures 12.14 through 12.17 are four sample business rules derived from the health care scenario from Chap. 1. These were derived from analysis of the data model shown in Fig. 12.9. Figure 12.14 indicates that all patients must be discharged from a hospital when being physically removed from the facilities. Discharge reasons range from being taken home after birth to transfer to another facility to patient death. Information stored in the disposition entity should be used to update the hospital census information.

Figure 12.15 presents the definition of an encounter. Encounters track to face-to-face contacts between providers and patients. From the role it is clear that an update to the encounter entity must also update the data with contact information must also update a record

```
Statement:  Disposition, Inpatient

Category:   Disposition Business Rule

    Text:   The removal of a patient (including live
            births) from the census of a hospital by
            reason of discharge, transfer to another
            medical facility, death, or other termination
            of inpatient care.

  Source:   Disposition function (SD component 1.3) from
            the patient administration component (1.0)

Data Links: date of death
            discharge comments
            disposition date
            disposition order
            dispositioning physician
            projected disposition date
            transferred moved to

Is Part of: Disposition Process
```

Figure 12.14   "Inpatient disposition" business rule.

indicating contact between at least one provider and at least one patient. Figure 12-16 indicates that the system must track an infinite list of potential aliases. Patients with multiple name changes must be traceable. When considered in context with the previous example, it is clear that these two combine to present system designers with

```
Statement:  Encounter Definition

Category:   Encounter Business Rule

    Text:   A face to face contact between a patient and a
            provider who has primary responsibility for
            assessing and treating the patient at a given
            contact, exercising independent judgment.

  Source:   Disposition function (SD component 1.3) from
            the patient administration component (1.0)

Data Links: admitting physician
            attending physician
            provider id

Is Part of: Admission Process
```

Figure 12.15   "Encounter" business rule.

```
Statement:    Former  Patient  Name

Category:    Registration Business Rule

    Text:    A patient's present and former name must be
             cross-referenced.

  Source:    Disposition function (SD component 1.3) from
             the patient administration component (1.0)

Data Links:  patient alias

Is Part of:  Registration
```

Figure 12.16 "Former patient name" business rule.

the challenge of associating patients having face-to-face encounters with health care providers while using multiple names. Finally, Fig. 12.17 presents a very specific system requirement—essentially describing a system requirement for an undo function that spans the previous 24-hour period.

Project Wrapup Phase Outputs

The wrapup phase is concerned with packaging the phase II outputs. It adds substantial value in addition to the models produced as a result of target system analysis activities. Recall models become assets when they are published in the organizational data bank. These include

- *Integrated data assets.* Data assets are combinations of models not previously integrated. Analysis of integration results permits understanding of similar data elements contained in the systems and the relationships among the systems as an integrated whole.

- *Technique and methodology effectiveness reports.* It is important to regularly assess the effectiveness of the technical process employed, particularly any changes, modification, or enhancements. To help to evaluate the effectiveness of the organizational investment in CASE technology, gather data on procedures, methods, tool usage, conventions, protocols, etc.

- *Shared and shareable data assets.* This is required to achieve desired organizational dexterity.

- *Project metrics data.* Historical production data is maintained to evaluate methodology and technique effectiveness.

- *Framework usage data.* The language, data management (or handling) systems, implementation complexity, and strategic plan can differ for each target system. For each project, develop a project-specific reverse engineering framework, methodology, and tool usage.

■ *Framework effectiveness reports*. The effectiveness of the methodology employed, especially any changes, modifications, or enhancements, must be reported to permit organizations to develop a means of assessing and improving the organizational reengineering efforts.

■ *Framework use data*. The project team publishes the models (normalized, "as is" business and conceptual data models) that resulted from the reverse engineering process. It captures and documents any changes to the conventions, procedures, and protocols that took place during this process. Data suggesting improvements for refining the methodological approach is analyzed. Also the data asset inventory from the CASE tool is published.

■ *CASE tool based data assets*. Portions of the system that are reverse engineered are documented in the organizational data bank, and when published as standards, these data items are used as the basis for developing new systems.

```
Statement:    Patient Discharged and Readmitted on
              Same Day

Category:     Disposition Business Rule

Text:         If a patient is readmitted on the same day as
              discharged (for the same diagnosis or
              condition related to the previous inpatient
              episode, the admission) ... may be reactived
              (by canceling the previous disposition).  The
              hospitalization may then be considered as one
              continuous period.  If a patient is readmitted
              after 24 hours a new record must be created.

Source:       Disposition function (SD component 1.3) from
              the patient administration component (1.0)

Data Links:   admission date
              disposition date
              register number

Is Part of:   Disposition Process
```

Figure 12.17 "Patient discharged and readmitted on the same day" business rule.

Data Administration–Related Outputs

Data administration–related outputs are by nature cumulative. That is, the value is dependent on a critical mass—sufficient understanding of the "as is" systems and the "to be" data architecture in order to produce useful information. So much is understood about the information that what is really understood is information about the information or what has often been labeled "meta-information." This class of data assets should be delivered in the format compatible with the data bank and the data architecture function. Delivery should be coordinated to complement other data administration–related projects.

What begins as an understanding of the terminology used in systems and processes evolved through target system analysis into candidate organizational data elements. These include organization-wide definitions to be used in the future. Lack of shared data is primarily a result of system brittleness. Use of shared data implies an evolutionary approach to change and orderly change management. It also implies a model-based system development structure permitting a greater degree of organizational of technological maturity.

Data integration, data exchange projects, business rule analysis, and data evolution use data assets from DRE projects. (Figure 13.6 illustrates the relationships between data integration, business rules, data evolution, data reverse engineering, and data architecture development.) All can help organizations to identify DRE opportunities satisfying multiple information requests.

Enterprise Integration Outputs

Enterprise integration outputs are DRE project outputs destined to become useful to other enterprise integration projects made accessible to the appropriate activity by the data administration group.

Technology insertion opportunities

This output identifies possible areas of technological opportunities to improve the existing systems. As long as these well-qualified teams are analyzing legacy information systems, it seems entirely appropriate to take note of major areas where technology insertion recommendations would be useful components as inputs to the resulting evolution plans. This information may be in categories such as hardware, communications and networking, database management, user-machine interface, data validation and integrity considerations, system maintainability, system migration-rehosting technology, database design tools, operating expense, and security. The report also identifies considerations warranting further, more detailed analysis. Technology constraints and opportunities information captured during DRE activities often provides a wealth of requirements information to subsequent enterprise integration activities such as infrastructure customization. Information such as transaction volume, data transfer content, and refresh rates are identified during DRE and stored in the data bank.

Data evolution

Systems evolution plans prescribe the steps necessary to make the existing legacy systems compliant with enterprise integration goals. They are plans for bridging the gap between the "as is" legacy information system and the "to be" integrated enterprise information systems. These are examined in Chap 13.

Reusable software requirements

Another by-product will be reusable software requirements identified, located, and referenced by data models, domain-specific rule sets, and perhaps, eventually, the software constructed to support the requirements.

Managing Reverse Engineering Project Outputs

Reverse engineering project outputs can occupy literally thousands of pages and (of more value) hundreds of megabytes of CASE tool data bank stored on disk. It is important to carefully manage these resources. It is crucial to ensure the correct information is made available to appropriate activities in time to be useful. Organizations have been reluctant to maintain models stored as stacks of paper-based output, preferring to duplicate electronic copies. Problems have nevertheless arisen when the only access to information is through CASE tools costing several thousand dollar per copy. Viewing-only capability is a welcome addition to CASE product offerings.

13

Indirect Outputs

In addition to the direct outputs described in Chap. 12, three indirect but related outputs receive special consideration in this chapter. *Data exchange* is the process of sharing data with other groups within and external to the organization. *Data evolution* is the process of changing the association of data from the target systems to the reengineering system. *Data integration* is required to achieve both data exchange and data evolution. Indirect outputs are not produced directly from DRE projects, but awareness of enterprise integration requirements permits organizations to plan their production and take the opportunity to produce multiple outputs. Indirect output is a product of specific information system (IS) planning, and professional management by a data administration staff. The cost benefit return of data administration overhead shows up in the quantity and quality of indirect outputs. Data administration effectiveness measures are, in part, measures of the gain directly related to the system development benefit attributed to the indirect output, and to those actions beyond design that the data administration team provides. The indirect benefits are the key elements that allow the output of a system operation to be considered as a service, and not just a series of paper based products. As the focus of organizational computing shifts from personal to workgroup computing, from islands of information to integrated systems, and from internal computing to interorganizational computing, the need for these three indirect DRE project outputs increases.

Data Evolution

In a systems reengineering context, at certain points the data associated with an old system will be required to be associated with a new system. *Data evolution* is the process of accomplishing this transfer of association. Aspects of data evolution are popularly described using the following terms:

■ *Data migration.* This is the process of changing the location of the data from one system to another.

■ *Data conversion.* This is the process of changing data into another form, state, or product.

■ *Data scrubbing.* This is the process of comprehensively inspecting and manipulating, manually recoding, or rekeying data in order to prepare it for subsequent use.

The size of the data evolution challenge facing the industry today can be summarized in a few statistics revealed by a 1993 Forrester Research survey of IS managers, planning directors, and information systems VPs reported by Lent [1994]. Respondents indicated approximately two-thirds of their corporate data resided in mainframe and minicomputers, but by the year 2000 more than 50 percent will be off-loaded to servers. Almost 70 percent of organizations still have transaction processing programs, 30 percent still have batch systems, and 10 percent still have decision support systems (DSSs) residing on mainframes.

■ Of the batch systems, 55 percent plan to rebuild in client/server environments, 15 percent will be moved to another computing platform, more than 20 percent will be left on their current hosts but improved, and more than 20 percent will be left alone.

■ Of the transaction processing systems, 65 percent will be rebuilt in client/server environments, 10 percent will be moved to another computing platform, 25 percent will be improved, and 15 percent left alone.

■ Of the DSSs, 60 percent will be rebuilt in client/server environments, 15 percent will be moved to another computing platform, 25 percent will be improved, and 15 percent will be left alone.

Data evolution is often called for when the legacy system programming language, database, teleprocessing monitor, or computing platform is changed [Sneed 1991]. According to the survey, the chief motivations for data evolution are (1) the amount of resources the organization must utilize to keep the legacy systems operational and (2) the difficulties experienced by users when accessing data. Data evolution necessarily involves bringing data and application software under control of enterprise data banks. Conceptual steps in data evolution planning include

1. Identifying valuable data assets requiring less resources to support or better user access.

2. Mapping specific "as is" data items to standards in the organizational data bank.

3. Determining specific migration, conversion, and scrubbing requirements by evaluating the "as is" data assets against the definitions.

4. Developing and implementing evolution paths including conversion, logic, condensation, summarization, filtering and other considerations.

Extraction tools and enterprise data banks figure prominently in data evolution. Reverse engineering tools and techniques are used to migrate an application into a repository.

Careful understanding of these issues will enable one using enterprise integration planning, to determine the nature of the data evolution challenges facing the organization. The size and scope of data evolution challenges can be assessed against an ideal situation where systems were developed in the context of enterprise integration activities using carefully modeled data and processes. In these cases system migration is easily accomplished. In less ideal situations, specific organizational needs can be forecast and planned to coincide with DRE projects to maximize their effectiveness.

Data Exchange Support

Many already belong or will soon belong to some form of frequent-flyer/frequent-purchaser programs (FFPs). A decade of real-time inventory control experience has enabled supermarket chains to develop frequent-buyer programs to track *individual* purchasing habits! (Watch as these direct marketing concepts spread across the World Wide Web as well.) These capabilities will eventually enable retail organizations to finely tune their promotional expenditures. Consider how different (how direct) the process of marketing could become if market researchers could track individual reactions to promotions. Imagine receiving this e-mail message from your local grocer:

> We noticed you have been buying brand x bread. How would you like to try out a free sample of brand y? Our computer has already programmed a discount for your next regular Tuesday afternoon shopping visit.

How is all this going to be performed? In the grocery industry it can be handled completely with internal systems, matching the items customers purchase against promotional items [Pastore 1989, Marx et al. 1990]. However, the success of the MARS and resulting industry-wide embrace of the frequent-buyer concept has spawned many similar programs. For example, cigarette companies have smokers mileage programs. With increasing frequency, organizations are sharing information across organizational boundaries. This is the essence of *interorganizational information systems* (IIS): uses of information technology transcending organizational boundaries [Cash et al. 1992]. An IIS represents a successful coordination of information and information system resources between organizations. As the influence and scope of FFPs have increased so has the sophistication of IIS requirements. These in turn dictate increased requirements for sharing data across organizational boundaries.

An examination of interface characteristics often leads to the conclusion that common types of interfaces are brittle—or likely to break under changes in operating conditions (this definition of *brittleness* is from Gallant [1986]). Actually, a safer way to deal with brittle interfaces is to consider them *likely to break* if only one of the two cooperating systems changes anything. Changes to the interface timing, currency, frequency, accuracy, completeness, scope, etc. made without corresponding changes at the other end of the pipeline will often prevent the exchange of data and result in errors. And keep in mind, these interfaces cross organizational boundaries, requiring both organizations to cooperate to keep the system functioning.

The MARS component of the IIS performs all information exchange tasks between the cooperating systems. The interface components are responsible for managing the automated information transfer between the information systems belonging to the cooperating organizations. The situation characterized here grows more troublesome because requirements to interface with other systems result in adding more interfaces to the IIS. Yet the IIS is only as strong as its weakest link—in this case the MARS. Thus, adding additional (often) brittle interfaces to systems causes the overall IIS brittleness to increase. Addressing this key vulnerability in an otherwise successful cooperative venture is one reason why data architecture development has become a key component of organizational strategy.

One of the requirements for successful exchange of information among World-Wide Airlines' IS and the business partners is the development of at least seven interfaces. Figure 13.1 shows the high-level data requirements for each of the seven interfaces among the five different organizations (bank card, hotel chain, airline, rental car, long distance) to produce periodic statements; that is, the figure summarizes what information must be exchanged between organizations to enable the production of the statement. There is actually only a small amount of data involved. For example, interface 2 could function effectively, sending a list containing the bank-card identification and amount of charges as shown in Fig. 13.2 (this was originally presented as Fig. 1.3). In addition, presumably the MARS currently maintains a list of FFP participants that is sent to the long-distance billing system so the long-distance company provider knows which account information to send across the interface. Value is added by the exchange occurring at all where it was previously infeasible. Consider how the information processing would have to change if the airline persuaded the long-distance company to send all account information over the interface. The MARS would require a filtering function added to separate the program participants from the remainder of the long-distance customers. (However, consider the value

Interface name	Satisfies requirement
1 Long-distance → bank card	Charges bank-card account for amount of monthly long-distance bill. (I prefer to have my monthly long-distance charges debited automatically to my credit-card bill each month: (1) I delay paying the bill until the bank card bill is due, and (2) I get additional FF miles as the long-distance bill is added to my bank-card tally each month.)
2 Long-distance → airline mileage	Copies monthly long-distance bill total to FF account. Shows up as additional miles. (My airline FF program "rewards" me with 5 FF miles for each dollar spent on long-distance monthly.)
3 Long-distance → hotel chain	Copies hotel long-distance information to hotel chain-affiliated default long-distance supplier for billing purposes.
4 Hotel chain → airline mileage	Supplies airline mileage accounting system with "reward" amount data. (Some hotel chains will "reward" a stay at their establishment with a number of FF miles.)
5 Rental car → airline mileage	Supplies airline mileage system with "reward" amount data. (Some operations will "reward" a rental with a number of FF miles.)
6 Rental car → bank card	Charges bank-card account for amount of rental card mileage from multiple rental organizations.
7 Bank card → airline mileage	Reports total amount of credit-card purchases each month to airline mileage accounting system. (I am "rewarded" with one FF mile for each dollar spent with the credit card.)

Figure 13.1 MARS interface requirements.

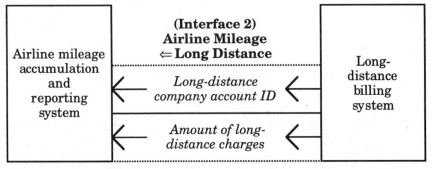

Figure 13.2 Close up view of interface 2—long-distance billing system sends data to the airline mileage reporting system.

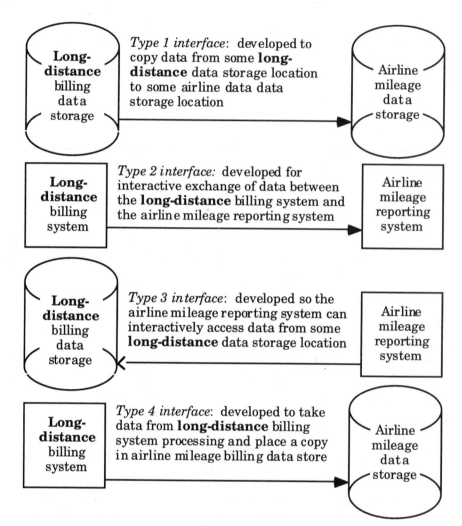

Figure 13.3 Four generic types of interorganizational information system interfaces.

to World-Wide of obtaining the complete list of customers—imagine having the ability to invite those customers spending more than $500/month in long-distance charges to participate in the FFP and increase World-Wide's business.)

Automation is the key to making this process economically feasible. Unfortunately, successful exchange of a small amount of data does not avoid the problem of interface brittleness. The problem is that the MARS is in such poor shape that this type of modification is unthinkable. If changes to either piece of information exchanged, the timing of the exchange, or the information content are not coordinated with the cooperating partner, the interface can fail. For example, consider one FFP feature: "rewarding" participants with 5 miles of travel for each dollar spent on long distance. If the long-distance company reports the gross amount of miles to be credited but now wants to report only the dollars spent, it must secure agreement from the cooperating airline. This situation can quickly turn into a mess if different FFPs with different reporting requirements force the long-distance companies to exchange data differently for each FFP interface developed. Lack of standardization can create expensively brittle operating conditions regardless of the amount of data exchanged.

To potentially further complicate the situation, note how each interface can be developed as one of at least four possible generic interface types that could be created for each of the seven interfaces (Fig. 13.3). Interface development can be a complicated and involved effort. For example, if interface type 2—the data in storage at the long-distance billing data store—is changed, then a change must be made to a functioning program across organizational boundaries. Sound a bit brittle? Value for this system is measured by meeting customer demand for accurate and timely accounting and available partnerships. Delivering this value while having to maintain the overall IIS functionality without the aid of a data architecture requires that each problem be individually addressed.

A major goal of the organizations participating in such interorganizational strategic alliances is to minimize program operation cost. The monthly production of these statements depends heavily on automation. The economic viability of the entire frequent-purchaser industry depends on successful automated functioning of all involved systems. If any one portion of the system breaks (i.e., long-distance reporting), complaints and queries are likely to be voiced by all program participants. The goal is zero complaints. Costs associated with handling any significant increase in the number of customer queries requiring human intervention could outweigh the benefits gained and quickly render these programs infeasible.

The successful coordination demonstrated by the smooth functioning of FFPs is an excellent milestone in assessing our position as an industry. We have come far enough down the road to enable us to obtain FF mileage from dollars we spend on long-distance telecommunications, rental car transactions, hotel stays, as well as virtually all of our other bank card transactions. These are occurrences I (for one) take for granted every day. On the other hand, this type of interorganizational information exchange is still sufficiently scarce and specialized to be classified as a business asset available only through participation in a strategic alliance among organizations.

The first FFPs were strategic attempts by organizations to give consumers an incentive to purchase their goods and services. However, consumers quickly made known that they expected this to be a standard feature for all competitors in certain industries. The popularity and persuasiveness of this type of information exchange will change the classification of a FFP from *strategic asset* to *basic commodity*, similar in character to automated billing. In the meantime, some organizations are clearly considering these intraorganizational information systems as strategic investments. The cost of not having a FFP has been loss of business.

The popularity of this type of service will lead to demand for more and more interorganizational data sharing. For example, customers will continue to ask their local governments why their airline can provide these types of services and yet the local utilities are sending out multiple bills each month—charging separately for gas and utilities.) The demand for this type of information sharing will place certain firms in the same position as the airlines. Compete on this level (i.e., enterprise integration), or you won't be able to remain in the competition.

Most information systems are so brittle because they were designed to support processes. According to Kerr [1991, p. 104], "Traditional, process-driven development tends to produce systems that tie data definition directly to program requirements. System modification therefore requires redefinition of databases as well as programs. This is not the case with systems developed with program/data independence in mind. The modular nature of architected data and process modeling logically separates data definition from program logic." The type 3 interface (presented previously) is an example of data definition tied to program requirements. In the type 3 interface example, the airline mileage reporting system reads data interactively from a long-distance billing data storage location. If MARS requirements change, so must the format of the data stored at the long-distance billing data storage location. In addition, any other programs reading or writing the data stored at the long-distance billing data storage location must be changed.

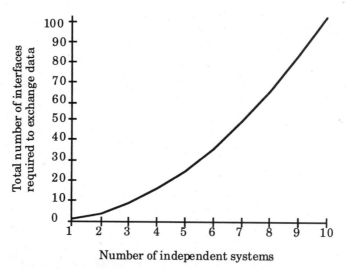

Number of independent systems

Figure 13.4   Cost of nonintegrated data (adapted from Durell *Data Administration: A practical guide to data management* © 1985 McGraw-Hill).

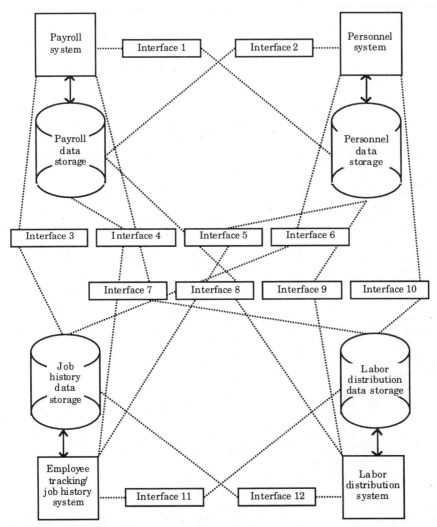

Figure 13.5 Gordian knot illustrating an organization constrained by brittle interfaces (adapted from Durell *Data Administration: A practical guide to data management* © 1985 McGraw-Hill).

A brief example from Durrell (also see Fig. 13.4) will demonstrate why so few organizations are currently able to develop information systems at a level of sophistication as high as that of the FFPs. Durell's often repeated example begins by describing how organizations seldom adopt long range information integration goals when developing their information systems.   Information sharing within the organization is then accomplished by building specific interfaces between existing systems. The result is demonstrated by his Gordian knot example (shown in Fig. 13.5).   It is easy to see how IS organizations quickly bog down with system maintenance responsibilities maintaining such brittle data structures. The growing new applications backlog is the result of 80 percent of information technology spending on maintenance activities. (In 1990, the average corporate application development backlog was 29 months [Software 1990, Deloitte & Touche 1994].)

Durell illustrates that the applications backlog results from piecemeal construction of four independent sets of data structures. The government pay and personnel scenario has become a complex web of complicated and redundant data stores. The system brittleness comes from the fact that it is extremely difficult to modify or expand any part of the system.

The efficient operation of the information system portrayed in the Gordian knot example is dependent on the smooth functioning of the system. But the system was not constructed to facilitate the sharing of information. Instead, the interfaces operate only on predetermined data characteristics. Change the data characteristics, and the brittle interface might break and have to be repaired. Or worse still, a change might have a ripple effect and force another system-interface combination to also break and require repair. The result is a tendency to modify the system only as much as is required to correct an error instead of configuring it to respond to changing competitive conditions. Quite simply, fewer changes to the system are attempted because of the possibility of breaking something.

Brittle information systems are quickly characterized by their users as unable to rapidly be configured to focus directly on attainment of objectives and therefore not useful except as information accumulators. The system's information is only used effectively when it precisely meets the needs of the decision makers. Systems characterized as unsupportive of organizational decision making become merely sources of information—similar to what comes in a regularly issued newspaper—our most valuable assets reduced to producing periodic reports instead of being used as a strategic organizational asset.

Effective sharing of data assets such as customer database information and promotional coordination among organizations requires smooth functioning of shared information systems resources to be cost effective. This level of performance will be surpassed by organizations operating in an environment designed for data sharing and exchange—organizations operating at the maturity level of Nolan's data processing growth stages.

Consider the data exchange challenge undertaken by Wal-Mart. The company processes 100,000 transactions each day from 5000 vendors [Wilson 1994]. To cite just two instances of data exchange, Wal-Mart and Wrangler (jeans) exchange 5 million characters of information each and every day [Haeckel and Nolan 1993] and GE Information Services maintains almost 13,000 electronic data interchange trading partners and this figure is growing at 40 percent annually [Stimart 1994]. Howe [1993] states:

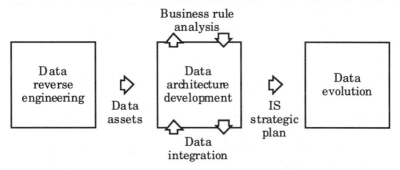

Figure 13.6 The relationship between data integration, business rules, data evolution, data reverse engineering, and data architecture development.

In most cases in the corporate world, this understanding is developed by one or more programmers when writing custom software to mediate the integration. This knowledge is rarely formalized and stored beyond the integration or conversion processes (that) the programmer develops.

Models are used capture this understanding. Without models, data exchanges are subject to the data problems described previously, while adding additional difficulties in correcting those problems through integration.

Data Integration

This section describes the contribution DRE has toward achieving the goal of integrated data. Figure 13.6 illustrates the relationships between data integration, business rules, data evolution, data reverse engineering, and data architecture development. Data integration, business rule analysis, and data evolution share two similarities:

1. They don't produce usable or useful results unless information reaches a critical mass.

---

integration n.

1. (a) The act or process of integrating; (b) The state of becoming integrated.

2. The bringing of people of different racial or ethnic groups into unrestricted and equal association, as in society or an organization; desegregation.

3. Psychology. The organization of the psychological or social traits and tendencies of a personality into a harmonious whole.

Synonym(s): noun—the act, process, or result of abolishing racial segregation. Desegregation.

Source: *American Heritage English Dictionary* © 1993 Houghton Mifflin Company

2. They deal with binary-true/false conditions: data is integrated or it isn't; data evolution is planned or unplanned; and business rule sets are validated or unvalidated.

Because models are defined by their relationships to each other, it generally isn't useful to talk about "almost" integrated data models. All three activities can help organizations identify DRE opportunities satisfying multiple information requests. In addition, all three processes depend on attaining a critical mass of understanding of the "as is" systems and the "to be" data architecture in order to produce useful information.

In a DRE output context, Howe [1993] defined the term *integration* as "the combination of information from multiple sources." Whether they are developed as DRE project outputs or in strategic planning sessions, various models will require integration in order to function as useful components of an organizational data architecture. Individual models, while better than none, are not fully exploitable until they are reconciled with models from other target systems. Until all terms are defined globally instead of locally, it is not possible to achieve shared data. Data integration is an area of cooperation between the functional community and the organizational data administration function. It is focused on unifying the models created by DRE projects and other data architecture development processes. Various types of data integration occur throughout data architecture development. Integration should be part of every DRE project.

There are three types of integration considerations:

1. Relationship to other modeling efforts.

2. Performing model integration along one of three dimensions.

3. Determining integration precedence or bias.

It is critical to gain an understanding of the relationships among models in order to integrate information among them. In the same manner that a specific DRE project is comprised of modeling cycles, each devoted to the development of a model component, so too, is a data architecture constructed partially of models. Two data integration activities are (1) resolving conflicts between the models and (2) specifying the relationships of separate models by formally associating their respective components.

Happily, the process of resolving model conflicts also provides indications of possible commonalty. The goal of data integration is the whole greater than the sum of its parts. The combinations of the two models being integrated should be greater than the two models that are not integrated. A typical taxonomy of organizational models is shown in Fig. 13.7. Data reverse engineering projects produce models that contribute to the development of the enterprise data architecture. At some point two models will have to be combined into a single model. Data integration is the process of establishing the relationships between previously unrelated models. Generally a required critical mass of information is obtained from the combined results of a series of DRE projects and some enterprise data architecture development. Integrating the models is the measure of progress toward organizational data maturity.

Integrating models

The primary reference on data-focused model integration is that of Batini et al. [1986] who describe the integration context along two axes.

■ *Interschema properties.* These involve comparing model components to determine whether they are describing the same business things. If they are, this provides a correspondence between the two models that didn't exist before. Consider the entity BED from the scenario 2 example presented in Chap. 12. Another model might contain the entity PATIENT.BED. Data integration attempts to determine whether the two describe the same formal entity defined across the organization.

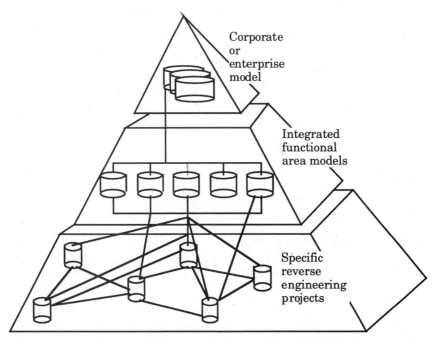

Figure 13.7   Three types of models maintained in support of corporate modeling efforts.

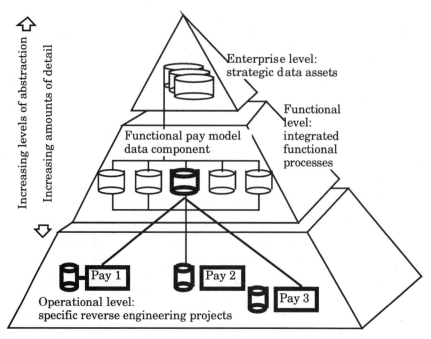

Figure 13.8 Enterprise model integration environment.

- *Intraschema properties.* These involve structural differences in the models used to represent similar concepts. Consider, for example, the differences in the structures developed to support information needs at different levels of the organization. Operational level users tend to require detailed information from specific systems while management requires trend analysis. Different data structures are required to maintain this data depending on their environment, perspective, assumptions, available tools, or abilities.

Data components have some structural characteristics that provide basic information about their relationships to other data components. Figure 13.8 illustrates one means of describing the relationships between data component types.

- The operational level corresponds to groups of models representing data assets of existing systems. The assets at this level are typically developed from DRE projects and other reengineering projects. There is a one-to-one correspondence between each data component and its real-life counterpart system component.

- The functional level represents integration required when operational data components cannot be mapped directly to strategic or enterprise-level models. Consider the case of an organization with three pay systems that aren't integrated. A functional level pay data component might be created to facilitate the integration. This situation is outlined in bold in Fig. 13.8.

- The strategic level, the top of Fig. 13.8, contains enterprise models. A one-to-many correspondence exists between the enterprise-level model and the functional components of level 2; that is, the single functional pay data component could be related to multiple individual data components.

All models can be characterized as strategic, functional, or operational in nature. Integration of models across these levels is one type of data integration challenge. Another is integration across functional boundaries. Pay systems often interface with personnel and accounting systems. Integration of data components from different organizational functions is often required to complete the enterprise model. Planning for data integration involves planning and organizing data architecture development to complement DRE projects and vice versa. The requirements for a strategic perspective should be obvious.

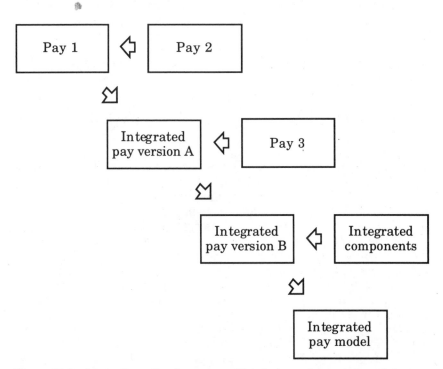

Figure 13.9   Integration option 1: one way of developing an integrated pay data component.

Priority sequencing

Consider a situation possible under the governmental pay and personnel scenario (Chap. 1, scenario 3), where three models representing the existing pay systems will be integrated to produce a single "as is" functional area pay model. When integrating separate but related models, organizational priorities can be used to provide appropriate bias and most conflicts can be easily solved. In instances requiring resolution, one key to successful data integration is to determine an order of precedence. Ordering the integration is often easily accomplished in a pair-wise fashion (what Batini et al. [1986] call "binary laddering"). This approach involves comparing the models requiring integration, two at a time. Figure 13.9 illustrates one way of developing an integrated functional pay data component by applying data component integration precedence.

First, perhaps because of more comprehensive functionality, "Pay 1" could be designated as having precedence over pay system 2. Thus, "Pay 2" would be integrated with "Pay 1" producing an interim integrated component designated "INTEGRATED PAY VERSION A." Next, "Pay 3" would be integrated into "INTEGRATED PAY VERSION A" again producing an interim version called "INTEGRATED PAY VERSION B." A final round of integration with other integrated components at the functional level would then result in the desired integrated pay component. By comparing only two models at once, this approach simplifies any conflict resolution by reducing the number of parties involved at any point in the integration process and by indicating a clear order of precedence for the integration to proceed. Precedence does not indicate dominance however, and care should be taken to not blindly permit one model to dominate another at the expense of model and/or data quality.

Conversely, Fig. 13.10 illustrates an alternate method of data integration. In this example, the organization has produced a comprehensive functional-level "to be" integrated pay component specifying the requirements for future pay systems to be developed. In the example, estimates for converting each pay system that is not integrated can be developed with information resulting from the integration of the three pay system models with the integrated pay model. The conversion estimates can also be used to determine whether the organization should attempt to modify one of the three existing pay systems or develop or acquire a new one. In the case of selecting a new acquisition option, the models already produced can be used to develop the application software specifications and then verify the correctness of the application once it has been developed or purchased. For instance, to designate one of the existing systems to be enhanced (say "Pay 1"), the integration results will determine both the modification required to "Pay 1" to make it meet the "to be" requirements specified in the integrated pay component and the data evolution considerations required to evolve the data from "Pay 2" and "Pay 3" to the new target system.

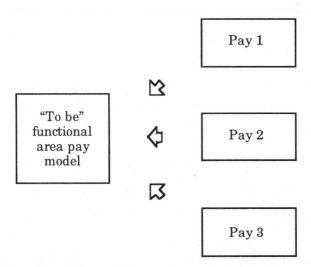

Figure 13.10   Integration scenario 2: selecting a new pay system.

Designating one data component as having precedence over another also has implications for data stewardship, that is, the designation of the responsibility for management of that portion of the organization's data assets. The steward ensures data quality and   currency. There are three types of stewardship roles: sole (controlling), joint (shared with one assigned superiority), and access-dependent (requiring access to data from associated   subject areas) [Richards 1994].   When combined with the three types of data ownership— private, shared, and common [Appleton 1983]—it is   possible to identify and categorize data across applications and organizations.

Data conflict

A dangerous misperception is that data integration can be achieved by matching and modifying data item labels.. It cannot. Integration implies meaning. The meaning of data items in application programs is coded in what Gane (as quoted by Pfrenzinger [1992]) says is 1 to 10 percent of the software and is rarely documented to desired levels. These are required to achieve data integration. Addressing just the data asset label does not permit understanding sufficient to achieve integration. There are several types of conflict described below.

To begin with, two primary types of data item naming conflicts exist:

- *Synonyms*—when a single concept is represented by two or more data items with different names (for example PAYROLL NUMBER and PR-ID)

■ *Homonyms*—when two different concepts are represented by data items with the same or similar names (for example location, which means an "office" in system A, but a "division's city" in system B)

Consider for just a minute the following terms; do they describe homonyms or synonyms in the context of a specific system?

Married couple	Children	Parent
Person		Married

Second, one must consider the following types of data conflicts:

■ *Structural conflicts.* These occur where data items are represented at different levels of detail between the two systems. For example, one system might represent a concept as a "business thing" about which we can describe various characteristics. Another system might "demote" the business thing to a characteristic of another data item.

■ *Type/subtype conflicts.* In one system, all values are tracked as a single concept; in the other system, usually because of additional details, the values are tracked according to a categorization of that concept (for example when one system tracks information about employees and another tracks different information about part-time and temporary employees).

■ *Stored versus calculated conflicts.* Some systems store data that could otherwise be calculated leading to data currency problems (age or length of service are common examples).

Finally, other potential conflict problems needing study and resolution include [Smith et al. 1981]:

■ *Inconsistency conflicts.* Inconsistencies in data item values resulting from use of different measuring units..

■ *Referential integrity conflicts.* Differences in multiple copies of the same data stored in multiple locations throughout the system.

The process of data integration is concerned with identifying each of the potential conflicts, bringing each issue to the individual(s) responsible for resolving it, recording the resolution (to assist in the transformation which occurs later as the "as is" data items are evolved to the "to be" system), and making the appropriate changes to the relevant data items.

Data integration cycles

When faced with sizable integration tasks, project teams perform integration cycles in the same manner as modeling cycles. This can take additional weeks of dedicated project team effort to complete. Models created can be integrated as soon as the project team validates them. Especially in instances where the integration parameters and guidance are known, this can represent an excellent opportunity to introduce parallelism into the enterprise integration activities. Model integration sessions are a variation of the standard MR/V sessions aimed at combining different data components by establishing and documenting the nature of the relationships between their respective models. The data engineers plan and hold one or more data integration sessions. End users are presented with data components that may be suitable candidates for integration. As a whole, the performance team identifies areas of commonalty between the models, performs the integration, and validates the results.

Data integration example using the government pay and personnel scenario

The decision of what to pay a person is represented in *personnel* policy encoded in the personnel   system, and the decision of how to pay a person is represented in pay policy encoded in the *pay* function.

Like puzzle pieces with straight edges, system interfaces are generally good places to begin integration efforts because there are usually two sources of evidence: the sending system and the receiving system. In addition, the cross functional nature of interfaces make it more likely that some of the documentation is maintained. If documentation is located, it often provides immediate candidate data item definitions and possibly some purpose statements. Analysis of data items shared across the interface leads, in turn, to identification of related data items, supporting the creation of the interface data items. This is shown in Fig. 13.11 where the interface data items provide information about the structure connecting the two systems.

The goal of this example is to reconstitute the data assets of the "Pay and personnel interface." At the interface there are three categories of data assets:

1. *Shared data items*. Data items shared between the two systems would include such items as employee identification and the associated pay grade.

2. *Directly supporting data items*. Data items supporting creation and use of the shared data items would include such items as time and attendance data.

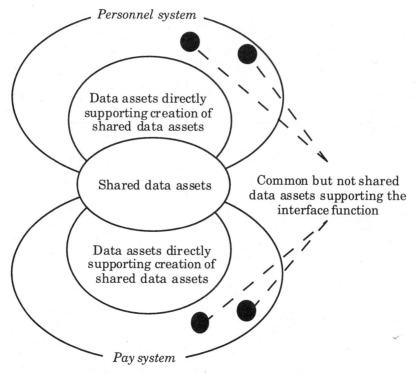

Figure 13.11   Scope of interface analysis.

3. *Common data items.* Data items common to both systems supporting the interface but not shared would include items such as salary limitations.

Analysis of the assets shared across the interface represents partially identified, shareable data that is able to be derived from the evidence. The analysis also identifies how the interface data elements were generated and used among systems and any other shareable noninterface data items. The existing interface data elements defined for transferring data instances do not represent completely identified, shareable data structure and semantic requirements among systems. In order to obtain a complete picture of the data sharing requirements, reverse engineering analysis must not only determine what data items .are shared among systems but also identify the sources and uses of the data items. The next three subsections present three examples of information learned about two systems as a result of interface analysis of the governmental pay and personnel scenario (presented in Chap. 1).

Example 13.1 presents an example where interface assets directly support the interface function. The personnel system sends a real Social Security account number (SSAN) if the employee has one job.

It sends a real SSAN and a pseudo-SSAN if the employee has two jobs. The pay system has to deal individually with every instance of multiple job appointments because of a lack of programmatic information coming from the personnel system. The fact that the personnel system uses a pseudo-SSAN indicates existence of another business rule that is currently incorrect. This second business rule is that every employee is uniquely identified by that employee's SSAN and that every employee can have one and only one job. This is illustrated in Fig. 13.12.

Example 13.2 presents an example where supporting data items .are exchanged between systems. An interesting discovery is the existence of an undocumented business rule requiring action claims to originate from personnel. This rule is derived from the fact that the pays claims subsystem uses some data shared across the interface. The pay system contains a data item used as input to the pay claims subsystem. This subsystem obtains the employee IDs and major claimant code from the personnel system. Only employee IDs generated by the personnel system are accepted by the claim subsystem. Figure 13.13 shows how, since the claim code is always transferred from the personnel system, no one could submit any sort of claim transaction using the pay system!

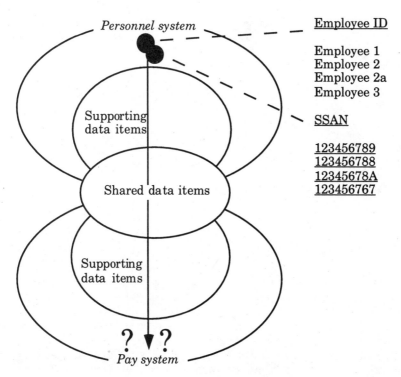

Figure 13.12 Example 13.1: interface assets directly supporting interface function.

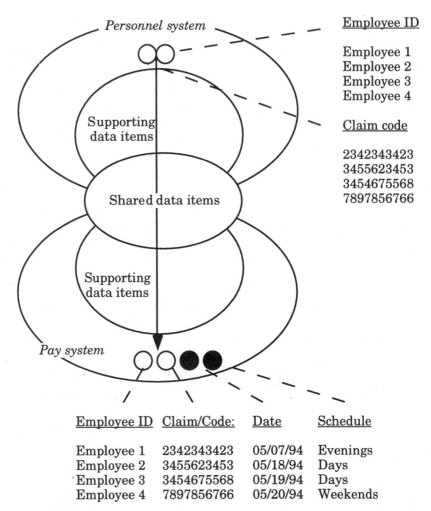

Figure 13.13   Example 13.2 : supporting data items are exchanged..

Example 13.3 (Fig. 13.14) presents an example where nonshared elements directly or indirectly support the interface. The personnel system maintains the employee actual geographic location on every individual record as shown in the figure. Data maintained in that fashion forces any changes to be applied to each record. In this example the pay system maintains employee geographic location encoded in a table. When the software runs, it loads the most current version of the table. Changes to geographic location are easier to make and control in the pay system. The fact that system A's riskier data is shared across the interface is significant. For that matter, no one really knows what happens inside system B. Perhaps the data was replaced? Who do you think knows? Certainly no one has iden-

tified this as an obvious point for single source of entry. And yet the
superior design of the table driven component of the pay system is
underutilized. Geographic location is stored in both systems but not
exchanged across the interface.

Integration analysis focused on data items exchanged across an
interface between systems will uncover these and other types of data
issues rapidly and lead to effective data conflict solutions as well as
effective model integration practices.

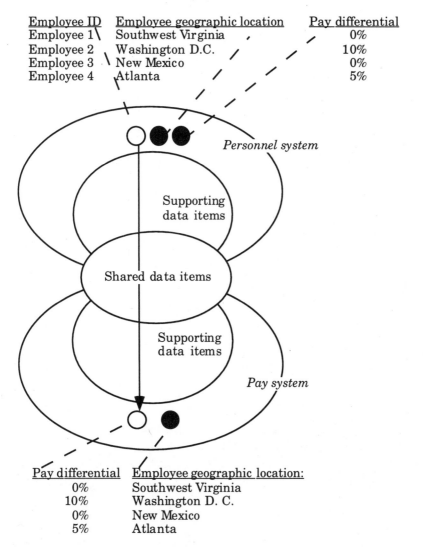

Employee ID	Employee geographic location	Pay differential
Employee 1	Southwest Virginia	0%
Employee 2	Washington D.C.	10%
Employee 3	New Mexico	0%
Employee 4	Atlanta	5%

Personnel system

Supporting
data items

Shared data items

Supporting
data items

Pay system

Pay differential	Employee geographic location:
0%	Southwest Virginia
10%	Washington D. C.
0%	New Mexico
5%	Atlanta

Figure 13.14   Example 13.3: nonshared elements directly or indirectly supporting
the interface.

14

Data Architecture Specifications

This chapter describes an approach to developing baseline architectural specifications for organizations desiring to improve their existing data architectures and data administration programs. Data architectures are concerned with the strategic coordination of individual efforts at achieving organizational goals using information technology. Evidence suggests that many organizations have not achieved desired levels of coordination and that they would benefit from an improved organizational data architecture. Organizations typically reengineer their existing architectures by first examining their existing assets, and then selectively rebuilding on the basis of that analysis. Under these conditions, reverse engineering analyses can effectively provide the information required to develop baseline data architecture specifications. Structured techniques are used to extract and validate data assets from the existing systems and organize them into architectural components. In addition, the approach can also provide useful information to other organizational strategic planning efforts. (For example, it can reveal areas not capable of meeting future information technology (IT)–based organizational objectives and thus requiring additional development work.) The second half of this chapter describes how previous organizational data administration experiences and existing data standardization efforts should influence the use of DRE in a data architecture development context.

In order to achieve synergistic performance, individual requirements engineering efforts are guided by an organizational data architecture. Data architectures are used to maintain information representing the organizational-level goals and functions of and constraints on the individual system development efforts.

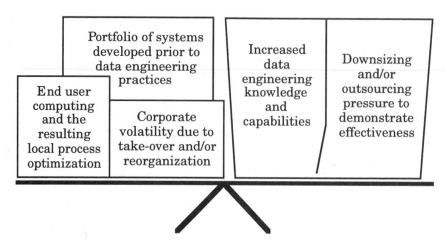

Figure 14.1 Organizational knowledge of architecture–based capabilities meeting implementation capabilities.

Figure 14.1 summarizes the combined demand for a corporate-wide requirements engineering capability and illustrates how increased information engineering knowledge and capabilities have combined with corporate downsizing and/or outsourcing pressures to result in the development of data architectures as a means of addressing the problems. Only recently have data engineering–based development capabilities become part of university curricula [Whitten et al. 1994], as has the introduction of the so-called upper CASE tools capable for maintaining and managing the complex data model required to implement these data architectures on a wide scale basis [GAO 1993]. The current trend toward corporate downsizing and outsourcing along with growing dissatisfaction with the evaluation, monitoring, and management of information system investments is putting pressure on developers to create systems capable of meeting organizational requirements [Brynjolfsson 1993].

Presented with the situation described above, is it any wonder that management has been reluctant to initiate data architecture development efforts? The same right sizing trend has also made it difficult to "sell" management on new development projects (such as the development of organizational data architectures). The key to developing an effective approach to is to demonstrate the fundamental soundness of the proposed approach.

From Legacy Systems to Architectural Components

Figure 14.2 illustrates an approach to reengineering organizational data architectures.

1. Analyze the accuracy, currency, and usefulness of the existing data architecture.

2. Survey the information contained in the legacy information systems.

3. Reverse engineer selected systems to obtain the desired data assets.

4. Where required, transform the data items into the desired data architecture components.

This approach can be repeated on a regular basis. Repetition enables the development of metrics, permitting qualification of the costs of developing the organizational data architecture components. Each step is described below.

Analyze the existing data architecture

Step 1 is to analyze the existing data architecture (see Fig. 14.3). The analysis should consider the accuracy, currency, and usefulness of the information contained in the architecture. The output is a pri-

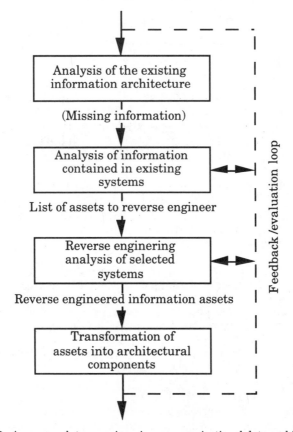

Figure 14.2 An approach to reengineering an organizational data architecture.

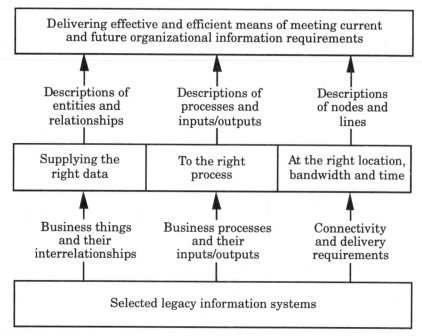

Figure 14.3 High-level components of a data architecture.

oritized list of data architecture deficiencies. While all organizations have data architectures, individual instances will fall along a continuum ranging from nonexistent to something in the range of data administration or maturity—stages 5 and 6 of Nolan's stages of data processing growth [Nolan 1979], with fewer occurring at the advanced stages of growth [Haeckel and Nolan 1993]. The remainder of this section presents a taxonomy of information constituting organizational data architectures. The taxonomy can be used as a standard for comparing and developing goals for existing data architectures.

There are six types of information represented in a data architecture. They occur in pairs with

- *Entities* and *relationships* describing the information about and interdependencies among things of concern to the organization

- *Processes* and *inputs/outputs* describing the value-added business functions in terms of respective inputs and outputs

- *Nodes* and *lines* describing the organizational operating nodes and connectivity and delivery requirements

Each of the 15 entries in the framework requires a different view of the respective descriptions of required data, functions, and communication. The complete taxonomy is described in Figs. 14.4 through

14.6. Each information category is analyzed with respect to accuracy, currency, and usefulness. Missing, inadequate, or otherwise deficient information is noted and passed to the next step.

Survey the legacy information system contents

The portfolio of organizational information systems is surveyed using the deficient architectural information as a shopping list. The survey is designed to identify systems where the missing information can be obtained. Often multiple information sources are noted. These are evaluated for analysis effectiveness with priority given to systems with more accurate or easy-to-obtain information. This survey can often be accomplished with a few conversations among system users. The output from this step is a list of system components from which the missing architectural information can be obtained.

Reverse engineer

Figure 14.7 illustrates the two remaining steps in the approach. First, the targeted system components are reverse engineered. Each individual reverse engineering project has the goal of improving one or more deficient information architectural components. Thus, separate architectural components can be combined into larger reverse engineering efforts while the focus of analysis can be at the system or system-component level. Successful projects will yield the IT–based assets.

Data view: What?		
Components	*Entities* are defined as:	*Relations* are defined as:
Ballpark	A list of classes of real-world things important to the organization	N/A
Owner	Descriptions of real-world entities	Business rules describing the interaction among real-world entities
Developer	Logical data–based descriptions of real-world entities	Business rules describing the interaction of logical entities
Builder	Physical implementation of characteristics of logical data entities such as segments or rows	Physical implementation of characteristics of logical data relationship such as pointers and keys
Maintainer	Definitional language describing entities in systems	Definitional language describing entity relationships in systems

Figure 14.4 Data column taxonomy.

Function view: How?		
Components	*Processes* are defined as:	*Inputs/Outputs* are defined as:
Ballpark	A list of classes of real-world organizational business processes	N/A
Owner	Descriptions of real-world organizational business processes	Descriptions of real-world organizational business resources
Developer	Descriptions of business application functionality	User views of business applications
Builder	Descriptions of computer–based functions supporting the business application	Descriptions of screen and other I/O devices supporting the business application
Maintainer	Programming language statements	Program sections dealing with I/O

Figure 14.5 Process column taxonomy.

Network view: Where?		
Components	*Nodes* are defined as:	*Lines* are defined as:
Ballpark	Business locations	N/A
Owner	Business units	Business relationships
Developer	IS functional support for processes	Connection characteristics
Builder	System hardware/software	Line specifications
Maintainer	Addresses	Protocols

Figure 14.6 Network column taxonomy.

Transform outputs for use as architectural components

At times the recovered assets will require additional transformations in order to become part of the existing data architecture. When required, these transformations can involve restructuring, rehosting, combining, dividing, or otherwise transforming the assets into forms suitable for integration with the data architecture. One particularly important function is a storage function where incomplete architectural components are placed on hold while waiting on the information required to complete the components. The output of this step is a new version of the organizational data architecture.

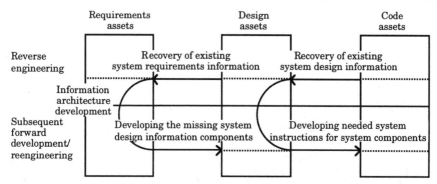

Figure 14.7 A reengineering–based approach to development of baseline organizational data architecture specifications (adapted from Chikofsky and Cross "Reverse Engineering and Design Recovery: A Taxonomy" © 1990 *IEEE Software*).

Significance and Use of Information Technology–Based Assets

The significance and use of data assets extracted from legacy information systems as they are transformed into data architecture components are shown in Fig. 14.8. There are three particular aspects of these IT–based assets: their characteristics, their sources and uses within the context of data architecture reengineering efforts, and their secondary uses beyond data architecture development.

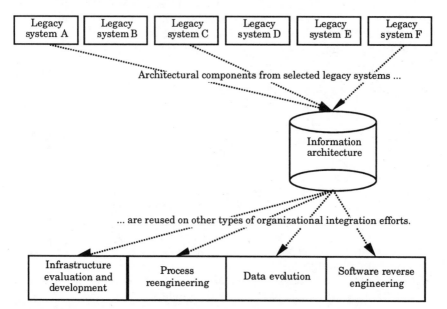

Figure 14.8 Multiple users of data assets developed as data architecture components.

Asset characteristics

Legacy information systems are the primary source of data architecture specifications because they contain the current, real-world implementation of the data that an information architect desires to populate the architecture. Much of the data required to populate the Zachman framework [1987] is contained in the legacy information systems. Assets from reverse engineering projects are typically represented as models derived from a particular information system. These models become the architectural components of the organizational data architecture.

The business rule would be contained in a model located at the coordinates ("Developer" row, "Data" column) of the framework. In a similar fashion, other types of information can be derived from the legacy systems and used in models. Once validated, the models, in turn, populate the data architecture. The data assets produced are quantifiable and verifiable because they reflect reality.

Developing the information base

Various types of specific data assets extracted as a result of DRE efforts are used in the development of data architectures as summarized in Fig. 14.9.

Other data asset uses

While the development of a data architecture has a primary direct benefit—reduction in data definition problems—an additional economic justification for the use of reverse engineering to populate organizational data architectures concerns the relatively high probability of reusing the information in another integration project at a future date. These information architectural development efforts become critically important during business reengineering and information engineering efforts. Much of the information required for either of these efforts stems from the same sources. (See Chap. 15 for a more complete description of the dependencies between enterprise integration phases and activities.) Stored in a CASE-based repository, various architectural components can be retrieved and used for other projects. Consider the following list.

- *Information system development information.* Reverse engineering analysis develops information architectural components that can be used to identify discrepancies between outmoded documentation and the present state of the system. In addition, it permits evaluation of the legacy system and associated business practices using an engineering discipline to determine system capabilities versus actual use. Actual uses of data architecture components occur in many places in the system development life cycle.

- *Improved system documentation.* Each system component that is reverse engineered will by definition move that system into the subset of systems maintained in a CASE-based repository environment. The analysis produces state-of-the-art documentation of aging systems and prepares them for the forward engineering activities. Often the reverse engineering analysis results in an integrated on-line functional description that surpasses existing system documentation in terms of accuracy and usefulness.

- *Reduced cost of achieving integrated shareable data.* The architectural components developed play a key role in controlling redundancy, fostering reuse and dependability, improving operational performance, and reducing costs.
  - Promotes data shareability and maintainability
  - Lowers the cost of data inventories by improving data quality
  - Enhances the shareability and maintainability of data, particularly in cases where data is shared across functional areas

View	Data: What?	Process: How?	Network: Where?
Ballpark	Should be detailed as products and/or services in the organizational mission and/or strategic plan	Should be detailed as value added in the organizational mission and/or strategic plan	Inventory of business locations and relationships traceable by lines of communication
Owner	Information required to support the organizational trade in products and/or services	Macroview of the basic business units described in terms of processing and resource utilization and production	Hierarchical arrangement of organizational components from the organizational chart
Developer	Derived from the physical models, in turn, derived from the builder or maintainer models	User perspectives of the system obtained from user manuals and other system documentation	Can be directly obtained from the system network architecture documentation
Builder	Analysis of the use of variables and storage accesses of actual code used to implement the system	Functional program and I/O descriptions obtained from program documentation	Accounting for the various system–based components by inventorying all system connections
Maintainer		Analysis of the transforms, processes, and program I/Os implemented in the system code	Examination of the network–based system code

Figure 14.9 Types of specific data assets extracted as a result of DRE efforts are used in the development of data architectures as summarized.

- Promotes integration of data models as a prerequisite to achieving large economies of scale associated with shareable data
- Accomplishes structuring and mapping of data, facilitating migration to other languages and platforms
- Improves data quality and accuracy by permitting data sharing across areas or applications using a single point of entry
- Enhances data shareability and maintainability across functional areas by reducing the "islands of automation" syndrome

Framework extensions

Since the Zachman framework was published [1979] it has been extended to also address the questions: Who, When, and Why [Sowa and Zachman 1992]. Since current CASE technology is only now reaching the level of maturity to be able to interrelate information about these three data architecture questions, these questions form the basis for the next area of investigation. Beyond that much remains to be accomplished. Perhaps most important is the development of metrics to establish a baseline for accurately assessing this type of technology–based investment. Other areas include the application of automated reverse engineering techniques, development of baseline productivity measurements, development of closer CASE repository-workgroup connections, and formulating indicators capable of revealing areas unable to meeting future IT–based organizational objectives—thus requiring additional development work.

Application of DRE to Organizational Data Architecture Component Development

The role of standards

IT–based processes and tools are developed as part of the attempt to understand the structure of nature (in general) and the local operating environment (in particular). A constant theme in IT development has been to increase individual abilities to manage the learning and information processes. From the development of the Gutenberg bible, to the personal workstation, the quest has been to develop more information using shareable formats. Once information is able to be shared, it is understandable by other users in different knowledge domains. Cross-domain knowledge sharing and resulting new information organization facilitates the development of new knowledge and thus becomes a major objective. *Data representation* is a generic process to formalize data for presentation in a data interchange electronic environment. The objective of data representation is to provide for data standardization.

Physical engineering depends increasingly upon standardization. Market globalization requires standardization. Our educational systems are geared toward imparting standards to students, and then students improving upon these standards or creating new standards. Communication, one of the major objectives of education, requires many technical and linguistic standards to be effective and meaningful. Communication technology requires standards and protocols for information interchange and interface management activities. Standardization of the technology and other components is required to make products reproducible in volume. A primary objective for data standardization is to facilitate interchange and use of data in response to organizational information requirements.

In spite of widespread use of standards–based structures, many organizations have not developed data standards–based data architectures as part of a coordinated data administration program. For these organizations, traditional data administration functions have not established a meaningful business case capable of justifying the required investment. To understand why, consider the factors presented in the following discussion.

Standardization of data within the contemporary IT community requires a registration process and a registrar, i.e., czar or umpire, for standards. Because data is a resource of significant value in business and government operations, the role of data administration is a constant requirement. One data administration function is to perform the role of data standards registrar, and encourage the use of standards. The cost of data administration must be measured and accounted for in business operations. Failing to account for or submerging data administration within an organization is a serious management oversight. When the standards development and/or adoption processes are efficient and the standards developed are effective, the cost for the data architecture development process can be low. To the extent feasible, automated tools can be used to aid the performance of verification, validation, edit, and audit tasks. Thus, data administration costs are lowest when standards are in use.

A good example of standards at work would be a business mailing house that is a vendor/contractor for mass mailings. The business uses a mix of U.S. government standards and standard business products to perform the repetitive process of mailing without having to invent, edit, and audit the standards and technology for mailing. The government standards for state codes, city names, ZIP codes, size of envelopes, stamps, package weights, etc. provide paper products vendors the standards and parameters required to interchange their products with the existing production systems. The vendor who complies with the government and business standards saves money by complying with standards. The mailing vendor who decides to reinvent all of these and create everything new must pay the costs of all that is new, and then pay the costs associated with the problems of interface, compatibility, and acceptance. The case for use of data standards should be equally clear. The way it works best is to have the data administration function identify the standards required for smooth organizational operation (dexterity) and provide conditionals encouraging use of the standards where appropriate—and simultaneously to the greatest extent possible.

Standards and data architecture development

The two major problems that have been associated with organizational data administration programs are:

1. The cost of staffing the effort at levels required to support the data administration have occasionally been high, especially if staff time is used to study, create, and implement a data architecture–based on local organizational standards. In the long run, the cost of data administration can be significantly lowered by appropriate use of standards. As an overhead task, or a cost of doing business, the role and staffing for data administration should be small. This can be encouraged and facilitated by adopting appropriate standards upon which to develop data architecture components.

2. Time delays have been encountered while obtaining standards committee concurrence or otherwise developing, analyzing, implementing, and maintaining local standards. Promulgation of local standards and their changes are often not prompt or far reaching. They can become particularly burdensome with high cost of publications and communication. The standards related delays can cause potential data administration customers to become disillusioned. If the struggle over concepts such as: the placement of man; or a product; or an object at the top; or the center; seems endless, then disillusioned users may develop their own local data standards subverting the organizational efforts in the process. To refer back to Ackoff's [1981] famous quote (cited originally in Chap. 4), slow moving discussions may seem to focus on improving the dancing, not the weather.

In addition, while data oriented development methodologies are predicated upon the fact that data items evolve at a slower rate than process methodologies, data does evolve. When the standards change, the cost of the change takes on different significance to different user classes.

- The users who can operate only with the change endorse the cost of change to standards as a one-time, low-cost bargain.

- The users of a standard who can profitably and efficiently operate for some period of time without adopting the update of the standards will view the cost of the change as a burden, and may withdraw from the standards community until their needs require adopting the new standard.

Developing a standards–based taxonomy is often a prerequisite to organizational standardization efforts. Unfortunately, too often the reverse occurs. A standard is imposed and then a taxonomy is developed and then the organization discovers what data it has. Under these circumstances, the taxonomy can suffer from too limited a vision of the relation of the business case to the rest of the business community, or the interest group market of the data. Perhaps more importantly, the user community can become disillusioned with the data administration capabilities.

Taxonomy definition is vital to creating the environment for the data standardization effort. Enterprise data engineering is used to relate the data of business process one to the data of business process two. Taxonomy and data architecture engineering are the starting point establishing logical relationships between data items. Taxonomies provide a structure in which the data architecture evolves.

The English language is the most flexible and expansive of the modern languages. The English speaking cultures accept new technology words and words from other languages quickly. The growth and change of the English language in industrialized countries confounds interchange of data as the growth and change varies between countries. The commonality of the English language has created international standards of communication. But automated data interchange has lagged because the terminology to describe the content has been confused.

Barriers to standardization

As the IS community describes the importance and the process of developing standards–based data architecture components, it reveals a few fundamental inconsistencies. The major problem in standardization relative to establishing data representation within a taxonomy is the definition of a noun. The English language definition of a noun is historically said to be the name of a person, place, or thing. Yet in other languages, and in the sciences, the noun can be extended to conditions of state of being, an intellectual subject, or a definable nonphysical object (object oriented). The terminology of language constructs is not yet standardized, but the desire is there to provide it. Data standardization processes suffer from the same problem of differing terms to define the process. There are two primary areas of disagreement within the data community. When attempting to carry on a dialog with a technical counterpart, agreement on use of these terms is prerequisite to exchanging information.

First, is a rather classic problem of attempting to apply the concept of a *data attribute* (see Fig. 14.10). Data attributes have different definitions because of the traceability required between the external, physical, and logical views of the data (traceability was described in Chap. 9). In some instances, attributes represent specific system implementation details used to create the data structures created by the data stores. A second use is that of the application programs accessing the stored data. A third use is as a component of the logical model linking the first two. Maintaining consistency and traceability among these levels has caused confusion about other structures built upon them (such as schema and subschema) and has been a barrier to communicating with others about the data architecture development process.

---

attribute n.

1. A quality or characteristic inherent in or ascribed to someone or something.
2. An object associated with and serving to identify a character, a personage, or an office: Lightning bolts are an attribute of Zeus.
3. Abbr. attrib. Grammar. A word or phrase syntactically subordinate to another word or phrase that it modifies; for example, my sister's and brown in my sister's brown dog.

Synonym(s):   noun—A distinctive element.   property, quality, character, feature, characteristic, mark, affection, trait, peculiarity, savor.

Figure 14.10 Definition of attribute (Source: *American Heritage English Dictionary* © 1993 Houghton Mifflin Company).

Second, use of the term *domain* is similarly applied to multiple concepts. *Domain* is used by some data standardization processes as the label for data item value options, e.g., the domain for the data item "color" could be red, green, blue, etc. In another popular and often simultaneous usage, *domain* is used to represent a sphere of activity, study, or interest. Using a term with such powerful taxonomic uses for such a low-level label for optional value further confuses the standardization dialog.

---

domain n.

2. A sphere of activity, concern, or function; a field: the domain of history. See Synonyms at field.

Synonym(s):   noun—A sphere of activity, study, or interest.   world, area, field, department, subject, territory, province, orbit, realm, arena, terrain.

Figure 14.11 Definition of domain (Source: *American Heritage English Dictionary* © 1993 Houghton Mifflin Company).

Mathematicians, scientists, and engineers have led the way on standards for measurement through the ages. The IS profession has not caught up with them to implement standards of data item descriptions, and is far behind in standards for data interchange of simple values. Metric measures can be sent for volumes and sizes, but try and come up with a standard for sequence in a data profile. Scientists can measure and communicate about distances of the

planets, but try and relate their studies by date.   Is it
month/day/year, or day/month/year, or year/month/day.   And is the
domain for month numeric or alphabetic?

Regardless of cause, business tolerance for delays in the IT and
date element standards process is short and delay can be costly, especially in terms of organizational perception.   The situation can de-
generate further if the authority of the data administration function
is constantly challenged.   In these situations, the user community
can fragment into groups wanting changes.   The focus can shift away
from effective and efficient information management and to typical
organizational power struggles.

Guidelines for the influence of standards

The costs and problems associated with adhering to data administration efforts can cause organizations to look to DRE as an alternate and more effective means of mapping existing data items to useful standards as part of data architectural components and making
steps toward enterprise integration.   Figure 14.12 illustrates how
previous organizational data administration experiences and existing
data standardization efforts should influence the use of DRE in a
data architecture development context.

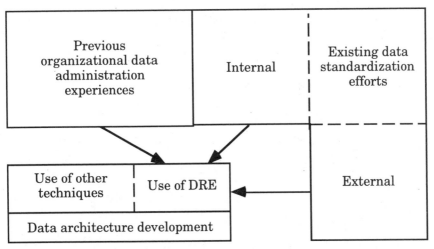

Figure 14.12 Experience and factors combining to influence organizational
application of DRE.

Over time, repeated use of certain data in production situations
constitutes *de facto* standards.   In some instances, standards will be
the primary focus of the organizational data administration effort
with little or no formal data architecture development ever required.
These situations focus DRE activities on identifying (really mapping)
existing internal data items to standards existing in the real world

and used by our business partners. In situations where the data administration organization has become bogged down, DRE is an appropriate vehicle for reinvigorating the program. In addition, organizations will occasionally find themselves in positions to promulgate their internally developed standards to the remainder of the community. In these circumstances, DRE can be used to help develop and implement standards and plans, and prepare documentation (in the form of an electronic data bank) to be made available to the remainder of the community.

What scope, or volume, or range of data standards is needed for a good beginning? What is the end objective of creating data standards? The answer to both of these is a limited number—an upward limit objective of numbers of data to generate is related to the objective—a few thousands, not tens of thousands [McCarthy 1995]. (Recall Appleton's leveraging example presented in Chap. 3—proper management of a relatively few data items can enable an organization to manage proportionately greater amounts of information.) So pick a limited subset of all of your data. Apply 80/20 Pareto analysis, attempting to identify 20 percent of your data needs that account for 80 percent usage, and focus on these initially. I found the following quote written about a large, ill-fated government data administration effort: "Only a government project run by a mad-person can generate tens of thousands of data items, as only the government can throw a lot of money at such an endeavor."

15

Enterprise Integration Information

This chapter defines enterprise integration in terms of achieving levels of organizational dexterity. Achieving desired dexterity depends on enterprise integration. One means of achieving enterprise integration is presented as 12 activities organized into 4 phases. Once the relationships and dependencies among the activities and phases are understood, organizations can begin to take the steps required to effect enterprise integration.

Phase-Activity Dependencies in Enterprise Integration

Understanding organizational dexterity as the goal, and development of an organizational data architecture to manage organizational data assets as the primary tool, the question becomes: How do enterprises achieve integration? This chapter presents one way of describing the activities involved in achieving enterprise integration.

A general enterprise integration procedure follows the form:

1. *What do you currently have?* Evaluate existing conditions by modeling "in place" assets supporting the achievement of enterprise integration objectives.

2. *What would you like to have?* Determine the specific enterprise information needs required to support business processes developed to achieve enterprise objectives.

3. *What do you need to get there?* Identify the gaps between the present condition and the desired condition.

4. *How do you get there?* Develop solutions to close the gaps.

Legacy systems: developed without enterprise data bank

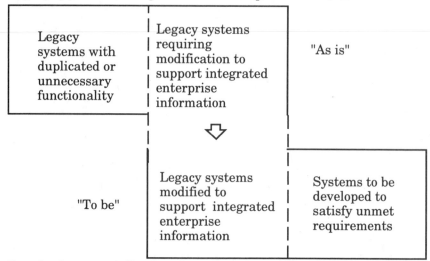

Required systems: developed in a enterprise data bank environment

Figure 15.1 The mathematics of integrated enterprise information.

(*Note*: These are similar to but more generalized than the inventory-analysis, positioning, and transforming postulated by Ulrich [1994].)

The gaps can be described according to Fig. 15.1, which shows the set of legacy systems consisting of existing systems with duplicated or unnecessary functionality and those applications meeting future requirements. The "to be" system required will consist of systems reengineered to meet new, usually organization-wide requirements and those to be derived from existing systems. Consider the situation when viewed from an information system management perspective. Coincidentally, assets in systems requiring reengineering can also be examined for providing opportunities to achieve savings due to software asset reuse [Yourdon 1994].

Figure 15.2 shows the four perspectives following this form: data, process, software, and infrastructure. The questions associated with each block on the figure indicate the enterprise integration goals viewed from that particular perspective. Typically reengineering each perspective (data, software, processes, and infrastructure) is required to achieve the desired organizational dexterity. Thus, each enterprise integration activity contains some "as is" analysis (reverse engineering), then some "to be" analysis (architecture development), and finally, some development using modern repository technology-based redevelopment (implementation). These same concepts are presented in Fig. 15.3, this time indicating the corresponding analysis technique used to answer the questions listed in Fig. 15.2.

The four basic enterprise integration reengineering "flavors" include the following:

	Data	Process	Software	Infrastructure
"As is" analysis (establish baseline)	What data assets do we currently have?	What processes are we currently supporting?	What software applications are we currently supporting	What is our technological infrastructure base?
"To be" analysis (radical change)	What data assets should we be maintaining?	What processes should be supported?	How should our software assets be employed?	What technological infrastructure will be required in the future?
Continuous implementation activities	How will we get from our current to our desired state?	How are we going to implement the new processes?	Transforming our software assets to the desired states?	How are we going to implement the required infrastructure?

Figure 15.2 Enterprise integration perspectives.

	Reengineering the:			
	Data	Processes	Software	Infrastructure
Reverse engineering activities	DRE		Software reverse engineering	Infrastructure evaluation
Architecture engineering activities	Data architecture engineering	Business process reengineering	Software architecture engineering	Infrastructure development/customization
Forward engineering activities	Data evolution		Application software development	Infrastructure modernization

Figure 15.3 Enterprise integration analysis tools and techniques.

Phase name	Phase description	Associated activities
1. *Baseline development*	Establishing an information base for further study and evaluation	■ Data reverse engineering ■ Infrastructure evaluation ■ "As is" process reverse engineering
2. *Architecture planning*	Creation of plans guiding the subsequent development activities	■ "To be" process engineering ■ Data architecture engineering ■ Infrastructure development ■ Software architecture development
3. *Architecture implementation*	Organizations creating working products based on the reengineered organizational architecture products	■ Infrastructure customization ■ Data evolution ■ Software reverse engineering
4. *Architecture population*	Create products capable of taking advantage of the features of the newly developed architecture	■ Infrastructure modernization ■ Application software development

Figure 15.4 A four-phase approach to enterprise integration.

■ *Data reengineering.* Must take place as the existing data are inventoried, structured into an architecture, and evolved into more flexible and process-independent support for business processes.

■ *Business process reengineering.* Inventories current supported business processes, corrects locally optimized processes, and focuses them on organization objectives.

■ *Software reengineering.* Selected software applications must be reengineered. Some to obtain targeted software assets, some to obtain design assets for reuse, and some for both reasons.

■ *Infrastructure reengineering.* The technological infrastructure must be evaluated for future opportunities such as matching organizational needs with solutions facilitating organizational dexterity or solving problems such as removing barriers to interoperability.

Each of the four contains a three-activity implementation:

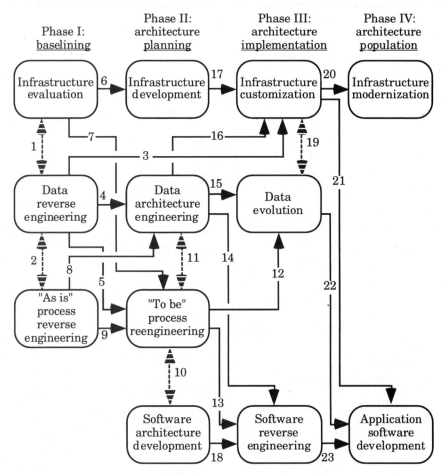

Figure 15.5 Enterprise integration phase/activity dependencies. (*Note:* Outputs 1 to 23 shown here and in Fig. 15.7 are described in the sections following this figure.)

- Reverse engineer existing assets from the existing base.

- Develop an architectural plan that will serve as a plan for future development activities.

- Implement and plan to keep it in synch with future system enhancements.

Enterprise integration can be divided into four phases as shown in Fig. 15.4.

Except in the case of organizations starting from scratch, enterprise integration must take place in organizations possessing legacy information systems. The question is how to begin integration with legacy systems in place. Ideally, we would like to integrate data, process, software, and infrastructure at the same time and achieve enterprise integration rapidly. Information products from some activities are required by others. These dependencies force specific phasing of enterprise integration activities. Figure 15.5 illustrates the discussion framework for the phase-activity dependencies in enterprise integration. Data flows are numbered for subsequent explanation.

Phase I: Baseline Development

Phase I of enterprise integration baseline development is establishing a basis for further study and evaluation. Organizational infrastructure issues, like all strategic-level issues, require careful evaluation of costs, benefits, and associated risks. Baselining activities are used to develop an information base permitting informed decision making on issues such as strategic direction of information system architectures, the business processes supported by the organization, and the current technological capabilities and limitations.

Data reverse engineering

Five specific DRE project outputs are useful to other enterprise integration activities.

1. Regular exchanges of information with any concurrent infrastructure evaluation activities. Many of these technology-based system characteristics are identified during a DRE analysis and are easily captured in the enterprise data bank for later use. The key is to track and store this type of information, making it available to any subsequent infrastructure evaluation activities.

2. Data assets exchanged with "as is" process reverse engineering efforts might include validated model decomposition hierarchies that can help guide or confirm the results of process reverse engineering activity. (See Chap. 7 for a description of validated model decomposition hierarchies and how they can be used to create representations of organizational processes, one of the goals of "as is" business process reverse engineering.)

3. System-related technology constraints and opportunities captured during DRE activities often provide a wealth of requirements information to subsequent infrastructure customization activities. Information such as transaction volume, data transfer content, and refresh rates is identified during DRE and stored in the enterprise data bank. These results typically come from a class of information collected during the system profile describing the system according to a number of specific technological criteria.

4. Validated data assets are developed with the presumption that they will be integrated with the corporate data architecture. An example might be the process of incorporating model components associated with a specific hospital into an overall model describing the functioning of the health care organization from the regional perspective. This model is in turn incorporated as a component of the enterprise model.

5. An inventory of existing data assets, containing the type and form of data currently maintained about the people, places, things, concepts, events, etc. of interest to the organization. The inventory can help "to be" process reengineering activities to evaluate alternative organizational process architecture configurations. For example, an existing database of competitor responses to organizational competitive moves might support a more aggressive pricing strategy of our organizational products and services.

Infrastructure evaluation

Infrastructure evaluation is process of detailing and assessing the organizational infrastructure assets including:

■ Database technologies

■ Network topology

■ Emerging technology

■ Processor technology

■ Operating systems and system software

■ Software development methods

■ Software development technology

These can also include such things as "smart" buildings, existing manufacturing expertise, or a customized data communications network. Many legacy systems include obsolete electronics, technology, and systems designs. Some systems are decades old and poorly documented. In addition, some systems are pushing the limits of their engineered capabilities, creating reliability and maintainability problems. Still more cannot be readily adapted to open architectures and current technologies.

Infrastructure evaluation often technically begins during DRE because so much information describing the infrastructure is actually recorded and verified as part of the PSS. This information can be used to form the basis of the infrastructure evaluation. One form of DRE product, a set of *technology-based recommendations*, takes note of major areas where application of technology could be used to gain either competitive advantage or production economies. Areas such as advanced database and communications network technologies are typical recommendations. Two types of outputs are useful in other enterprise integration activities.

6. Infrastructure evaluation produces information directly useful to subsequent infrastructure development and customization activities. For example, how large is the organizational dial-up user population and what are its present growth rate and capacity?

7. Infrastructure evaluation also can provide "to be" process reengineering efforts with information permitting better-informed evaluation of alternative courses of action. For example, it can answer questions such as "Can our current network handle a doubling of message traffic?"

"As is" process reverse engineering

The "as is" portion of business process reengineering is not quite as popular as the "to be" portion. Often, it is more interesting to ponder what should be than what is. Nevertheless, it is often quite useful to examine the organizational processes as they currently exist [Davenport and Short 1990]. "As is" process reverse engineering can produce two outputs useful to subsequent enterprise integration activities.

8. Information describing and validating some data assets produced by DRE activities. The ability to trace data assets between the existing processes and aspects of the organizational data architecture facilitates the ability to implement architectural changes. Consider the value of information linking data model components to data architecture components, which are linked further to specific screen and report elements, linked still further to policies and procedures. Changes to one can be evaluated on other model components.

9. The process of establishing baseline business processes provides an indication of any gap to be addressed after the "to be" processes have been decided. Identification of gaps is a necessary prerequisite to taking steps to close them.

Phase I milestones

A strategic milestone in phase I activities will have been accomplished when DRE projects produce validated business decompositions useful to a "to be" process reengineering effort. These milestones can be used to assess the effectiveness of enterprise integration efforts. Architecturally based planning activities involve the development of plans guiding subsequent development activities.

Phase II: Architecture Planning

Phase II activities are dependent on information from phase I activities.

"To be" process engineering

While many process reengineering activities are designed to begin with "to be" process engineering activities, it is useful to obtain the three inputs from the phase I baselining activities:

■ The inventory of existing data assets (flow 5 on Fig. 15.5)

■ An objective and realistic evaluation of the existing organizational infrastructure (flow 7 on Fig. 15.5)

■ A model of the baseline business processes (flow 9 on Fig. 15.5)

"To be" business process reengineering is most effectively accomplished after DRE analysis has produced validated business process decompositions. While not a required input, these decompositions represent validated representations of logical groupings of processes and related data about which the organization is interested in maintaining information. If these products are not available, they must be derived and validated from the target system as the first part of "to be" business process reengineering. "To be" business process reengineering results in the definition of what the enterprise should do to add maximum value to its products and services.

It is significant that both DRE analysis and business reengineering support the fundamental need to identify the essence of an enterprise. This can be accomplished only by creating the enterprise model in a logical environment that is free from physical implementation details. Logical models are used to free the reengineering efforts from constraints such as "We have always done it that way." Consider the following brief example of the representation of a logical modeling concept.

Physical models might represent an item with an identifying label such as "Form Y (3-Part)." A parallel logical representation of the same object could be *purchase request*. Note the concept of purchase request might take several different forms, including electronic mail (E-mail), U.S. postal service mail (s-mail), voice mail (v-mail), terminal dialog, a phone call, and voice recognition. All of these are alternatives to the current implementation that might not have been considered if the object had remained labeled "Form Y (3-part)." "To be" process reengineering activities produce four outputs used by other enterprise integration activities:

10. Timely software architecture development activities include those developed to support reengineered processes.

11. Similarly, knowledge of reengineered processes should guide data architecture development activities.

12. Business process reengineering results will certainly need to be combined with the resulting data architecture to determine what data currently exists and what and how data needs to be transformed to achieve organization-wide data sharing.

13. Process reengineering outputs must provide the focus of software reverse engineering efforts. Processes of no interest can be excluded while those directly supporting the reengineered "to be" processes can provide information such as the relative future value of specific systems and possible software reuse and data sharing opportunities.

Data architecture engineering

Recall that Chap. 14 described data architecture engineering as the development of a data architecture that will, in turn, facilitate the development of shareable data.

14. Data architecture–based data assets are combined with the software architecture specifications. The resulting information can be used to assess the relative worth of each software system, identifying suitable candidates for subsequent software reverse engineering projects.

15. The data architecture provides strategic guidance for evolving data from its baseline state to the desired state, indicating the destination and format of the desired data. The architecture can be considered to be the plan for achieving the "to be" implementation of the organization's data assets.

16. Data architectures provide organizational requirements and guide infrastructure customization efforts. For example, converting telecommunication systems to open architectures could reduce the subsequent data migration efforts by an order of magnitude due to increased interoperability.

Infrastructure development

There are several strategic initiatives that organizations can take, such as planning the transition to open systems or increased levels of security that can be implemented separately from reengineering outputs. These infrastructure development activities depend on infrastructure evaluation but can be initiated independently of data architecture development, and refined with little effort if the architecture dictates subsequent changes.

17. Infrastructure development activities will set the boundaries and/or standards for subsequent infrastructure customization activities. For example, specifying use of ultrasecure communications channels may constrain the overall use of electronic communication.

Software architecture development

Software architecture development includes such dimensions as the degree of centralization versus decentralization, distribution, or parallelism in the software.

18. The software architecture development is a prerequisite to reverse engineering software programs because the reengineered business processes define the new organizational priorities. Applications not directly supporting the new process will probably not be important candidate software reverse engineering projects.

Phase II milestones

Phase II milestones have been reached when the first software reverse engineering project is identified largely from the information gained from DRE analysis and the enterprise integration project is influenced by "to be" process reengineering activities and the software architecture. From a strategic management perspective, significant enterprise integration milestones will have been reached when the products listed in Fig. 15.6 have been produced and embraced by the organization's strategic management.

Phase II product	Description
Technological infrastructure	Specifies technological hardware and software base and other considerations for future development
Data architecture	Describes the structure and content of the enterprise's data assets
"To be" reengineered processes	Specifies what the organization would do to add value to its products and services if freed from current operating constraints
Software architecture	Specifies subsequent system implementation requirements including language, platform, and other prerequisites

Figure 15.6 Phase II milestones.

Phase III: Architectural Implementation

Infrastructure customization

Infrastructure customization activities refer to those specific enhancements required to "tune" the organizational infrastructure to support the newly defined business processes. Two outputs of infrastructure customization are used in other enterprise integration activities.

19. The infrastructure customization activities include close coordination with any concurrent data evolution as it could result in architectural changes in the data location, storage media, currency, etc. For example; processing reengineering could indicate greater reliance on real-time data. This has obvious implications on the infrastructure requirements, especially in the database area.

20. Infrastructure customization also produces information required to guide subsequent infrastructure growth, evolution, and migration. Phase IV infrastructure modernization activities will include items such as upgrading manufacturing operations through just-in-time inventory control and developing transportation network capabilities.

21. Infrastructure customization also defines and describes constraints and requirements for subsequent application software development activities. For example, decisions such as implementing various layers of the telecommunications infrastructure in hardware or software will drive organizational software development priorities.

Data evolution

Data evolution deals with restructuring data in its physical condition while not loosing meaning and accuracy. In situations calling for consolidation of multiple systems, data must be evolved from the systems being shut down to new "locations" affiliated with other systems and sometimes to new formats. These activities can include data migration, data transformation, and data scrubbing.

22. Data evolution will produce guidelines and requirements for application software development and will also describe test data requirements to be used to verify the system functionality.

Software reverse engineering

As defined in Chap. 1, *software reverse engineering* is concerned with obtaining software assets from existing systems.

23. Software reverse engineering outputs can be thought of as a potential source of reusable software assets. These can be reengineered to produce new application software conforming to soft-

ware, data, and infrastructure architectures and supporting "to be" business processes.

Phase III milestones

Phase III milestones can be demonstrated successfully when

- The organization can provide a suitable infrastructure for hosting the new application software developed

- Data evolution plans indicated destinations

- You are reusing software assets from legacy systems in application software development activities

- The organization can provide formats for existing data in the new systems

Phase IV: Instantiation

Infrastructure modernization

The term *modernization* indicates that the organizational infrastructure must be constantly maintained and upgraded to keep it up to date. Modeling and simulation can help most capacity planning with projections of growth in demand and capacity.

Application software development

Application software development is most useful after all these prerequisites are complete. While it isn't always possible or desirable to cease system development activities, often certain projects can be postponed or coordinated so that they can benefit from enterprise integration activities.

Phase IV milestones

The four phases of enterprise integration presented in this chapter can also be used as organizational milestones, each representing progress towards enterprise integration goals. Figure 15.7 presents an enhanced version of Fig. 15.5 showing several strategic milestones useful for assessing progress toward enterprise integration. (Outputs and milestones were introduced in Chap. 12.)

Figure 15.8 contains another illustration of the activity dependencies. Consider, for example, the first sending enterprise integration activity: data reverse engineering. It sends enterprise integration output 1 to the receiving activity infrastructure evaluation. The process infrastructure evaluation can also send information back to the DRE activity, resulting in two-matrix entries showing possible two-way communication between the activities. Enterprise integration outputs 1, 2, 10, 11, and 19 are exchanged. This is indicated by the dashed arrows on Figs. 15.5 and 15.7. In addition, they show up twice on the matrix. All other enterprise outputs are shown only once.

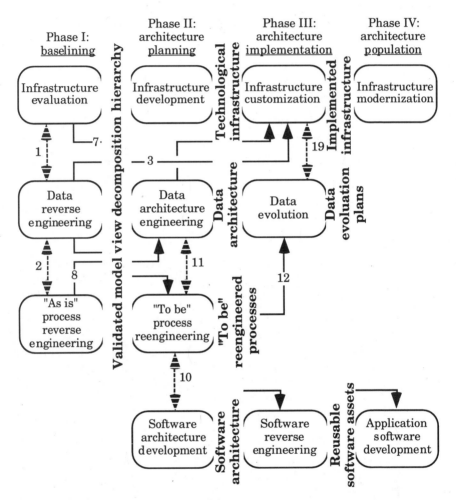

Figure 15.7 Enterprise integration milestones.

Sending process \ Receiving process	Data reverse engineering	Infrastructure evaluation	"As is" process reverse engineering	"To-be" process engineering	Data architecture engineering	Infrastructure development	Software architecture development	Infrastructure customization	Data evolution	Software reverse engineering	Infrastructure modernization	Application software development
Data reverse engineering	1	2	5	4			3					
Infrastructure evaluation	1		7		6							
"As is" process reverse engineering	2			9	8							
"To be" process rengineering					11		10		12	13		
Data architecture engineering					11			16	15			
Infrastructure development								17				
Software architecture development					10					18		
Infrastructure customization									19		20	21
Data evolution								19				22
Software reverse engineering												23
Infrastructure modernization												
Application software development												

Figure 15.8 Another view of enterprise integration activity dependencies.

Investments

investment n.

1. The act of investing.

2. An amount invested.

3. Property or another possession acquired for future financial return or benefit.

4. A commitment, as of time or support.

    Often used to modify another noun: investment analysis; investment dollars. To produce or manufacture (something) during a certain time.

Synonym(s): noun—something expended to obtain a benefit or desired result; cost, expense, expenditure, disbursement, outlay.

Source: *American Heritage English Dictionary* © 1993 Houghton Mifflin Company.

Data reverse engineering (DRE) can be justified in many cases on the basis of the improved system understanding and and/or improved system documentation resulting in decreased maintenance costs. However, the greatest synergy will be derived when DRE is performed as a coordinated investment in enterprise integration. The chapters in this part of the book describe several DRE considerations in this context. Accordingly:

Chapter	*Summary*
16	*Presents the process of estimating DRE projects as an important component in reengineering decisions.*
17	*Details a number of considerations organizations might adopt when evaluating DRE opportunities.*
18	*Examines the symbiosis existing between organizational CASE implementation and reengineering efforts.*

(continued)

Chapter	Summary
19	*Details metadata obtainable during DRE projects that can be used to develop client/server architectures.*
20	*Surveys the reengineering literature and presents pointers to additional information on reengineering trends and research.*
21	*Discusses the widely diverse results reported in the reengineering community and presents what is known and what is unknown about reengineering.*

16

Estimating DRE Projects

The cost of the reverse engineering projects can determine the ultimate viability of reengineering. Like all analysis problems, useful project estimates are best established after preliminary study of the project. As a result, it is necessary to invest a relatively small amount of resources in a preliminary system survey prior to attempting to develop project estimates. This chapter describes an approach to developing DRE project estimates based on project experience. When combined with the forward engineering estimate, it provides a system reengineering cost estimate.

Reengineering Decision Characteristics

The chapter begins by presenting reengineering decision situation characteristics. The following subsections present information useful for identifying key characteristics of potential projects that will inform the investment decision. Sneed [1991b] has described three types of situations in which reengineering should be considered. Although not covering all possible instances where DRE should be considered, they describe the more common situations.

Situation A: system obsolescence

In situation A the existing system has become obsolete, and must be replaced. The reengineering economics are calculated as follows:

Reengineering benefits = [existing system value –
(reengineering costs × reengineering risks)] –
[expected new system value – (development
cost × development risk)]

In situation A decision makers have a choice of developing a new system with or without the benefits of information gained from DRE analysis. If the functionality provided by the system is unstable, undocumented, or unknown, DRE may be required to ensure the effectiveness of subsequent development efforts. The governmental pay and personnel scenario corresponds to this situation.

Situation B: technical problems

In situation B the existing system has severe technical problems but conditions are not forcing replacement of the system as in situation A. Instead the organization is motivated to investigate reengineering to attempt to reduce the costs associated with system operation. The reengineering economics are calculated as follows:

Reengineering benefits = [existing maintenance –
maintenance costs after reengineering] +
[existing system value –
(reengineering costs ×
reengineering risks)] –
[expected new system value –
(development cost × development risk)]

Under these circumstances system management has four options:

1. Replacing the system with a commercial off the shelf (COTS) software package

2. Redeveloping the system from scratch without reverse engineering components of the existing system

3. Reengineering the system

4. Continuing to pay the high cost of maintaining the existing system

DRE can play a role in all four options; it can be used to

1. Determine the requirements for the COTS package

2. Validate the requirements for a new system

3. Inform the reengineering effort

4. Reduce maintenance in situations where no immediate development is forecast

The MARS scenario corresponds to this situation.

Situation C: voluntary reengineering

In situation C there is no motivation to reengineer the system, but it might make economic sense if the cost of reengineering will result in savings in the maintenance costs. Assuming a 24-month payback period, the reengineering economics are calculated as follows:

Organizations addressing or pursuing:			
Maintenance problems	Data migration challenges	Inter-organizational information systems	Integrated enterprise information

————————————————————————————————▶

are taking increasingly proactive approaches to achieving
enterprise integration

Figure 16.1 Organizations likely to benefit from DRE projects. (*Note:* organizations to the right of the scale are increasingly likely to benefit from DRE as are organizations with multiple characteristics.)

Reengineering benefits = 2 × (annual projected savings from
  reengineering) –
  (reengineering costs × reengineering risks)

The health care scenario (Chap. 1, scenario 2) is an example of this situation C. Figure 16.1 lists organizations that probably would benefit from DRE projects:

■ Organizations with large maintenance problems

■ Organizations faced with data evolution challenges

■ Organizations participating in strategic data interchange via interorganizational information systems or electronic data interchange (EDI)

■ Organizations consciously attempting to achieve integrated enterprise information

Useful Estimates

The adjective *useful* is often paired with the noun *estimate* to imply that some estimates are useful and others are not. Analysis problems have posed dilemmas because organizational management often wants to know how much proposed reengineering projects will cost before approving them. Project estimates developed before sufficient system knowledge has been acquired are likely to be incorrect and thus are not useful. Project estimation involves a number of variables, including those in the following list (from Brooks [1975] and Sneed [1991b]):

– Availability of users
– Complexity of the system or product

– Content of documentation to be compiled
– Database

- Experience with system complexity
- Geographic dispersion of users
- Language
- Level of security to be incorporated
- Number of databases or files
- Number of functions
- Number of persons involved
- Number of queries to develop
- Number of reports or displays
- Personnel
- Personnel turnover
- Programming language

- Project management environment
- Project management structure
- Quality of user needs identification
- Stability of technological environment
- System scope and size
- Time constraints
- Type of processing
- Use of productivity tools
- User types and familiarity with the system

Combining these variables into useful estimates can be difficult. The next section presents an example from the governmental pay and personnel scenario.

Sample Project Estimate

An estimate for the government pay-personnel DRE project is shown in Fig. 16.2. Three components of this project estimate—resource commitments, personnel availability, and hardware/software—are described in the following sections. (*Please note*: For the sample project all data including the costs and the participation levels are illustrative, substitute specific organizational numbers where appropriate.)

Resource commitments

The sample project estimate is composed largely of the cost of obtaining key system personnel participation. A total of $162,000 is slated to cover the cost of human participation. Of this, more than $80,000 has been allocated to cover the key technical personnel participation costs. The number of weeks of required participation is obtained from the project participation diagram (shown later as Fig. 16.7). In Fig. 16.2, two junior data engineers are to receive training, resulting in slightly higher data engineering support requirements.

Personnel availability

Being able to account for key system personnel participation is important, but sometimes it can be difficult to secure their participation at all. (I have observed this situation when key system personnel have been unavailable to participate on a DRE project because they were more urgently needed on a forward development effort occurring simultaneously.) In this era of organizational downsizing it is important to identify and secure sufficient organizational resource commitments to support their participation, ensuring that the project is viable and has proper management endorsement [Van Kirk 1992, Delligatta 1992, and Ning 1990].

Technology related costs

Ten thousand dollars (also an illustrative cost) is allocated to cover the cost of an additional copy of a CASE tool for the data engineering trainee. Other potential technology related costs might include

- Videoconferencing, e-mail, long distance, or other expenses for "virtually" including distant participants

- Workstation, software acquisition, training, or maintenance expenses associated with the use of CASE technology

- Consultants or other project-specific expertise

Data Reverse Engineering Project Characteristics

As shown previously, four project-specific characteristics (system size, evidence condition, participation levels, and automation impact) are derived and assessed to determine project characteristics. Variations in metadata values describing the system size, condition of the evidence, participation levels of key personnel, and the net impact of automation combine in various ways to create individual project characteristics. Understanding these characteristics is key to developing useful project estimates. Although no component has total dominance over the others, individual component influences can be strong. For example, it is possible for the *participation* component to render a proposed project infeasible because of lack of key system personnel availability. The four project characteristics are described in more detail in the following sections.

Resource	Quantity	Weekly unit cost, U.S. $	Weeks required	Cost, U.S. $
CASE tool	1	10,000		10,000
Senior data engineer	1	2,000	18	36,000
Junior data engineer	2	1,500	14	42,000
Business analyst	1	2,000	14	28,000
Database manager	1	2,000	5	28,000
System analyst	1	2,000	5	28,000
Totals	6		56	172,000

Figure 16.2   Government pay-personnel DRE project estimate.

System size

The system size project characteristic provides gross measures of system scope and complexity by determining the relevant dimensions of the system to be reengineered. Figure 16.3 illustrates three dimensions succinctly describing the system physical implementation, user and technology base, and system procedural operational and technical complexity. Examples include

- A small compact system used by a small group of collocated users for a specific function such as a group decision support system.

- A small compact system used by thousands of users distributed around the world for a focused task such as an automatic teller machine (ATM) control program.

Component	Desired result	Characteristic range or dimension
System user base	An understanding of both the number and the type of system users.	The upper range of both key system technical and functional expertise indicates the potential worst-case scenario for system and project complexities. Large, diverse user populations imply complexity challenges, while a small technical support staff can imply difficulties obtaining access to technical expertise.
System technical complexity	An understanding of the system's technological implementation details, including the data structures, complexity of the system algorithms, operating system(s), or the programming language(s)	Complex technological implementations imply more difficult analysis. The system may be technically complex as typified by the on-line, instantaneous update nature of real-time monitoring systems, or it may be an unsophisticated batch transaction program periodically updating an indexed file. (Practitioners may find McCabe's work on complexity measurement useful in analyzing some situations [McCabe 1976].)
System operational complexity	An understanding of the system's host environment and implementation details.	System features such as lack of a macro-language, 24-hour daily availability requirements, or the fact that system communication must occur via magnetic tapes can further complicate the analysis if key information must be extracted from or using nonstandard features.

Figure 16.3 Components of the system size project characteristic.

Component	Desired result	Characteristic range or dimension
System installed base/ popularity	An understanding of the degree to which the operating environment obscurity and availability of knowledgeable technical support staff will impact the project.	Less "popular/standard" technological implementations imply a smaller degrees of tool and technical support (e.g., there are more COBOL based reverse engineering products and considerably fewer for EDISON. In a similar fashion there are numerous COBOL programmers and considerably fewer EDISON programmers.
Physical implementation	An understanding of the volume of evidence requiring analysis typically includes such items as pages of code, file-based data items, reports, screens, fields, data structures, schemas, and business rules.	The physical implementation can help or hinder, but having documentation regardless of its condition is preferable to not having it. The existence of 500,000 pages of system documentation in hard-copy format might be considered a barrier to effective analysis in some reverse engineering situations. The same 500,000 pages of documentation stored in ASCII on a CD-ROM would be considered more useful evidence. Still more useful would be the hypertext browsing capabilities added when documentation is maintained in a CASE tool environment (see Roth et al. [1994]).
Evidence existence	A checklist of all evidence categorized as existent available, and verified.	Existence of evidence is good news to the data engineers. Most useful to DRE analysis are schemas, file specifications, and other data-related evidence.
Evidence relevance	An assessment of the state of the system documentation as: *in sync* with the current state of the system or *not in sync* with the system state.	Evidence that is synchronized with the current system state is better, but it still must provide the desired information.

Figure 16.4 Components of the evidence condition project characteristic.

■ A large distributed interorganizational information system such as an airline mileage accounting and reporting system (MARS) used monthly by a few technicians to generate statements.

Evidence condition

The condition of the evidence is key to any investigation. What is desired is a measure of the expected contribution of the evidence to the overall project information. Information not obtainable from evidence must be obtained using key systems personnel in more resource-intensive model refinement-validation sessions (MR/V). Figure 16.4 describes the four components describing analysis of the existing evidence. System documentation can range from not useful to useful.

Where in between the two extremes does this system lie? Is it completely undocumented? Or has the organization been able to apply the resources required to keep key documentation synchronized with the system changes? Some evidence may exist only in the heads of key system personnel. Additional factors such as organizational technical knowledge, version control, and configuration management procedures must also be factored in. Each piece of desired evidence must eventually be categorized as available or not available. When its status is unknown, this assessment is best accomplished by first-hand examination, performing a series of comparisons with the existing system to verify correctness, and matching the system change history with the documentation changes. System volatility can also be a confounding analysis factor. In the sample project estimate, changes for these systems are implemented semiannually. If system updates were implemented monthly, the analysis—taking longer than a month to complete—would have to capture the state of the system at some point in time to establish a baseline analysis requiring an update to regain synchronization with the evolving system.

Participation levels

Key specialist participation can be the most important and costly aspect of DRE analysis. Failure to acquire key specialist participation at the minimum required levels has been a primary cause of DRE project failure. As shown in Fig. 16.5, the key specialist participation characteristic comprises subject area coverage, key system personnel availability, and management sponsorship. This project characteristic describes the specific participation levels required of specific individuals possessing expert system knowledge and who will play key roles in the reverse engineering analysis. It addressees issues such as

■ The desirability of transporting (virtually or physically) key system personnel who work in different parts of the world—are they available? (Travel funding should become part of the project estimate if appropriate.)

■ Multiple stakeholders can create conditions where it is important to consider all perspectives—have they all been identified?

■ Appropriate levels of participation by key system personnel including requisite management sponsorship. (*Note*: "Appropriate" means enough participation to ensure efficient and effective use of organizational resources.

As mentioned above, obtaining adequate key user participation levels is crucial to project success. However, levels of key system personnel participation can be increased only to a point—diminishing returns are experienced beyond this point.

Component	Desired result	Characteristic range or dimension
Subject area coverage	An understanding of the user expertise of relevant aspects of the system and its implementation	User understanding of systems can range from no understanding through sophisticated understanding (such as awareness of certain database insertion and deletion anomalies).
Key system personnel availability	An understanding of the likely availability of key system personnel required to achieve project objectives	Useful user participation ranges from full project team member to a guest subject area expert. Project estimates are based on and tied to the specified levels of participation of specific key system personnel.
Management sponsorship	An understanding of the nature and status of management support for the project	Useful management participation can range from sponsorship to champion. Perhaps the least desirable circumstances occurred when management didn't understand the project context.

Figure 16.5 Components of the participation-level project characteristic.

Automation impact

The last primary factor assesses the potential due to any available automation. The question is "To what degree will automation in the form of CASE technology or other tools contribute to the effectiveness and efficiency of the analyses?" The answer will range between:

- *No support.* No automated tools support the platform/language combination.

- *Fully supported.* The popularity of the system has created a market for the automated tool support that can be used to accomplish certain specific tasks.

Combining Data into Project Estimates

Figure 16.6 shows how information from the PSS can be combined to yield a description of individual project characteristics. These are then combined with historical organizational reverse engineering performance data to obtain the project estimate. To obtain a useful assessment of the project characteristics, follow this procedure:

1. Develop a baseline assessment of the evidence analysis requirements.

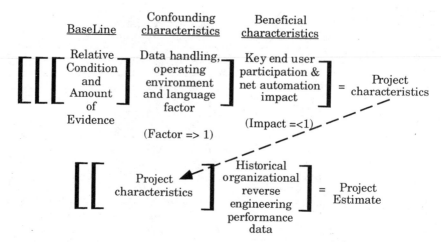

Figure 16.6 Developing project estimates from project characteristics.

2. Identify any negative characteristics which will tend to extend time or resources required to complete the project.

3. Factor in beneficial characteristics.

4. Apply productivity statistics in the form of historical organizational reverse engineering performance data.

Each step is described in the following subsections.

Step 1: develop a baseline evidence assessment

Combine the facts describing the amount of evidence and the facts describing its relative condition into a baseline DRE project assessment. This assessment describes the relative resources required to analyze the evidence on the basis of its quantity and quality. Analysis of the relative condition and amount of evidence consists of inventorying the number of system data items. Over a series of projects the organization will develop expertise making these metrics more useful. This results in evidence assessed on two conditions: synchronization and existence; that is, evidence can exist or not exist, and if it exists, it can be accurate or inaccurate. Many available statistics can be obtained from the system maintenance and personnel log files.

The second baseline component is an assessment of the availability, accessibility, and condition of the system documentation. The goal of this portion of the analysis is an assessment of the condition of the system data assets. This output is usually developed as a by-product of the system context model development. The assessment is best accomplished by examining the documentation first hand, performing a series of comparisons with the existing system to verify correctness, and following the change history with the documentation changes to get a feel for the system volatility.

To jump back into the development of the example project estimate, recall that it was $172,000 invested in a 19-week project. It involved $10,000 for additional CASE tool support and the participation of three data engineers and three personnel members involved with the system in some capacity. For the example, these individuals include (1) a business analyst, (2) the personnel system's database manager, and (3) a pay system analyst. For all these individuals, an hourly rate based on their cost to the organization (including overhead) is multiplied by the number of hours required to accomplish the DRE task. Hours required for project participation are obtained from a project participation diagram (see Fig. 16.7).

The hours required to complete individual project duties correspond to the amount of work required to complete the analysis. It is derived by summing the time required to analyze the various system components. The specific computations for the example project estimate are shown later in Fig. 16.9.

This task is a good place to practice some sensitivity because it involves assessing and reporting on the state of the system and the associated documentation. These tasks have sometimes been uncomfortable to professionals who might wish for the resources required to keep it up-to-date. Try to be a lot like a good detective; concentrate on the facts without judging. Future enthusiastic participation of these individuals on the performance team is likely to be a key determinant of project success.

| | | | Participation | | | | | |
| | | | Data engineers | | | Key technical participation | | |
Week	Date	Activity	Senior engr.	Jr. engr. 1	Jr. engr. 2	Business analyst	Database mgr.	System analyst
1	1/9	MR/V session 1 Planning						
2	1/16	MR/V session 1						
3	1/23	MR/V session 2 Planning						
4	1/30	MR/V session 2						
5	2/6	MR/V session 3 Planning						
6	2/13	MR/V session 3						
7	2/20	MR/V session 4 Planning						
8	2/27	MR/V session 4						
9	3/6	MR/V session 5 Planning						
10	3/13	MR/V session 5						
12	3/20	MR/V session Assessment						
13	3/27	Data asset packaging						
14	4/3	Data asset integration planning						
15	4/10	Data asset integration session						
16	4/17	Data asset integration assessment						
17	4/24	Data asset transfer						
18	5/1	Project metric collection						
19	5/8	Framework-methodology refinement						
		Total weeks required	18	13	14	5	5	5

Key = participation rate (Full, Half)

Figure 16.7 Project participation diagram.

Step 2:   Factor in negative characteristics

Any potential negative impact of system characteristics must be factored into the analysis requirements. For example, if the project goals require some analysis of the source code, the specific programming language requiring analysis can adversely impact the project. If applicable, a language factor is assigned according to the class of programming language. Again, the more popular or standard the programming language, the more likely it is that automated tools supporting DRE will be available.

The degree of platform-specific support for the DRE project can also negatively impact the analysis efficiency. An MVS operating-system specialist thrown at a Unix workstation can become technically challenged. Working with an unfamiliar operating system environment can adversely affect productivity. The relative familiarity and popularity of operating environment respectively affect the number of available experts and the general comprehensiveness of the reverse engineering tool support for the language. A data-handling system factor can be developed similarly according to the category of data-handling system. Similar to the programming language classification, the more obscure, obsolete, or otherwise nonstandard the data-handling system, the more difficult it has been to perform the required analysis. Factor in project characteristics capable of negatively impacting the analysis such as use of obscure programming languages, operating systems, and operating environments. The net result of this step will be to increase the baseline data by some factor greater than 1.

Step 3:   Factor in beneficial characteristics

The positive impacts of specific system characteristics must also be factored into the analysis requirements. This project characteristic has components along two dimensions: availability and coverage. Key system personnel availability levels are assigned according to the level of participation available. Participation requirements for each of the following categories must be defined, and the participation of individuals possessing the required knowledge must be secured:

- Effect on productivity due to database expert participation

- Effect on productivity due to functional participation

- Effect on productivity due to application program expert participation

- Net effect on productivity due to domain expert participation

Both the degree of key system personnel participation and the net impact of automation should contribute to reducing the combined baseline assessment and any negative characteristics. An indirect goal of the PSS is to, as much as possible, verify the anticipated participation level of the key system personnel. Similar to available key system personnel participation levels, automation can also positively affect DRE project estimates. The goal is to determine the potential technological leverage in light of likely project goals.

Step 4: Applying productivity statistics

Figure 16.8 illustrates the sample problem (based on an accurate project estimate). Once obtained, the project characteristics were transformed into an estimate by applying data describing previous organizational reverse engineering productivity. Thus the PSS provides a baseline estimate of the number of total data assets to be analyzed to produce the desired project outputs. The example PSS determined that there were a total of 120 file-based data items to be analyzed and added as components of the system model. Previous organizational experience indicated that an average of six file-based data items could be added to the system models each hour, requiring a total of 20 hours of analysis to incorporate the 120 file-based data items into the system model.

Preliminary system survey result	Available statistic	Hourly productivity estimate, $	Hours of analysis required
File-based data items	120	6	20.00
Report-based data items	142	10	14.20
Screen-based data items	84	8	10.50
Application schema data items	117	6	19.50
Relevant pages of documentation to review	90	6	15.08
Total hours required to analyze all data items	553	7.2	79.28
System development language	Assembly		+50.00
Net effect expert participation (database, functional application, and system analyst)			-50.00
Time required to refine and verify all data items as system model components	553	4	138.25
Number of MR/V sessions	138	28	4.94

Figure 16.8 Government pay and personnel example project estimate calculations.

ID	Name	Quarter 1						
		Nov	Dec	Jan	Feb	Mar	Apr	May
1	Project Implementation							
2	MR/V session 1 planning							
3	MR/V session 1							
4	MR/V session 2 planning							
5	MR/V session 2							
6	MR/V session 3 planning							
7	MR/V session 3							
8	MR/V session 4 planning							
9	MR/V session 4							
10	MR/V session 5 planning							
11	MR/V session 5							
12	MR/V session assessment							
13	Project wrapup activities							
14	Data asset packaging							
15	Data asset integration planning							
16	Data asset integration session							
17	Data asset integration assessment							
18	Data asset transfer							
19	Project metric collection							
20	Framework/methodology refinement							

Figure 16.9 Sample project schedule resulting from estimate.

The time required to construct a system model consisted of the 553 relevant data items, taking a total of 90 hours of the three participating data engineers. A possible complication is the additional analysis required by use of a relatively obscure programming language adding some additional hours onto the analysis. For the sample problem, the increase in project resources required to deal with the operating system environment is offset by the participation of the system personnel—in this case the programmers who originally coded it. The number of total data items provides an additional project measurement: the number of MR/V sessions required to complete the analysis. This is derived by dividing the total number of data items by the historical hourly rate required to refine and validate each data item as a model component during MR/V sessions. For the sample problem this figure is four per hour, indicating a total of 138 hours of MR/V session time required to complete the analysis. An average of 28 hours per week are scheduled in MR/V sessions indicating a total of five (4.94) sessions required to complete the analysis. The MR/V sessions are scheduled as shown in Fig. 16.9.

Considerations

Some of the project variables can come only from your organization. These include the productivity of the DRE specialists and the cost of key system personnel participation. Also, since the historical data won't exist in organizations that have not performed DRE projects, it will be difficult to estimate the first project. The numbers used in this chapter can be considered as representative of those associated with the reverse engineering of large mainframe-based information systems entering their second decade of service. The projects were conducted with information engineering-based CASE tool support [IESC 1994]. Use these numbers as estimates for your first project, and then compare them with your own results to evaluate their usefulness and accuracy and adjust accordingly.

One obvious extension of this work is to extend this initially proposed framework to include components from areas such as database and software reengineering to build a more comprehensive reverse engineering project estimation framework. In addition, the costs to properly reverse engineer systems and value of the reverse engineering products are consistently underestimated by management. A common misperception is that we just "run the code through a CASE tool, and the tool will produce new systems." It has been challenging to convince management that reverse engineering is a substantially broader and more complex task than merely "restructuring the code." Should the organization be in a position to, key system personnel can quickly be trained to perform some data engineering functions (i.e., entering project information directly into the project data bank). This form of support can be used to leverage the performance team efforts. It represents an opportunity to save considerable project time and also perform some technology transfer as the key system personnel discover how much easier it can be to maintain CASE-based system documentation.

17

Evaluating Investment Opportunities

Certain situations, particular times in the system and organizational life cycle, and other conditions have created DRE project opportunities. These conditions include data interchange requirements, process changes, chronic neglect, rapidly changing technology, or fortuitous project timing. Understanding the nature and characteristics of each candidate DRE project situation—such as a requirement that suitable CASE technology will provide project feasibility—indicates to decision makers that further investigation is warranted. This chapter describes the characteristics of these situations from the system management, developer, and functional user perspectives, providing readers with information to evaluate against their own situations and presents the cost assessment criteria using a series of matrices.

Outputs (Direct or Indirect) versus Product versus Service

Defining "outputs" from an information perspective has occasionally been difficult. The perception of output in the physical sense has had a tendency to obscure the intellectual reality of output in the information world. In the physical world, an output is something familiar to us like a car, a chair, a comb, a gadget, etc. Defining an output in the information realm has been more complex. Originally, outputs were thought to be reports, usually on paper. In the 1990s, automatic data processing (ADP) has grown into information technology (IT), and the very nature of output has dramatically changed.

Early ADP was primarily process focused, the output was a product of the process. To change the output, the computer programmer had to change the process. Programmer skills led the way to indirect output initially. Then, data structuring led to more types of indirect outputs with multiple direct outputs being also possible. Today data structure, definition, and manipulation tools have greatly expanded the potential concepts of output.

In the discussion of output there is a further search for a description of output as a product. Product definition is difficult because of a lack of a cohesive taxonomy linking management funded programs, at the top, to subprograms, containing subprograms, and projects, and user products, at the bottom, of a management pyramid. Organizations have long struggled to create taxonomies to resolve the internal communication management problem.

When management tasks the creation, and funding, of an automated information system (AIS) to provide a management information system (MIS), the search for defining the output and the product of the management tasking gets very interesting. Is the AIS a process-oriented automation system? If so, the MIS may be equivalent to the AIS? If the AIS is truly an information-oriented system that is modularly designed, then how many applications of it are documented as MISs? One AIS may have three applications with separate MIS names; e.g., Footwear AIS supporting the Shoestring MIS, the Leather MIS, and the Thread MIS. In this instance the question of output and product gets interesting depending upon who is the user of the AIS/MIS.

- The senior manager(s) providing the tasking to create for the organization an AIS, see themselves creating a funded program to create an AIS. In this way management sees the AIS as a product, e.g., like a truck that delivers many sizes of packages. The users of the AIS/MIS see the AIS/MIS as a tool that delivers products, e.g., the truck brings the store some products. The view of the item as a product is relative to an individual's relation, e.g., tasker, operator, or user, to the program, product, tool, output (whether it is direct or indirect).

- The user, e.g., citizen, who steps up to an ATM kiosk and gets back a piece of paper for a transaction is convinced the paper is the product and the output of the transaction.

- The AIS manager sees the user entering a data transaction into a system that he calls a software tool, and the paper the user walked away with is a product or an output that managers are tasked to provide to customers. The executive tasker of the AIS of the funded program sees the AIS as the product, and sees all activity performed via the product as a service to the community of users, and wants to impose a service charge on the user. The user may say that the piece of paper is too small for the service charge. The executive tasker says the user fails to see the importance of the service and the value of the information provided.

The discussion is important in many ways to understand the nature of dialog between system stakeholders. They are important relative to evaluating, and measuring, the activity so performance and success rate can be stated in simple economic terms. If the AIS is the product, and not the receipt or the report the customer gets, then the measure of the cost of the AIS versus the benefits can be stated.

The output considerations are very important as they relate to cost considerations. Analysts look at the output and then divide the items into the total cost and derive some indicator of value for the output and see if the output is justified by the cost. Hopefully the customer base supports the output and that will justify the cost. In a fee-for-service business environment this works well, but in a government or a business in-house situation, the fee-for-service computation may not exist to justify the cost of the output and the business process that generates output.

What is the product of an AIS/MIS or any Information System (IS), is it the output? In the more recent integrated data systems design where the product may be considered as the service that question becomes harder to answer. If this is the product then the output is either a report on paper or a service. Thus considering the AIS as the product that produces services simplifies the dialog on output, product, and service.

How does an AIS manager measure cost benefit return for IS when information exchange is the objective of the IS? The management answer is, you measure the service benefit and the number of titled reports or reams of paper. This is where the Indirect Output items of data migration, data conversion, and data scrubbing are performed by Data Administration. The results of this are where overhead cost makes or breaks the AIS and the business budget.

So, the computer with an IS, hence an AIS, becomes a utility, like an electric power plant. The generators are the computer and the electricity is information. The problem is the output of information is not as easily measured as electricity. In electricity we measure watts and amperes, and in communications we measure baud rates and bit patterns. What do we measure for IS output effectiveness? The customer dollar is prime if there is a fee-for-service situation. But what about the Executive Information System (EIS) computing selected values on a screen?

One measure of output value and cost benefit return is to look at the IS in relation to how the customers are served. The traditional process approach has the IS serving the MIS staff. The customer gets output from the MIS staff that interacts with the MIS. The MIS thus justifies the existence of the staff, and the staff pays for itself by exacting fees for reports from customers. In the case of government no-fee for service, the value is the satisfaction of citizens with questions to be answered.

Staff control of output is acceptable as it is so traditional, like the librarian who controls the release of books to citizens. Staff control of AIS and MIS is defensible in security and classified projects where the staff must evaluate the data before the release of the data. This situation is common in intelligence, banking, and personnel privacy data activity.

One consideration to measure the output value is to separate the staff elements that support the customer from the AIS staff if possible. Some AIS environments provide all services with a unified and integrated staff. The staff number distributions between performing indirect output and customer service is critical to understanding the cost benefit of the funded program, the program product, IS services, and the role of the staff.

The big question is, does the AIS operator charge the customer support staff to the IS product cost, or to customer support? In terms of Indirect Output the answer is to charge to customer support. But, in most accounting criteria such fine distinctions are lost, and all AIS component activity is lumped in with the AIS. This lack of a distinction balloons costs for AIS into very high numbers and understates the cost of providing information services.

Defining and measuring a service in the information realm is thus a major challenge to IT and IS activity. The definition of product in relation to management concepts of program and project will impact on how to measure the performance and quality of service compared to the cost of providing the service, especially when a lot of staff and the benefit of the service is related to overhead and management, and not the external customer. The definition of product also impacts on the understanding of the nature of the service provided. If service is the major product, then the overhead of indirect output is justified with the fee for service charge. Developing a taxonomy for defining products in relation to management programs is vital to understanding costs of AIS/MIS/IS on a corporate basis.

Output as a data administration function has a significant relation to indirect output as a critical element of providing a DRE service. Within a data engineering environment, and certainly within DRE, a prime example of indirect output (data exchange, data evolution, and data migration) is attaining an Inter-Component Data Transfer (ICDT), a generic functional data throughput as a cross-reference service (see Chap. 15). An ICDT is a primary service function of correlating, interfacing, and integrating multiple data elements, data profiles, and files. The objective of an ICDT may be to track movement/relocation of units/types of information between disparate data files, so that a history summary of movement or people or supplies may be logged. The ICDT may be a direct capability, but it is based on indirect functional processes. The ICDT may be a hidden data procedure for providing selected services to specified users.

Data Reverse Engineering Investment Considerations

Data reverse engineering projects should be considered as organizational investments. Securing advance commitment from management for the anticipated resource levels required to feasibly complete the project has not been an easy task. There are two management issues:

1. Educating management to the role of DRE as a key aspect of enterprise integration—that is, demonstrating that DRE is an effective means of contributing to enterprise integration efforts and redirecting resources previously spent on system maintenance.

2. Demonstrating project efficiencies to management. Management must also be convinced that the project will produce the desired outcomes, on time, and within the planned budget—paying back the investment within a reasonable time period.

Organizational management must recognize also the industry-wide need to not only correct massive software maintenance expenses, but also understand it in terms of examples specific to the organization. This kind of evidence is not refutable and tends to be useful in gaining project approval. These organization-specific DRE project proposals show management something as specific as

> Look, Boss! If we invest $w into this data reverse engineering project, it will save us $y within z months.

(Assume: $w < $y and z < 24.) Presented with such compelling arguments, management is more likely to interest themselves in DRE projects. After a few successful projects, management will come to realize the value in data reverse engineering.

System Developer Considerations

Considerations evaluated by the system developer are summarized in Fig. 17.1 and discussed below. Although the system developers might intuitively know these characteristics, it is better to document them for posterity. Rather than attempt to quantify each characteristic, the system developer should use them as criteria, looking for outlying information indicating that the DRE project is opportune or perhaps timely. If an individual characteristic is either strongly favorable or strongly against, that characteristic is likely to weigh heavily in the overall decision. Low payoff indicates that continuing to deal with the existing situation will likely be more effective than reverse engineering.

Organizational knowledge of data

The first consideration is the extent of organizational knowledge of the data in the current system. The less known about the data found in the system, the greater the potential DRE payoff. DRE will provide a better understanding of the data associated with the system. If the system data is understood and accurately documented,

	High payoff	Neutral payoff	Low payoff
Organizational knowledge of data	Data not understood	Data somewhat understood	Data understood and documented
Use of structured methodologies during development	Low use of structured development methodologies	Moderate use of structured development methodologies	High use of structured development methodologies
System documentation quality	Nonexistent or poor-quality system documentation	Fair-quality system documentation	Complete, accurate, and synchronized system documentation
Development personnel system knowledge	Low development personnel system knowledge	Moderate development personnel system knowledge	Excellent development personnel system knowledge
System size and complexity	Large system size or high system complexity	Moderate system size and complexity	Small system size and low system complexity
System portability	Low system portability	Moderate system portability	High system portability
System maintenance history	Poor maintenance history	Fair maintenance history	Good maintenance history
Personpower costs of new system	New "from scratch" system will incur high relative IS resource costs	New from scratch system will incur moderate relative IS resource costs	New from scratch system will incur low relative IS resource costs
Dollar costs of new system	New from scratch system will incur high IS dollar costs	New from scratch system will incur moderate IS dollar costs	New from scratch system will incur low IS dollar costs
Reverse engineering project costs	DRE project will incur relatively low personpower costs	DRE project will incur relatively moderate personpower costs	DRE project will incur relatively high personpower costs
Dollar project costs	DRE project will incur low relative dollar costs	DRE project will incur moderate relative dollar costs	DRE project will incur high relative dollar costs

Figure 17.1 Developer DRE decision considerations.

the relative value of the system as a DRE candidate is much less, reducing its relative attractiveness as an investment. (The three matrices presented in this chapter present the considerations from the three system perspectives. For example—the payoff is higher where the organization has little knowledge of data. The payoff is lower in situations where organizational is greater.)

Use of structure during system development

Generally, the less structured the methodology used to develop the system, the greater the need to reverse engineer. One variable to consider in determining where the system code is at is the extent of code modularity. The less modular, the harder it is to rework the code without data reverse engineering.

System documentation quality

Existence of good system documentation is a key to being accurately able to transform an existing system to a new system or a rework of the current system in an orderly fashion. It also allows for verification of the mapping of business rules to the system's functions. Lack of good documentation leads to the need to spend time analyzing what the system does and how it relates to the business practice at hand. As has been mentioned earlier, when resources are allocated to dissect or analyze a current system de facto DRE is at work. The greater the need to perform this de facto data reverse engineering, the greater the need to adopt DRE, and the more knowledge to be gained by developers the higher the potential project payoff.

Development personnel knowledge

The more knowledge to be gained by developers, the higher the potential project payoff.

System size and complexity

Much the same as data knowledge, knowledge of the system is complicated by the system's size and complexity. Size can affect system development or rework from the sheer magnitude of the system involved. System complexity, based on complex business rules, likewise can raise the difficulty of understanding the system workings. The smaller and the less complex the system, the more likely that one will be able to reengineer without performing much analysis or system dissection.

System portability

Another characteristic is the extent to which the current system is portable to new hardware architectures under enterprise integration efforts. In today's environment, as corporations move from mainframe-based computing to distributed network computing, the need to move systems from one hardware architecture to another becomes compelling. In this situation, the greater the reliance of the system under consideration on a specific architecture, the greater the need to reverse engineer to capture the essence of the program for migration to a new architecture.

System maintenance history

The more a system has exhibited maintenance trouble, the greater the need to investigate data reverse engineering. Data reverse engineering provides a formal means of reviewing the system to recapture that which is useful prior to moving to rework the system or develop a new system. Systems consuming disproportional shares of maintenance expenditures are good candidates for DRE projects.

Personpower cost of new system development

If the cost of the human component of building the replacement systems is high then DRE can often produce a higher payoff.

Dollar costs of new system

If the dollar costs of a new system aren't as high as those of the DRE project, payoffs are likely to be higher under conditions requiring relatively low key specialist participation.

Reverse engineering personpower costs

Data reverse engineering project payoffs are likely to be higher under conditions requiring relatively low key specialist participation.

Dollar project costs

Data reverse engineering project payoffs will appear similarly attractive when associated with relative low project costs.

Relative project cost

The personpower costs include not only the salaries of those programmers assigned to the DRE project, but also the person-hours unavailable to support other projects.

Other developer concerns

Other developer concerns include the following:

- The technical integrity of the system

- Efficiency of the system, i.e., use of hardware resources

- Cost of system failure in lost opportunities for other system maintenance; new system development

- Centralized versus decentralized decision-making structure

- Where we are going: changing platform, e.g., mainframe to client/server

- Planned growth; staff downsizing, or centralized functions

- Whether we provide services to other organizations using this system

- Whether the system makes us unique in the industry and/or the organization

- Whether the system is a market necessity, e.g., airline reservation system

- Time spent maintaining system database(s)

- Personnel costs related to using or supporting the system

- Chargeback revenues for IS maintenance and day-to-day IS support of system in light of maintenance rework

- Efficiency of hardware and software by the current computer system: CPU time, I/O reads, I/O writes, etc.

- What percent of systems support is demanded by this system compared to its percentage of total systems used or maintained by IS (systems consuming inordinate percentages are more likely DRE candidates)

- How usage of computer resources in relation to other systems is essential to the business or functional area

- Level of security to be incorporated

- Number of databases or files

- Experience with system complexity

- Personnel turnover history

- Stability of technological environment

- Type of processing

- Number of queries to develop

- Use of productivity tools

- Number of persons involved

- Complexity of the system or product

- Training costs incurred to support the system

- Training costs involved with an expanded use of the system

- Losses due to inefficiencies in the system, e.g., sales support not having available on-line lookup of products

- Readability and understandability of screens and reports produced

System Management Considerations

The system management can evaluate the considerations presented in Fig. 17.2, again as a consideration checklist in addition to using it as a means of organizing relevant information.

Organization stability

Is the organization stable; for instance, are no major changes seen in the nature of the business or business ownership? Organizations operating under uncertain conditions shouldn't (and probably aren't) pursuing enterprise integration.

System role in organizational strategy

Does the system play a role in the corporate strategy? The more essential the system is to the corporate strategy, the greater the need to reverse engineer in light of needed changes. The greater the role of the system in organization strategy, the higher the demands for effective performance. While the first project has some decidedly different considerations, in general the greater the role the system plays in organizational strategy the more likely it is a candidate for data reverse engineering.

System importance in day-to-day operations

How essential is the system to day-to-day operations? The more a system is a necessity for day-to-day operations, the greater the need for data reverse engineering. Similarly, the more important the system is to daily operations, the higher is the potential need for DRE payoffs.

IS function maturity

The more mature the organizational IS and/or data administration function is, the better potential candidate the system is for data reverse engineering.

	High payoff	Neutral payoff	Low payoff
Organizational stability	Organization in stable state	Org. moderately stable	Organization in unstable state
System role in organizational strategy	System key to organizational strategy	System important to org. strategy	System strategically unimportant
System important to day-to-day operations	System necessary for day-to-day operations	System is a "player" in day-to-day ops.	System is not needed for day-to-day ops.
Information technology effectiveness	Effective application of IT results in competitive leverage	Some application of IT to compete	Ineffective application of IT
IS function maturity	High IS maturity	Moderate IS maturity	Low IS maturity
Overall system development or maintenance workload	Low org. system development or maintenance workload	Moderate org. system development or maintenance workload	Heavy org. system development or maintenance workload
Org. maintenance history	Good org. maintenance history	Fair maintenance history	Poor maintenance history
DRE cost as a % of organizational resources	DRE cost low as % of organizational resources	DRE cost moderate as % of organizational resources	DRE cost high as % of organizational resources
Reengineering cost compared to new development cost	Reengineering costs are less than cost to build new	Reengineering costs are similar to cost to build new	Reengineering costs are greater than cost to build new
Personpower cost	Low with respect to org. personpower requirement	Moderate with respect to org. requirement	High with respect to org. personpower requirement
Personpower cost of DRE compared to building	Personpower cost of DRE less than the cost to build	Personpower cost of DRE is similar to the cost to build	Personpower cost of DRE is higher than the cost to build
Organizational vision	Organization has a clear vision of its future	Organization has formed vision of its future	Organization is groping to develop a vision of its future

Figure 17.2 System management DRE decision considerations.

Overall system development or maintenance workload

Is the organization's IS organization swamped with maintenance problems? If so, high payoff is indicated.

Organizational maintenance history

Does the organization have a good maintenance history? If so, it will likely be a poor candidate for DRE.

Dollar cost of data reverse engineering as a percentage of resources

Where does the cost of the DRE option fall in the overall corporate picture? The greater the cost as a percentage of resources (e.g., revenues), the less likely that a DRE project will find viable financial support.

Organization application of information technology (IT)

The more effectively the system represents the application of IT, the better the candidate it is for data reverse engineering.

Data reverse engineering and new system development costs

This is the dollar cost of DRE compared to the dollar cost of new system development. If the cost of new development is less than that of data reverse engineering, the choice may seem clear.

Other development or rework projects the organization has planned

What percentage of staff is dedicated to the upkeep of the system in light of other maintenance needs and system development needs? What other projects does the organization have up for development or rework? The greater the workload facing the IS department, the less likely that personpower will be available for data reverse engineering. However, one then needs to look at the priority of the various systems with regard to market advantage, day-to-day operation support, and other factors to make the final decision.

Personpower costs

What personpower costs will be incurred by the system data reverse engineering? These costs are those incurred not only by the IS department, but by all departments involved in the DRE project, including end users and management. How do these costs compare with other corporate personpower costs and costs of other options such as new system development?

Strategic vision

Finally, does the organization have a clear vision of its future? While things may be stable at the present, what does the organization have in mind as it moves ahead through time? Is there a corporate plan? Where is it going? The vision of a organization that is clear lends itself to DRE by laying a foundation of what to expect future operations to be and what will be required of the system. The less clear the future, the less desirable the action to invest in any changes, let alone a DRE project.

Indirect output provided by combined staff and automated data administration

If an organization controls and measures its indirect output then the key system specialists become a primary reference to DRE efforts. Also, these present good opportunities to assess ICDTs.

Intercomponent Data Transfers (ICDT)

Does this indirect output service capability exist? If not, what are the costs required to achieve it? If so, what are the various ICDT profiles?

Other organizational resource management considerations

These include:

- The value of the information provided as measured by the impact on corporate revenues or on loss prevention.

- The value of the information provided as measured by the cost incurred versus the cost to be incurred to gain the same information from an alternate means.

- The losses to be incurred from system failure, e.g., factory production support system: idling time of workers, equipment, lost customer orders, etc.

- Current and future strategic values of the system.

- Value received from system in light of corporate outlays for system use and maintenance.

- Current system reliability.

- Corporate risk associated with modifying the system.

- Costs of system failure incurred by corporation.

- Does system give us a competitive advantage or disadvantage? Does system make us unique in the industry or the organization?

- Is the system a market necessity, e.g., airline reservation system?

- Are products essential to organization produced or supported by the system?

- What is the strategic outlook for the organization? Is the organization going to, merge, takeover, grow, or downsize?

- Input costs versus value of output produced, need to look at:
  - Time spent collecting system data
  - Functional area personnel costs related to using/supporting the system

- Information system maintenance and day-to-day support of system.

- Timeliness of outputs generated to the business process supported.

- Value of output received, based on any of the following:
  - Why you need the data produced by the system and whether the data is timely
  - Whether the system is the only available source and will soon be out of date
  - Need for data for day-to-day production runs
  - How long business could operate without the system
  - Need of data for financial planning
  - Need of output for business management control
  - Accuracy of data is known, or unknown
  - Value of services or product supported directly by system
  - Value of alternate means of providing the output, e.g., outsourcing, economic consequences of system failure

- Use of computer resources in relation to other systems essential to the business.

- Current and future tactical values of current system.

- Given a chargeback system, value received from current system in light of functional area outlays for the system's use and maintenance.

- Reliability of the current system.

- Functional area risk of changing the current system.

- Costs of system failure incurred by functional area.

- Does system give us a power position in the market or organization advantage (or disadvantage)?

- Is the product essential to business produced or supported by the system?

- Are we going, at the functional level to either merge, grow, or downsize?

System Functional User Considerations

For the end-user community weighing the opportunity to invest in a DRE project, review of the considerations shown in Fig. 17.3 will be useful.

	High Payoff	Neutral Payoff	Low Payoff
System workgroup function	System essential to workgroup function	System supports workgroup functioning	System supports relatively small amount of work
Workplace stability	Workplace stable	Workplace moderately stable	Workplace unstable
System support for functionality	System provides good support for required functional tasks	System provides moderate support for required functional tasks	System provides little support for required functional tasks
System understandability	System not easily understood	System understood with effort	System easily understood
System support for business practices	System does not currently support business practices	System currently supports some business practices	System directly supports business practices
End user cost of supporting data reverse engineering	End user cost of supporting DRE is low	End user cost of supporting DRE is moderate	End user cost of supporting DRE is high
Probability of productivity enhancement	Productivity enhancement probability is high	Productivity enhancement probability is moderate	Productivity enhancement probability is low
Current system maintenance costs	Current system maintenance costs are relatively high	Current system maintenance costs are moderate	Current system maintenance costs are relatively low
Relative system training costs	Relative training costs of system are high	Relative training costs of system are moderate	Relative training costs of system are low

Figure 17.3 End user's DRE decision chart.

System work group function situation factors

How important is the system to the workgroup using it? If the system is essential, DRE is likely to have higher payoff.

Workplace stability

Is the end user's workplace stable? The less stable the workplace, the less likely they will be interested in data reverse engineering. This comes from the inability to plan for the future, let alone strike out on a new venture such as data reverse engineering.

System support for functionality

Is the current system functional? The more satisfaction you have with the system at present, the less you will gain for this aspect through data reverse engineering. It should be noted that DRE for other reasons will not harm the functionality.

System understandability

Is the candidate system easily understood? If so, DRE will not gain you significantly more understanding: however, as noted earlier, it likewise will not cause harm to the understandability. If the system is incomprehensible, then DRE will lead to a better understanding of the system.

System support for business practices

How does the candidate system map to your business practice? If there is a clear disconnect, then DRE is the answer. The core of DRE is developing replacement systems capable of harmonizing system functions and business practice.

End user cost of supporting data reverse engineering

If the function's users cannot use the system, the project has potentially high payoff.

Probability of productivity enhancement versus personpower versus productivity costs

What will the candidate DRE project cost you in lost personpower and/or productivity? If you figure that the time spent by you and your staff will not result in payoffs higher than what will be lost to participation in data reverse engineering, you shouldn't participate. However, what appears to be a greater cost now may actually be an investment in a greater future payoff.

Current maintenance costs

What is maintenance costing now? *Cost* is defined in this case as lost productivity or lost sales due to system downtime, chargeback costs to information systems, and similar costs. If you aren't experiencing much of this, DRE won't improve a good record. (If it ain't broke ...) On the other hand, large maintenance costs are generally related to system design and implementation errors that can be corrected by data reverse engineering.

Relative training costs

Finally, what does it cost to train your staff on the system? Data reverse engineering offers the opportunity to better understand the system and impart this to users through better training.

Other end user perspective considerations

These include the value of the information provided as measured by the impact on corporate revenues and loss prevention. The value of the information provided is measured by the cost already incurred versus the cost to be incurred to gain the same information from an alternate source. Losses incurred from system failure in a factory production support system, for example, include idling time of workers, equipment downtime, and lost customer orders.

Chapter

18

CASE-Reengineering Symbiosis

---

symbiosis n.
A relationship of mutual benefit or dependence.
Synonym(s): no synonyms found for symbiosis.

Source: *American Heritage English Dictionary* © 1993 Houghton Mifflin Company.

This chapter describes how organizations can benefit from the potential symbiosis between organizational CASE and systems reengineering efforts. Organizational use of CASE has increased from 30 percent in 1989 to 62 percent in 1993 according to the annual Deloitte & Touche survey of CIOs [1994], but only 17 percent use it extensively. Organizations implement CASE as a strategy in hopes of favorably influencing the technological aspects of mission support. Many CASE implementations occur in a systems reengineering context. The nature of the reengineering challenges can influence short- and long-term requirements for organization-wide CASE implementation. As part of the reengineering efforts, the reengineering projects can also be used to prototype CASE implementation projects to determine the goodness of the "fit" of the tool in response to organizational needs. Thus, analysis and reengineering of organizational legacy portfolios can help determine the requirements for and appropriateness of CASE technologies, helping organizations evolve from current to desired technology bases. Organizational benefits include more robust reengineering efforts and lower risks associated with CASE implementation.

Figure 18.1 illustrates the potential information flows between CASE adoption and implementation efforts and organizational systems reengineering efforts. (I'll use the shorter labels *CASE efforts* and *reengineering efforts* from here on.) These three information metaflows—occurring in sequence from top to bottom—are the basis for the potential symbiosis between CASE and reengineering efforts. Briefly, understanding the reengineering challenges can inform and facilitate organization-wide CASE requirements. Adoption of CASE technologies can, in turn, influence the selection of the reengineering projects. Finally, use of CASE technologies on reengineering projects should be evaluated for goodness of "fit" between organizational needs and CASE capabilities. This shared information facilitates symbiosis between two organizational efforts that are often related but not as often coordinated.

Next a background section describes the motivation for organization-wide CASE technology implementation, the challenges of implementing CASE in a legacy environment, the systems reengineering process and its dependence on CASE technologies, and the CASE schema elements adopted as a framework for organizing the information flows. The next three sections each describe one of the three potential information metaflows capable of producing beneficial results if CASE and reengineering efforts are coordinated:

■ How a legacy portfolio analysis can provide indications as to the organizational CASE requirements

■ How organizational CASE technology guidance can influence selection of reengineering efforts.

■ Feedback that use of CASE technologies on reengineering projects can provide organizations prior to organization-wide implementation.

The chapter concludes with a general assessment of the potential CASE-reengineering symbiosis and some suggestions for future research.

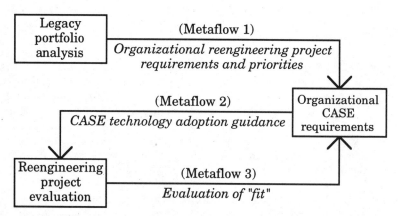

Figure 18.1 A representation of the information metaflows facilitating the symbiosis between organizational CASE and reengineering efforts.

CASE, Systems Reengineering, and Legacy Systems

Both systems reengineering and CASE are technologies of increasing importance to system developers. A lot of effort and resources are going into both systems reengineering and CASE technology support for it. This perhaps is the motivation behind the growth in both the reengineering market and the market for CASE technologies supporting it. Pfrenzinger [1992] estimates that the annual market for reengineering tools will grow to $650 million by 1996, while Caldwell [1994] estimated the 1994 reengineering market at $32 billion with a large amount going to information systems reengineering.

Organizations implement CASE technologies in hopes of achieving increased effectiveness and efficiency of their technology-based operations. These increases can come in many forms, including lowered system maintenance costs due to better understanding of how existing systems work [Sneed 1991b], improved quality in system development practices [QED 1989], improved system development productivity [Zarrella et al. 1992], and new and innovative information technology-based applications, products, and services [Haeckel and Nolan 1993].

CASE has many proponents and some success stories [Banker and Kauffman 1991, Necco et al. 1989, Norman and Nunamaker 1988, and Swanson et al. 1991]. There are also those who contend that CASE has yet to achieve its full potential [Card et al. 1987, Yellen 1990, Norman et al. 1989, Orlikowski 1988, and Vesset et al. 1992]. Problems associated with CASE implementation include lack of training, lack of experience, developer resistance, and increased design and testing time.

The cost of CASE is also an important factor. To implement a $2,500/seat CASE technology across a 75-person organization, Huff [1992] recommended a 5-year budget of more than $2.5 million— quite a bit more than the $187,000 cost of the tool itself. Figure 18.2 illustrates what Huff terms the "iceberg" effect of CASE technology implementation, which presents opportunities for phased implementation and permits organizations to learn from pilot project experiences before committing to any particular technology. As the true nature of the investment is understood, organizations are beginning to wait the requisite 2- or 3-year investment period required to evaluate a CASE investment.

Legacy systems have often been seen as barriers to organizational CASE implementation because their consumption of resources for maintenance purposes was often seen as conflicting with CASE implementation projects. The argument has often gone something like "How can we invest millions in CASE technology when so much of our information technology spending goes to maintaining our legacy systems?"

One barrier to CASE has been that it has tended to be associated with new systems development. When one considers that 80 percent

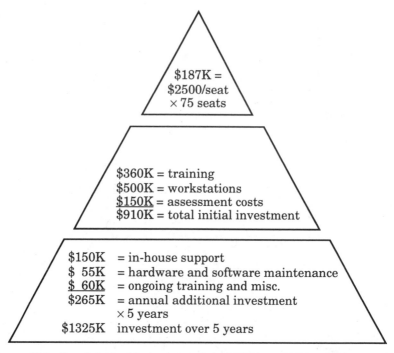

Figure 18.2 Sample budget for implementing a $2500/seat CASE technology can be $2.5 million over a 5-year period (adapted from Huff "Elements of a Realistic CASE Tool Adoption Budget" © 1992 *Communications of the ACM*).

of all IS spending is for system maintenance [Pressman 1993], a relatively small amount of resources remains to be invested in new systems development. New development has been seen as the place to invest in technology and it has been difficult to obtain this level of resources for existing systems.

If not replaced, software does not age gracefully. As Jones [1992] noted, the standard rate of change of software is between 5 and 7 percent each year for as long as the software is operational and in use. Over time this tends to degrade the program's original structure. Both the maintenance and reengineering tasks become more difficult as a result. These types of situations—where aging legacy systems have fostered stagnant, unresponsive, or dysfunctional operational environments—have led to a number of systems reengineering efforts (see for example Hammer and Champy [1993], Cash et al. [1994], or IIE [1994]).

CASE is used to support the processes of capturing, organizing, and evaluating the information gained from reverse engineering and make it available for the forward engineering phase. Reverse engineering information is stored in a CASE-based data bank (also known as a library, dictionary, encyclopedia, repository, or ware-

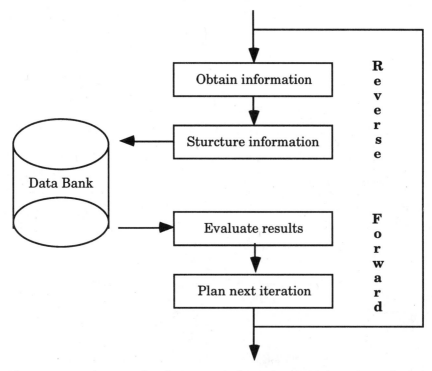

Figure 18.3 Information flow during a typical reengineering information gathering cycle.

house). In this manner, it is made available to the forward engineering activities. This process is shown in Fig. 18.3 in the context of a typical reengineering information-gathering cycle.

The types of reengineering projects called for will drive the types of reengineering tools. Data, processes, and software are the primary foci of reengineering efforts. This is perhaps the most obvious place to begin the examination of the process of informing the CASE technology adoption and implementation process. We can begin with some very simple heuristics shown in Fig. 18.4.

Called for by reengineering plan:	CASE technology support required:
Process reverse engineering	Process modeling
Data reverse	Entity relationship diagramming
Software reverse	Extraction tools

Figure 18.4 Obvious mapping between reengineering needs and CASE technology support.

	Organizations having legacy systems in need of reengineering	Organizations having no systems in need of reengineering
Organizations that have not adopted or implemented organization-wide CASE technologies	1	4
Organizations that have adopted but not implemented organization-wide CASE technologies	2	5
Organizations that have adopted and implemented organization-wide CASE technologies	3	6

Figure 18.5   Categories of organizational CASE and legacy systems.

Determining what form of CASE support becomes of interest, particularly to organizations that have not adopted CASE technology organizationwide—even more so to organizations involved with underway reengineering efforts. Recently, organizational data administration functions have tended to be responsible for taking the lead on CASE because according to Tucker [1993] (1) it has been easier to implement data-driven approaches to information systems development and (2) the data administration function has tended to be populated with change specialists. While some (as quoted in Caldwell [1994]) are correct to criticize exclusive dependence on CASE technologies and inappropriate CASE methodologies to perform reengineering, there are some obvious places for features found in CASE technologies on reengineering projects. This adds additional incentive to examine these reengineering and CASE efforts for possible symbiosis, especially when one considers that both of these efforts are likely to be controlled out of the data administration function, increasing the possibility of performing these two activities in close synchronization.

Organizations not possessing legacy systems in need of reengineering (categories 4–6 of Fig. 18.5) are less likely to benefit from the potential symbiosis between CASE and reengineering efforts. Of the remaining categories, number 3 is the easiest to explain. Organizations having already adopted and implemented organization-wide CASE technologies will likely use the organizational CASE technology to support any reengineering. Project evaluation can indicate how well their adopted CASE technology worked in the context of their reengineering projects. Lessons learned might range from confirmation of the appropriateness of the selection, to influencing the process of rethinking their CASE technology investment. Consider, for example, the situation where the organizational CASE technology does not support the reengineering project well and the organization faces additional reengineering challenges. Organizations falling into categories 1 and 2 have a strong motivation to learn what they can from their legacy environment before attempting to adopt and implement organization-wide CASE technologies.

Figure 18.6 presents a basic CASE tool schema comprising elements related both horizontally and vertically (adapted from Jones [1994]). The framework is used to illustrate the various types of

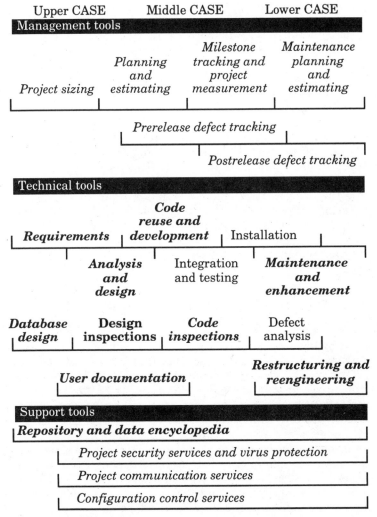

Figure 18.6 CASE technology schema (adapted from Jones *Assessment and Control of Software* © 1994 Prentice-Hall) .

CASE tool information that can be exchanged with reengineering activities. Each element is characterized from the CASE perspective as

- Senders (elements shown in **boldface**)—flows from the CASE effort that can inform the reengineering effort.

- Receivers (elements shown in *italics*)—flows from the reengineering project that can inform the CASE effort.

- Senders and receivers (elements shown in ***boldface italics***)—some elements, such as restructuring and reengineering, are both senders and receivers.

- Neither senders nor receivers (elements shown in plain text)—some elements are apparently not involved in the symbiosis.

The next three sections explain how subsets of these elements make up each of the three information metaflows shown in Fig. 18.1 capable of producing symbiosis between the reengineering and CASE efforts.

Figure 18.7 presents a direct mapping between metaflows and CASE schema framework elements. Listing the 22 elements moving from the top left, a mark in any of the first three columns indicates presence of a potential flow between reengineering and CASE efforts involving that particular element. While most of the flows are from reengineering efforts to CASE efforts ($\leftarrow$), there is some flow from CASE to reengineering ($\uparrow$). A third icon used on the figure ($\lrcorner$) indicates potential feedback of previous guidance that has been attempted on a reengineering project.

Organizational Reengineering Project Requirements and Priorities

Organizational reengineering project requirements and priorities are developed by legacy portfolio analysis described as a part of the DRE project framework. Performing regular analysis on data collected on the performance of the organizational systems portfolio is a feedback loop typically desired by management. Some subset of the portfolio—systems or system components—is identified as reverse engineering candidates with project-specific objectives contributing toward organizational objectives. When analyzed for dependencies, the reengineering projects can be ranked and instantiated as objectives in a strategic reengineering plan. The metaflow labeled "Organizational reengineering project requirements and priorities" in Fig. 18.1 can be decomposed into three individual flows, illustrating information that can inform and influence the process of adopting and influencing organization-wide CASE implementation. CASE schema framework elements representing these information flows are shown in italics on Fig. 18.1.

CASE tool schema element:	Legacy portfolio analysis	Organizational CASE requirements	Reengineering project evaluations	CASE level	CASE function	Schema element number
Project sizing	←	↑	⌐	U	M	1
Planning and estimating	←	↑	⌐	U	M	2
Milestone tracking and project measurement	←	↑	⌐	M	M	3
Maintenance planning and estimating	←	↑	⌐	L	M	4
Pre-release defect tracking	←		⌐	U/M	M	5
Post-release defect tracking	←		⌐	L	M	6
Requirements	←	↑	⌐	U	T	7
Analysis and design	←	↑	⌐	U	T	8
Code reuse and development	←	↑	⌐	M	T	9
Integration and testing		↑	⌐	M	T	10
Installation			⌐	M/L	T	11
Maintenance and enhancement	←	↑	⌐	L	T	12
Database design	←	↑	⌐	U	T	13
Design inspections		↑	⌐	U/M	T	14
Code inspections		↑	⌐	M	T	15
Defect Analysis		↑	⌐	M	T	16
Restructuring and reengineering	←	↑	⌐	L	T	17
User documentation	←	↑	⌐	M	T	18
Repository and data encyclopedia	←	↑	⌐	U/L	S	19
Project security services and virus protection	←		⌐	U/L	S	20
Project communication services	←	↑	⌐	U/L	S	21
Configuration control services	←	↑	⌐	U/L	S	22

Legend: Flow direction   CASE level: CASE function:
← = reengineering to CASE   M = management   U = upper
↑ = CASE to reengineering   T = technical   M = middle
⌐ = feedback   S = support   L = lower

Figure 18.7 Mapping information flows to and from CASE schema elements.

Reengineering CASE technology requirements

The reengineering priorities will anticipate the size, scope, and focus of specific reengineering projects. These projects will indicate specific technical programming language, database, and documentation-based CASE technology features required to effectively to perform the reengineering effort.

Restructuring and reengineering

Information about requirements for CASE restructuring and reengineering requirements is the most obvious information flow from reengineering efforts to CASE efforts. The reengineering objectives will include plans for reengineering specific systems or system components. These should be factored into the organizational CASE capability requirements by providing information determining the number of seats required, parallel tool usage considerations, training requirements, and other CASE technology requirements. An obvious example—an organization with a portfolio consisting largely of assembly language code—will be interested in CASE technology supporting assembly language reengineering capabilities.

Code reuse and development

The most rudimentary legacy portfolio analysis contains information such as that shown in Fig. 18.8. From this information, it is clear that appropriate CASE technology support for translating the COBOL code into system models or perhaps even into restructured code might be a prudent investment of resources. Naturally, it would be nice to have tool support for each system language, but a more realistic situation would have a limited budget.

User documentation

The state of the user documentation can also influence the CASE technology acquisition priorities. User documentation currently maintained on-line and off-line represents a valuable organizational data asset. Each asset's future should be specifically addressed in the legacy portfolio analysis and plans developed for migrating existing assets toward new CASE standards or adopting an existing CASE technology as standard. For example, the existence of well-maintained CASE-based system documentation on a unsupported 286-based CASE technology can be of sufficient organizational value

Priority	Quantity	Language	Lines of code (LOC)	Avg. age
1	13	COBOL	~650K LOC each	17 years
2	2	Assembly	122-155K LOC	13 years
3	5	RPG	< 250K LOC each	6 years
4	4	HyperCard	~50K LOC each	5 years
5	10	C	~255K LOC each	4 years
	34	Total		

Figure 18.8 A sample list of reengineering candidate groupings.

to warrant keeping the obsolete CASE technology operational beyond a typical life span. Of the CIOs surveyed by Deloitte & Touche [1994], 57 percent indicated the greatest benefit was improved documentation, indicating the value placed on the results by the CIOs.

Repository and data encyclopedia

The amount of data to be acquired, as well as the number and the timing of reengineering activities, can influence the timing of the organizational data bank implementation. Many reengineering plans call for early and/or heavy acquisition of data from reverse engineering efforts. This data needs to be organized and stored someplace where it can be accessed by other reengineering activities. In situations where a lot of reverse engineering is scheduled early on, the organization may become in a position to benefit from the data bank early in its implementation. While it is a natural desire not to jump into the technology too rapidly, in these situations it often makes sense to invest earlier in a corporate repository technology to make the reverse engineering economically justifiable. For example, use of a single integrated repository can obviate the need for large model integration exercises as separately developed models are integrated.

Project security services and virus protection

The legacy environment will influence the types of strengths of the various organizational CASE technology security requirements. Systems to be reengineered and operating under heavy security requirements will require comparable features from the organizational CASE technology.

Project communication services

Reengineering projects and priorities will dictate specific communications service requirements. For example, electronic mail (e-mail) may play an important role in distributed projects. Simultaneous access and/or traffic volume requirements are also potentially derivable from this information.

Configuration control services

In a similar fashion, information on the change control and configuration management practices of the legacy systems will indicate what the organization has practiced in the past. This information can be examined and used to modify current practice.

Legacy Portfolio Data

The data characterizing the portfolio of legacy systems contains valuable information that should influence the CASE adoption process supporting both management and technical functions. Each element comprising the flow is described below.

Project sizing

The reengineering implementation schedule and size plan will help inform the CASE implementers as to the size and scope of the projects they will ask to be undertaken by the CASE technology eventually selected for organization-wide implementation. For example, a very ambitious reengineering plan calling for numerous individual projects can be used to justify the requirement that the CASE technology be able to manage projects from both strategic and operational levels. The reengineering implementation schedule indicates the minimum volume of the CASE technology usage.

Planning and estimating

The legacy portfolio analysis will provide information on the types of planning and estimated data that can be obtained from the existing environment. These and other information requirements can be used to assess the relative utility of specific CASE features.

Milestone tracking and project measurement

Information used to track project milestones and otherwise measure progress can be more easily shared between reengineering and CASE efforts if it occurs in the same format with corresponding units of measure, etc.

Maintenance planning and estimating

Information describing the type and amount of maintenance requirements obtainable from the legacy portfolio analysis can be similarly shared.

Prerelease and postrelease defect tracking

Information describing the volume and nature of defect tracking requirements is also obtainable from the legacy portfolio analysis.

Anticipated Data Assets

Some reengineering projects can deliver data assets—data of value to the organization in the same fashion that human and financial resources are valuable. Elements comprising this flow are described below.

Analysis and design

In a similar manner, much analysis, design, and code reuse and development information describing the organizational environment will have been collected.

Code reuse and development

The relative volume as well as language and computing environment coverage can be used to confirm the anticipated organizational CASE technology usage patterns.

Requirements

The business rules [Appleton 1984] recovered as part of any reengineering activity can have a relatively profound influence on the organizational strategies used to implement CASE. For example, stated organizational policy may be to vest local operations with policy interpretation authority. When applied to software implementation policy, it may be clear from the business rules that organization effectiveness and ability to achieve organizational objectives hinge on strict control and coordination of software releases. This implies that a centralized approach to the CASE technology configuration management is of more use to the organization.

Maintenance and enhancement

The legacy portfolio analysis will contain information on anticipated system maintenance and enhancement issues that can be used to guide CASE technology feature selection supporting those issues.

Code inspections

Similarly, it makes sense that the organizational code analyzers to be used in any software reverse engineering project be integrated into the organization-wide CASE suite. Tools lacking integration run the risk of stranding results outside the organizational CASE environment, requiring manual input.

Database design

Heavy database reverse engineering requirements may influence the choice of CASE technology adopted. Support for organizing and maintaining reengineering database designs can help differentiate certain competing CASE technologies. This one is obvious; if we are creating database schemas from existing databases in situations where the schemas don't already exist, this information is most appropriately maintained in the tool that will be used to develop the reengineered database and associated systems.

CASE Technology Adoption Guidance

Adoption of CASE technologies can influence an organizational reengineering implementation plan.   Consider a situation where there are several candidate reengineering projects.   Because of the interdependencies between the various aspects of reengineering, the organization's first problem may be identifying a suitable starting point to begin the reengineering process.   Organizations having already adopted but not yet implemented organization-wide CASE technologies (category 2 of Fig. 18.5) will likely use the adopted CASE technology as part of any reengineering efforts.   The adopted CASE technology will have specific technical abilities encompassing the representation of system requirements, analysis and designs, code, and maintenance issues.   Matches between these technical abilities and information desired from the reengineering projects will facilitate reengineering efforts. Matches can be used to select from among candidate reengineering projects.   A combined CASE-reengineering project will permit both efforts to demonstrate tangible achievements. Demonstrating early successes can benefit both reengineering and CASE efforts.

Evaluation of "Fit"

If the organization has adopted a CASE technology, the reengineering projects should use it to the extent that it supports project planning and estimation.   Project evaluation can indicate how well their adopted CASE technology worked in the context of their reengineering projects.   Lessons learned might range from confirmation of the appropriateness of the selection to rethinking CASE technology investments.   The information metaflow labeled "Evaluation of 'fit'" on Fig. 18.1 is comprised of information that can be used to assess the performance of the CASE tool in support of the reengineering effort. CASE schema framework elements included are discussed below under the categories of management, technical, and support tools.

Management tools

Information as to how well the project planning and estimating aspects of the reengineering activities worked will be useful.   Specifics might include how well various system measures and data items worked as part of the forecasting process.   Feedback comes from the original estimates.   Similarly, if the organizationally adopted standards for the CASE technology were used as the planning and estimation metrics, some sort of formal evaluation as to their suitability, should be transmitted back to the CASE group as feedback.   The usefulness of the metrics used to assess progress during reengineering activities should be evaluated in light of the assumptions made during the adoption decision. Metric and project management information exchange should be shared between CASE and reengineering efforts.

Technical tools

Experience gained with the use of extraction tools can provide useful indications as to the correctness of the fit between the tools and the organizational CASE requirements. If the experience with the tools was unproductive, was technically complex, or otherwise contraindicated the direction in which the organization is moving with its CASE adoption plan, then the plan should be reexamined. In some situations the organization may be able to gain experience examining the system documentation using a CASE technology that has not been implemented organization wide. This project experience can be compared against the assumptions made during the adoption decision. Confirming (or refuting) these assumptions can be an important source of feedback to the CASE implementation process.

Support tools

The experience of the CASE support features must be evaluated as part of the reengineering project. How well did the CASE product function in light of organizational reengineering needs for the following?

- A project repository
- Security services
- Communication services
- Configuration control services

Implications for Organizational CASE Implementation

The potential symbiosis between CASE and reengineering efforts implies that organizations should carefully examine the CASE schema framework elements to determine their applicability to the organizational situation. Several broad types of information that can be gained from this process are described below.

Methodology considerations

Since the CASE technology is often closely tied to an associated methodology, organizations will have to carefully examine both their organizational system development methodology and their reengineering methodology to ensure that the two are symbiotic.

CASE technology usage

Actual CASE technology usage can be observed during these preliminary projects to both improve training efforts and evaluate effectiveness. Usage data from the CASE project can be used to assess the
anticipated reengineering project productivity rates.

Training considerations

Jones [1992] notes that without significant investment in training in
more than 50 percent of CASE deployments, either the tool was
abandoned after use, users were dissatisfied, or the tangible results
were either zero (nil) or negative. Since training is a major factor in
CASE implementation costs, it must be assessed.

Probably the most significant indicator is the fact that legacy portfolio analysis occurred at all. This indicates that the organization
has reached a level of maturity sufficient to recognize its installed
base as an asset and that they are thinking about or perhaps are
already implementing an organizational data architecture. This involves time and commitment. Organizations unwilling to commit to
the preparatory work may be similarly unwilling or unable to perform
the requisite reverse engineering and unwilling or unable to focus the
required time and attention on CASE technology implementation.
Organizations that conduct analysis of legacy portfolios have typically
reached sufficient technological maturity that they recognize data as
an organizational resource and have defined or at least assessed the
state of the organizational data architecture. Related information
concerns an assessment of the CASE technology's fit with the organizational culture.

Future CASE Reengineering Research

There is a symbiotic relationship between organizational CASE and
reengineering efforts. Failure to recognize this can result in a loss of
organizational effectiveness. Indeed, reengineering may offer an excellent context in which to carefully introduce CASE technology and
profit from the lessons learned. It seems worthwhile to pursue this
line of research by determining a means of coordinating these two
related efforts. Developing organizational reengineering and CASE
implementation planning under the data administration function
would seem a promising approach. Examination of CASE support for
the four basic reengineering project goal types [Bush 1990] could lead
to a more robust match between reengineering project needs and
CASE tool support. Of particular interest are those areas where
Jones [1992] noted that CASE technology support was not available
or was inadequate: project sizing, planning and estimating, mile-

stone tracking and project measurement, prerelease defect tracking, and defect analysis. Examining them to see if the reengineering efforts may be able to facilitate CASE implementation of these elements would also seem a worthwhile investigation.

19

Implications for Client/Server Architecture Development

Client/server applications are increasing, according to the results of a 1994 Deloitte & Touche survey of more than 400 CIOs in 1993—5 percent of them reported running client/server applications in 1992; and 27 percent, in 1993. Many reengineering efforts are also examining distributed environments as technological destinations. This chapter describes what can be learned from reverse engineering of existing systems when the analysis is targeted toward distributed environments. Capturing just a bit more data in the models developed during reverse engineering can provide guidance to subsequent forward engineering efforts. Sources of information from various reverse engineering activities are linked to various distributed environment development decisions using a framework developed by Inmon [1993]. The contributions of data reverse engineering to various development decisions are also indicated. This chapter describes 16 metadata items which, if collected during reverse engineering, can influence the development of distributed systems.

In the best-case scenario, certain additional system metadata (i.e., data about the data processed by the system [Brackett 1994]) would be collected during reverse engineering analyses. This metadata would be useful (and thus used) to plan certain aspects of the distributed system. These 16 metadata items influence several critical distributed systems development characteristics.

Figure 19.1 presents an overview of the generalized process. Reverse engineering legacy system(s) can produce metadata that enhances the specifications for distributed systems. This metadata can be used to validate comparable data contained in the system specifications—an activity likely to be valuable if the specifications were developed early on in the project, as they are commonly. The result should be enhanced system specifications and facilitated data evolution.

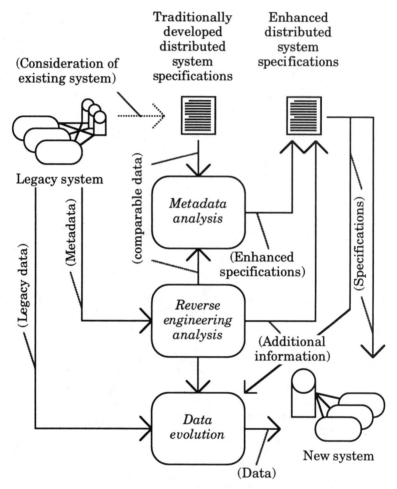

Figure 19.1 Overview of the generalized process of using the additional metadata gained from reverse engineering analyses in the development of distributed applications.

The remainder of this chapter presents an analysis of the sources and uses of the 16 metadata items obtainable from reverse engineering and useful to distributed systems development. They are addressed in three groups corresponding to the classes of metadata usage. The next four sections provide (1) an overview of the metadata, (2) a review of the metadata used in the distributed system architecture, (3) a review of the metadata used in applications development, and (4) a discussion of how reverse engineering experiences can provide indications as to organizational ability to successfully implement distributed applications.

#	Primary use	Metadatum	Domain value
1	Architectural development	Data quality type	- Public - Private
2	Architectural development	Data usage type	- Operational - DSS I: single server node - DSS II: multiple server nodes - DSS III: distributed data and processing
3	Architectural development	Data residency type	- Functional - Subject - Geographic - Other
4	Application development	Archival data type	- Continuous - Event-discrete - Periodic-discrete
5	Application development	Data granularity type	Smallest unit of addressable data is an - Attribute - Element - Some other unit of measure

Figure 19.2   Common domain value metadata useful in planning distributed systems and obtainable as part of reverse engineering analysis (metadata adapted from Inmon *Data Architecture: The Information Paradigm* © 1993 QED Technical Publishing Group).

Metadata Framework

There are numerous distributed application development methodologies (e.g., see Armstrong [1994], Brackett [1994], Croxton [1994], Flood [1994], and Vaughn [1994]).   Inmon [1993] presents distributed application development from the data perspective as a series decision serving primarily to steer the planning efforts into the correct development context.   These decisions were used to identify the information required to make those decisions.   The 16 metadata items are the result.   Figures 19.2 through 19.4 provide an overview (organized into three categories) of the 16 metadata items useful in planning distributed systems and obtainable as part of reverse engineering analysis.

■ *Common domain value.*   These metadata items can take on only restricted, preexisting domain values applicable regardless of data usage, platform, or development context.   They use common domain values across all applications development.   For example, all *data quality* types are classified as either *public* (available to others in the organization) or *private* (not available outside of the organization).

#	Primary use	Metadatum	Domain value
6	Architectural development	Data performance issues	Performance measurement/ period of measurement
7	Application development	Data access frequency	Accesses/period of measurement
8	Application development	Data update frequency	Update/period of measurement
9	Application development	Data access probability	Likeliness that an individual data element of the total population will be accessed during a processing period
10	Application development	Data update probability	Likeliness that an individual data element of the total population will be updated during a processing period

Figure 19.3 Quantifiable metadata useful in planning distributed systems and obtainable as part of reverse engineering analysis (metadata adapted from Inmon *Data Architecture: The Information Paradigm* © 1993 QED Technical Publishing Group).

■ *Quantifiable.* These metadata items are characterized by measurements describing probability and frequency of data access and update. Metadata in this category are characterized by measurements obtained by studying historical and statistical system performance. By obtaining the proper conversion values, one can compare quantifiable metadata items across systems development projects. For example, while the values indicating that a specific datum has a high likelihood of access will fluctuate among systems, systems are likely to have data access characteristics roughly corresponding to a Pareto (80/20) distribution—with a relatively small portion of the data accessed much of the time [Boehm 1987].

■ *Organization specific.* These metadata items consist of six specific classes of system requirements. Both the values and measures characterizing this information vary from system to system but retain consistency within the context of a specific system. For example, while typical subject area divisions include functional, subject-specific, or geographic classes, each system could also possess its own data subject area classification.

Sources and uses of the 16 metadata items are examined in the next sections, corresponding to their respective primary usage category in distributed systems development. The upcoming sections de-

#	Primary use	Metadatum	Domain value
11	Architectural development	Data integration requirements	Number and possible classes of nodes
12	Architectural development	Data subject area	Number and possible subject area breakdowns
13	Architectural development	Data grouping	Useful for cataloging user-defined clusters
14	Application development	Data location	Number and availability of possible node locations
15	Application development	Data stewardship	Range of all business units
16	Application development	Data system of record	System responsible for maintaining data element's data

Figure 19.4 Organization-specific metadata useful in planning distributed systems and obtainable as part of reverse engineering analysis (metadata adapted from Inmon *Data Architecture: The Information Paradigm* © 1993 QED Technical Publishing Group).

scribe metadata influencing the development of the (1) distributed system architecture and (2) individual application components in distributed systems, as well as metadata that can be used to reassess the reengineering project in light of the organization's achievements to date.

Architectural Considerations

In today's environment, an organization's technical architecture is often more important than individual applications. This is because a sufficiently flexible architecture will permit the organization to react more rapidly than the competition, enabling it to take advantage of situations arising from the environment. The technical architecture will answer the questions of *what, how, where, who, when, and why* to place services and applications within the architecture [Sowa and Zachman 1992]. This analysis has identified six metadata items specifically influencing the architectural development of distributed systems.

Common domain values: data quality, data usage, and data residency

Three metadata items have common domain values: data quality, data usage, and data residency.

Data quality is a binary indicator of quality—either *pubic* or *private*. Private data quality indicates that the data is not for use beyond the boundaries of the owner's application. It has not been standardized or otherwise made suitable for sharing within the organization. A public quality indicator designates data that has been recognized and is maintained as an organizational data asset (with suitable quality controls, etc.).

Data usage has two potential values: *operational* or *decision support*, the value indicating in which of two basic distributed system modes the data will be accessed. As shown in Fig 19.2, the DSS category is composed of three subtypes (they are DSS data):

■ Only at a single server node

■ At multiple server nodes

■ Data and processing are distributed

Data residency is the state in which an organization prefers to maintain its data. The three most common are

■ *Functional.* Each functional area in the organization has stewardship over its own data.

■ *Subject.* Similar to functional organizations (referenced above), organizations adopting this model generally consider data as organized by, and consequently the responsibility of, subject areas. Consider, as an example, divisions in the publishing industry between the textbook and the professional markets.

■ *Geographic.* In this paradigm data is organized according to physical region with the operational concept of local offices processing locally resident subsets of data.

When combined, data quality, data usage, and data residency can influence one of the most basic distributed developmental decisions, the identification of which quadrant(s) of the distributed systems development context components of the current project occupy. Figure 19.5 illustrates the four quadrants. *Operational distributed* systems process current transactions, while *DSS* focuses on retrieval of archival data. Thus current-value data and archival data must be separated and processed differently. *Private* indicates the data is relevant at only a particular processing node; while *public* indicates broader possible organization-wide usage.

	Private	Public
DSS	I	II
Operational	III	IV

Figure 19.5 Distributed systems development contexts.

- Quadrant I represents DSS applications that are completely self-contained within a specific node. Although rarely considered part of the distributed system under development, these can still be influential to the distributed system architecture if they consume inordinate system resources. (The probability for this is high considering the low standards enforced for these applications.)

- In today's environment quadrant II systems are typically found as extensions to today's legacy systems focused generally on time-based analysis for executive management, grafted onto main-frame-based, transaction processing applications with distributed connectivity.

- Quadrant III houses most of the end user applications. These should also be examined for possible resource consumption and factored into the overall system architecture.

- Applications in quadrant IV constitute today's legacy systems, providing real-time support for daily operations.

Each quadrant represents a different class of applications development. These metadata items should be captured during reverse engineering analyses. They can be obtained from a matrix indicating which processes create, read, update, or delete (CRUD) which entities. Entities defined during reverse engineering analyses can be examined by accessing processes to determine sources and uses of data. Process definitions indicate whether the data usage and/or processing is DSS or operational in nature.

Data quality can also be used to determine project sizing characteristics, such as determining the amount of public data as a percentage of the total data. One of the more common discoveries during reverse engineering analysis is that a private data source has somehow become crucial to system operation. Consider, as an example, an instance where a julian date routine was encoded incorrectly and a third shift operator knew how to perform the correct calculation and enter the data through the console at the appropriate time. In addition, since mixing public and private data and use of operational and DSS data within nodes is discouraged, the metadata can be examined programmatically to see if system designs confirm to organizational specifications. When developing distributed systems support decision support, the system architecture can take several "flavors." The simplest system architecture has data existing at only a single server node. Either volume of data or access requirements can force data on a single server to be split across multiple servers. The third option, distributed data and processing (subtype 3), requires just a little data, a little access, and a little processing, to work well. If more than a little of data, accessing, or processing are required then subtype 3 won't work. To determine which is most appropriate, the set of accessing processes can be mapped to specific nodes in various configurations using the same sources and uses of data described earlier.

Quantifiable: data performance

Data performance is the only quantifiable metadata item contributing toward architectural development. Since distributed environments typically use conventional WANs and LANs (wide and local area networks) to move data around, the transfer rate may be slower than the mainframe bus speed, requiring careful placement of data and services across the network. Data performance metadata is concerned with characterizing the performance requirements of the data element. While these can include specifics such as access and update frequency, this metadata is most often expressed in terms of access time specifications from

- Source node to destination node

- External storage to internal storage

- Internal storage to the screen

These drive the requirements, dictating, in turn, specific access and update requirements. For example, data performance metadata is obtained most often through regular interaction with users in interview or joint modeling sessions. It can even be included as part of a checklist used to ensure completeness of transaction descriptions. Performance metadata robustness can be evaluated by attempting to determine the effects on the system of doubling the data and processing requirements. Robust performance metadata will permit the calculation of this information.

Organization-specific: data integration requirements and data subject area

The organization-specific metadata define the general parameters of processing guidelines with the goal of enabling the specification of optimal system processing—balancing typically between processing and storage economies of scale and the local responsiveness requirements.

- *Data integration requirements.* Metadata is concerned with characterizing the number and type of transformations a datum must undergo to make itself accessible for use by other systems or system components. A general data integration requirement is that a datum must not lose precision or accuracy in order to reach its destination. Functional or other system decomposition usually forms the basis for development of a hierarchy of model views, also known as "node trees." Matrices linking these nodes to elements contained within each view provide reliable indications of integration requirements.

■ *Data subject area.* Metadata is concerned with linking each data element to a specific subject area to facilitate the organization of the data relationships. These relationships can be supported by either applications or a database management system. This additional metadata is a pointer that is easier to capture up front and maintain on-line than to revisit on an instance-by-instance basis at a later date. The data subject area also serves as a candidate system of record in absence of organizational policy in this area. Finally, it facilitates organization of the data into archival format in preparation for the transfer between an operational environment and a distributed DSS environment.

Application Development Guidance

In addition to the differences between the data and the resource utilization, very different system development life cycles (SDLCs) exist for distributed applications being considered for the operational and DSS context. Distributed systems supporting operational needs use the standard "waterfall" model SDLC, consisting of analysis, design, implementation, testing, and maintenance phases. For distributed DSS development, the classic SDLC is somewhat reversed to include the following phases:

■ Implementation of archival, time variant data

■ Testing of the data for completeness, etc.

■ Rapid development of programs

■ User analysis of the results of the programs developed

In a further simplification of the distributed DSS application planning, DSS data isn't considered updatable, thus permitting developers freedom to trade items such as database table size for fewer system inputs and outputs. The distributed DSS development process is iterative, ending with the user identifying the desired results. Attempting to apply the wrong method will lead to unpredictable results. Different SDLCs reinforce the guidance against mixing operational and DSS data within systems. Once the context has been verified, application development is influenced by the matrix shown in Fig. 19.6, defining and influencing system aspects such as system modularity definition and composition. Where such CASE support as cluster analysis exists, it should be used to determine the initial module composition characteristics. Figure 19.6 illustrates application characteristics of distributed DSS and operational systems. Two dimensions report *DSS* and *operational* on the vertical axis (ordinate) and use *corporate wide code* versus *node autonomous code* on the horizontal axis (abscissa). Analysis has identified 10 metadata items capable of influencing and facilitating the development of individual applications in a distributed environment. Reverse engineering process modeling techniques can be used to identify processes matching the descriptions belonging to the specific quadrants of Fig. 19.6.

Common domain values: archival data and data granularity

Archival data classifications focus development on specific application types. Current-value data is processed by the transaction processing systems of the operational distributed system. Archival data is relevant only to distributed DSS systems. Data slated to be included in distributed operations can be screened out using this metadata.

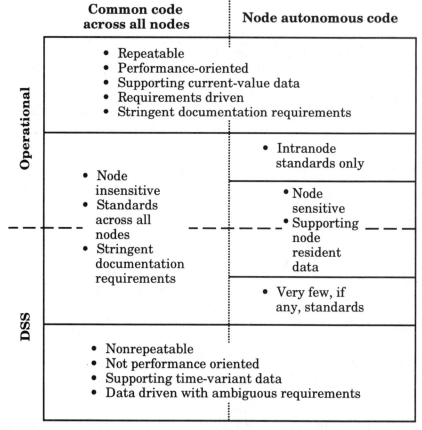

Figure 19.6 Distributed application characteristics (adapted from Inmon *Data Architecture: The Information Paradigm* © 1993 QED Technical Publishing Group).

The three types of archival data—continuous, event-discrete, and periodic-discrete—each influence the organization of archival DSS data into a data warehouse. As DSS data is considered to be read-only, keys must be designed to accommodate system growth. Reverse engineering will permit classification of the data requirements.

■ If data requirements are discovered as *continuous*, the key structure of the archived data must incorporate a *from/to date* attribute.

■ If data requirements are discovered as *event discrete*, the key structure of the archived data must incorporate an *effective date* attribute.

■ If data requirements are discovered as *periodic discrete*, the key structure of the archived data must incorporate an *as of date* attribute.

Data granularity represents the lowest level at which the data can be accessed. Usually it consists of the binary values: *data element* and *data attribute*. However, it can be, and is, also used to define larger data structures. Basic distributed system design principles encourage programs to access the smallest possible unit of data in order to reduce the potential system impact of data access and update processes. Data granularity encourages development of appropriate data access options so that efficient programs can be developed.

A third use for archival data and data granularity metadata in distributed system development concerns developing required support for transforming the current value data processed by operational distributed systems into archival DSS data. The archival processing can involve integrated conversion, logic, condensation, summarization, and filtering operations that are better understood with the aid of archival data and data granularity metadata.

Quantifiable: data access/update frequency and probability

Data access/update frequency (Fig. 19.7) and the probability of data access/update are considered in this section. Data access information is easily collected during reverse engineering analysis. For example, much information can come from system maintenance and operation records (such as system management data). In general these indicators should provide strong positive confirmation as to whether the physical data should be stored in normalized forms or denormalized, typically to achieve better performance characteristics. According to Inmon [1993], the following heuristics can be applied:

■ Data that is frequently accessed and not frequently updated
  should be denormalized for performance by
  — Adding redundant data to reduce inputs and outputs.
  — Grouping tables by like keys.
  — Creating arrays of data in rows.

	Frequently accessed	Infrequently accessed
Frequently updated		
Infrequently updated		

Figure 19.7   Quantifiable metadata characterizing access and update requirements.

— Separating data into smaller tables on the basis of access.
— Introducing derived or calculated data when it is accessed frequently.

■ Data that is frequently updated and not accessed should be normalized.

■ Data that doesn't fit either of the above categories should be modeled and operationally simulated under various likely current and future conditions to determine proper normalization.

Probability of access is determined by comparing the access/update frequency with other system data to calculate an overall probability of access/update for each data item. This information can be used to determine node residency by simulating operational conditions and other application development issues.

Organization-specific: data stewardship and data system of record

Data groupings are user-defined groupings possibly unrelated to subject areas or locations. These provide information as to informal uses of data. *Data location* provides links between data and usage. The *data stewardship* must be recorded because it is often different from the data residency characteristic. Data stewards are responsible for protecting the value of a specific data asset. The *system of record* is an operating protocol indicating that at any point in time there can be one and only one process responsible for maintaining any one collection of data.

When combined with data access/update and data frequency/probability metadata, these last four metadata items provide crucial links, determining candidate arrangements of processing data throughout the system and documenting connections between data items, functional stewardship, and system access. Data locations can also be determined using the CRUD matrices linking data to processes developed during reverse engineering. Development principles indicate that data should be located at the node containing the highest probability of access. Frequently accessed and frequently updated physical data groupings can then be distributed throughout the system via load balancing or other task distribution techniques.

Organizational Capability Assessment

In addition to the information provided specifically to distributed architecture and application development, a third category of more-or-less unspoken and undocumented metadata can be used to perform a reality check on the suitability of the application under consideration to (1) be successfully implemented by the organization and (2) meet the needs of the project sponsor. Distributed system development challenges are combined systems and process challenges. For example, the process of migrating toward networked systems management represents a three-stage process of first managing organizational networks, then managing the organizational systems, and finally combining both forms of management into networked systems management. Organizational maturity will play a role in development and implementation success [Nolan 1979]. Organizations reaching toward higher levels of maturity will be leaving the firefighting stage behind and are headed toward optimal organizational performance [Caldwell 1994]. The very concepts that enable distributed systems to appear appealing to organizational management— uniformity of corporate processing, lower hardware processing costs, ownership of data, and organizational discipline—are often more difficult to implement than are the technical aspects of systems development. Some organizations have been unprepared, for example, to fund requisite technical specialist positions required to keep distributed systems operating efficiently. Organizations unable to demonstrate success at reverse engineering probably will fail as well at their attempts to implement distributed systems.

Organizational Guidance

Organizational guidance may come from a number of areas, depending on organizational experience. For the following areas, tradeoff analysis and selection are facilitated since just a few vendors dominate the markets for

■ Organizational standards for operating platform hardware

■ Network operating systems

■ Network management applications

■ Systems integration support

Identifying .... how much can be learned
Subtracting .... (– how much was learned)
Resulting in assessments of ... what was learned and what wasn't learned
What was learned is .... (+ applied to the problem at hand)
Resulting in evaluation
of the process .... lessons learned

Figure 19.8   Assessing metadata usage effectiveness.

When this guidance exists and is combined with the 16 metadata items, the amount and kind of guidance available to systems developers become clear. Understanding this metadata and its usage (Fig. 19.8) can result in project management's ability to develop plans to ensure that maximum effectiveness is obtained during the reengineering effort. This includes developing a plan for ensuring that information sources are identified, obtaining the information, adding it to the project or organizational data bank, and finally applying it usefully to the development of the target system.

Development methodologies often produce system specifications as an early step. These specifications are used as the basis for new system development. The process is generally no different for the development of distributed systems. Increasingly, however, new systems development is being viewed as reengineering efforts and includes plans for the reverse engineering of specific system components in order to obtain information useful for informing the development planning and guiding the implementation. When viewed as a reengineering project, there are two possible implications: (1) insertion of a formal step in the development methodology used to enhance the quality of the system specifications (Fig. 19.1) and (2) collection of additional metadata that can useful for informing the development planning and guiding the implementation (Figs. 19.2 through 19.4). From an operational perspective:

■ If the project has already begun and has transformed or been recognized as a reengineering effort instead of a new systems development effort, the question to be addressed is "What can we learn from the reverse engineered system components that will inform the development planning and guide the implementation?"
  – If reverse engineering analyses have already been performed, then capture the metadata from the reverse engineering analysis of those components.
  – If reverse engineering analyses have not been performed yet, then plan to capture the additional metadata items as described.

■ If the project is planned as a reengineering project from the start, the reverse engineering plans should include capture of these additional metadata items during the reverse engineering analysis.

Chapter

20

DRE Trends and Research

This chapter is a resource for locating additional information about reverse engineering and related topics. Many findings came from extensive literature searches—some sources are shown in Fig. 20.1. An initial version of a reverse engineering bibliography is available from the author upon request or by visiting my World Wide Web home page at

    http://128.172.188.1/isydept/faculty/paiken/paiken.htm

Figure 20.2 adds the results of extensive searches of publications listed in Fig. 20.1, among others. Although the authors of some articles mixed up the terms a little, the results indicate eight topic groupings of more than 250 entries. I included the 42 nonduplicated articles from Arnold's *Software Reengineering* [1993] collection, the special issues of the *Communications of the ACM* (May 1994) and *IEEE Software* (January 1995) yielding more than 300 entries. The chapter presents a representative example for each topic grouping, followed by some more general pointers to other topic areas. (The references presented are not intended to be comprehensive, and omission

- *Communications of the ACM*
- *Computerworld*
- *Computing Canada*
- *Corporate Computing*
- *Database Programming & Design*
- *Datamation*
- *High Performance Systems*
- *Government Computer News*
- *Federal Computer Week*
- *IBM Systems Journal*

- *The IEEE publications database*
- *InformationWEEK*
- *Journal of Strategic Information Systems*
- *Microprocessors and Microsystems*
- *Management Information Systems Quarterly*
- *Office Systems and Technology*
- *PC Week*
- *Software—Practice and Experience*
- *Software Magazine*

Figure 20.1 Representative information sources for the literature survey.

of any particular work does not imply that the work is any less significant than those appearing in this chapter.)

Reverse Engineering Research Topic Groupings

Tool-focused

The most popular category consisted of papers and articles describing a tool-based approach to some aspect of software reverse engineering (see Fig. 20.2). Typically these articles focused on:

- The development and usage of environments facilitating software reengineering [Desclaux and Ribault 1991, Choi and Scacchi 1991, Kozaczynski et al. 1991, Abd-El-Hafiz et al. 1991, and Lanubile et al. 1991]

- Computer-aided reengineering tool surveys [Krallmann and Wohrle 1992, and Fogel 1992]

- The impact of reverse engineering on CASE technologies [Drake 1992, Usowicz 1990, and Warden 1991]

- Automated support of software development environments [Jones 1992, Canfora et al. 1991, Karakostas 1991, and Slusky 1991]

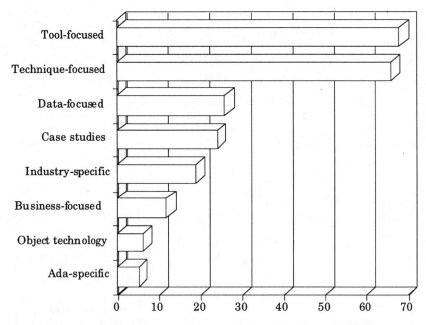

Figure 20.2   Data reverse engineering paper and article topic groupings.

It is perhaps significant that this first group of articles seems to be attempting to demonstrate success at the process of reverse engineering. This has indicated to the rest of the community that reverse engineering can be accomplished.

Technique-focused

The second largest group of topics described reverse engineering techniques. Again, representative of these were papers and articles on

- Integrated reengineering/migration frameworks—For example, The Systems Redevelopment Methodology (TSRM) is a proprietary systems redevelopment methodology that has been successfully applied in a number of contexts. (TSRM is a registered trademark of James Martin and Co. [Ulrich 1990, 1994])

- Approaches to software reengineering [Warden 1989, Lerner 1991, and Shagam 1991]

- Integrating reengineering concepts in traditional development methodologies [St-Denis 1991]

- Economics of software reengineering [Sneed 1991b]

- User involvement in software reengineering [Ning 1990, and Delligatta 1992]

- Research overviews [Hall 1992]

- Reengineering perils [Cafasso 1993, and McPartlin 1993]

Writers on topics in this category were intent on describing how some aspect of reverse engineering was or ought to be occurring. They help illustrate how the reverse engineering process occurs.

Data-focused

This group carries a central theme that data-architecture-based development will provide the means organization need to develop the dexterity required to achieve enterprise integration. Representative of the 25 or so articles were the following discussions of

- Data warehousing and other data management oriented topics [Inmon 1992b, Stodder 1992]

- Data migration issues [Ulrich 1990, and Van Kirk 1992]

- Producing different types of data assets (object- and process-oriented) from systems [Breuer and Lano 1991]

- Data integration issues [Howe 1993]

- Modeling of intermodular data flow [Canfora and Cimitile 1992]

- Extraction of business knowledge from programs [Chikofsky 1990, and Karakostas 1992]

- Schema transformations into relational format [Fong 1992]

- Data modeling—the basis for integration [Hars and Scheer 1991]

Data-oriented topics typically didn't try to "preach to the choir." Instead, they attempted to extend the basic information engineering principles and clarify certain aspects of existing procedures.

Case studies

The fourth category of more than 20 entries consisted of descriptions of reverse engineering projects in organizations. Figure 20.3 summarizes these contributions. The case study approach is typically used to help readers understand the application of a concept in the context of its environment. Another effect occurs from the description of the performance of any products used in the projects. While not direct endorsements, they do serve to highlight the use of certain products and can assist readers to predict their performance in the reader's context. Case studies also tend to be truthful. Organizations participating in the studies often receive correspondence from others wanting to know more. The same number of category entries appeared in trade publications and conference proceedings and, perhaps not surprisingly, most reported success stories.

Industry-specific focus

Another popular class of entries concerned a broader focus on the impact of reverse engineering on specific industries. Taken together, these two categories would have been the third most popular category. The strategic level or otherwise broader focus of entries in this category served to differentiate them. Examples included

- Health care
  - The application of software reengineering techniques to health information systems [Muller et al. 1991]
  - The importance of addressing maintenance costs in health care information systems [Helppie 1992, and Morris and Brandon 1991]

- Insurance and Finance
  - Reengineering the insurance industry [Brady 1992, Lawrence 1991, and Wilson 1992b]
  - How the finance market is making use of reengineering [Schmerken 1992]

— How banks are investing in CASE software reengineering tools
[Radding 1990]

■ Government Systems
— Large scale system migration [Caldwell 1992, and Smith 1993]
— The concept of "creeping complexity" in complex software systems [Weil 1992]
— Government practices shared among agencies [Moore 1993]

Organization	Project	Products/vendors	Reference
(Anonymous)	System's complexity and the difficulties that were encountered in originally installing it become exaggerated	Microsoft Excel	*Corporate Computing* [Chivvis and Geyer 1992]
Allnet Communication Services Inc.	Reengineering a mission-critical billing application result in a reduction from 6 million records processed to 500,000	VIA/Renaissance/ Viasoft Inc.'s products	*Datamation* [Kador 1992]
Australia	Specific legal ruling on the effects of 'reverse engineering' under Australian law		*Tolley's Computer Law and Practice* [Hughes 1992]
CNUCE-CNR	Redesign of a general-purpose data-processing center management program	• AD/Cycle "family" CASE tool • SYSTEM 2000 • SQL/DS	*Proceedings SHARE Europe Spring Meeting.* [Signore and Celiano 1991]
Columbia University	Downsize university computer systems to a client/server architecture		*Computerworld* [Ballou 1992]
Dept. of Computers and Information Sci., Kansas State Univ.	Reengineering a FORTRAN program into an Ada program		*Software— Practice and Experience* [Byrne 1991]
Dept. of Computer Sci., Northern Illinois Univ.	A methodology for reverse engineering an existing IMS database into the entity-relationship model	IMS	*Proceedings of the Ninth International Conference* [Winans and Davis 1991]

Figure 20.3 Descriptions of reverse engineering projects in organizations.

Organization	Project	Products/vendors	Reference
ESPRIT METKIT laboratory experiment	Laboratory experiment provided data enabling the assessment of the benefits of reengineering old programs		*Proceedings. Conference on Software Maintenance 1990* [Sneed and Kaposi 1990]
Federal Aviation Administration	Reengineer a major portion of the New York terminal approach control (TRACON) real-time application software to IBM/370		*IBM Systems Journal* [Britcher 1990]
Internal Revenue Service	A case study that examines the feasibility and cost-effectiveness of CASE tool use for reengineering.		NIST Special Publication [Ruhl and Gunn 1991]
Kimberly-Clark Cigna Systems	Discussion of practices at respective organizations		*Computerworld* [Margolis 1992] [Caron et al. 1994]
Kimberly-Clark	Internally developed product marketed by IS to outsiders turns out to be a new business venture	K-C Enable/DB2 converts programs based on Computer Associates International Inc.'s Datacom/DB to IBM's DB2 database	*Datamation* [Francis 1990]
Los Alamos National Lab.	Reengineering the Los Alamos common file system	Unix-type file system	*Digest of Papers. Tenth IEEE Symposium on Mass Storage Systems.* [Christman et al. 1990]
Miltope Corp.	Integrating manufacturing and other business processes	• Cimcenter/ Cincom • Lexel • MAPICS DB/IBM • VMS/DEC	*Corporate Computing* [Pelton 1993]
Pacific Bell	GEMSTAR C-based software reengineering project—modeling PacBell's systems as a finite state machine	• Code Check • Tandem Computers Inc.	*LAN Technology* [Stapleton and Sarasin 1992]

Figure 20.3 (*Continued*) Descriptions of reverse engineering projects in organizations.

Organization	Project	Products/vendors	Reference
Reasoning Systems	What aspects of the reengineering process seem to be most amenable to automation and what productivity gains can be expected		*Proceedings, 14th Annual International Computer Software and Applications Conference* [Markosian et al. 1990]
San Diego Gas	A "to be" reengineering project		*Computerworld* [Hoffman 1993]
Siemens	The roots and intentions, the advantages and disadvantages of CASE and CASE standardization issues	DOMINO GRAPES /Siemens	*European Symposium on Software Development Environments and CASE Technology; Proceedings* [Wagner 1991]
The Travelers Co.	Reengineering mainframe-based COBOL	• Renaissance /Viasoft Inc. • Via/Insight, Via/Smart/ Compuware Corp. • InterPort Software Corp.	*Software Magazine* [Bucken 1992]
Chevron Information Technology Co.	Upgrade an accounts-payable application	PowerBuilder/ PowerSoft Corp.	*PC Week* [Comaford 1992]
Union Bank of Switzerland	Seven bank applications with 203 programs and 432 files were renovated and migrated from a UNIVAC-494 to a UNISYS-1100	JSP-DELTA	*Conference on Software Maintenance 1991* [Sneed 1991a]
Mutual Benefit Life	Classic reengineering success story		*Journal of Strategic Information Systems* [Cliff 1992]
USAF	The Air Force is modernizing its Computer-Aided Load Manifesting (CALM) system	Reengineering will involve converting the software from C to Ada and running CALM in an open systems environment	*Government Computer News* [Endoso 1993]
Union Pacific Railroad	"Screen-scrape" reengineering	• RAIL • OS/2 Oracle	*PC Week* [Comaford 1992]

Figure 20.3 (*Continued*)   Descriptions of reverse engineering projects in organizations.

Business Process Reengineering

The sixth category consisted of articles focusing on business process reengineering, either explaining its use in context or attempting to sell people on the concept. Some additional examples include

- Reports on the "young discipline" of process modeling [Curtis et al. 1992]

- Information Engineering (IE)–based projects benefiting from reengineering [Errico and Sullivan 1992]

- Debating whether process reengineering can be accomplished separate from information technology considerations [Wilson 1992a]

- The need for computer literacy at the CEO level [McClatchy 1990]

Business process reengineering currently goes under a number of names, but since Hammer and Champy's [1993] text sold 100,000 copies "business process reengineering" is now the most common term.

Object technology–specific and Ada-specific

The handful of object technology–specific and Ada-specific entries illustrated how well reverse engineering has instantiated itself into these respective and sometimes overlapping communities. The major conferences regularly run reengineering tracks [van Lamsweerde and Fugetta 1991, Norman and Van Ghent 1991, and Dekleva 1991], and there are examples of synergistic research [Lee 1991] between the Ada and object technology communities. (Readers interested in a discussion of the application of enterprise-level object technology should consult Mattison [1994].

Other Topic Sources

In addition to the preceding very brief look at the results of a snapshot of part of the literature, it will be useful to briefly note some informative literature on the following subjects.

Software reengineering literature

Arnold has complied "a substantial body of software reengineering literature" in his contributed text, *Software Reengineering* [1993]. This 600-page collection contains chapters specific to business process reengineering, reengineering experiences, reengineering technology, software code analysis, restructuring and translation, program understanding, and knowledge-based program analysis, as well as many others. The collection makes a good starting place for further research into the software side of reengineering.

Software reengineering economics

An excellent starting place to learn further about the economics of software reengineering is a series of papers by Sneed [Sneed 1984, Sneed and Kaposi 1990, Sneed 1991a, Sneed 1991b, and Sneed 1995].

Software engineering tools

Sharon's [1993] regular column, "Tool Box," in *IEEE Software* is a good place to go for assistance understanding and evaluating software engineering tools. Francett [1989] provides a description of a narrow range of conversion tools. Don't forget about the previously mentioned (Chap. 12) STSC *Reengineering Tools Report* [Sittenauer et al. 1992].

Information engineering

Perhaps most notable are the volumes available from Clive Finkelstein [1993] and James Martin [1989]. In particular, Finkelstein has provided support for object as well as processed-based analysis components in his methodology.

Data administration

Durrell [1985] wrote what was probably the first text on data administration. Although it is out of print, it is still possible to locate copies and worth reading. In addition, the Data Administration Management Association (DAMA), with regional branches internationally, is an excellent source of information on this important topic. Contact them at the address below or any other regional location.

DAMA
National Capital Region
6729 Curran Street
McLean, VA 22101 USA

Data modeling/data analysis

While practically all college-level system analysis and design texts contain chapters on data modeling and data analysis, more often better explanations are to be found in other sources, including Finkelstein [1993]. Information specific to data integration can be found in Hars and Scheer [1991], and Batini et al. [1986] among others. Hay [1995] has a publication with the intriguing title *Data Model Patterns: Conventions of Thought* to be issued shortly from

Dorset House Publishing. It indicates that it will offer ways of gaining insight into business structure using (and reusing) data model patterns found in many types of businesses.

Business rules

Not a terrifically popular topic but one of growing importance. Appleton's writings in *Datamation* during the early 1980s are an excellent starting place (see for example Appleton [1983, 1984, 1985, and 1986]). Von Halle and Kull have included several excellent articles in their *Handbook of Data Management* [1993]. Recent issues of *Data Management Review* and *Database Programming and Design* have also contained good articles. Ross [1994] has recently issued the third version of *The Business Rule Book*. Subtitled *Classifying, Defining And Modeling Rules,* it is a comprehensive presentation of Ross' classification scheme for business rule types.

Data and information architectures

John Zachman wrote the most popular systems architecture paper in 1987 and updated it five years later [Sowa and Zachman 1992]. This description of a number of perspectives to be addressed when developing architected products is required reading for anyone wishing to be conversant in this field. Other examples include Spewak's [1993] *Enterprise Architecture Planning*, Inmon's [1992] *Data Architecture: The Information Paradigm*, and more technically, the previously mentioned *Enterprise Integration Modeling: Proceedings of the First International Conference* [Petrie 1992].

Data warehousing

Inmon [1992] has written widely quoted articles endorsing the concept of a data warehouse.

GOV SIG as a source of data assets

Government representatives are organizing a group (see Fig. 20.4) intended to facilitate the exchange of information among government organizations. After all, they reason, why model the federal acquisition regulations again if this has been already been accomplished? Contact them at the addresses below for further information about the government special interest group.

DAMA-NCR /GOV-SIG
Attention: Pam Piper
6729 Curran Street
McLean, VA 22101
E-mail: piper1p@cc.ims.disa.mil

Government Special Interest Group (GOV-SIG) About to Be Launched

With the assistance of NIST and DISA/CIM, DAMA is preparing to launch a Government Special Interest Group (GOV-SIG) under the DAMA-NCR umbrella. The purpose of the GOV-SIG is to promote networking, information exchange, and self-help to SHARE/RE-USE existing data administration (DA) products and experience that would be useful during any business reengineering efforts among members. While the SIG will be affiliated with the National Capital Region we welcome a broad range of both interest and participation from DA groups around the country including but not limited to government representatives who would like to network between, exchange information and lessons learned among, provide assistance to, or receive assistance from other government affiliated DA groups.

Figure 20.4 Government SIG approach to data asset sharing.

Dissertations

Eighteen dissertations and theses of interest are listed in Fig. 20.5. No doubt more have been written since this list was compiled.

Title	Author	School/degree
A Component Factory for Software Source Code Reengineering and Reuse (Reusable Components)	Bailey, John Winston	University of Maryland College Park (Ph.D.)
Reverse Engineering of VA Fileman/Mumps Specifications to Conceptual Extended Entity Relationship Schema	Kalyanpur, Gaurang Suresh	The University of Texas at Arlington (M.S.)
The Identification of Key Business Processes	Updike, Lianne Renee	San Jose State University (M.S.)
Group Matrix: A Collaborative Modeling Tool (Electronic Meeting Systems)	Hayes, Glenda Sue	The University of Arizona (Ph.D.)
A Presentation Environment for Improving Software Understanding	Duncan, Robert Paul	The University of Alabama Huntsville (M.S.)
APEX: Ada Programming Expert System, a Computer-Aided System Engineering Tool	Lee, Rosalind Hua	California State University, Long Beach (M.S.)
Knowledge-Based Adaptive Software Automation Using Programming Knowledge Tools of Mat and Pmat: Theory and Implementation Design	Han, David Chiao Do	Illinois Institute of Technology (Ph.D.)

Figure 20.5 Relevant dissertations and theses.

Title	Author	School/degree
Software Maintenance Environment and Its Supporting Tools for Assembly Programs (Tools)	Chen, Shuyuan	University of Minnesota (Ph.D.)
Automatic Control Understanding for Natural Programs (Program Understanding, Software Maintenance, Reverse Engineering)	Hartman, John Edwin	The University of Texas at Austin (Ph.D.)
A Procedure for Software Module Upgrades	Li, Marvin Xuewen	University of Victoria (Canada) M.S.C.
A Vision System Model (Edge Detection, Color, Attention Mechanisms, VLSI Circuits)	Fretheim, Erik J.	Air Force Institute of Technology (Ph.D.)
Modeling and Manufacturing of Multiple Featured Objects Based on Measurement Data (CAD)	Sarkar, Biplab	The Ohio State University (Ph.D.)
Integrating Reverse Engineering into Computer-Aided Software Engineering (CASE)	Usowicz, Thaddeus W.	University of California, San Francisco (Ph.D.)
Reverse Engineering in CASE	Bierman, David Stuart	The University of New Brunswick (Canada) (M.S. CCS)
A Persistent Environment for Micro-Incremental Reuse (Software Reuse, Version Management)	Kazerooni-Zand, Mansour	Oklahoma State University (Ph.D.)
SOFTMAN: An Environment Supporting the Engineering and Reverse Engineering of Large Scale Software Systems	Choi, Song Chol	University of Southern California (Ph.D.)
Reverse Engineering of Databases: Extraction of Domain Semantics	Chaing, R. L.	University of Rochester (Ph.D.)
Role of Reverse Engineering in the Development of Functional Tests for Microprocessors (Controllability, Observability, Cooling)	Lin, Ming-Guan	Rensselaer Polytechnic Institute (Ph.D.)

Figure 20.5 (*Continued*)   Relevant dissertations and theses.

21

Reengineering's Indeterminate Results

Indeterminate adj.

1. a. Not precisely determined, determinable, or established—a person of indeterminate age. b. not precisely fixed, as to extent, size, nature, or number—an indeterminate number of plant species in the jungle. c. lacking clarity or precision, as in meaning; vague—an indeterminate turn of phrase. d. not fixed or known in advance—an indeterminate future. e. not leading up to a definite result or ending—an indeterminate campaign.

Synonym(s): adjective—Lacking precise limits; indefinite, inexact, undetermined.

Source: *American Heritage English Dictionary* © 1993 Houghton Mifflin Company.

In the Fall 1994 issue of the *CALS/Enterprise Integration Journal,* Oracle Corporation ran an advertisement. Over the caption "Can you remember why reengineering was such a good idea in the first place?" it showed a photograph of an individual sitting on a bench—alone. An overcoat is draped to one side and a paper cup sits on the other side. The individual's head rests face down on a pair of hands with intertwined fingers—a worried posture. The implication is that the head-hanging individual is apparently attempting to determine where the reengineering project had gone wrong and how to get it back on track. Oracle is advertising its reengineering capabilities and has apparently decided the "fix the reengineering projects gone astray business" is a good one to pursue.

Much has been written about reengineering in the last few years. Ulrich [1991] summarized it well, stating (a software perspective):

Reengineering has received widespread attention as of late. Unfortunately, not all the coverage has been favorable. Reengineering successes, and failures, have been exaggerated beyond reasonable hype Slang. n.

1. Excessive publicity and the ensuing commotion: the hype surrounding the murder trial.

2. Exaggerated or extravagant claims made especially in advertising or promotional material: "It is pure hype, a gigantic PR job" (*Saturday Review*).

3. An advertising or promotional ploy: "Some restaurant owners in town are cooking up a $75,000 hype to promote New York as 'Restaurant City, USA'" (*New York*).

4. Something deliberately misleading; a deception: "[He] says that there isn't any energy crisis at all, that it's all a hype, to maintain outrageous profits for the oil companies" (Joel Oppenheimer).

To publicize or promote, especially by extravagant, inflated, or misleading claims: hyped the new book by sending its author on a promotional tour. [Partly from hype, a swindle (perhaps from HYPER-) and partly from HYPE(RBOLE).]

Synonym(s): no synonyms found for hype.

Figure 21.1 Searching for reengineering facts involves sorting reality from hype (Source: *American Heritage English Dictionary* © 1993 Houghton Mifflin Company).

proportion leading to two potentially serious problems. First, certain organizations have written off reengineering as a build/buy alternative without clearly investigating how it can help. Others view reengineering as a panacea for solving every MIS problem. Somewhere between these two views lies a realistic approach for systematically changing current information systems to meet ever changing business needs.

Many organizations have initiated reengineering projects, and a variety of results have been reported. There has been much excitement about reengineering. Some organizations have reported substantial gains in efficiency and productivity. However, even proponents have been quoted as explaining why project failure rates could be as high as 70 percent [Caldwell 1994]. What follows is an overview of what has been reported about reengineering results (both software and business process). Understanding the nature of the available facts will lead to better-informed decision making.

Reengineering Hype

Reengineering received tremendous publicity resulting in and as a result of the sales of *Reengineering the Corporation* [Hammer and Champy 1993]. As Strassman [1994] asks rhetorically, "What manager wouldn't support the notion of taking something that is defective and fixing it?" But attempts to sort reality from hype (Fig. 21.1) have so far had limited success. Literature searches reveal hundreds of reports of individual success and/or failure stories; for example, consider a 1994 Internet posting summarizing an article originally in *The Wall Street Journal* (Fig. 21.2). And the various surveys detailed in the next section present a variety of sometimes confusing and conflicting results (from a business process reengineering perspective).

Date: Thu, 20 Oct 1994 Subject: Computer Mess at Greyhound

The 20 Oct 1994 Wall Street Journal contains an article about computerization at Greyhound that you'll have to read to believe. The full reference is: Robert Tomsho, How Greyhound Lines re-engineered itself right into a deep hole, *The Wall Street Journal*, 20 October 1994, pages A1, A10.

After Greyhound came out of bankruptcy a few years ago, a new management team declared that they would revolutionize the company by cutting costs and creating a huge computerized reservations system to replace the existing collection of incompatible systems and things done by hand. They called it "re-engineering". Wall Street liked this idea and bid up the company's stock price. The managers, feeling obliged to keep the stock price up, promised that the system would work on schedule.

But of course it didn't, for reasons that won't surprise Risks readers. The main problem is that buses make many more stops than airplanes, meaning that a bus scheduling system is an order of magnitude harder to build than an airline scheduling system, which is already one of the most complex things anybody ever built. The system started slipping behind schedule, and the prototype had a terrible interface, crashed all the time, and hung up on people.

Meanwhile, Greyhound was falling apart. Employee turnover was very high, customer service was terrible, the computer was messing up everything it touched, and the company advertised a discount program even though it had no chance of handling the expected volume of business. Yet the stock price stayed high because stock analysts, who make dramatically more money than Greyhound's customers, don't ride buses and so didn't see the problems. This postponed the day of reckoning long enough to cause tremendous disruption for the customers -- and long enough for the top managers of the company to cash in a pile of options while the stock was still at its highest level.

"Looking back, Mr. [Thomas] Thompson [the vice president in charge of developing the system] says, "I should have quit or just said that I couldn't do it." Instead, most copies of his report [warning of difficulties with the system] were destroyed, and any mention of it was purged from many Greyhound agendas, calendars and computer files, many people say."

It's distressing that words like "reengineering" can have such magical force for so many people that well-known pitfalls in system implementation can go undetected for so long -- except, of course, by the working people who have to use the systems or get around on the bus.

Figure 21.2 Internet posting of a reengineering effort and poster's comments.

Activity modeling
Business process analysis
Business process improvement
Business process reengineering
IDEFing
Industrial engineering
Process modeling
Reengineering
Reinvention

Figure 21.3   Terms often used interchangeably.

Interestingly, much of the contradictory information can probably be explained as a data synonym problem. Fig. 21.3 is an incomplete list of terms often used interchangeably by a community encompassing the consulting–systems integration industry—the computer science community focused on software reengineering research—and the Office of the Vice President's Reinventing Government Initiative.

Differing definitions and interchangeable usage across the reengineering community have led to interesting results. Consider the statistic noted by Deloitte & Touche in their 1994 CIO survey. The term *reengineering* was undefined in the 1991 and 1992 surveys but was defined as "the radical change of critical business processes and their supporting systems to effect breakthrough gains in performance" for the 1993 survey. Reengineering projects launched per company rose from 1.6 in 1991 to 4.4. in 1992 but fell to 3.2 in 1993 [Deloitte & Touche 1994]. Similarly, a Forrester Research survey (as reported by Caldwell [1994]) of 50 companies claiming to be sponsoring reengineering projects determined that 42 percent were really "just tweaking things here and there, looking for incremental improvements to ongoing operations." Nevertheless, reengineering (of all sorts) is a $32 billion industry—with spending forecast to rise to $52 billion by 1997 and of that $40 billion will be spent for information systems. With the wide use of the term *reengineering* and the growing marketplace, it isn't surprising that so many different results are reported. Useful results range from careful research studies such as those conducted by Sneed [1991b] and Caron et al. [1994] to a series of reengineering surveys. The next section presents a summary of the surveys as reported in the literature. It is followed by a series of questions that might be considered by an organization considering reengineering as a strategy. The questions are addressed using the reengineering survey facts.

Reengineering Surveys

Literature reviews revealed widely reported and quoted surveys attempting to assess organizational reengineering practices. When

Survey	Survey performed by	Useful facts
ALD	Arthur D. Little	2
B&C	Baine & Company	1
CE	Computer Economics	1
CSC	CSC/Index Corporation	7
D&T	Deloitte & Touche	10
GMC	Gateway Management Consulting	10
IBM	IBM	1
IDC	International Data Corporation	1
PBMS	Pitney Bowes Management Services	4

Figure 21.4 Fact source key.

possible, the original survey results were obtained. What follows are relevant facts from these surveys. Facts were numbered with unique identifiers according to Fig. 21.4.

Arthur D. Little

Who was surveyed: 350 executives in more than a dozen industries

Reported by: Currid [1994] and Caldwell [1994]

Findings:

ALD-1   85% were unhappy with their company's reengineering efforts

ALD-2   16% were "fully satisfied" with their company's reengineering efforts

Unanswered questions:

■ What industries were surveyed?

■ What was the cause of the "unhappiness": not enough reengineering efforts, inadequate reengineering, insufficient results or something else?

■ In what state of completion were the reengineering projects?

Baine & Company

Who was surveyed: 500 business executives

Reported by: King [1995]

Findings:

B&C-1 Ranking of management tools:
  1.   Mission statements
  2.   Customer surveys

3.   Total quality management
4.   Pay for performance
5.   Reengineering
6.   Strategic alliances
7.   Self-directed teams
8.   Cycle time reduction
9.   Core competencies
10.   Competitor profiling

Unanswered questions:

■ What industries?

■ Was the term *reengineering* defined?

Computer Economics, Inc.

Who was surveyed: 1200 organizations

Reported by: Caldwell [1994]

Findings:

CE-1   Total spending on business reengineering will grow by
        20% each year during the years 1994–1996.

Unanswered questions:

■ What industries?

■ What was the basis for the conclusion?

CSC/Index Corporation

Who was surveyed: 497 North American and 124 European chief
                       operating officers

Reported by: CSC [1994], Currid [1994], and Caldwell
                  [1994]

Findings:

CSC-1   69% of North American and 75% of European chief oper-
         ating officers reported at least one reengineering project
         under way.

CSC-2   The North American respondents reported an average of
         3.3 projects; the Europeans reported an average of 3.8.

CSC-3   Of those who weren't reengineering, 51% were planning to
         launch one in the next 12 months or were considering one.

CSC-4   71% of the reengineering initiatives were incomplete at
         survey time.

CSC-5   "The majority of companies that were reengineering reported that they were meeting or exceeding most or all of their project goals."

CSC-6   Almost half the respondents were dissatisfied with their reengineering.

CSC-7   Of North American reengineering projects, 38% had reduced costs (by an average of 18%), 15% had increased revenues (by an average of 18%), 23% had reduced cycle times (by an average of 37%), 27% had increased productivity (by an average of 23%).

Unanswered questions:

■ When were the executives surveyed?

■ Was the term *reengineering* defined on the survey?

Deloitte & Touche

Who was surveyed: 400 (+) CIOs

Reported by: Deloitte & Touche [1994], Currid [1994]

Findings:

D&T-1   68% reported satisfaction.

D&T-2   5% reported dissatisfaction.

D&T-3   27% indicated the jury was still out.

D&T-4   After "organizational resistance to change" (indicated by 59% of respondents), the "limitations of existing systems" were ranked as the next most important obstacle to reengineering success (40% of respondents).

D&T-5   80% had at least one reengineering project under way in 1993.

D&T-6   On average organizations started 3.2 reengineering projects in 1993.

D&T-7   Most popular reengineering foci: accounting and finance, order processing, and customer service.

D&T-8   Respondents listed "communication and networking" more frequently that any other enabling technologies.

D&T-9   Respondents indicated 60% of mission-critical applications need to be replaced or radically improved.

D&T-10   59% of respondents said resistance to change was a significant obstacle.

Gateway Management Consulting

Who was surveyed: 514 top executives throughout the country: 128 CEOs and COOs, 133 CFOs, 127 CIOs, and 126 HR directors; industry types were manufacturing (210), utilities (102), and insurance (202).

Reported by: Gateway [1993], Smith [1992], McPartlin [1993], Currid [1994]

Findings:

GMC-1   Reengineering is the most popular initiative taken by senior management when attempting to achieve strategic objectives: 88% reported reengineering, 78% reported automation, 77% reported restructuring, 67% reported downsizing, and 40% reported outsourcing.

GMC-2   About 70% of survey participants are familiar with the concept of reengineering.

GMC-3   There are 41.2% currently involved in reengineering.

GMC-4   Another 6.8% are actively considering reengineering.

GMC-5   Almost 30% were unfamiliar with the term *reengineering*.

GMC-6   22% had no plans to reengineer.

GMC-7   Insurance companies are more involved in reengineering than are other industries.

GMC-8   70% of the companies with revenues of $1 billion or more are reengineering, while only 44% of those with revenue of less than $99 million are reengineering.

GMC-9   Over 70% of the companies with revenues of $1 billion or more are reengineering, while only 44% of those with revenue less than $99 million are reengineering.

GMC-10   The Gateway CEO was going to tell audiences in a 7-month lecture series for the American Management Association that only 5% of all companies embarking on reengineering efforts will succeed.

Unanswered questions:

■ When were the executives surveyed?

■ Was the term *reengineering* defined on the survey?

International Business Machines

Who was surveyed: A year long study of organizations using a combination of process, organizational, and client/server technologies.

Reported by: Currid [1994]

Findings:

IBM-1   84% were happy with results

Unanswered questions:

- What industries?

- When?

- Who was "happy?" Users, managers, the vendor?

International Data Corporation

Who was surveyed: 200 sites

Reported by: Currid [1994]

Findings:

IDC-1   40% consider reengineering a high priority

Unanswered questions:

- Whom did the sites represent?

Pitney Bowes Management Services

Who was surveyed: 100 of the largest *Fortune* 500 firms involved in reengineering initiatives with 32% responding.

Reported by: King [1995]

Findings:

PBMS-1   70% experienced an increase in employee productivity.

PBMS-2   38% stated that the single biggest challenge was motivation and encouraging employees to change.

PBMS-3   60% believed employees felt empowered as a result of reengineering.

PBMS-4   68% reported negative outcomes.

Unanswered questions:

■ What industries?

■ In what state of completion were the reengineering projects?

Reengineering Results

The primary problem with the facts about reengineering is that they either are very detailed about one or a few specific projects or are at a relatively high level of abstraction as evidenced by the surveys. Individual experience reports are easy to locate. But consider the integration difficulties and subsequent usefulness of individual reports. The results of three organizations results were reported in the same publication [Caldwell 1994]; for example:

■ Citibank N.A. admits wasting $50 million in a year-long effort to reengineer its back office security processing.

■ American Express made mistakes at first but has managed to trim $1.2 billion as a result of completing 150 of more than 250 separate reengineering efforts.

■ Amoco failed twice during 1986 and 1990 and 'got it right the third time' in 1992 by chopping its capital budget allocation process and staffing by one third.

Presented as raw data, these results seem to indicate little more than the following broad based conclusions.

1. Many organizations are attempting reengineering.

2. Even more organizations are calling what they are doing "reengineering," but it isn't.

3. Some organizations are achieving remarkable results doing what they call "reengineering."

Not much guidance is available for a CEO or CIO facing a potential reengineering challenge (presented by any of the three proposals presented in Chap. 1). A list of questions to be addressed could include those presented below. Facts and interpretations supporting information answering each question are noted for each answer.

What percent of companies in the United States have been or are involved in reengineering projects?

■ A survey of 500 business executives reported in 1995 that reengineering was ranked as the fifth most popular management tool [B&C-1].

■ When 514 top executives in the manufacturing, utilities, and insurance industries were surveyed, reengineering was the most popular initiative taken by senior management when attempting to achieve strategic objectives [GMC-1].

■ Organizational reengineering spending is forecast to grow [CE-1].

How much organizational reengineering experience has been accumulated?

■ Of 497 North American and 124 European chief operating officers surveyed, 69 and 75 percent, respectively, reported at least one reengineering project under way [CSC-1].

■ The North American respondents reported an average of 3.3 projects; the Europeans reported an average of 3.8 reengineering projects under way [CSC-2].

■ Of the 621 North American and European chief operating officers surveyed, 51 percent who were not already reengineering were planning to launch a project in the next 12 months or were considering one [CSC-3].

■ A survey of more than 400 CIOs using a precise definition of the term reengineering reported that 80 percent had at least one reengineering project under way in 1993 [D&T-5].

■ The same survey reported an average of 3.2 "business process reengineering" projects launched per organization [D&T-6].

■ Of 514 top executives in the manufacturing, utilities, and insurance industries 41 percent are currently involved in reengineering [GMC-3].

■ Of same executives, almost 7 percent are actively considering reengineering [GMC-4].

■ Of same executives, 22 percent did not have any plans to reengineer [GMC-6].

■ Of more than 350 executives in more than a dozen unspecified industries, 85 percent were unhappy with their organizational reengineering efforts—implying that 85 percent were sufficiently involved in reengineering to be unhappy with it—the terms "unhappy" and *reengineering* were undefined in the reported results [ALD-1].

What type of organization is reengineering?

- Larger organizations (defined as revenues greater than $1 billion) are apparently more likely to be reengineering or considering doing so than are smaller organizations [GMC-8].

- Quite a number of manufacturing, utilities, and insurance industry reengineering experiences have been reported [GMC-3].

What kinds of results have been reported?

- The majority of the 480 chief operating officers in North America and Europe surveyed who were reengineering reported that they were meeting or exceeding most or all of their project goals [CSC-5] but 71 percent of the reengineering initiatives were incomplete at the time of the survey [CSC-4].

- Of the same survey group almost half were dissatisfied with their reengineering projects [CSC-6].

- A yearlong study of organizations using a combination of process, organizational, and client-server technologies indicated that 84 percent were "happy" with the results [IBM-1].

- A 1993 survey of more than 400 CIOs reported 68 percent satisfaction [D&T-1], 5 percent dissatisfaction [D&T-2], and 27 percent indeterminate results [D&T-3].

- Of more than 350 executives in more than a dozen industries, 85 percent were unhappy with their organizational reengineering efforts (the terms "unhappy" and *reengineering* were undefined in the reported results) [ALD-1].

- A survey of 32 of 100 of the largest *Fortune* 500 firms involved in reengineering initiatives indicated that 68 percent reported negative outcomes [PBMS-4].

- The same survey indicated that 70 percent of the 32 firms experienced an increase in employee productivity and attributed it to reengineering [PBMS-1].

What technologies are employed in reengineering solutions?

- A yearlong study of organizations using a combination of process, organizational, and client/server technologies indicated that 84 percent were happy with the results [IBM-1].

- A 1993 survey of more than 400 CIOs reported communication and networking were the most popular enabling technologies [D&T-8].

How is the reengineering challenge perceived by other executives?

■ A 1993 survey of more than 400 CIOs reported more than 60 percent of their mission-critical applications need to be replaced or radically improved [D&T-9].

What are some popular reengineering focus areas?

■ A 1993 survey of more than 400 CIOs reported that accounting and finance, order processing, and customer service were the most popular [D&T-7].

What were some specific reengineering project goals and results?

■ Of the 480 chief operating officers in North America surveyed and reporting reengineering results (71 percent were incomplete), 38 percent had reduced costs (by an average of 18 percent), 15 percent had increased revenues (by an average of 18 percent), 23 percent had reduced cycle times (by an average of 37 percent), and 27 percent had increased organizational productivity (by an average of 23 percent) [CSC-7].

Have applicable reengineering critical success factors been identified?

■ A 1993 survey of more than 400 CIOs 59 percent of respondents reported that resistance to change was a significant obstacle [D&T-10].

■ A survey of 32 of 100 of the largest *Fortune* 500 firms involved in reengineering initiatives indicated 38 percent believed motivating and encouraging employees to change was the single biggest challenge to reengineering success [PBMS-2].

Where To Next?

It is clear that the community will be well served by a comprehensive survey of reengineering in practice. What is lacking are more detailed reengineering effectiveness results. Such a survey has been undertaken by my colleagues at the Air Force's Software Technology Support Center (STSC). The survey was intended to help organizations evaluate return on investment in reengineering projects. The project managers for more than 150 reengineering projects were identified and agreed to provide data for the survey. Unfortunately, the survey results have been returned at a slower rate than planned. Eighteen months after the study was initiated, about 20 surveys had been returned in time to present the results at the Fifth Systems Reengineering Technology Workshop in February 1995 [Olsem and Sittenauer 1995]. Although not enough from which to draw substantive conclusions, the most favorable results indicate 50 percent lower system maintenance costs. Other lessons gleaned from the returned surveys include

1. The need for an organizational champion to promote reengineering within the organization.

2. Organizations benefit from starting with pilot projects and progressing to larger efforts. This gives them time to develop expertise with the reengineering tools and techniques. (Interestingly, this finding contradicts a key CSC Index finding that indicated organizations targeting higher goals have a better record achieving them than do organizations setting more modest goals [CSC 1994].)

3. Organizations need to look beyond automated tools for support for their projects. Successful tools application has been accompanied by the problems mentioned previously: lack of data exchanged between the tools, lack of exact tool fit for intended applications, lack of support for development paradigm shifts, and significant human intervention required.

In the meanwhile, the investigators Olsem and Sittenauer have teamed up with an academic team led by Tilley and Kontogiannis to pool their data in hopes of achieving more significant results. It will be interesting to see if the numerous results of failed reengineering projects overcome the positive results achieved by some organizations. (Commenting on a draft of this chapter Mike Olsem wrote of his concern for "the gray distinction between business process reengineering and software reengineering." He further indicated that readers would benefit from qualifying the more general term "reengineering" by adding the qualifiers "software" and "business process" whereever the term was used in the chapter. I couldn't agree more, it will be interesting to see how long it takes the community to sort through the data synonym problems. Organizations successfully performing organizational reengineering efforts will continue to perform them regardless of what they are called. It would be a shame to base decisions on hype instead of facts. Until these or similar results have been achieved, the community will be left with broad surveys and individualized success stories. We are anxiously waiting further results. Until then, we may continue to experience confusion about reengineering effectiveness and results.)

References

[Abd-El-Hafiz et al.1991] S. Abd-El-Hafiz, V. Basili, G. Caldiera "Towards automated support for extraction of reusable components" *Proceedings. Conference on Software Maintenance 1991* (Catalog No. 91CH3047-8) p. 212-19 IEEE Computer Society Press, Los Alamitos, CA, USA.

[Abella 1991] R. Abella, J. Daschbach, L. Pawlicki "Human skill interface in reverse engineering" *Computers & Industrial Engineering* 21(1-4):495-9.

[Ackoff 1967] R. Ackoff "Management Misinformation Systems" *Management Science* December 1967, 14(4):B147-B156.

[Ackoff 1981] R. Ackoff "On the use of models in corporate planning" *Strategic Management Journal* Oct-Dec 1981 2(4):353-359.

[AHED 1993] *American Heritage English Dictionary*, Deluxe Edition, Boston: Houghton Mifflin Company, 1983

[Aiken 1987] P. Aiken "Planning for Requirements Analysis: The Straw Man Approach" *Proceedings of the 1987 IEEE International Conference on Systems, Man, and Cybernetics*, IEEE Publishing Services, pp. 329-333.

[Aiken 1989] P. Aiken *A Hypermedia Workstation for Requirements Engineering*, Ph. D. Dissertation: George Mason University, 1989.

[Aiken 1991] P. Aiken "Hypermedia-based Requirements Engineering," chapter in (Stephen J. Andriole, editor) *Advanced Technology for Command and Control Systems Engineering*, AFCEA International, 1991.

[Aiken and Bach 1993] P. Aiken, J. Bach "'Hypermedia-based Support For Requirements Analysis: Promise And Problems" *Southeast Decision Sciences Institute 1994 Annual Meeting Proceedings* March 2-4, 1994, pp. 463-465.

[Aiken and Piper 1995] P. Aiken, P. Piper "Estimating Data Reverse Engineering Projects" *Proceedings of the 5th annual Systems Reengineering Workshop* (Johns Hopkins University Applied Physics Laboratory Research Center Report RSI-95-001) February 7-9, 1995, Monterey CA, pp. 133-145.

[Aiken et al. 1994] P. Aiken, A. Muntz, R. Richards "DoD Legacy Systems: Reverse Engineering Data Requirements" *Communications of the ACM* May 1994 37(5):26-41.

[Allen 1988] M. Allen "Strategic Management of Consumer Services" *Long Range Planning* Dec 1988, v21n6, p. 20-25.

[Allen and Boynton 1991] B. Allen, A. Boynton "Information Architecture: In Search of Efficient Flexibility" *MIS Quarterly* December 1991 15(4):435-445.

[American 1993] *American Heritage Dictionary*, Deluxe Edition, Boston: Houghton Mifflin Company, 1983

[Andriole 1989] S. Andriole *Storyboard Prototyping: A New Approach to User Requirements Analysis*, QED Information Sciences, Wesley, MA, 1992.

[Appleton 1983] D. Appleton "Law of the Data Jungle" *Datamation* October 1983, 29(10):225-230.

[Appleton 1984] D. Appleton "Business Rules: The Missing Link" *Datamation* October 1984, 30(16):145-150.

[Appleton 1985] D. Appleton Company, Inc. "IISS (Integrated Information Support System) Information Modeling Manual, IDEF1 - EXTENDED (IDEF1X)," December 31, 1985.

[Appleton 1986] D. Appleton " Rule-based Data Resource Management" *Datamation* May 1986, 32(9):86-99.

[Armstrong 1994] M. Armstrong "Application Design in a Client-Server Environment" chapter in Barbara von Halle and David Kull (editors, *Handbook of Data Management*, Auerback, 1993.

[Arnold 1993] R. Arnold *Software Reengineering* IEEE Computer Society Press Los Alamitos, CA, 1994.

[Atkinson, 1992] Robert A. Atkinson "Applying the 80/20 Rule : Making It Work for IS Plans" *Information Systems Management* Summer 1992, 9(3):57-59.

[Bachman 1988] Bachman C, "A CASE for reverse engineering" *Datamation* July 1988, 34(13):49-56.

[Ballou 1992] M. Ballou "Assignment: re-engineering. (Columbia University) *Computerworld* Nov 9 1992 , 26 (45):71(2).

[Banker and Kauffman 1991] R. Banker, R. Kauffman "Reuse and Productivity in Integrated Computer-Aided Software Engineering: An Empirical Study" *MIS Quarterly* September 1991 15(3):375-401.

[Basili 1990] V. Basili "Viewing Maintenance as Reuse-Oriented Software Development" *IEEE Software* January 1990, SE-8(3):19-25.

[Basili and Mills 1982] V. Basili, H. Mills "Understanding and Documenting Programs" *IEEE Transactions on Software Engineering* May 1982, SE-8(3):270-283.

[Batini et al. 1986] C. Batini, M. Lenzerini, S. Navathe "A Comparative Analysis of Methodologies for Database Schema Integration," *ACM Computing Surveys* December 1986, 18(4).

[Beese 1988] S. Beese et al. *Software Engineering Standards and Procedures Manual*, McLean, VA: The MITRE Corporation, November 1988.

[Bergeron and St-Arnaud 1992] F. Bergeron, J. St-Arnaud "Estimation of information systems development efforts," *Information & Management* April 1992, 22(4):239-254.

[Berry 1994] J. Berry "A Potent New Tool for Selling: Database Marketing" *Business Week* September 5, 1994, pp. 56-62.

[Biggerstaff 1989] T. Biggerstaff "Design Recovery for Maintenance and Reuse" *IEEE Computer* July 1989, pp. 36-49.

[Biggerstaff et al.1993] T. Biggerstaff, B. Mitbander, D. Webster "The Concept Assignment Problem in Program Understanding" *Proceedings of the Working Conference on Reverse Engineering* May 21-23, 1993, Baltimore MD pp. 27-43.

[Boehm 1987] B. Boehm "Industrial software metrics top 10 list" *IEEE Software*, September 1987.

[Boehm and Papaccio 1988] B. Boehm, P. Papaccio "Understanding and Controlling Software Costs" *IEEE Transactions on Software Engineering* October 1988, 14(10):1463-1477.

[Bohm and Jacopini 1966] Bohm and Jacopini "Flow Diagrams, Turning Machines and Languages with Only Two Formation Rules" *Communications of the ACM* May 1966.

[Brackett 1994] M. Brackett *Data Sharing using a Common Data Architecture* New York: John Wiley & Sons, 1994.

[Brady 1992] M. Brady "Planning for workflow management-analysing and re-engineering business processes with the insurance industry" *OIS Document Management 92. Proceedings of the Conference* pp. 189-94 Meckler, London, UK, 1992.

[Breuer and Lano 1991] P. Breuer, K. Lano "Creating specifications from code: reverse-engineering techniques" *Journal of Sofware Maintenance: Research and Practice* September 1991, 3(3):145-62.

[Britcher 1990] R. Britcher "Re-engineering software: a case study" *IBM Systems Journal* 1990, 29(4):551-67.

[Brooks 1974] F. Brooks "The Mythical Man-Month" *Datamation* December 1974, 20(12):45-52.

[Brooks 1975] F. Brooks *The mythical man-month; essays on software engineering* Reading, MA, Addison-Wesley, 1975.

[Bruce 1992] T. Bruce "Simplicity and Complexity in the Zachman Framework" *Database Newsletter* May/June, 1992, Database Research Group, Boston.

[Brynjolfsson 1993] E. Brynjolfsson "The Productivity Paradox of Information Technology" *Communications of the ACM* December 1993 36(12):67-77.

[Brynjolfsson et al. 1994] E. Brynjolfsson, T. Malone, V. Gurbaxani, A. Kambil "Does Information Technology Lead to Smaller Firms?" *Management Science* December 1994, 40(12):1645-1662.

[Buchanan 1994] Leigh Buchanan "In for a penny - in for a pound" *CIO* November 1994 p. 42- 51.

[Bucken 1992] M. Bucken "Travelers preserving programming pillars; insurance giant pushes reengineering pilot successes to IS skeptics" *Software Magazine* October 1992 , 12(14):48(2).

[Bullen and Rockart 1986] C. Bullen, J. Rockart "A Primer on Critical Success Factors" in *The Rise of Managerial Computing* (Rockart and Bullen, editors) Homewood, Illinois: Dow Jones-Irwin, 1986, pp. 383-422.

[Bush 1990] E. Bush "Reverse Engineering: What and Why" Language Technology Inc., 1990.

[Buss 1994] E. Buss. R. De Mori, W. Gentleman, J. Henshaw "Investigating reverse engineering technologies for the CAS program understanding project" *IBM Systems Journal* 33(3):477-500.

[Byrne 1991] E. Byrne "Software reverse engineering: A case study" *Software— Practice and Experience* December 1991, 21(12):1349-64.

[Cafasso 1993] R. Cafasso "Rethinking re-engineering" *Computerworld* March 15 1993, 27(11):102(4).

[Caldwell 1992] B. Caldwell "Battleground: an attempt to streamline the Pentagon's operations has triggered a fight for control" *InformationWeek* November 30 1992, 402:12(2).

[Caldwell 1994] B. Caldwell "Missteps, Miscues: Business reengineeing failures have cost corporations billions, and spending is still on the rise" *InformationWeek* June 20, 1994, pp. 50-60.

[Canfora and Cimitile 1992] G. Canfora, A. Cimitile "Reverse-engineering and intermodular data flow: a theoretical approach" *Journal of Sofware Maintenance: Research and Practice* March 1992, 4(1):37-59.

[Canfora et al.1991] G. Canfora, A. Cimitile, U. De Carlini "A logic based approach to reverse engineering tools production" *Proceedings. Conference on Software Maintenance* 1991 (Cat. No.91CH3047-8) p. 83-91, IEEE Computer Society Press, Los Alamitos, CA, USA.

[Card et al. 1987] D. Card, F. McGarry. G. Page "Evaluating Software Engineering Technologies" *IEEE Transactions on Software Engineering* July 1987, SE-13(7):845-851.

[Carmel et al. 1993] E. Carmel, R. Whitaker, J. George "PD and Joint Application Design: A Transatlantic Comparison" *Communications of the ACM* June 1993, 36(4):40-47.

[Caron et al. 1994] J. Caron, S. Jarvenpaa, D. Stoddard "Business Reengineering at CIGNA Corporation: Experiences and Lessons Learned from the First Five Years" *Management Information Systems Quarterly* September 1994, 18(3):233-247.

[Cash et al. 1992] J. Cash, F. McFarlan, J. McKenney, and L. Applegate *Corporate Information Systems Management: Text and Cases*, Irwin, Homewood, IL 1992.

[Cash et al. 1994] J. Cash, F. McFarlan, N. Nohria, R. Nolan "CASE 8-2: Capital Holding Corporation-Reengineering the Direct Response Group" (in) *Building the Information-Age Organization: Structure, Control, and Information Technologies* Irwin, 1994.

[Chen 1989] P. Chen "Entity-Relationship Model: Towards a Unified View of Data" *ACM Transactions on Database Systems* 1989 1(1).

[Chikofsky 1990] E. Chikofsky "The database as a business road map" *Database Programming and Design* May 1990, 3(5):62-67.

[Chikofsky and Cross 1990] Elliot Chikofsky and James H. Cross II "Reverse Engineering and Design Recovery: A Taxonomy" *IEEE Software* January 1990 7(1):13-17.

[Chivvis and Geyer 1992] A. Chivvis, J. Geyer "Folklore kills: You know those stories about the application too complex to reengineer? Don't believe everything you hear" *Corporate Computing* October 1992 1(4):57(1).

[Choi and Scacchi 1990] S. Choi, W. Scacchi "Extracting and Restructuring the Design of Large Systems" *IEEE Software* January 1990, pp. 66-71.

[Choi and Scacchi 1991] S. Choi, W. Scacchi "SOFTMAN: environment for forward and reverse CASE" *Information and Software Technology* Nov. 1991, 33 (9)664-74 .

[Christman, et al. 1990] R. Christman, D. Cook, C. Mercier "Reengineering the Los Alamos common file system" *Digest of Papers. Tenth IEEE Symposium on Mass Storage Systems. Crisis in Mass Storage* (Cat. No.90CH2844-9) , p. 122-5 Editors: K.D. Friedman, B.T. O'Lear, IEEE Computer Society Press Washington, DC, 1990.

[Clark 1992] T. Clark "Corporate Systems Management: An Overview and Research Perspective" *Communications of the ACM* February 1992, 35(2):61-75.

[Cliff 1992] V. Cliff "Re-engineering becomes the CEO's policy at Mutual Benefit Life" *Journal of Strategic Information Systems* March 1992, 1(2):102-5.

[Coad and Yourdon 1989] P. Coad, E. Yourdon *Object-Oriented Analysis* Prentice Hall 1989.

[Colbrook et al. 1990] A. Colbrook, C. Smythe, A. Darlison "Data abstraction in a software re-engineering reference model" *Proceedings. Conference on Software Maintenance* 1990, Los Alamitos, CA, USA IEEE Computer Society Press Publication Date: 26-29 Nov. 1990, p. 2-11.

[Comaford 1992] C. Comaford "Revitalizing legacy apps with minimal hassle" *PC Week* November 16 1992, 9(46):74(1).

[Connall and Burns, 1993] D. Connall D. Burns "Reverse Engineering: Getting a Grip on Legacy Systems" *Data Management Review* October 1993, pp. 24-27.

[Cooke and Parrish] D. Cooke, E. Parrish "Not Measuring Up" *CIO* June 15, 1992 pp. 84-85.

[Croxton 1994] M. Croxton "Migrating Legacy Systems to Client/Server and Other Architectures" *Proceedings of the 4th Reengineering Forum*, Victoria, BC, Canada, September 19-21, 1994.

[CSC 1994] CSC Index Inc. *State of Reengineering Report Executive Summary* Cambridge MA, 1994.

[Currid 1994] C. Currid "Battling the Naysayers" *Informationweek* July 11, 1994, p. 83.

[Curtis et al. 1992] B. Curtis, M. Kellner, J. Over "Process modeling" *Communications of the ACM* September 1992, 35(9):75(16).

[Cusumano 1991] M. Cusumano *Japan's Software Factories: A challange to US management* Oxford University Press, 1991.

[Davenport and Short 1990] T. Davenport, J. Short "The New Industrial Engineering: Information Technology and Business Process Redesign" *Sloan Management Review* Summer 1990, 31(4):11-27.

[Davis 1990] A. Davis *Software Requirements: Analysis and Specification* Prentice Hall, Englewood Cliffs, NJ, 1990.

[Dekleva 1991] S. Dekleva *Software Maintenance Proceedings 1991. Proceedings of the Annual Meeting and Conference of the Software Maintenance Association* Software Maintenance Assoc Vallejo, CA, USA 1991.

[Deloitte & Touche 1994] Deloitte & Touche *Leading Trends in Information Services* National Office Ten Westport Road, Wilton CT, 203/761-3000.

[Delligatta 1992] A. Delligatta "System reengineering and the user" *Information Systems Management* Winter 1992, 9(1):76-7.

[DeMarco 1979] T. DeMarco *Structured Analysis and System Specification* Prentice-Hall, 1979.

[Desclaux and Ribault 1991] C. Desclaux, M. Ribault "MACS: maintenance assistance capability for software-a KADME" *Proceedings. Conference on Software Maintenance 1991* p. 2-12 IEEE Computer Society Press, Los Alamitos, CA, USA.

[Dijkstra 1965] E. Dijkstra "Programming Considered as a Human Activity" *Proceedings of the 1965 IFIP Congress*, 1965.

[DoDa92] DoD Directive 8320.1-M *Data Standardization*, August 1992 (Draft).

[DoDb92] *Status of the Department of Defense Corporate Information Management (CIM) Initiative*, October 1992 - reprint edition.

[DoDc92] DoD Directive 8020.1-M *Functional Process Improvement (for Implementing the Information Management Program of the Department of Defense*, August 1992 (Draft).

[Drake 1992] K. Drake "Is software re-engineering the savior of CASE?" *Computing Canada* October 26 1992, 18(22):38.

[Durell 1985] W. Durell *Data Administration: A practical guide to data management* McGraw-Hill, 1985.

[Eastwood 1992] A. Eastwood "It's a hard sell - and hard work too. (software reengineering)" *Computing Canada* October 26 1992, 18(22):35.

[Eliason 1990] A. Eliason *Systems Development Analysis, Design, and Implementation* (second edition) Scott, Foresman and Company, 1990.

[Eliot 1994] L. Eliot "Critical Success Factors for Assessing CASE Readiness" *Software Engineering Strategies* March/April 1994, 2(1):154-160.

[Endoso 1993] J. Endoso "Air Force retools logistics system that configures aircraft cargo loads" *Government Computer News* February 15 1993, 12(4):45.

[Errico and Sullivan 1992] S. Errico, A. Sullivan "Redevelop in pieces (Business Process Reengineering must be implemented by corporate information systems departments)" *Software Magazine* December 1992 12(17):6.

[Evered 1983] R. Evered "So What *Is* Strategy?" *Long Range Planning* 1983, 16(3):57-72.

[Fairley 1985] R. Fairley *Software Engineering Concepts* New York: McGraw-Hill, 1985.

[Finkelstein 1989] C. Finkelstein *An Introduction to Information Engineering:* Addision Wesley 1989

[Finkelstein 1993] C. Finkelstein *Information Engineering: Strategic Systems Development*, Addision Wesley, 1993.

[Flood 1994] S. Flood "Managing Data in a Distributed Processing Environment" chapter in Barbara von Halle and David Kull (editors, *Handbook of Data Management*, Auerback, 1993.

[Fogel 1992] S. Fogel "Data modeling with Macintosh CASE tools" *Database Programming & Design* Nov 1992, 5(11):43(6).

[Fong 1992] J. Fong "Methodology for schema translation from hierarchical or network into relational" *Information and Software Technology* March 1992, 34(3):159-74.

[Forte and Norman 1992] G. Forte, R. Norman "A Self Assessment by the Software Engineering Community" *Communications of the ACM* April 1992, 35(4):28-32.

[Francett 1989] B. Francett "From IMS or Non-IBM, the Move Is on to DB2" *Software Magazine* September 1992, pp. 50-61.

[Francis 1990] B. Francis "Kimberly-Clark sees profits in IS" *Datamation* May 15, 1990, 36(10):53-4.

[Frank, 1993] M. Frank "CASE for client/server" *DBMS* March 1993 6(3):57(7).

[Freeman 1994] M. Freeman and P. Layzell "A meta-model of information systems to support reverse engineering" *Information and Software Technology* May 1994, 36(5):283-294.

[Gallant 1986] S. Gallant "Brittleness and Machine Learning" *Proceedings of the International Meeting on Advances in Learning,* July 1986, pp. 140-156.

[GAO 1979] General Accounting Office *Contracting for Computer Software Development--Serious Problems Require Management Attention To Avoid Wasting Additional Millions* Report to the Congress of the United States by the Comptroller General FGMSD-80-4, November 9, 1979.

[GAO 1992] General Accounding Office *Information Management and Technology Issues* - December 1992 General Accounting Office Report GAO/OCG-93-5TR.

[GAO 1993] Software Tools: Defense is not ready to implement I-CASE Departmentwide (GAO/IMTEC 93-27).

[Gateway 1993] Gateway Management Consulting *Reengineering Survey Report: Survey Methodology and Objectives* New York, 1993.

[Gause and Weinberg 1989] D. Gause, G. Weinberg *Exploring Requirements: Quality Before Design*, Dorset House Publishing, New York, 1989.

[Gibbs 1994] W. Gibbs "Software's Chronic Crisis" *Scientific American* September 1994, 271:86-95.

[Gomoll and Wong 1994] T. Gomoll, I. Wong "User-Aided Design at Apple Computer" (chapter in Michael Wiklund - editor) *Usability in Practice: How Companies Develop User-Friendly Products* Boston: AP Professional, 1994.

[Grammas 1985] G. Grammas, J. Klein "Software Productivity as a Strategic Variable" *Interfaces* May-June 1985, 15(3):116-126.

[GSA 1993] General Services Administration/Information Resources Management Service/Policy Analysis Division Robert N. Karr Jr. *Data Management Issues Associated with Stovepiper Systems* October 1993, KMP-94-1-I.

[Hackathorn 1993] R. Hackathorn *Enterprise database connectivity : the key to enterprise applications on the desktop* New York: Wiley, c1993.

[Haeckel and Nolan 1993] S. Haeckel, R. Nolan "Managing by wire" *Harvard Business Review* September/October 1993, 71(5):122-132.

[Hainaut et. al. 1993] J. Hainaut, M. Chandelon, C. Tonneau, M. Jorris "Contribution to a Theory of Database Reverse Engineering" *Proceedings of the Working Conference on Reverse Engineering* May 21-23, 1993, Baltimore MD pp. 161-170.

[Hall 1992] P. Hall "Overview of reverse engineering and reuse research" *Information and Software Technology* April 1992, 34(4):239-49.

[Hammer 1990] M. Hammer "Reengineering Work: Don't Automate, Obliterate" *Harvard Business Review* July-August 1990 68(4):104-112.

[Hammer and Champy 1993] M. Hammer, J. Champy *Reengineering the Corporation: A Manifesto for Business Revolution* HarperBusiness, New York, 1993.

[Hars and Scheer 1991] A. Hars, A. Scheer "Enterprise-wide data modeling-the basis for integration" *Engineering Systems with Intelligence, Concepts, Tools and*

Applications p. 541-8, Editors: S.G. Tzafestas, Kluwer Academic Publishers Dordrecht, Netherlands 1991.

[Hay 1995] D. Hay *Data Model Patterns: Conventions of Thought* Dorset House Publishing, 1995.

[Heemstra 1992] F. Heemstra "Software cost estimation" *Information and Software Technology* October 1992 34(10):627-639.

[Heller 1993] D. Heller *Cross System Functional Integration: Final Report*, Phase I Hughes Information Technology Company, February 8, 1993.

[Helppie 1992] R. Helppie "A time for reengineering (in health care)" *Computers in Healthcare* January 1992, 13(1):22-4.

[Henderson 1989] B. Henderson "The Origin of Strategy" *Harvard Business Review* 89(6):139-144.

[Henderson 1994] L. Henderson "Use of Groupware to Accelerate Data Standardization" ACFEA 1994 Database Colloquium, San Diego CA August 1994.

[Hoffman 1993] T. Hoffman "San Diego Gas to re-engineer: technology unit will be used as test bed for processes changes" *Computerworld* Feb 8 1993, 27(6):6.

[Hopper 1990] M. Hopper "Rattling SABRE-New Ways to Compete on Information" *Harvard Business Review* May/June 1990 90(3):118-125.

[Howe 1993] G. Howe "A collision of semantics? (semantic issues in data integration)" *Database Programming & Design* February 1993, 6(2):54(6).

[Huff 1992] C. Huff "Elements of a Realistic CASE Tool Adoption Budget" *Communications of the ACM* April 1992 35(4):45-54.

[Hughes 1992] G. Hughes "Reverse engineering in Australia" *Tolley's Computer Law and Practice* 1992, 8(2):46-9.

[Humphrey 1989] W. Humphrey *Managing the Software Process* Addision-Wesley Publishing Company, Reading MA, 1990.

[IEEE 1983] Institute of Electrical and Electronics Engineers *IEEE Standard Glossary of Software Engineering Terminology* ANSI/IEEE Standard 729-1983, New York 1983.

[IESC 1994] Information Engineering Systems Corporation *IE:Advantage Reference Manual* and *Users Guide* Version 6.1 Alexandria, VA 1994.

[IIE 1994] Institute of Industrial Engineers "Corning Asahi Video Products Co." in *Beyond the Basics of Reengineering: Survival tactics for the '90s* Institute of Industrial Engineers Press, 1994.

[Inmon 1988] W. Inmon *Information Engineering for the Practitioner, Putting Theory Into Practice*, Englewood Cliffs, NJ Prentice-Hall 1988.

[Inmon 1992a] W. H. Inmon *Data Architecture: The Information Paradigm* QED Technical Publishing Group Wellesley, MA 1992.

[Inmon 1992b] W. H. Inmon "Dawn of a new age: Why everyone is building a data warehouse" *Database Programming & Design* December 1992, 5(12):76.

[Inmon 1993] W. Inmon *Developing Client/Server Applications* Boston: QED Publishing Group, 1993.

[Jones 1993] T. Jones "Equipping the software engineer. (lack of automation of software engineers)" (edited abstract of chapter of Jones' book, *Assessment and Control of Software Risks*) *Software Magazine* Jan 1993 13(1):100(2).

[Jones 1994] T. Jones *Assessment and Control of Software Risks* Englewood Cliffs, NJ: Yourdon Press, 1994.

[Kador 1992] J. Kador "Reengineer to boost software productivity (reengineering at Allnet Communication Services Inc.) *Datamation* December 15 1992, 38(25):57(2).

[Karakostas 1991] V. Karakostas "Automated business knowledge acquisition from programs" Third International Conference on Tools for Artificial Intelligence TAI

'91 (Cat. No.91CH3054-4) pp. 40-7 IEEE Computer Society Press, Los Alamitos, CA, USA.

[Karakostas 1992] V. Karakostas "Intelligent search and acquisition of business knowledge from programs" *Journal of Sofware Maintenance: Research and Practice* March 1992, 4(1):1-17.

[Kent 1978] W. Kent *Data and reality: basic assumptions in data processing reconsidered* New York: North-Holland Pub. Co. 1978.

[Kerr 1991] J. Kerr *The IRM Imperative* John Wiley, 1991.

[Kettinger 1994] W. Kettinger, W. Grover, S. Guha, A. Segars "Strategic Information Systems Revisited: A Study in Sustainability and Performance" *MIS Quarterly* March 1994, 18(1):31-59.

[Keuffel 1991] W. Keuffel, "House of Structure," *Unix Review* 1991, 9(2):28-36.

[Kimball 1994] R. Kimball, K. Strehlo "Why decision support fails and how to fix it" *Datamation* June 1, 1994, 40(11):40-43.

[King 1983] J. King "Centralized versus Decentralized Computing: Organizational Considerations and Management Options" *Computing Surveys* December 1983, 15(4):319-349.

[King 1995] S. King "How to Fail" *NAPM Insights* February 1995 pp. 50-52.

[Kirkbride 1994] L. Kirkbride "Reengineering Customer Support in a Client/Server Environment" *Proceedings of the 4th Reengineering Forum*, Victoria, BC, Canada, September 19-21, 1994.

[Klien 1993] M. Klein "IEs Fill Facilitator Role in Benchmarking Operations to Improve Performance" *Industrial Engineering* September 1993, pp. 12-15.

[Koberg and Bagnall 1972] D. Koberg, J. Bagnall *The All New Universal Traveler—a soft systems guide to: creativity, problem-solving and the process of reaching goals* William Kaufman Publishing, 1972.

[Kozaczynski et al. 1991] W. Kozaczynski, E. Liongosari, J. Ning "BAL/SRW: Assembler re-engineering workbench" *Information and Software Technology* November 1991, 33 (9):675-84.

[Krallmann and Wohrle 1992] H. Krallmann, G, Wohrle "Market survey CASE tools" *Wirtschaftsinformatik* April 1992, 34(2):181-9.

[Krasner 1994] H. Krasner "The payoff for software improvement (SPI): What it is and how to get it" *Software Process Newsletter* September 1994, p. 3-7.

[Lanubile et al.1991] F. Lanubile, P. Maresca, G. Visaggio "An environment for the reengineering of Pascal programs" *Proceedings. Conference on Software Maintenance 1991* (Cat. No.91CH3047-8) pp. 23-30 IEEE Computer Society Press, Los Alamitos, CA, USA.

[LaPlante 1993] A. LaPlante "The Big Deal About Thinking Small" *Forbes* ASAP March 28, 1993, pp. 22-43.

[Lawrence 1991] P. Lawrence "Reengineering the insurance industry" *Best's Review— Life/Health Insurance Edition* May 1991, 92(1):36-8, 40.

[Lee 1991] R. Lee *Apex: Ada Programming Expert System, A Computer Aided System Engineering Tool* CA State University, Long Beach (6080) Degree: Ms 1991.

[Lent 1994] A. Lent "Migration Strategies: A Legacy Worth Protecting" *InformationWeek* June 20, 1994, 62-70.

[Lerner 1991] M. Lerner "A process of re-engineering large and complicated systems" *Conference Proceedings 1991 IEEE International Conference on Systems, Man, and Cybernetics. Decision Aiding for Complex Systems* (Cat. No.91CH3067-6) p. 479-85 vol.1

[Lerner 1994] M. Lerner "Software Maintenance Crisis Resolution: The New IEEE Standard" *Software Development* August 1994 2(8):65-72.

[Licklider 1960] J. Licklider "Man-Computer Symbiosis," *IRE (now IEEE) Transactions on Human Factors In Electronics* March 1960, pp. 4-11.

[Liddell-Hart 1954] B. Liddell-Hart *Strategy* Frederick A. Praeger, New York, 1954.

[Loosley 1992] C. Loosley, "Separation and Integration in the Zachman Framework," *Database Newsletter*, Database Research Group, Boston 20, No. 1, 3-9 (1992).

[Madsen and Aiken 1993] K. Madsen, P. Aiken "Some Experiences Using Cooperative Interactive Storyboard Prototyping" *Communications of the ACM* June 1993 36(4):57-67.

[Margolis 1992] N. Margolis "Voices of experience (two information systems executives discuss re-engineering projects)" *Computerworld* Dec 28 1992, 27(1):16(2).

[Markosian et al. 1990] L. Markosian, T. Driscoll, R. Hunter-Duvar, J. Hartman, W. Kozaczynski, J. Ning "Industrial experience in automating software re-engineering" *Proceedings. Fourteenth Annual International Computer Software and Applications Conference* (Cat. No.90CH2923-1) p. 611-16 Editor: G. Knafl, IEEE Computer Society Press Los Alamitos, CA, 1990.

[Martin 1989] J. Martin *Information Engineering Book I: Introduction* Prentice Hall, Englewood Cliffs NJ, 1989.

[Marx et al.1990] G. Marx, J. Moderow, S. Zuboff, B. Howard, K. Nussbaum "The Case of the Omniscient Organization" *Harvard Business Review* Mar-April 1990, 68(2):12-30 (9 pages).

[Mattison 1994] R. Mattison *The Object-Oriented Enterprise: Making Corporate Information Systems Work* McGraw-Hill, 1994.

[McCabe 1976] T. McCabe, "A Complexity Measure," *IEEE Transactions on Software Engineering* December 1976, SE-2(4):308-320.

[McCarthy 1995] S. McCarthy "Martin promotes the common ground" *Government Computer News* June 1955 14(11): 5, p. 20.

[McClatchy 1990] W. McClatchy "Reengineering the CEO" *InformationWeek* November 5, 1990, 294:34, 38.

[McLean et al. 1993] McLean, Kappleman and Thompson "Converging End-User and Corporate Computing" *Communications of the ACM* December 1993 36(12):78-92.

[McPartlin 1993] J. McPartlin "Just chasing rainbows: critics brand much of the reengineering clamor as sheer marketing hype" *InformationWeek* February 1 1993, 410:55(1).

[Moad 1993a] J. Moad "Does Reengineering Really Work?" *Datamation* August 1, 1993, pp. 22-28.

[Moad 1993b] J. Moad "New Rules, New Ratings As IS Reengineers" *Datamation* November 1, 1993, pp. 85-87.

[Moore 1993] J. Moore "DOD extends CIM help to civilian agencies; business process re-engineering hot topic in government" *Federal Computer Week* March 1 1993, 7(5):14(1).

[Moriarty 1992] T. Moriarty "Migrating the legacy: as the industry migrates to the PC, don't give up your mainframe products yet" *Database Programming & Design* Dec 1992, 5(12):73(2).

[Morris and Brandon 1991] D. Morris, J. Brandon "Reengineering the hospital: making change work for you *Computers in Healthcare* November 1991, 12(11):59, 64.

[Muller et al. 1991] H. Muller, J. Mohr, J. McDaniel "Applying software re-engineering techniques to health information systems" *Software Engineering In Medical Informatics Proceedings of the Imia Working Conference*, Amsterdam, Netherlands North-Holland, 1991, p. 91-110

[Nadeau 1988] L. Nadeau, J. Rogers "Evaluating Tools: CASE Studies" *Computer Decisions* March 1988, 20(3): 42-44.

[Narayan 1988] R. Narayan, *Data Dictionary, Implementation, Use and Maintenance*, Englewood Cliffs, NJ Prentice-Hall 1988.

[Nardi 1993] B. Nardi *A Small Matter of Programming* MIT Press, Boston, 1993.

[NBS 1988] *Guide to Information Resource Dictionary System Applications: General Concepts and Strategic Systems Planning* National Bureau of Standards (NBS) Special Publication 500-512, April 1988.

[Necco, et al. 1989] C. Necco, N. Tasi, K. Holgeson "Current Usage of CASE Software" *Journal of Systems Management* May 1989 40(5):6-11.

[Neiderman et al. 1991] F. Neiderman, J. Brancheau, J. Wetherbe "Information Systems Management Issues of the '90s" *MIS Quarterly* December 1991 pp. 475-499.

[Ning 1990] J. Q. Ning "User involvement in software re-engineering" *Fourth International Workshop on Computer-Aided Software Engineering. Advance Working Papers* (Cat. No.90CH2956-1) p. 28-9 Editors: R. Norman, R. Van Ghent IEEE Computer Society Press Los Alamitos, CA, USA 1990.

[Nolan 1979] R. Nolan "Managing the Crisis in Data Processing" *Harvard Business Review*, March/April 1979 pp. 115-126.

[Norman and Nunamaker 1988] R. Norman, J. Nunamaker "An Empirical Study of Information Systems Professionals Productivity Perception of CASE Technology" *Proceedings of the Ninth International Conference on Information Systems* 1988, pp. 11-118.

[Norman and Van Ghent 1991] R. Norman, R. Van Ghent (Editors) *Fourth International Workshop on Computer-Aided Software Engineering. Advance Working Papers* (Cat. No.90CH2956-1) IEEE Computer Society Press Los Alamitos, CA, USA, 1990.

[Norman et al. 1989] R. Norman, G. Corbitt, M. Butler, and D. McElroy "CASE Technology Transfer: A Case Study of Unsuccessful Change" *Journal of Systems Management* May 1989 40(5):33-37.

[O'Brien 1989] C. O'Brien "Run-time reverse engineering speeds software troubleshooting" *High Performance Systems* November 8 1989, 10(11): 41, 44, 46.

[O'Brien 1993] J. O'Brien *Management Information Systems: a managerial end user perspective* Irwin 1993.

[Olsem and Sittenauer 1995] M. Olsem, C. Sittenauer "STSC's Reengineering Project Data Repository" *Proceedings of the 5th Annual Systems Reengineering Workshop* February 7-9, 1995, Monterey CA, (Johns Hopkins University Applied Physics Laboratory Research Center Report RSI-95-001) pp. 146-149.

[Orlikowski 1988] W. Orlikowski "CASE technologys and the IS Workplace: Some Findings from Empirical Research" *Proceedings of the ACM SIGCPR Conference* ACM Press, Baltimore MD, April 1988, pp. 88-97.

[Orlikowski 1993] W. Orlikowski "CASE Technologies as Organizational Change: Investigating Incremental and Radical Changes in Systems Development" *MIS Quarterly* September 1993, 17(3):309-340.

[Parker and Benson, 1990] M. Parker, R. Benson "A Strategic Planning Methodology: Enterprisewide Inform ation Management" *Data Resource Management* Summer 1990, pp. 6-15.

[Parker et al. 1994] B. Parker, D. Smith, D. Satterthwaite "Data Management Capability Maturity Model (DM SMM)" *Proceedings of the ACFEA Database '94 Colloquium*, August 29-31 1994.

[Parker et al. 1995] B. Parker, L. Chambless, D. Smith, D. Satterthwaite, D. Duvall *Data Management Capability Maturity Model* (March 1995) MITRE Document MP95W0000088, MITRE Software Engineering Center 7525 Colshire Drive, McLean, VA 22102.

[Parnas 1972] D. Parnas "A Technique for Software Model Specification with Examples" *Communications of the ACM* May 1972.

[Parnas and Clements 1986] D. Parnas, P. Clements "A Rational Design Process: How and Why to Fake It" *IEEE Transactions on Software Engineering* February 1986 SE-12(2):251-257.

[Pastore 1989] R. Pastore "Coffee, Tea and a Sales Pitch" *Computerworld* July 3, 1989, 23(27):1,14.

[Pelton 1993] C. Pelton "Integration battle (reengineering at Miltope Corp.) *Corporate Computing* Jan 1993, 2(1):116(11).

[Peterson 1993] I. Peterson "Reviving Software Dinosaurs: Learning to decipher antiquated computer programs" *Science News*, August 7 1993 144(6):88-89.

[Petrie 1992] C. Petrie (editor) *Enterprise Integration Modeling: Proceedings of the First International Conference* The MIT Press, Cambridge, MA 1992.

[Pfrenzinger 1992] S. Pfrenzinger "Reengineering goals shift toward analysis, transition; users adjust expectations as suppliers work on next-generation capture tools" *Software Magazine* October 1992, 12(14):44(9).

[Porter 1980] M. Porter *Competitive Strategy: Techniques for Analyzing Industries and Competitors* The Free Press New York, 1980.

[Premerlani 1993] W. Premerlani, M. Blaha "An Approach to Reverse Engineering of Relational Databases" *First Working Conference on Reverse Engineering* May 21-23, 1993, Baltimore, MD pp. 151-160.

[Pressman 1993] R. Pressman *Software Engineering: A Practitioner's Approach* (3rd edition), New York: McGraw-Hill Book Company, 1993.

[Pressman and Herron 1991] R. Pressman, S. Herron *Software Shock* Dorset House, 1991.

[QED 1989] *CASE, The Potential and the Pitfalls* Wellesley, MA: QED Information Sciences, 1989.

[Radding 1990] A. Radding "CASE cuts software development costs, but receives slow acceptance at banks" *Bank Management* February 1990, 66(2):50.

[Richards 1994] R. Richards *Data Architecture Development* unpublished monograph available from the author 1951 Kidwell Drive, Fifth Floor, Vienna, VA 23182.

[Ricketts et al. 1989] J. Ricketts, J. DelMonaco, M. Weeks "Data Reengineering for Application Systems" *Proc. Conference on Software Maintenance—1989* IEEE Computer Society Press pp. 174-179.

[Ross 1987] R. Ross *Entity Modeling: Techniques and Application* Database Research Group, Inc. Boston, MA 1987.

[Ross 1992] R. Ross, W. Michaels *Resource Life Cycle Analyisi—A Business Modeling Technique for IS Planning* Database Research Group, Inc. Boston, MA 1994.

[Ross 1994] R. Ross *The Business Rule Book—Classifying, Defining, and Modeling Rules Version 3.0* Database Research Group, Inc. Boston, MA 1994.

[Roth et al. 1994] T. Roth, P. Aiken, S. Hobbs "Hypertext Support for Software Development: A Retrospective Assessment" *Hypermedia* Winter 1994 6(3).

[Rugaber 1992] S. Rugaber "Reverse Engineering Projects at Georgia Tech" *Reverse Engineering Newsletter* #3, October 1992, pp. Rev-1/Rev-4.

[Ruhl and Gunn 1991] M. Ruhl, M. Gunn *Software Reengineering: A Case Study And Lessons Learned*, Washington, DC, National Institute of Standards and Technology, September 1991.

[Sandifer and von Halle 1991] A. Sandifer, B. von Halle "Collecting business rules: A case study" *Database Design* March 1991 pp. 11-16.

[Scandura 1990] J. Scandura "Cognitive approach to systems engineering and re-engineering: integrating new designs with old systems" *Journal of Software Maintenance: Research and Practice* September 1990, 2(3):145-156.

[Schmerken 1992] I. Schmerken "Reengineering Wall Street's systems" *Wall Street Computer Review* January 1992, 9(4):14-18, 20, 22 .

[Selfridge et al. 1993] P. Selfridge, R. Waters, E. Chikofsky "Challenges to the Field of Reverse Engineering" *Proceedings of the Working Conference on Reverse Engineering* IEEE Computer Society Press, 1993, pp. 144-150.

[Selkow 1990] W. Selkow "Strategic Information Planning: A New Framework" *Enterprise Systems Journal* 1990.

[Seymour 1994] P. Seymour "Critical Success Factors in Reengineering Legacy Systems" *Software Engineering Strategies* March/April 1994, 2(1):5-17.

[Shagam 1991] E. Shagam "Software re-engineering using hierarchical-client-server paradigm (HCS) and BUBBLES" *Proceedings. The Fifth Israel Conference on Computer Systems and Software Engineering* (Cat. No.91TH0349-1) p. 50-6 IEEE Computer Society Press Los Alamitos, CA, USA 1991.

[Sharon 1992] D. Sharon "Developing and Applying a Tool Classification Scheme and Evaluation Criteria for Reverse Engineering and Re-engineering Tools" (Presentation #29) *Proceedings of the 3rd Reverse Engineering Forum* September 15-17, 1992 Northeastern University, Burlington, MA.

[Sharon 1993a] D. Sharon "A Reverse Engineering and Reengineering Tool Classification Scheme" *Reverse Engineering Newsletter* #4 January 1993.

[Sharon 1993b] David Sharon "Software-Engineering Tool Classification" *IEEE Software* September 1993 pp. 106-109.

[Signore and Celiano 1991] O. Signore, F. Celiano, "From a 'well designed' database to AD/Cycle tools: a reengineering experience" *Proceedings SHARE Europe Spring Meeting. CASE and Applications Development in Practice* pp. 1-8 SHARE Europe Geneva, Switzerland 1991.

[Sittenauer et al. 1994] C. Sittenauer, M. Olsem, D. Murdock *Reengineering Tools Report* Software Technology Support Center, Ogden ALC/TISE, Hill AFB, Utah 84056

[Slofstra 1993] M. Slofstra "Re-engineering tops list of IS concerns: study" *Computing Canada* Feb 15 1993, 19(4):14(1).

[Slonim 1994] J. Slonim "The Program Understanding Project" *Proceedings of the 4th Reengineering Forum*, Victoria BC Canada September 19-21 1994, pp. 7-1/7-4.

[Slusky 1991] L. Slusky "Modelling of I-CASE Platform" *Information and Software Technology* October 1991. 33(8):549-58.

[Smith 1992] B. Smith "Business Process Reengineering: More than a buzzword" *HR Focus* December 1992, p 17.

[Smith 1993] J. Smith "Outside DOD, CIM has put down some roots and may yet flourish" *Government Computer News* Feb 1 1993, 12(3):80(1).

[Smith et al 1981] J. Smith, P. Bernstein, U. Dayal, N. Goodman, T. Landers, K. W., T. Lin, E. Wong "Multibase--Integrating Heterogeneous Distributed Database Systems," *Proceedings of AFIPS*, 1981, pp. 487-499.

[Sneed 1984] H. Sneed "Software renewal—a case study" *IEEE Software* 1(3):56.

[Sneed 1991a] H. Sneed "Bank application reengineering and conversion at the Union Bank of Switzerland" *Proceedings of the Conference on Software Maintenance 1991* (Cat. No.91CH3047-8) p. 60-72 IEEE Computer Society Press Los Alamitos, CA, USA 1991.

[Sneed 1991b] H. Sneed "Economics of software re-engineering" *Journal of Sofware Maintenance: Research and Practice* September 1991 3(3):163-82.

[Sneed 1995] H. Sneed "Planning the Reengineeing of Legacy Systems" *IEEE Computer* January 1995 12(1):24-35.

[Sneed and Kaposi 1990] H. Sneed, A. Kaposi "A study on the effect of reengineering upon software maintainability" *Proceedings. Conference on Software Maintenance*

1990 (Cat. No.90CH2921-5) p. 91-9 IEEE Computer Society Press Los Alamitos, CA, USA 1990

[Software 1990] "Newsfront: Backlog still flat at 29 months" *Software Magazine* March 1990 p. 12.

[Sowa and Zachman 1992] J. Sowa, J. Zachman "Extending and formalizing the framework for information systems architecture" *IBM Systems Journal* September 1992 31(3):590-617.

[Spewak 1993] S. Spewak *Enterprise Architecture Planning* QED Publishing, Boston, 1993.

[Sprague and Carlson 1982] R. Sprague, E. Carlson *Building Effective Decision Support Systems* Englewood Cliffs, NJ: Prentice-Hall, Inc., 1982.

[St-Denis 1991] R. St-Denis "Capturing design-related decisions in JSD methodology" *Information and Software Technology* September 1991, 33 (7):509-17.

[Staiti 1992] C. Staiti, P. Pinella "DoD's Strassmann: The Politics of Downsizing" *Datamation* October 15, 1992, pp. 107-110.

[Stapleton and Sarasin 1992] L. Stapleton, G. Sarasin "Pacific Bell gets competitive. (how programmers redesigned software for telephone company)" *LAN Technology* November 1992, 8(12):8(12).

[Stevens et al. 1974] W. Stevens, G. Myers, L. Constantine "Structure Design" *IBM Systems Journal* May 1974.

[Stodder 1992] D. Stodder "Linchpin of the enterprise: database technology will be called upon to pull the enterprise together" *Database Programming & Design* November 1992, 5(11):7(2).

[Strassmann 1994] P. Strassmann "The Hocus-Pocus of Reengineering" *Across the Board* June 1994 pp. 35-38.

[Subcommittee 1989] Subcommittee on Investigations and Oversight *Bugs In The Program: Problems in Federal Government Computer Software Development and Regulation* U.S. Government Printing Office, Washington, DC September 1989.

[Swanson et al. 1991] K .Swanson, D. McComb, J. Smith, and D. McCubbrey "The Applications Software Factory: Applying Total Quality Techniques to Systems Development" *MIS Quarterly* December 1991 15(4):567-579.

[Tannenbaum 1994] A. Tannenbaum *Implementing a corporate repository: the models meet reality* New York: J. Wiley, 1994.

[Tapscott and Caston 1993] D. Tapscott, A. Caston *Paradigm Shift: The New Promise of Information Technology* McGraw-Hill 1993.

[Taylor 1992] A. Taylor "A sampling of solutions for the forward thinker" *Computing Canada* October 26 1992, 18(22):39(1).

[Tomic and Tilley 1995] M. Tomic, S. Tilley "Seven Issues for the next generation of program understanding systems" *Proceedings of the 5th Annual Systems Reengineering Workshop* February 7-9, 1995, Monterey CA, (Johns Hopkins University Applied Physics Laboratory Research Center Report RSI-95-001) pp. 150-155.

[Tucker 1993] J. Tucker "Data Administrators: Guardians of the Corporate Data Asset" (chapter in von Halle and Kull, editors) *Handbook of Data Management*, Auerback, 1993, pp. 159-165.

[Ulrich 1990a] W. Ulrich "Re-engineering: a requirement for an integrated migration framework" *Fourth International Workshop on Computer-Aided Software Engineering. Advance Working Papers* (Cat. No.90CH2956-1) p. 35-6 Editors: R. Norman, R. Van Ghent IEEE Computer Society Press Los Alamitos, CA, USA 1990.

[Ulrich 1991] W. Ulrich "Reengeering: Defining an Integrated Migration Framework" *CASE Trends* November/December 1990 - May/June 1991.

[Ulrich 1992] W. Ulrich "Software Re-engineering The Methodology Gap" (Presentation #17) *Proceedings of the 3rd Reverse Engineering Forum* September 15-17, 1992 Northeastern University, Burlington, MA.

[Ulrich 1993] W. Ulrich "Formal Method Needed to Assist Reeengineering, Redevelopment Effort" *CASE Trends* November 1993.

[Ulrich 1994] W. Ulrich "From Legacy Systems to Strategic Architectures" *Software Engineering Strategies* March/April 1994, 2(1):18-30.

[Usowicz 1990] T. Usowicz "Integrating design recovery into CASE" *Fourth International Workshop on Computer-Aided Software Engineering. Advance Working Papers* (Cat. No.90CH2956-1) p. 37-8 Editors: J. Norman, R. Van Ghent IEEE Computer Society Press Los Alamitos, CA, USA 1990 xvii+553 pp.

[Van Kirk 1992] D. Van Kirk "Downsizing host applications; data conversion is often the last but most critical step in re-engineering" *InfoWorld* Dec 28 1992, 14(52-1):39(2).

[van Lamsweerde and Fugetta 1991] A. van Lamsweerde, A. Fugetta (Editors) *ESEC '91. 3rd European Software Engineering Conference Proceedings* Springer-Verlag Berlin, Germany 1991.

[Vaughn 1994] L. Vaughn *Client/server system design and implementation* New York : McGraw-Hill, 1994.

[Verdugo 1988] G. Verdugo "Portfolio analysis—managing software as an asset" *Proceedings of the 6th International Conference on Software Maintenance Software Management Association* New York, 1988.

[Vessey et al. 1992] I. Vessey, S. Jarvenpaa, M. Tractinsky "Evaluation of Vendor Products: CASE Tools as Methodology Companions" *Communications of the ACM* April 1992 35(4):90-105.

[Voelcker 1988] J. Voelcker "Automating Software: Proceed with caution" *IEEE Spectrum* July 1988 25(7):25-27.

[von Halle 1992] B. von Halle "Leap of Faith: Building a Shared-Data Environment from the Ground Up" *Database Programming & Design* September 1992,

[von Halle and Kull 1993] B. von Halle, D. Kull (editors, *Handbook of Data Management*, Auerback, 1993.

[von Halle and Kull 1994] B. von Halle, D. Kull (editors, *Handbook of Data Management 1994-1995 Yearbook*, Auerback, 1994.

[Wagner 1991] J. Wagner "Lessons learned from DOMINO and GRAPES (CASE tools)" *Software Development Environments and CASE Technology. European Symposium Proceedings* p. 130-42 Editors: A. Endres, H. Weber Springer-Verlag, 1991.

[Warden 1989] R. Warden "Software re-engineering: a practical approach" *Software Tools '89. Proceedings of the Conference* pp. 423-34 Blenheim Online, London, UK 1989.

[Warden 1991] R. Warden "Software re-engineering-methods first CASE second" *Eurocase II. The 2nd European CASE Conference. Conference Proceedings. Putting CASE to Work* pp. 1-10 vol. 2.

[Weil 1992] U. Weil "IT's 'creeping complexity' stalls investment" *Government Computer News* November 9 1992, 11(23):21(1).

[Whiting 1994] J. Whiting "Reengineering the Corporation: A Historical Perspective and Critique" *Industrial Management* December 1994, 36(6):14-16.

[Whitten et al. 1994] Whitten, Bentley, and Barlow *Systems Analysis and Design* (3rd edition) Irwin 1994.

[Wilson 1992a] J. Wilson "Reengineering business performance: is technology needed?" *Networks 92. Networking People. Proceedings of the International Conference* pp. 249-62 vol.3 Blenheim Online London, UK 1992 3 vol.

[Wilson 1992b] L. Wilson "Premium on reengineering (the *Information Week* 500: insurance)" *Information WEEK* September 1992, 392:58, 62 21.

[Wilson 1994] L. Wilson "Cautious Change for Retailers" *Information Week* October 10, 1994, pp. 177-180.

[Winans and Davis 1991] J. Winans, K. Davis "Software reverse engineering from a currently existing IMS database to an entity-relationship model" *Entity-Relationship Approach: the Core of Conceptual Modelling. Proceedings of the Ninth International Conference* p. 333-48 Editor: H. Kangassalo North-Holland Amsterdam, Netherlands, 1991.

[Wolkomir 1994] R. Wolkomir "The chips are coming, the chips are coming ... " *Smithsonian* September 1994 25(6):82-93.

[Wood 1992] M. Wood "Software Reengineering Cost Models" (Presentation #5) *Proceedings of the 3rd Reverse Engineering Forum* September 15-17, 1992 Northeastern University, Burlington, MA.

[Wu 1944] S. Wu *The Art of War* The Military Service Publishing Company, Harrisburg Pennsylvania, 1944.

[Yellen 1990] R. Yellen "Systems Analysts Performance Using CASE versus Manaual Methods" *Proceedings of the Twenty-Third Annual Hawaii International Conference on System Sciences* IEEE Computer Society Press, Los Alamitos, CA 1990.

[Yourdon 1988] E. Yourdon *Modern Structured Analysis* Yourdon Press, 1988.

[Yourdon 1994] E. Yourdon "Software Reuse" *Application Development Strategies* 6(12):1-16.

[Yourdon 1995] E. Yourdon "Business Process Reengineering: Tools and Techniqes" *Application Development Strategies* January 1995 7(1):1-16.

[Zachman 1987] J. Zachman "A framework for information systems architecture" *IBM Systems Journal* 26(3):276-292.

[Zarrella et al. 1992] P. Zarrella, D. Brown, E. Morris *Issues in Tool Acquisition* Technical Report CMU/SEI-91-TR-8 available from the Software Engineering Institute, September 1991.

Index

About the Author

Dr. Peter Aiken has been continuously employed since 1975 and in information technology/management related positions since 1980. During the early 1980's he managed the Information Center of a major research university, providing consulting and support services to a distributed user population. Later he was promoted a position responsible for the distributed on-line program development and telecommunications systems for the University's mainframe operations. From 1985 to 1993 he participated in research and development projects at George Mason University (GMU) in Fairfax, VA. His dissertation was one of the first research projects illustrating how hypermedia technologies could be applied to software requirements. His primary experience and publications have been in the areas of data reverse engineering, software requirements engineering, information engineering, human-computer interaction, systems integration/systems engineering, strategic planning, and decision support systems. As Director of the GMU Hypermedia Technologies Laboratory, he led a research team investigating the application of tools and techniques to the process of software requirements engineering, and developed applications supporting group consensus building. In 1992 he was recruited by the Department of Defense to work in the Center for Information Management's (CIM) Information Engineering Directorate. At CIM, he directed a multi-million dollar DOD-wide reverse engineering program and participated in the development of a DOD-wide strategic level data model, as well as other efforts. Dr. Aiken has more than a decade of university-level teaching and course/curricula development experience and has chaired both doctoral and masters committees. In 1993 he switched his academic base to the Department of Information Systems in the School of Business at Virginia Commonwealth University. His achievements have resulted in recognition in *The Dictionary of International Biographies, Who's Who in American Education, Who's Who in Science and Engineering, Who's Who of Emerging Leaders in America*. He can be reached via the Internet at

paiken@cabell.vcu.edu

or visit his home page at

http://128.172.188.1/isydept/faculty/paiken/paiken.htm